Sites of Desire ❧
❧ Economies of Pleasure

The Chicago Series on Sexuality, History, and Society
a series edited by John C. Fout

Also in the series:
Improper Advances
Rape and Heterosexual Conflict in Ontario, 1880–1929
by Karen Dubinsky

A Prescription for Murder
The Victorian Serial Killings of Dr. Thomas Neill Cream
by Angus McLaren

The Language of Sex
Five Voices from Northern France around 1200
by John W. Baldwin

Crossing Over the Line
Legislating Morality and the Mann Act
by David J. Langum

Sexual Nature / Sexual Culture
edited by Paul R. Abramson and Steven D. Pinkerton

Love Between Women
Early Christian Responses to Female Homoeroticism
by Bernadette J. Brooten

The Invention of Sodomy in Christian Theology
by Mark D. Jordan

The Trials of Masculinity
Policing Sexual Boundaries, 1870–1930
by Angus McLaren

Sites of Desire ⇝
⇜ Economies of Pleasure

Sexualities in Asia and the Pacific

EDITED BY

Lenore Manderson
and Margaret Jolly

THE

UNIVERSITY OF CHICAGO

PRESS

CHICAGO AND

LONDON

LENORE MANDERSON is Professor of Tropical Health at the Australian Centre for International and Tropical Health and Nutrition, the University of Queensland. MARGARET JOLLY is Senior Fellow and Convenor of the Gender Relations Project in the Research School of Pacific and Asian Studies, the Australian National University.

The University of Chicago Press, Chicago 60637
The University of Chicago Press, Ltd., London
© 1997 by The University of Chicago
All rights reserved. Published 1997
Printed in the United States of America
06 05 04 03 02 01 00 99 98 97   1 2 3 4 5

ISBN: 0-226-50303-8 (cloth)
ISBN: 0-226-50304-6 (paper)

Library of Congress Cataloging-in-Publication Data

Sites of desire, economies of pleasure : sexualities in Asia and the
   Pacific / edited by Lenore Manderson and Margaret Jolly.
        p.   cm. — (The Chicago series on sexuality, history, and society)
     Includes bibliographical references and index.
     ISBN 0-226-50303-8. — ISBN 0-226-50304-6 (pbk.)
     1. Sex customs—Asia—History.   2. Sex customs—Pacific Area—
   History.   3. Sex role—Asia—History.   4. Sex role—Pacific Area—
   History.   5. Ethnology—Asia.   6. Ethnology—Pacific Area.
   I. Manderson, Lenore.   II. Jolly, Margaret.   III. Series.
   HQ18.A8S58   1997
   306.7'095——dc21   96-40938
                                                                                      CIP

in memory of
Jeffrey Clark

CONTENTS

ILLUSTRATIONS

◆≡ PREFACE ≡◆

This volume arose from a conference organized by the Gender Relations Project at the Australian National University in July 1993, "The State, Sexuality, and Reproduction in Asia and the Pacific," and from a prior meeting, "Sexuality and Gender in East and Southeast Asia," organized by the Center for Research on Women at the University of California, Los Angeles, in December 1990.[1] The meetings and the less formal discussions that surrounded them, and the emerging discourse that informed our thinking on the subject matter, highlighted both the elasticity and the Eurocentrism of the language. Sex and sexuality came to include a vast array of topics, leaving us confused, finally, as to what sexuality really was, in our own or other cultures.

This is not a mere semantic game. What meanings are attached to sexual acts? Can we apply Western understandings of *sexuality* to describe sexual practices in other cultures, when we are so hazy about the utility of the concept in our own cultures? What happens under particular conditions— for example, under colonialism—when sexual relations are imbricated with those of class? In applying Western theories of sexuality and its language to sexual acts and gendered identities in other cultures, or to making sense of individual conjugations across time and space, are we any less guilty of ethnocentrism than those who have woven fantasies of licentiousness or repression around these same cultures? This collection of essays represents our desire to pose these questions, although not necessarily to answer them.

We would like to thank the following people for their help: the series editor, John Fout, for his suggestion that we consider this volume for the University of Chicago Press; Matt Howard, whose interest and encouragement through Internet was invaluable. We thank Duke University Press for permission to republish Ann Stoler's essay, which is chapter 6 of her book *Race and the Education of Desire: Foucault's History of Sexuality and the Colonial Order of Things*. At the University of Queensland, we thank Jenny Cooper and Gwen MacCartie for their meticulous word processing and warm support, Tanya Mark and John Richter for their skillful and generous research assistance, and Gulcin Cribb and her colleagues for their timely responses to requests for films and production details. At the Australian National University, we wish to thank Annegret Schemberg for her consummate research assistance and conference organization, and Ria van de Zandt for her excellent word processing. We are grateful to Megan Jennaway, whose phraseology and conceptualization of the Balinese "pleasure economy" inspired the title of this book. We thank also Pat, Toby, Kerith, Nick, and Anna for suffering our preoccupation, especially in the final stages of editing, and to the authors of the contributed chapters for their scholarship, timeliness, and good humor.

The chapter by Jeffrey Clark was one of the last pieces he wrote; he was terminally ill as he finished the manuscript. We dedicate this book to him.

Lenore Manderson, Brisbane
Margaret Jolly, Canberra

⊰ INTRODUCTION ⊱

Sites of Desire/Economies of Pleasure in Asia and the Pacific

MARGARET JOLLY AND LENORE MANDERSON

The study of sexuality, like the study of gender, has been caught in vertiginous controversies between biological essentialism and cultural constructionism. On the one hand is the language of instincts and corporeal essences, and on the other the language of malleable desires, of bodies molded and disposed by history and culture. There has been of late a proliferation of constructionist approaches[1] to sexuality—or rather sexualities—that are seen to vary across time and place. Constructionism typically proceeds by offering an array of diversities.

In this volume, we are not so much concerned to challenge universalist and essentialist views of sexuality by documenting the diversity of indigenous sexualities in Asia and the Pacific;[2] universalism and essentialism have lately been much challenged. In opposing sexuality as a natural universal, as an unthinking projection of a Western eros (Vance 1991), there is an obverse danger of exoticism and of overemphasizing difference. Paradoxically, both those who argue biological sameness and those who argue cultural difference typically proceed from a Western viewpoint, from which vantage such sameness or difference is measured. They also equally elide the deep histories of sexual contact and erotic entanglement between Europeans and "others." We query both an easy universalism and an easy relativism by focusing on cross-cultural *exchanges* in sexualities—exchanges of meanings and fantasies as well as the erotic liaisons of bodies. We explore "sites of desire" formed by confluences of cultures, be they the tidal waves of European colonialism or the smaller eddies of sexual contacts and erotic imaginings created between cultures. It is this border crossing, this fluid terrain in the exchange of desires, which this volume highlights.

The essays included here explore several sites of desire in both Asia and the Pacific—Thailand, the Philippines, Burma/Myanmar, Japan, Fiji, Papua New Guinea, and the islands of Polynesia. They traverse equally diverse epochs too—from the first explorations of Europeans, through the climax and withdrawal of colonial power, to the contemporary connections of the global and the local in the circuits of sexual tourism, prostitution, and the

HIV/AIDS pandemic. Our concern in all this is not so much with theoretical abstractions about desire as with the historically and culturally specific circumstances of erotic encounters between European, Asian, and Pacific peoples in these regions. But we also suggest how the history of sexuality in the West was configured by the experience of and knowledge about the sex of "others." Thus, Stoler has recently argued (1995, and chap. 1 in this volume) that the question is not just how a Foucauldian history/theory might be transposed to non-European sites, but also how the eros of the "West" is itself constituted by encounters with and images of those "othered" by race or culture.

How do the essays in this volume relate to recent debates about sexuality emerging from those other sites of desire—Europe, North America, and Australia (where the editors of this volume and many of its contributors are situated)? In recent discussions, both activist and academic, there has been much controversy about the terms *sex, gender,* and *sexuality* (e.g., Butler 1990a; Connell 1987; Connell and Dowsett 1992; de Lauretis 1984, 1994; Gallop 1988; Grosz 1989, 1994; Pringle 1992; Segal 1994). We first scrutinize these debates and then consider how this present volume might relate to them.

A Holy Trinity?

Pringle proclaims that the relation of gender and sexuality is not so much autonomous and overlapping (see Rubin 1992) as volatile, even schizophrenic (Pringle 1992, 76). This schizophrenia derives, she suggests, from their shared relation to that ambiguous third term, *sex,* which is used to mean either bodily desire undifferentiated by gender *or* corporeal sexual difference. It refers "both to an act and a category of a person, male or female" (Pringle 1992, 88).[3] In either case it denotes a refractory "nature" which seems to resist or to escape cultural construction.

Early feminist writings of the 1970s (e.g., Oakley 1972; Millett 1972) often strongly distinguished sex and gender.[4] This distinction was derived from Stoller's distinction between the biological and social elements of sexual difference in his study of transsexualism (1968) and perhaps more broadly from the pervasive Western opposition of nature and culture (Ortner 1974; MacCormack and Strathern 1980). This distinction between male/female and masculinity/femininity came under serious challenge from a number of theoretical directions in the 1980s—from persisting essentialist strands within radical feminism, from feminist philosophers influenced by Lacan and Irigaray, and from American theorists like Butler and de Lauretis.

Radical feminists like MacKinnon (1987) continued to talk about "sex," and to insist on absolute differences between men and women and the irreducible fact of male power most clearly manifested in heterosexuality, rape, and pornography.[5] Feminist philosophers like Gatens (1983, 1991) and Grosz (1989, 1994) also opposed the sex/gender distinction, but on rather different grounds—that it reinscribed a Cartesian split between body and mind, and continued to devalue or deny the body, often gendered feminine, in contrast to the mind or reason, gendered masculine. Being masculine or feminine was, they argued, very differently embodied by men and women.

In stressing sexual difference, such feminists often critically reinterpreted psychoanalysis, through Lacan or Irigaray. They veered between a view that identity was tenuous and unstable and the presumption that there was an invariance in "the law of the father" (see Butler 1990a, 332). Lacanian semiotic reinterpretations of Freud still left the girl child with "lack," and the feminine as that which was not only not represented but unrepresentable. Irigaray (1985) opposed all such language whereby women were positioned as the "other," the objects of knowledge, while men were the knowers or the subjects of knowledge. She inspired many feminist philosophers, including Gatens and Grosz, to develop an autonomous value of the female which did not derive from the male.

But psychoanalytic theories of sexual difference were subsequently challenged by Butler (1990a, 1990b), who insisted that they were trapped within the binaries they were trying to deconstruct and were still premised on compulsory heterosexuality, which they were trying to refuse in the name of female sexual pleasure. The result was, she argued, "a narrativised myth of origins in which primary bisexuality is arduously rendered into a melancholic heterosexuality through the inexorable force of the [paternal] law[;] . . . it reduces finally to the coincidence of two heterosexual desires, each proceeding from oppositional identifications or dispositions . . . so that desire strictly speaking, can issue only from a male identification to a female object or from a female identification to a male object" (1990a, 332–33). Butler's *Gender Trouble* (1990b) tried to recover not just the unrepresentable female, but the invisible lesbian. Although de Lauretis (1986) was less certain about the political benefits of subverting identity, she likewise argued for the contextual and fluid character of gender and sexual identities as well as those of ethnicity and class.

Debates about sexuality, like those of gender, have often proceeded from the problem of sex—conceived either as a biological foundation or a corporeal ground shared by all humans, male or female. Notions of instincts or drives were deployed by many early sexual theorists—not just Freud (1953 [1905], 1963 [1930]) but also Havelock Ellis (1923 [1897]), Kinsey et al. (1948, 1953), and Masters and Johnson (1966). But whereas Freud ultimately suggested a more layered and nuanced theory—of desire and its repression, the relation of mind and body, and the centrality of the difference between male and female in this process—later sex researchers often employed a simple "hydraulic" theory (Vicinus 1982) and focused on how, in the physiology of orgasmic pleasure, there were fundamental similarities between women and men.[6] This gender-neutral conception of sex as good in itself, as a drive which should not be repressed, was reformulated into a theory of sex as revolution in the emancipatory promises of theorists like Marcuse (1955).

Feminists critiqued such views as gender-blind rather than gender-neutral, suggesting that both sexological research and sexual revolution were supremely masculinist, encoding male notions of desire, with an emphasis on penetration and performance (e.g., Stimpson and Person 1980). Not only was the clitoral orgasm vaunted above the vaginal, but the very notion of the erotic as genitally focused was adjudged supremely masculinist. Marcuse's notions of sexual liberation as promiscuity not only presumed a natural sexuality waiting to be let out, but assimilated women to a male model of desire and elided questions of male sexual power or exploitation.

Such emancipatory theories had an uncertain relation to the liberation of homosexual desire, which was still often marginalized as unnatural or else portrayed in stereotypes of masculine/feminine or heterosexual desire—poofters/dykes, active/passive.[7] Excavations into past times and other places uncovered the difficulties with any simple notion of the homosexual as having a given identity (Weeks 1985, 1987; Halperin 1990; Herdt 1981, 1984, 1987; and see below).[8] An emergent cultural constructionism seemed to threaten the integrity of homosexual movements almost as surely as some feminists were threatened by the dissolution of the category "woman," in the face of the differences among women arising from ethnicity and class, culture or epoch. Then, from the early 1980s, the emergence of the HIV/AIDS epidemic in the gay male subcultures of the West had a rather contrary effect. On the one hand essentialisms were reinforced through engagement with biomedical models as gay activists cooperated with medical and sex researchers and sexologists to stem the tide of the epidemic, thereby also reassociating sexuality with disease and death (Vance 1991, 880–81). Claims about the gay brain or the gay gene, flimsy as the evidence was, provided ironic comfort in the midst of trauma and death that anatomy might, after all, be destiny. This seemed to some to absolve gay men from the guilt which homophobes laid upon them, by locating the blame in nature. Simultaneously, however, the new research into sexualities spawned by the HIV/AIDS pandemic subverted essentialisms. Sociological and psychological research focused on individual and collective practices to spread knowledge of HIV/AIDS and provide a firmer basis for public health campaigns advocating safer sex. This challenged many orthodoxies and exposed gaps between ideologies and experience, between acts and identities. Stable or fixed notions of homosexuals, bisexuals, and heterosexuals became increasingly problematic (see Vance 1991, 881; Altman 1992, 36).

Essentialisms and Constructionisms—Hard and Soft

Thus, in both academic and activist discussions of sex, gender, and sexuality in the West, recurrent tensions emerge between natural essences and cultural constructs. Although we, like most contemporary authors, espouse cultural constructionism, it is often too easy simply to dismiss competing stances as "essentialist."[9] Carol Vance (1984, 1989, 1991) has distinguished differences among a hard essentialism, a softer cultural influence model prevalent in anthropology, and a more strenuous constructionism. Hard essentialisms are of course to be found in those theories which posit biology as a determining force or substratum in what constitutes the "human," or "male" and "female." In contrast, Vance argues that the cultural influence model that has been pervasive in anthropology from the 1920s to the 1990s perceives sexuality not so much as bedrock but as "a kind of universal Play Doh" (1991, 878) molded by culture.

Although anthropologists have stressed since early in this century the roles of culture and learning in shaping sexual behavior and attitudes (e.g., Mead 1923, Malinowski 1929), they have still preserved a notion of a naturalized sex drive or impulse. Variation was the chronic refrain in titles devoted to cross-cultural research on sexuality (e.g., Frayser 1985), but often these were variations on a monotonous melody which wafted from the Euro-American conjugal bedroom. Not only did such surveys privilege exotic sexual customs which differed from Euro-American practices (the harem, postpartum taboos, ritual homosexuality), but the core of sexuality was often presumed to be reproductive heterosexual intercourse, with nonreproductive eroticism or homosexuality seen as minor variations. Vance (1991) suggests that sexuality and gender were thus typically conflated or seen as mutually constituted rather than separable. Moreover such research leaves certain key concepts untheorized—variations are admitted in terms of incidences and attitudes but not in individual subjective meaning or collective social significance (but see Ortner and Whitehead 1981). Some categories remain unquestioned as natural universals—for example, heterosexual and homosexual, male and female sexuality and sexual drive. Moreover, there is an epistemic as well as a sociopolitical sexual hierarchy[10] whereby certain practices require explanation while others do not. Comparative work on homosexuality was perhaps more vigorously pursued than that on heterosexuality, since homosexuality was perceived as a mystery or a problem, while heterosexuality was not. Thus Vance and Snitow quipped that "it would seem that certain behaviors are more constructed than others" (1984, 128).

Social constructionism in Vance's view must go further to "problematize and question Euro-American folk and scientific beliefs about sexuality. . . . Thus, statements about the universally compelling force of sexual impulse, the importance of sexuality in human life, the universally private status of sexual behavior, or its quintessentially reproductive nature need to be presented as hypotheses, not *a priori* assumptions" (1991, 879–80). Moreover she asserts that social constructionism is not simply arguing for nurture against nature; rather, it deconstructs these very dichotomies, which are part of hegemonic contemporary Western views.

But the hegemony of the West saturates much recent research on sexuality. Much of the abstract theorizing remains firmly grounded in Western traditions of thought (be it Freud or Foucault, Irigaray or Butler), and even more of the empirical, activist research on sexuality has been less willing to admit the differences of ethnicity and class than parallel work on gender. It is paradoxical perhaps that constructionism in both theoretical and action-based research on Western sexualities was initially inspired more by studies of past times and exotic sites than by the complexities of sexual experience as lived and witnessed in sites like San Francisco or Sydney. Only the most recent empirical and activist research, responding primarily to the global threat of HIV/AIDS, has treated ethnicity and class as central to the terrain of gender and sexuality (e.g., Dowsett 1990; Patton 1990; Watney 1989a, 1989b; Treichler 1992a). This volume likewise considers ethnicity and class as integral to the historical and cultural construction of gender and sexuality—both in colonial and postcolonial moments. But we also have to confront the question of Western hegemony—as a historical process and in our persisting imperialisms in theorizing about sexuality—a question to which we return below.

Colonialism as Sexual Urge—The License of the Other, the License in the Self

Stoler (1995, and chap. 1 in this volume) consummately shows how Western colonialism has been chronically sexualized and frequently analyzed in psychoanalytic terms—in concepts borrowed, if in bowdlerized form, from Freud. Colonial power is often naturalized as an instinct by notions of a repressed, sublimated and projected sexual impulse. She discusses several writers who variously see colonialism itself as a sublimation of sexuality, the colonies as places where desire repressed in Europe can be released,[11] and the projection of the desires and fears of the colonizer onto the colonized, who is imagined as licentious and unrepressed (1995, and chap. 1 in this volume). In such scenarios the colonizing subject is typically imagined as male—in masculinist tropes of penetration of dark interiors or the virile extension of male members into foreign places. In Said's *Orientalism* (1978) for instance, the Orient is portrayed as passive and female, prone to the masculine penetration of the West (see Kabbani 1986; for critiques, Jolly 1994; McClintock 1995).[12]

But as Stoler suggests, this is to tell a story far simpler than most sexual scenarios in the colonies, where the fluid fantasies of sexual license spilled across a more convoluted terrain of class, gender, and race. Such a view of sexuality as a natural urge and of civilization as repressive locates others (infants, "primitives," and lower classes) in oceans of desire which are unrepressed and dispersed in polymorphous currents. The attribution of uncontrolled desire, of untrammelled sexuality and animalistic urges, was variously applied to those others of the adult, white bourgeois (and masculine) self. As Stoler has so persuasively suggested, the "hydraulic" theory of sexuality depended not just on a dam within the male body, but also on the attribution of release and freedom to others—to working-class or racial "others" of the bourgeois European self. Not only were natives seen to be driven by insatiable instincts, but certain Europeans were as well—lower-class men in particular—and there was always the risk that respectable bourgeois men and women might "go native."

In some Enlightenment theories of the late eighteenth century in Europe, the sexual promiscuity of the aristocracy signaled the excess of culture as corruption (see Forster 1778). From the mid-nineteenth century, the bourgeois self differentiated its disciplined habits not just from those of decadent nobles but from the sexually untrammeled lives of the working class and those exotic others of Africa, Asia, and the Pacific. In each of these sites of desire there was a local inflection, and from the late nineteenth century such theories were often imbued with social Darwinist precepts which justified colonialism by attributions of "primitive promiscuity," of animalistic lust, to racial others (Gilman 1986; Pratt 1992; Stoler 1995, and chap. 1 in this volume). In Africa the sexuality of black people, and of black women in particular, was linked with the sense of a dark, threatening, and mysterious interior (Comaroff and Comaroff 1991, 86–124). This was most palpably expressed in the extraordinary story of Saartje Baartman, the !Kung woman, the "Hottentot Venus" whose protruding buttocks and overdeveloped genitalia signaled not just corporeal excess but erotic indulgence, signifying both black woman and Africa. The appalling history of her display as an object of the gaze of both circus crowds and Parisian scientists affords a particular point of view on the intimate relation between popular and scientific spectacle, the prurient voyeurism of the masses and of "objective" scientists. As Gilman (1986, 1988) has shown, however, it also links the essentialism of race and class types—the essence of the black woman and the prostitute as phenotypes, with attributes to be inspected and tabulated, painted and photographed, and cadavers collected after death, with genitalia distilled in bottles in the Musée de l'Homme (see also Jolly 1994; Wiss 1994).

The image of the African woman as the site of erotic excess is not the only formation of the erotics of the exotic. Constructs of Polynesian women in the Pacific from the exploratory voyages of the eighteenth century onwards regularly conferred on them the propensity for sexual excess, although usually in the image of the exotically beautiful rather than the grotesque (see Jolly, chap. 4 in this volume). This was not a familiar beauty, despite the constant classical allusions in depicting the bodies of Polynesian women and men as akin to the bodies of ancient Greeks or Romans. And although the women of the Western Pacific/Melanesia were rarely accorded such classical beauty, they were later also depicted as licentious. Thus Reed (chap. 2 in this volume), writing of the Massim region in Papua at the turn of the century, suggests that although adults and children alike were portrayed as promiscuous, women were singled out for their licentiousness and irresponsibility as mothers. He analyzes how the indigenous regime of sexuality was construed in the texts of missionaries, colonial officials, and Malinowski's ethnographic writings. Although they all focus on the early erotic life of Trobrianders, premarital "promiscuity," and adultery, especially of women, they did so with different colonial agendas—the missionaries intended to institute Christian notions of modesty and monogamy, the colonial officers to control the spread of venereal diseases and thereby discipline the population, and the ethnographer to document and portray Trobriand license in opposition to the sexual repression of civilization (and thereby to debate with Freud).[13]

Similar elaborations of Western-imagined Oriental sexuality were influenced by its medicalization, contributing to the mythic creation of prostitute physiology and the construction of racial/sexual typologies that continued into late-twentieth-century psychology and sociobiology (Rushton and Bogaert 1989). Different constructs emerged from different areas and in response to different phenotypes: the difference between black and Asian (cf. Tasker 1993), Melanesian/Polynesian, the reputed polymorphic desires among morphologically similar Balinese men and women, and so on.[14]

Stoler, in chapter 1 of this volume, documents the gynecological voyeurism of Stratz in his study, *Women on Java,* which infuses racial taxonomy and sexual science with the pleasures of pornography. She also cautions about the "double exposure" inherent in recirculating such voyeuristic images and texts, as in Gilman's writing on the iconography of prostitutes and Hottentot (!Kung) women (1986) and Alloula's *Colonial Harem* (1986), a glossy representation of the "greedy gaze" of French postcards of Algerian women (cf. Marcus 1992, 54–58).[15] There is no doubt about the risk of recreating the prurience of a masculinist colonialist gaze as a postcolonial theorist. But there is also the risk of being wrong: Stoler suggests that the story of the powerful, white male subject looking upon native women as sexual objects is again too simple.

Kelly (chap. 3 in this volume) argues that there has been an obsessive focus on the gaze as against the grasp, the embodied, material, and dialogical relation between European men and colonized women. He quips, "Gazes don't scar." Drawing on court documents and memoirs of Fijian colonists, Kelly highlights the tensions that exist over issues of race, sex, and colonial inequalities that ignore certain transgressors and punish others. In particular, European men seem exempted from blame in sexual coercions of Indian women by a racializing typology which constructs indentured Indian men as prone to sexual jealousy and sexual violence and indentured Indian women as embodying not just exotic sensuality but predatory promiscuity. His complex argument, developed around a court case involving an indentured Indian woman in colonial Fiji, is not just that allegations of rape invited judicial and medical voyeurism, but also that a focus on the gaze elides the power of the "looking" and "talking back" of colonized women (in exchanges with the overseer Gill, for instance). He perceives in much colonial history an overemphasis on the panoptic and all-powerful gaze (e.g., in Mitchell 1988) as scripting the colonized as victim, and as presuming the colonizer had the power not only to reshape the world but to reinscribe the consciousness of the colonized. Following Guha (1989) on India, he doubts that colonial rule ever achieved hegemony.

Jolly (1994) has elsewhere argued that such a focus in postcolonial theory can confer more power on the white male gaze (or better, Kelly's "phallic leer") than it had in the realities and fantasies of colonial life. In chapter 4 of this volume, she considers the painting of the Polynesian woman Poedua in the context of her kidnap by Captain Cook, a situation where colonial coercion and voyeurism seem tightly joined. Here, still, we might struggle to recuperate the agency of the woman in her "looking back" and even of female resistance as well as accommodation to male colonizers. Jolly tries to further unsettle the Manichean terms by asking to what extent white women were complicit in such colonial voyeurisms, not just as viewers and readers, but as authors and painters. Beatrice Grimshaw, a lady traveler in the Pacific in the early twentieth century, depicts Polynesian women with all the prurience we associate with the male gaze (1907a, 1907b, 1921, 1922). Jolly thus finds a fracturing and a fogginess in the lens of the male colonial gaze. This entails bringing into the picture not just white women, and black men and white women, but also class differences among whites. It also entails considering not just the "gaze" of visual and textual representations, but how such representations were articulated with the lived and embodied experience of sexual liaisons and reproductive relations between races. How were interracial sexual and reproductive relations constituted in the colonies? Let us now consider some of the dramatic shifts by epoch, site, and ethnicity (see Stoler 1989, 1991).

Sexual and Reproductive Liaisons—Race, Class, and Gender

Portuguese men who settled in Asia in the sixteenth century, like their counterparts in South America, moved seemingly comfortably into the local sexual milieu. In nineteenth-century Indochina and Java, too, there was little insistence on racial segregation, and indeed Dutch and French men were often urged to take local women as concubines, both to ease their corporeal and medical needs and to ease the merging of the imperial into the local culture. As Hellwig has argued for the Dutch East Indies in this period, men's sexual needs were seen to be enhanced by the hot climate and the spicy food, and they were urged for their physical and mental health to find release by taking local women as *nyai* (concubines/housekeepers). From these liaisons of Dutch men and Indonesian women were born children of mixed ancestry (Indos; those born of Chinese and Indonesian ancestry were called *peranakan*). Such intimacies were not necessarily less racist than the casual, commercial, or violent sexual relations that occurred elsewhere, but were predicated on a logic of racial assimilation rather than segregation. Moreover, as in the earlier Portuguese colonies, they often generated complicated hierarchies of racial difference and mixing (see Thomas 1994a). Similarly in the Pacific the earliest sexual patterns were of European men—sailors, beachcombers, planters, or traders—having liaisons with local women and, where these were more enduring and domestic in character, parenting children of mixed race. There are differences among European colonists, too: the French in Indochina were inclined to legitimize such relations and to recognize the children (although not necessarily in a legal form); the British and Australians in the Pacific were more inclined to a segregationist sentiment about the "half-caste" rather than the French as-similiationist sentiment about the *metis* (*metisse* [f]; see Jolly n.d.).

Along with these differences in the ethnicity of the colonizers, there were significant transformations in colonial patterns of sexuality and reproduction over time. In many colonies in Asia and the Pacific, there was a dramatic shift in the late colonial period. In both Indochina and in the Dutch East Indies, concubinage of the form predominant in the nineteenth century gave way in the twentieth century to a pattern in which upper-class men were able to take wives to the colonies, while lower-class men engaged prostitutes rather than establishing *de facto* marriages with local women. The more segregationist pattern which developed from around the turn of the twentieth century coincided with the arrival of white women in the colonies, and it is probable that their arrival coincided with an imperial push and a renewed codification of nationality (Callaway 1987; Knapman 1986). As Stoler (1992) has shown, this reflected both new bourgeois nationalist sentiments within Europe and a need to redraw racial boundaries in the colonies as "natives," Indos, *metis,* and half-castes challenged and even violently opposed colonial rule. Thus the difficulty which some white women might have faced in dealing with local women as prior lovers or concubines of their husbands is paralleled and perhaps exceeded by the sexual panics which developed around the alleged threat that indigenous men presented to white women. These perils condensed the menace of sexual license and colonial resistance (witness both the novel and the film of *A Passage to India*). As Inglis (1974) has shown for Papua, the enactment of the White Women's Protection Ordinance in 1926 derived from male commercial interests in Port Moresby, rather than women's own desire to be protected. Indeed, prior to the ordinance there had been few attacks on white women; sexual violence was more likely to involve white men raping black women, although this was underreported and rarely punished (see also Kelly, chap. 3 in this volume, for Fiji, but cf. Reed, chap. 2 in this volume on Papua). When Papuan men made advances towards white women or children, they were punitively dealt with—by hanging or life imprisonment—punishments which simultaneously inscribed the virtue of white women and the power of white men.

The ideal of the chaste white woman was in need of constant policing not just against the menace of native men but also against the risk that white women might be unduly affected by the tropical climate, suffering enervation, nervous excitation, and perhaps even "going native," lapsing into sensuality, laziness, and seduction. Moreover, the rigid stereotypes of white female chastity and native female license shifted dramatically in the postcolonial period so that, today, in several countries in southern and Southeast Asia, Western women are often cast as promiscuous and local women as restrained or sequestered. But the fear of the sexuality and allure of black/Asian men, and the possibility of white women's attraction to them, generated not just colonial edicts but extraordinary, lingering images of them as rapists and of white women as vulnerable and in need of protection. Older sexual stereotypes of black men, originating in the period of Afro-American slavery and white supremacy, still recirculate—for example, in contemporary sensitivities in the United States about the "lynching mentality" triggered by representations of black men in harassment, rape, or murder trials; in black feminist critiques of black macho; and in more playful if incendiary form in the films of Spike Lee.

Contemporary Sexualities—Occidentalism and Crossing the Borders of Hetero and Homo

The fluid and contested terrain of sexualities emerging from racial, class, and sexual difference is not just characteristic of the colonial period. Such fluidity is perhaps most obvious today in the context of migration, travel, and sexual tourism, both as lived and fantasized in novels and films (see below). The exchange of desires is also apparent in the remote valleys of Papua New Guinea (see Clark, chap. 8 in this volume) as well as the rural and urban spaces of Thailand, a nation more obviously and deeply enmeshed in the global economy of sex (Jackson, chap. 7 in this volume). Clark focuses on heterosexuality and Jackson on homosexuality, but both suggest that contemporary sexualities are not simply indigenous. Rather than being sites of exotic desire insulated from outside forces, both countries are places where contemporary sexualities negotiate the border between inside and outside.

Clark's chapter boldly confronts the question of the universality of the notion of sexuality and of Western constructs of sex as a natural urge or an instinct. He satirizes Heider's (1976) portrayal of Dani sexuality as a "low energy system" as one which not only presumes a "hydraulic" theory of desire as an urge, but also an emasculated male subject with low urges. Among the Huli, Clark finds nothing which he can translate as urge or instinct. Rather he insists on the centrality of erotic and moral aesthetics in the constitution of Huli sexuality. Moreover, while the Huli sexual regime emphasizes the dangers of "pollution" inherent in heterosexual contact and conjugal coitus, this does not make it a puritanical and repressive "low energy" system. Against a positivistic sexology which would measure only sexual contact and coital rates, Clark emphasizes the diffuse indigenous notions of desire which link erotic practice, fantasy, and mythic narratives to the aestheticization of human bodies in decoration and dance. Here, allure is focused on the male body—it is men who dress up as birds, whose glossy skins and plumage denote not just a line of attractive, spunky individuals, but an erotic affirmation of group strength, a collectivity of bachelors whose control, power, and knowledge are concentrated in their beautiful wigs. Women by contrast are made beautiful and pure by the elimination of blood in menstruation and parturition, although this is not culturally elaborated or celebrated. Further, while women are seen to lose their sexual allure with natural maturation and age, men lose their beauty because of contact with women and their blood.[16]

All of this suggests a profoundly exotic indigenous imagination, but Huli sexuality has also been influenced by forces emanating from and fantasies about the world beyond these highland valleys and ridges. We have already discussed Western or European fantasies about the Orient, but here reciprocal fantasies of the Occident are manifest. Clark documents not just the huge impact of Christian missions, capitalist economy, and state incorporation on indigenous models of sexuality and gendered bodies, but associated Occidentalist images. Two rather different images of Western sexuality emerge: one of the intimate conjugal couple promoted by missions; the other of modern uncontrolled sexuality, especially in the context of sex for money. The processes of missionization and commoditization were equally destructive of the older regimes of Huli sexual and gender relations, but they were linked with antithetical images of the white or Western woman. The Christian woman, the good woman, wife, or mother, is in many ways continuous with indigenous ideas of "good women": chaste, modest, and dressed to deemphasize beauty and sexual allure—unrevealing clothes, no jewelry, and no cosmetics. The other, the image of the modern liberated woman, comes close to that of a prostitute, or *pamuk*. Local women who are perceived as *pamuks* are seen to endanger men, especially beautiful young men, through their hot vaginas and uncontrolled sexuality, and they are seen too as flighty foreigners, dangerously mobile like witches. Such women are seen as "like European women" in their style of dress, scanty clothes, and makeup. These women are not good or beautiful; being dangerously hot and uncontrolled, they are linked with money and to the space and the values of the *nambis,* the coast, Port Moresby, and the state.

Jackson's chapter offers another perspective on the problematic relationship between biological sex, gender identity, and sexual orientation. He considers the fluid relations between indigenous regimes of sexuality in Thailand and recent European/American ideas of "gay" sexuality. Indigenous Thai sexuality seems to have celebrated simultaneously virile promiscuity for men and chastity and fidelity for women (a similar dichotomy exists in Japan, where women accommodate their husbands visiting brothels or having lovers; see Buckley, chap. 11 in this volume). Jackson notes that Thai men are expected to have both wives and other sexual partners—minor wives—and casual sexual liaisons with women and with "not-men"—*kathoey.* This category seems to have been labile enough to denote biological hermaphroditism, a third sex/gender and homosexual orientation (cf. Shore 1981 for Samoa; Coleman, Colgan, and Gooren 1992 for Burma). Even so, the accommodation was not complete; hence the homo-erotic impulse was still marginalized, its expression perceived as feminizing most particularly for the *kathoey,* the receptive or passive partner in a variety of erotic acts. The assumption of the category of *gay* reflects here not an internationalization (and commercialization) of "the homosexual" (cf. Altman 1982), but a local reconfiguration of the ambiguities of sex, gender, and sexual identity.

Such ambiguity is not an unfamiliar theme in Thai society: Gray (1990), for example, refers to the transvestite buffoonery of a bawdy theatrical performance at a village wedding in northern Thailand; and in northeastern Thailand, young men seek to ward off the "widow ghosts" (*phii mae mii*) by painting their nails and sleeping in women's sarongs (McMorran 1984). This cross-dressing differs, however, from a construction of self built around sexual preference or gender identity, and in these cases the inversion sustains the boundaries, thereby reinforcing normative heterosexuality. In Thailand, homosociality is the norm because of pervasive notions of pollution and the segregation that occurs between women and monks, but as discussed above, heterosexuality is privileged and normative. The lived experience in villages allows for some blurring of these boundaries. But homosociality is quite distinct from homosexuality, and Thai men are represented as polysexual only in terms of the number of partners and not, especially in public, in terms of the sex of their partners. The imputed and internalized meanings have little relationship to those that apply in the West—such as homosexual, transsexual, or tranvestite. Neither *kathoey* nor *gay,* for example, necessarily embrace commercial sex workers or theatre transvestites (Manderson 1995).

As Jackson shows, in the indigenous sexual regime, female sexuality was more circumscribed, and in particular lesbianism was muted. Despite some allusions to lesbian practice in depictions of *kathoey,* lesbianism was rarely named and never institutionalized. The influence of Euro-American notions of "gay" identity for lesbians and for homosexual men in Thailand has interacted with these preexisting constructs, allowing the novel possibility for men of being both homosexual and masculine, and perhaps even for the invisible lesbian to appear.

Images of the Occident also emerge in Thailand, as in Malaysia. The construction here owes little to Christian missionary discourses about sexuality and the family, and more to the contrary images of Western modernity as sexual liberation. In Malaysia, and among Malays in southern Thailand, sexual relations are imbued with political, economic, religious, and ethnic tensions. The promotion of Islam in contradistinction to Western materialism and sexual liberation, supported by the Malaysian state from the mid-1970s, offered many urban Malays an oppositional cultural identity, providing especially disaffected Malay youth a fundamentalist framework in which to forge their identity as men. Islamic fundamentalist beliefs, as advocated during this time, redefined and restrained male/female interactions in their insistence on strict adherence to propriety and respect for the boundaries of the body and, through increased insistence on adherence to the rules of association and dress, they affected women's public presentation of self and their expression of sexuality (Nagata 1984; Ong 1990). In this conservative modern environment, discussion about sex has been circumscribed. Yet during the same period, "tiger" (live sex) shows flourished in the inner city area of Chow-Kit, monitored by the Police, Officers of the Department of Religious Affairs, and the Kuala Lumpur City Council, and although women might be arrested for soliciting, there was little to prevent other forms of commodity sex. Similarly, despite state emphasis on both heterosexuality and reproduction, both the Ministry of Health and the Pink Triangle, an association of gay men and lesbians, have been active in HIV/AIDS prevention work.

Lingering Orientalisms in Movies and Novels

Just as we witness Occidentalisms in contemporary Asia and the Pacific, lingering, sometimes nostalgic Orientalisms persist in Western popular culture and especially in movies and novels. This is the culmination of a continuing, emerging discourse on the erotic/exotic, translated in popular form through cinematic and textual fictions. As in the earliest travel writings, an eroticization of exotic place pervades the metropolitan imagination of viewers and readers, reaching a larger audience than those able to "be there." In their chapters in this volume, Jolly, Manderson, and Hamilton explore the representations of sex, gender, and sexuality from eighteenth-century explorers to twentieth-century tourists in Polynesia and in Thailand. Contemporary film texts offer an evolving Western commentary on sex, a twentieth-century analogue to (and indeed sometimes directly based on) the travel writing and novels of the eighteenth and nineteenth centuries (as in *The King and I*).

Such images of exotic sites of desire depend not just on the values, expectations, and presumed practices of the anticipated audience but on the practical, cultural, and political context. Thus Jolly (chap. 4 in this volume) argues that similar tropes, for instance of sexually saturated Polynesian women, can have different effects in the journals and paintings of eighteenth-century explorers, in the texts and photos of a "lady traveler" of the twentieth century, and in postwar American cinema such as *South Pacific*. Jolly in her discussion of *South Pacific*, and Manderson (chap. 5 in this volume) on *The King and I, Emmanuelle*, and *The Good Woman of Bangkok*, are concerned with the cinematographic representations of women, ethnicity, and sexuality. Are indigenous women rendered without agency? As Berger (1972, 47) argues, "*men act* and *women appear*" (see also Mulvey 1989; Stacey 1994, among others). In the films discussed by Jolly and Manderson, the heterosexual gaze is complicated by that of race. Indigenous men or women are sometimes rendered invisible or as nonindividuated objects of desire,[17] although Bloody Mary, the Indochinese woman of *South Pacific* (1958), contradicts this tendency, being both very visible and very sexually active.

Jolly is concerned with the projection of images of a generic Pacific as a site for romance in *South Pacific*, and with the way that this acts to legitimate a Western presence and ultimately American military control. Manderson is similarly concerned with the economic and political context in representations of Thai gender and sexuality on film. She depicts the eroticization of Thailand in the successive cinematic scripts of *The King and I* (1956), *Emmanuelle* (1974), and *The Good Woman of Bangkok* (1991). The first entails not just an erotics of place, but evocations of the mysterious erotic practices of the court—the harem of wives and the role of eunuchs under the control of the monarch. *Emmanuelle* modernizes the erotic imagery of Thailand in a way which prefigures and enables sex tourism. Thailand is now the geographic site of sexual adventure and license; Thai men (not women) are vehicles for European fantasies and actions. In *The Good Woman of Bangkok* Thai men are displaced with the Thai woman, who is granted a central role; like her namesake in Brecht's play *The Good Woman of Setzuan*, the prostitute in this film is portrayed as "the good woman in a wicked world."[18] The erotics of the exotic—as represented on film over time—appear to provide templates, even moral charters, for contemporary interactions. And in the *The Good Woman of Bangkok* fact and fiction slide into and out of each other.

Hamilton (chap. 6 in this volume) considers more closely contemporary Western men's accounts of Thai women and their sexuality, drawing on popular books and short stories in which the lives of Western men, often long-term residents of Thailand, and their Thai lovers are enmeshed.

The works that she includes, and others of their genre (e.g., Dawson 1988; O'Merry 1990), complement film accounts of the Orient, and in particular caricaturizations of Thai women (or Asian women generally) as pliable and submissive yet sexually skillful and experienced, contradictorily submissive yet manipulative. Hence the contrary images of a Thai woman folding a man's clothes after coitus "with a smile on her face" (see Manderson, this volume) on the one hand, and extracting money and favors on the other (Krich 1989; Barnes 1993; Odzer 1994). Yet the foreign (*farang*) man seems also to be in search of his identity as a "real" man, through relating to a truly feminine woman, and also even in search of love and long-term commitment. Given the confoundings and confusions about love and money, such relations are often seen to degenerate into mutual misrecognitions and disappointments.

For Love or Money? The Political Economy of Sex

Hamilton (this volume) suggests that this long libidinization of Thailand reached its zenith in 1993, with the Longman dictionary definition of Bangkok as a "place where there are a lot of prostitutes." Westerners often associate Thailand with "sex-for-sale, play-for-pay" and indeed Southeast Asia more generally with the commodification of sexuality and, by implication, the presumed low status of women (Seidler 1987; O'Neill 1989). The literature on prostitution—historical, sociological, and ethnographic—is substantial;[19] however, it has often created rather dramatic, ahistorical, and overstated images of the institutions and the people involved—both sex workers and clients. Gronewold, for example, described the sexual economy of prerevolutionary China as one that was unchanging in its treatment of women and girls as commodities. Stories of Japanese prostitution offer, for poor families, the same accounts (Hirschfeld 1935; Sone 1992). While traffic in women (and children) certainly occurred, there were a number of very different reasons for women's migration from family homes and their involvement in prostitution (Manderson 1995).

The traffic in women has been a particular feature of colonial and postcolonial Southeast Asia, and to a much lesser extent, of the ports, commercial, and administrative centers of the Pacific. Colonial attitudes and policies toward prostitution were based on an understanding of masculinity which decreed that regular heterosexual intercourse was normal and desirable. But they were also artifacts of early colonial migration policy whereby men but not women were recruited both as colonial administrators and as laborers. Sexual arrangements, including the accommodation of brothels and the medical surveillance of the women who worked in them, were made to placate and maintain the workforce through the provision of recreational sex and to limit infection among white settlers and troops (e.g., Walkowitz 1980; Warren 1993; Manderson 1996).

The arrival of foreigners powerfully influenced the history of sexualities more generally in complex and sometimes contradictory ways. As noted above, commercial sex transactions between indigenous women and colonial men proliferated and were sometimes officially endorsed while also subject to surveillance and control, with certain interesting contradictions in policies towards prostitution and the timing of repressions. The registration of brothels, rules and regulations regarding medical examinations, and the establishment of "lock hospitals" for the isolation of people with infectious diseases in the British colonies in the nineteenth and early twentieth centuries related both to practical economic and public health concerns in the colonies, as noted above (and see Reed, chap. 2 in this volume). But in the face of international and British-based pressure, prostitution was suppressed in the mid-1920s. In contrast, Japan suppressed mixed bathing in the 1870s as part of a gesture of "modernization," and in the Pacific from the early nineteenth century, missionaries proscribed behavior construed as sexual license and pushed to make prostitution illegal.

In "The Time of AIDS"

Imagined sexual license may have lured male colonists to spend time in the East, and colonial contact frequently led to sexual liaisons with local women and associated erotic fantasies. But along with the first sexual exchanges in Asia and the Pacific, there was the associated spectre of infection and especially of venereal diseases. HIV/AIDS is simply the most recent arrival in a long history of other sexually transmitted infections—infections which have often been spread by travel and migration, as with the spread of venereal disease by the sexual explorations of sailors on Cook's voyages in the Pacific. While Cook tried to stop this sexual commerce and its deadly consequences (see Jolly 1996), the primary goal of governments in the Pacific and in Asia was, as suggested above, to regulate commercial sex and inspect women in order to minimize morbidity and mortality and monitor transmission. The case of HIV/AIDS is no different.

In "the time of AIDS" (Herdt and Lindenbaum 1992), it is impossible not to address HIV/AIDS and to ponder how much the epidemic has changed not just sexual practices but sexual meanings and indeed the shape of research on sexualities (Manderson 1994). The epidemic in North

America, Europe, and Australia has not only spawned much more dedicated and empirical research on sexualities, but it has also tended to reassociate sexuality with disease, pathology, and death. As the burgeoning work in Africa has shown, HIV/AIDS is different not just in its epidemiological manifestation but in its discursive constitution in places remote from Europe, America, or Australia (Patton 1990; Farmer 1992; Daniel and Parker 1993). Whereas in the West, AIDS has been discursively linked with the fears of homosexuality, prostitution, and drugs, Western discourses on AIDS in Africa have often condensed the horror of the disease with fears of "the dark continent" that are reminiscent of earlier constructions of Africa and "African sexuality" (see above). There has also been a tendency to naturalize the epidemic, as pestilence, drought, and famine have been treated as natural rather than social disasters in that afflicted continent. For Treichler (1988, 1992a), HIV/AIDS is an epidemic of signification, but the discursive epidemiology shifts from site to site.

In Asia, stories of AIDS situate its spread in the context of globalization and development, and in perceptions of the "other." The long history of public health and in particular of past approaches to other STDs (Arnold 1993; Bamber, Hewison, and Underwood 1993) provides a backdrop to contemporary HIV/AIDS policies and programs in Southeast Asia and the Pacific. This is nowhere clearer than in the current proliferation of studies of the spread of HIV/AIDS in Asia and of associated public health programs, with their emphasis on the control of transmission through behavioral interventions in the lives of sex workers, migrant women, intravenous drug users, and gays in particular.

The social history of HIV/AIDS in Asia begins with an initial denial of its incidence in the region. Then came allegations that cases were "imported" (Law and Buckley, chaps. 10 and 11 in this volume), leading in turn to a brief period of speculation that Asians were in some way genetically resistant to infection. A growing number of cases led to local political acknowledgement of the epidemic, a shift in categorizing Asia epidemiologically, and the creation of new epidemiological patterns. The current explosion of infection, first in Thailand, then in India, Burma, and China, and then elsewhere in the region, highlights certain parallels with Africa, where HIV is transmitted heterosexually along the lines of trucking routes, but it also points to the significance of homosexual transmission, transmission through needle-sharing, the opportunistic and casual basis of "prostitution," and the political, economic, and cultural contexts of commercial sex (see Lyttleton 1994a; Savage 1996; Porter, chap. 9 in this volume).

The chapters by Porter on the Thai-Burmese border and by Law on the

Philippines explore several dimensions of these issues. Porter investigates the massive spread of the epidemic on the borders of Thailand and Burma, which are rendered permeable by the extensive trade, drug trafficking, movement of militia, and pervasive mobility in the region. Just as trucks cross over and connect "the golden triangle" with the interiors of Myanmar, China, and India, so HIV/AIDS is spreading across the region. As in Africa, the epidemic is moving on major trucking routes, gruesomely metaphoric of a process of globalization across national borders. Prostitution and intravenous drug use are implicated. But Porter perceives a tendency to presume categories of commercial sex worker (CSW) and intravenous drug user (IDU) in a way which occludes the fluidity of identities and which perpetuates the essentialization and stigmatization of "risk groups" rather than "risk behaviors or situations." Constructing epicentres of "core transmitters" provides an illusory cartographic certainty in a turbulent terrain. Porter argues, as he has regarding participatory development programs more generally, that rather than enabling and ennobling, such interventions may secure control by both governments and international agencies and "encircle" rather than empower those who are its targets.

Law similarly pursues the problematic dichotomies of choice and determination in a study of prostitution in the Philippines. Her chapter is focused on Cebu City in the period after the closure of the American bases and explores the relationship between the growth of sex work (including bar work and dancing), tourism, and the city's expansion inside a "bubble economy." Prostitution in the Philippines has typically been viewed in terms of the political economy of colonialism, militarism, and sex tourism. Although such structural determinants are important, Law argues that such analyses tend to cast women as victims rather than agents. But equally problematic is a construction which sees sex work simply as a job and asserts the free will of women to enter the industry without regard to poverty and debt. The dichotomies of agency and determination are traced not just through the life stories of female sex workers, but also in the variant discourses of development agencies and foreign and local nongovernment organizations (NGOs) working with female prostitutes in the context of HIV/AIDs. She critically assesses the relevance of "peer education" models derived from the West and especially from the experience of the gay community within Australia. There is a real danger here not only of presuming the universal meaning of sexuality and prostitution but also of fostering a new kind of colonialism in development aid whereby inapposite concepts of community and choice are transplanted from Sydney to Cebu City (cf. Murray and Robinson 1996).

In the final chapter of this volume, Sandra Buckley turns our attention to Japan, which—because of its economic and political position, and its reticence regarding local transmission—has sought and received little attention regarding HIV/AIDS. Like Thailand, the Philippines, and other countries in the region, Japan has construed AIDS as a "foreign" disease, both because it was introduced from the outside (through infected blood products) and because its sexual transmission within Japan is associated with and blamed on foreigners, particularly migrant sex workers. Buckley offers a cultural critique of Japan's response to its epidemic, which associates infection and the outside, while muting and thereby stigmatizing homosexuality and valorizing the nuclear heterosexual household within Japan.

Like Porter, she critically analyzes "the story in the statistics." These are not neutral numbers; by their very categorization of modes of transmission they signal the distinctive status of hemophiliacs as innocent victims deserving of state compensation, in contrast to the guilty, those who contracted the disease via sexual or drug-related transmission. The infected blood came primarily from the United States, thus underlining the foreignness of the epidemic. Moreover, the official figures always signal foreigners in parentheses, thus separating and enabling the stigmatization of those illegal immigrant women who work in the entertainment and sex industry. These are now primarily Thai with fewer Filipinas, Koreans, Taiwanese, and Chinese. Both media debate and public health progams tend to construct these women as the "source" of HIV/AIDS, and they are policed by blood testing and periodic raids, thereby "protecting" their Japanese male clients from them. There are probably patterns of underreporting of Japanese nationals as seropositive, because of shame, doctor's protocols of nondisclosure to terminal patients, and medical corruption.

Such patterns of blaming foreigners rather than Japanese are also reflected in newspaper stories and images, and in the videos, brochures, and *manga* comics used for AIDS education. In representations of AIDS in the United States, the emphasis is constantly on the importance of choosing the right life style, that is avoiding gay sex, sex work, and drug use. Even when the focus is on Japanese nationals, it is on "coming home," on reconciliation with family and homeland, rather than "coming out." A widely used AIDS education video assiduously avoids discussion of homosexuality, while other official brochures deploy strong antihomosexual images and language. They constantly construct homosexuals, foreigners, and drug users as threats to the happy, risk-free, heterosexual family. Canonically, it is the body of the mother, the heart of the family and Japan, which is depicted as a zone of sanctity and safety. But rather than accepting such a clear border between inside and outside, with carriers moving on "black lines of contagion," Buckley insists on the oozing through the cracks, and on the porous permeable boundaries of bodies, spaces, and national borders.

From Malinowski to Foucault—Sameness, Difference and Sexualities

We trust that in this volume we have rendered problematic any easy presumptions about the universality of sexuality as a natural instinct and about what constitutes male or female sexuality, heterosexuality,or homosexuality. But we have been equally insistent on avoiding a facile relativism, whereby cultural differences in sexualities are reified to such an extent that they defy mutual translation. In terms of both embracing bodies and desiring minds, there has been a long history of sexual contact and mutual erotic influence between Europe and the regions of Asia and the Pacific. Such contact has of course not always involved parity or mutuality in pleasures. Colonial sexual regimes were saturated with colonial power, but such power was often contested and was rarely hegemonic. Is there the risk, in this allegedly postcolonial moment, of recreating a Western hegemony in theory which was never there in practice? This brings us back to the recent Western theorizing about sexualities discussed at the start.

All of these concerns proceed from a presumption about "our part of the world." But as Stoler's chapter suggests, this imagined site is "more than innocuous convention, but a porous and problematic boundary to sustain." Who is speaking in the creation of this geopolitical map of subjects and objects of desire? As researchers and theorists of sexuality, we often not only occupy the site of the West but take it as our point of view as the normative measure of sameness and difference. We thereby presume our global centrality and deny our global connections.

We want to illustrate this by two theorists at a temporal and theoretical remove—Malinowski and Foucault. The first was a zealous ethnographer of the sexual customs of Melanesia, who strongly contrasted the "sexual lives of savages" with those of his own allegedly repressed Europe. Foucault, in contrast, never did empirical research in Asia or the Pacific, but his theory and speculative history of sexuality in Europe has often been moved to these places. These movements have sometimes presumed that the history of sexuality as he depicts it in Europe might be repeated, as in those theories of development which conceive a teleological trajectory whereby Europe becomes a dress rehearsal for the rest of the world. Several papers in this volume deploy and critically evaluate such Foucauldian transpositions (Stoler, Reed, Clark, and Porter).

Vance (1991, 875) has recently challenged the way in which anthropologists have portrayed themselves as fearless investigators of sexual customs and mores throughout the world, as breaking through the erotophobic intellectual taboos in other, more timid disciplines. She suggests that this is at odds with a more pervasive disciplinary tendency either to deny centrality or legitimacy to the study of sexuality or else to assimilate it to discussions of kinship and heterosexual reproduction and marriage. This is no doubt true of much anthropological work of the twentieth century. But Malinowski's early classics on the Trobriands, *Sex and Repression in Savage Society* (1927) and *The Sexual Life of Savages in North Western Melanesia* (1929),[20] not only precisely struck the posture of the fearless sexual scientist, but secured his ethnographic authority and captured popular imagination and a large readership. Moreover, in his obsessive attention to the physical facts of Trobriand sex, sexuality was presented as autonomous and never just as a part of heterosexual marriage. The directness of his works makes them rare and valuable too, in contrast to anthropological accounts wherein sexuality (and certainly sexual behavior) was considered only implicitly in structural and institutional terms, with respect to courtship, kinship, marriage, fertility, adoption, divorce, and inheritance. But as Reed argues in chapter 2, Malinowski's ethnography was complicit with broader colonial agendas, and he objectified his subjects as much as do the authors of parallel studies of physical anthropology and anthropometry, and the sexual sciences of doctors and medical researchers (Gilman 1985, 1988; Stoler 1995; Manderson 1996). This objectification was no doubt enhanced by his own sexual silences, at least until the publication of his diaries (Malinowski 1967) in which—as Kulick puts it—his "brazen fantasies" were revealed (Kulick and Willson 1995, 2). Until that time there was only the shocking detail of infantile promiscuity, of Trobriand love magic, and of erotic positions to titillate European audiences with their exoticism as well as physicality. No wonder his works became central texts in debates with Freud about the repressive nature of civilization.

But Malinowski's corpus was much more than this, debating as it did the questions of "virgin birth," theories of procreation in a matrilineal society, and the nature of the family. Malinowski perhaps managed temporarily to dislocate the secure patriarchal father of the Viennese family with the figure of an uncertain Trobriand father. Thus, in this case and perhaps more generally, we must ask again how far we can securely separate sexuality and reproduction. This has been a shibboleth of much feminist and gay theory in recent time, for obvious reasons. But this new orthodoxy makes it hard to concede their connectedness in other sites, in ways which relate not just to heterosexual marriage but to broader notions of social reproduction, fecundity, and growth. Was the embedding of sex in kinship a silencing of the sexual, or was it appropriate?

Le Guin has recently observed how the production of discourses on sexuality by men in particular have elided reproduction from sex and limited it to "copulation as if it knew nothing about pregnancy, birth, nursing, mothering, puberty, menstruation, or menopause" (1992, 228). She insists on meshing the sexuality of women-as-lovers with that of women-as-mothers, thus refusing the differentiation of pleasure and reproduction. This is not to deny womanhood or sexual pleasure to nonreproductive women (celibate, lesbian, or childless) but rather to insist on the pleasures of reproductive heterosexual women. Perhaps this is important not just for the heterosexual mother, but also for homosexual lovers in similar sites. Thus, by Herdt's account, homosexual practices in Sambia are markedly about growth as well as pleasure, and in "making men," sexuality and reproduction are again connected, although in different ways.

The issue extends beyond the separation of sexuality and reproduction to the broader supposition that sexuality has ontological status in all times and places, that it is a thing that can be named and to which a set of behaviors, feelings, and desires can be attached. But can sexual desire and action be segmented and reified, as a "thing" unto itself (cf. Ram 1993). Here we presume that sexuality is much more than corporeal acts of vaginal or anal copulation, fellatio or cunnilingus, caressing another or oneself. The images and fantasies of a desiring subject are much more than these corporeal acts, creating an atmosphere around their anticipation, deferment, and realization. Sexual desire is entangled with broader questions of pleasure, with the aesthetics of the body, with the pleasures of a more diffuse sensuality and collective sociality, and sometimes with the pleasures of fecundity. We must be wary of imputing a Western model of an individuated subject of sexuality. The indigenous sexual regimes of both the Pacific and Asia make it hard to sustain this idea of a sexual self. As Marilyn Strathern (1988) has argued for Melanesian constructs of the person in general, there is no clear distinction of object and subject, but rather a permeable person constituted by gendered debts of substance and interactions between persons inscribed with gender. In part her argument opposes Herdt's depiction of Sambian sexualities (1981), finding there a propensity to presume a masculine ego as sexed subject and a tendency to apply too readily the psychological and psychiatric theories derived from the West.

Rather different questions of theoretical imperialism can be posed in relation to Foucault. Foucault (1979) challenged the repressive hypothesis posited by Freud, arguing that the alleged repression of the Victorian period was in fact an excitation of desire produced through discursive excess. He discerns four "strategic unities" in the transformation of sexuality in Europe—the hysterization of women's bodies, the psychiatrization of perverse pleasure, the surveillance of the procreative couple, and the pedagogization of children's sexuality. We should note in passing how central the contested linkages between sexuality and reproduction are in such processes: all rely both on the excitation of desire through its policing and the notion that sex is constituted as a deep secret to be discovered, revealed, and confessed.

In drawing on Foucauldian notions of how the recent history of sexuality in Europe has been constituted by a surfeit of sexual talk rather than its repression, Clark (chap. 8 in this volume) also ponders what sexuality might be in places beyond the West, particularly for the Huli of Papua New Guinea, who through the processes of colonization and missionization have had to confront the differences in Western notions of desire and practice. As he illustrates, such differences are activated in the postcolonial state most obviously in public health and safe sex programs devised to contain the spread of HIV/AIDS. But prior to these recent regimes, the technologies were concentrated in the Christian confession, which relied heavily on the notion of sex as *the* secret to be confessed. Yet as Reed shows (chap. 2 in this volume), in their efforts to extract confessions, Christian missionaries in Papua tried to create an individuated sexual subject, prone to guilt, and often failed miserably.

Unlike Freud, Foucault does not believe that sex is *the* secret. In Freud, the subject preexists as an originary source with erotic urges or instincts; in Foucault, the subject is interpellated, constituted, created through discourse. The theories they have produced and the practices, behaviors, and identities that they seek to explain are antithetical in their conceptions of sexuality and their constitution of "the subject." But, espoused or denied, celebrated or subverted, sexuality is still seen as being at the core of the modern Western self, constituting both its objects of desire and its subject of sexed identity.

Yet both the theories of Freud and Foucault are awkward and inapposite in construing non-Western sexualities, particularly the way in which a sexual subject relates to the collectivity. We will not rehearse the difficulties of extrapolating Foucauldian theory of the history of sexuality in western Europe to the colonial context. Ann Stoler's introductory essay and a number of others in this volume (Reed, Clark, and Kelly most especially) contribute admirably to this. But we do want to highlight the more general problems—the lingering imperialism in our presumption of adjudging sameness and difference from the West, our unstated premises about the centrality of sex, its dissociation from reproduction, and its concentration in the private interiority of a sexed subject.

Some Final Thoughts

There are clearly other theories of sexuality which originate from sites beyond the West. Asian philosophies and aesthetics of sexuality in Confucian, Hindu, and Islamic modes we know about vaguely. The sanctification of sex in Hawaiian cosmogonic chants and hula dances, or New Guinea Highlands concepts of the lustre of skin as a sign of health, virility, and morality, are perhaps less understood. We need to credit the diversity and resilience of such non-Western theories of sexuality, although we have barely started a consideration of them here. In this volume we have explored the ways in which sexualities, embodied practices, and sexual meanings have been constituted across the borders of cultures in the Asian and Pacific regions. Our desire is to view sexuality not just as an autonomous realm of the senses, but as embedded in a social world structured and saturated by relations of power, not just of gender and sexual orientation but also of race and class. Shifts in political and economic circumstances are reflected in the contructions of the eros of "others"—from the intimate relations among and between male and female bodies to sexual exchanges between countries. Indeed the construction of the "self-other" dichotomies along these several axes might require simultaneous deconstruction. In exploring sexualities across borders in Asia and the Pacific, we trust we have also contributed to debates about gender, race, and class and the historically and culturally constituted character of the body in the context of broader political transformations of colonial and postcolonial history. Our original aim was to understand how Western ideas and images were projected onto Asian and Pacific peoples, but ultimately we had to imagine how such ideas and fantasies had to contend with the refractory realities and alternative philosophies of "other peoples." In the contemporary globalizing culture of which we are all a part, a reverse process of Occidentalism resists a lingering Orientalism. These reciprocal processes are not necessarily of equal force. Thus the problem remains as to how far cross-cultural sexual relations betray exploitation and misrecognition, and how far they allow a mutual translation of pleasure.

CHAPTER ONE

Educating Desire in Colonial Southeast Asia: Foucault, Freud, and Imperial Sexualities

ANN STOLER

One should not think that desire is repressed, for the simple reason that the law is what constitutes desire and the lack on which it is predicated. Where there is desire, the power relation is already present; an illusion, then to denounce this relation for a repression exerted after the event; but vanity as well, to go questing after a desire that is beyond the reach of power.

Foucault, *The History of Sexuality,* vol. 1 (1978, 81)

Judith Butler (1987, 186–229) has characterized volume 1 of Foucault's *The History of Sexuality* as a history of Western desire, but I am not sure this is the case. In fact desire is one of the most elusive concepts in the book, the shibboleth that Foucault discards and disclaims. For Foucault there is no "original" desire that juridical law must respond to and repress; rather desire follows from and is generated out of the law, out of the power-laden discourses of sexuality where it is animated and addressed.[1] In contrast to Freud's contention that "civilization is built up upon a renunciation of instinct," Foucault's task has been to specify the historical moment in the midnineteenth century when "instinct" emerged into discourse, to specify the cultural production of the notion of "sexual desire" as an index of individual and collective identity (Freud 1961, 45).[2] Since the "truth" of our sexual desire (the premise that we can know ourselves if we know the truth of that primal sexual instinct hidden within us) is not a starting point for Foucault, knowledge of our "true desires" cannot be a condition of critique; it must be a historically constituted *object* of enquiry (Rajchman 1985, 91). Foucault does not dismiss Freudian models entirely, but, as Rajchman notes, assumes a "kind of practical and historical doubt about their use . . . with the suggestion that there may be more to the historical determination of sexual desire than the prevention of our capacity to publicly formulate it."

The paradox of volume 1, however, is that while sexuality is that which inscribes desire in discourse, the discourses and technologies of sex that

Foucault describes tell us very little about what sorts of desires are produced in the nineteenth century and what people do with them.[3] We know that the confessional apparatus of "medical exams, psychiatric investigations, pedagogical reports, and family controls" were mechanisms of both pleasure and power, but it is left for us to examine in particular political contexts how that pleasure is distributed, how desire is structurally motivated, and what specific "spirals" of pleasure and power are displayed (Foucault 1978, 45).[4] Foucault defines his project as one that will "define the regime of power-knowledge-pleasure that sustains the discourse on human sexuality *in our part of the world*" (11). But once we turn to question the distributions of desires, to "discover who does the speaking" in the geopolitical mapping of desiring subjects and desired objects, "our part of the world" becomes more than an innocuous convention, but a porous and problematic boundary to sustain. For that boundary itself, as we know, took as much discursive and political energy to produce as that which bound sex to power and the "truth" of identity to sex.[5]

If the founding premise of Foucault's analysis is to trace how sexual desire is incited by regulatory discourses, one might expect the field of colonial studies, so influenced by him, to have embraced more of his critique than it has actually done. We have looked more to the regulation and release of desire than to its manufacture. We have hardly even registered the fact that the writing of colonial history has often been predicated on just the assumption that Foucault attacked: the premise that colonial power relations can be accounted for and explained as a sublimated expression of repressed desires in the West, of desires that resurface in moralizing missions, myths of the "wild woman," in a romance with the rural "primitive," or in other more violent, virile, substitute form.

In most colonial historiography, questions of desire occupy a curious place. While the regulation of sexuality has taken center stage, Foucault's reworking of the repressive hypothesis and thus the cultural production of desire has not. Although sexual desire, as expressed, repressed, made illicit, misdirected, inherited, and otherwise controlled has underwritten European folk theories of race from the seventeenth to twentieth centuries, desire is often suspended as a precultural instinct to which social controls are applied, a *deus ex machina,* given and unexplained. Much mainstream colonial history has proceeded not from a Foucauldian premise that desire is a social construct and sex a nineteenth-century invention, but from an implicitly Freudian one.[6] While Freudian language has certainly permeated other branches of history and other disciplines, the specific and varied invocations of Freudian models in colonial studies—and the effects of their often silent presence—have been neither fully acknowledged nor explored (see La-Capra 1989).

The relationship between Freudian models and Foucauldian critiques in the writing of colonial history has been more complicated than one might expect. Some analytic debts have been more quickly acknowledged than others. But saying yes to Foucault has not always meant saying no to Freud, not even for Foucault himself. Despite Foucault's rejection of the repressive hypothesis, there are surprising ways in which their projects can and do converge. For Freud, sexual desire is a cause; for Foucault, an effect. Freud accounts for the psychological etiology of perversions; Foucault looks to the cultural production and historical specificity of the notions of sexual pathology and perversion themselves. The differences are striking, but so are some of the points at which they are complementary, if not the same. Both were concerned with boundary formation, with the "enemy" within. For Freud, cultural conventions arise out of the psychological contortions of the individual at war with her or his own subliminal desires. As Kristeva writes, "Freud does not speak of foreigners: he teaches us how to detect foreignness in ourselves" (1991, 191). For Foucault, the cultural conventions of racism emerge out of social bodies at war with themselves. Thus when Rogin, in a paper on liberal society and the Indian question, argues that attitudes to native Americans were personalized and conceived as a "defense of the [American] self" (1971, 284)—what Foucault would call a defense of society against itself—it is Freud he draws on, but Foucault might have subscribed to Rogin's language of "defense" as well. Or, inversely, we might look to Edward Said's (1978) supremely Foucauldian analysis of Orientalist discourse and Western domination, where Freud's notion of projection, of the Orient as a "surrogate self" for the West, is a crucial but buried part of his argument.

In this essay I am interested in two problems: the ways in which the language of Freud has entrenched itself in the general field of colonial studies, and the tangled coexistence of Freud and Foucault, more specifically, in analyses of colonial racism. If Foucault has led us to the power of discourse, it is Freud who has, albeit indirectly, turned us toward the power of fantasy, to imagined terror, to perceived assaults on the European self that made up the anxious and ambivalent world in which European colonials lived.[7] It is Freud after all, on whom Fanon so effectively draws, who located, as Homi Bhabha writes (1994), how "the deep fear of the Black figured in the psychic trembling of Western sexuality." Fanon was not alone. Octavio Mannoni (1950), Albert Memmi, and Ashis Nandy (1983) have each drawn on Freudian psychoanalytics to provide a *contre-histoire* of colonialism, a way to access the subjugated knowledges and psychology of domination of colonized "Man." I am not proposing that our task in colonial studies is to abandon Freudian concepts—only the unreflexive use of them. We need to be aware of the varied analytic work we expect them to do—to distinguish, for example, when the concepts of repression, displacement, identification, and projection that saturate so much of colonial historiography serve to clarify historical processes of empire—and when, more frequently, they are invoked to substitute for an analysis of them.[8]

If we subject the use of Freudian models to scrutiny, we must scrutinize the use of Foucauldian models as well. If we embrace Foucault's statement that "sexuality is a dense transfer of power," charged with "instrumentality," do we not risk reproducing the very terms of colonial discourse itself, where everything and anything can be reduced to sex? Is Baudrillard's snipe valid that Foucault merely replaced the fiction of *homo economicus* with another, that of *homo sexualis*? And what is precluded by an economy of sex in which the genealogy of desiring subjects is only desiring men (Baudrillard 1977, 30)? While it may be that, in much colonial discourse, issues of sexuality were often metonymic of a wider set of relations, and sex was invariably about power, power was not always about sex. In these colonial contexts, discourses of sexuality often glossed, colonized, appropriated, and erased a much more complicated set of sentiments that, boiled down to sex, were easily served up for immediate consumption.

There is overwhelming evidence that much colonial discourse, as Foucault's argument would suggest, has been framed by a search for the "truth" of the European bourgeois self through sex. This is not surprising. What is disturbing is that colonial historiography has inadvertently embraced this notion of truth as well. Students of colonialism have often taken their readings of European sexual conduct in the colonies from colonial scripts themselves. Freudian notions of a repressed, sublimated, and projected sexual impulse are invoked to explain political projects in instinctual, psychosocial terms. In one version, desire is a basic biological drive, restricted and repressed by a civilization that forces our sublimation of it. Thus Fredrickson (1981, 100) in his history of white supremacy in the United States and South Africa suggests that Elizabethan repression of English sexuality may have incited the "secret or subliminal attractions" that were "projected onto Africans," and Gann and Duignan (1978, 240) in their work on colonial Africa write that British imperial expansion was possibly "a sublimation or alternative to sex."[9]

If the repressive hypothesis is unacknowledged by these authors, it is not by others. Mannoni's postwar study (1950) of French-Malagasy colonial relations was centrally figured around the psychological coordinates and political consequences of European repression.[10] Fanon (1967), too, explicitly called on psychoanalytic theory to explain racism as the projection of the white man's desires onto the Negro, where "the white man behaves 'as if' the Negro really had them." Freyre is perhaps most notorious for having attributed varied manifestations of colonial racial prejudice to the active libidos of the Portuguese, to the fact that they were so "highly sexed," in contrast to the more sexually conservative Anglo-Saxons (1946, 94). According to Jordan (1968, 40), Englishmen in the Renaissance projected onto the African "libidinal man" what "they could not speak of in themselves." Drinnon's study of the metaphysics of Indian-hating and empire-building in U.S. history (*Facing West*, 1980) takes a systemic "repression" as the underlying theme of racial violence.[11] So too did Rawick (1972, 132), who compared the Englishman's meeting with the West African to the experience of a "reformed sinner" who creates "a pornography of his former life." By Rawick's account, this "great act of repression" left the Englishman identifying with "those who live as he once did or as he still consciously desires to live."

For both Rawick and Jordan, racism emerged out of the unconscious realization by the English not that Africans were so different, but that they were frighteningly the same. As Jordan put it, there was an "irreconcilable conflict between desire and aversion for interracial sexual union. . . . [It] rested on the bedrock fact that white men perceived Negroes as being *both alike and different* from themselves. . . . Without perceptions of similarity, no desire and no widespread gratification was possible" (1968, 137–38). For Jordan, some form of sexual desire is a given, while for Rawick, there is a hint that other motivating desires may have been at issue as well. Roediger takes up just that theme in *Wages of Whiteness* (1991) to specify the sort of nostalgic longings that racist "projections" entailed. He contends that the consensus achieved by a heterogeneous white working class in the nineteenth-century United States rested on an idea of blackness that embodied "the preindustrial past that they scorned and missed."[12] In Roediger's nuanced analysis, it is not *sexual* license that is longed for, nor *sexual* desire that is repressed, but desire in other forms, "longing for a rural past and the need to adapt to the urban present" of industrial discipline (109, 117).

In each of these versions of the repressive hypothesis, some combination of the Freudian notions of sublimated and projected desire is offered to account for racism and Europe's imperial expansion. Racism is treated as a historical construct, but repression of instinct remains the engine. The libidinal qualities imputed to the Other are understood as a product of racist fears, but sexual desire itself remains biologically driven, assumed and unexplained. The underlying assumption is, as Martha Vicinus once so aptly put it, a "hydraulic model of sexuality" where "sex is always something to be released or controlled; if controlled it is sublimated, or deflected, or distorted" (1982, 136).

The notion that Western civilization has become increasingly restrictive and that the colonies have provided escape hatches from it runs deep in early Orientalist traditions and remains resonant in their contemporary popular forms.[13] White (1972, 7), among others, points to a modern cultural anthropology that "has conceptualized the idea of wildness as the repressed content of *both* civilized *and* primitive humanity," of the "Wild Man . . . lurking within every man." Tiffany and Adams have similarly argued that the anthropological idea of the sexualized "Wild Woman" has provided the "mirror in which we perceive ourselves" (1985, 6). Gay's recent study of the bourgeois cultivation of hatred portrays male agents of empire as those who "satisfied their aggressive needs with abandon" (1993, 85–86).[14] Buruma, in an otherwise wonderful review of perhaps the best Dutch colonial novel ever written, Louis Couperus's *The Hidden Force,* writes that "the European fear of letting go, of being 'corrupted,' of going native, was to a large extent, I suspect, the northern puritan's fear of his (or her) own sexuality" (1994, 30–32). Mason similarly notes that Rhodesian whites in the early twentieth century attributed to the "native," to "some dark and shadowy figure which they fear and hate, the desires they disapprove of most strongly in themselves . . . and when desire emerged, fear was not far away" (1958, 244).[15]

Eroticized native bodies densely occupy the landscape of Western literature, and in the wake of Said's powerful critique of Orientalism (1978), a profusion of literary and historical studies have catalogued the wide range of sexual and gendered metaphors in which the feminized colonies, and the women in them, were to be penetrated, raped, silenced, and (dis)possessed (Mill 1991; Mellman 1992; Behdad 1994). The sexual assault on women has provided more than the foundational imagery of imperial domination. Colonialism itself has been construed as the sublimated sexual outlet of virile and homoerotic energies in the West.[16] But to argue that different notions of bourgeois manhood were merely confirmed by colonial ventures is to dilute a more complicated story. For if the colonies were construed as sites where European virility could be boldly demonstrated, it was because they were also thought to crystallize those conditions of isolation, inactivity, decadence, and intense male comradery where heterosexual definitions of manliness could as easily be unmade.

Freudian assumptions about the relationship between repression and desire hold fast. While Said (1978, 190) rightly notes how much the Orient has been conceived as a "place where one could look for sexual experiences unobtainable in Europe," Hyam has taken that colonial discourse not as an object of critique but as a transparent social fact and basis for his own analysis. Hyam's *Empire and Sexuality* (1990, 158) exemplifies a recent twist on the theme of an unrestrictive colony and a restricted West. He holds that empire provided "sexual opportunities" for European men when those in Britain were severely reduced. While explicitly deferring to Foucault's "model of sexual politics" to describe sexual attitudes in nineteenth-century Britain, he frames his argument with the repressive hypothesis, and questions of power and racism drop out of his account (1990, 58). For Hyam, among others, the colonies are a site for the "revenge of the repressed," an open terrain for European male ejaculations curtailed in the West.[17] Hyam's narrow focus on genitalia rather than gender, on the sexual fantasies of elite white males, on "sexual relaxation" rather than rape, is only part of his problem.[18] The sexual politics of empire has never been reduced to the opportunistic possibilities prompted by repressions in Europe alone.[19] What gets clouded in such accounts is precisely where Foucault's analysis would lead us. Colonial discourses of sexuality were productive of class and racial power, not mere reflections of them. The management of European sexuality in the colonies was a class-and gender-specific project that animated a range of longings as much as it was a consequence of them. Nor were these confined to the colonies alone; for how else can we understand the production of desire that continued to surround Eurasian "half-caste" girls who, Buruma tells us (1994, 32), were still considered "hot" when he was growing up in The Hague in the 1940s and 1950s? But attention to the discourses on sexual desire only captures a small part of the psychological complexities that turned imitation into mockery, ambivalence into aggression, and reduced cultural nostalgia to a desire for—or prohibitions against—sex.[20]

Discourses about sexual contagions, moral contamination, and reproductive sterility were not applicable to any and all whites; nor were they free-floating, generalized pronouncements that treated all bodies as equally susceptible and the same. These discourses circulated in a racially charged magnetic field in which debates about sexual contamination, sexual abstinence, or spermatic depletion produced moral clusters of judgment and distinction that defined the boundaries of middle-class virtue, lower-class immorality, and the deprivations of those of colonial birth or of mixed race.

Whiteness, Class, and the Sexual Truth
Claims of Being European

It is the pull of this racially charged field that I turn to here. The range of competing and converging myths of the sexualized Other that riddle Euro-

pean *belles-lettres,* colonial official texts, and the subdisciplines of nineteenth-
century science have been the subject of a contemporary critical tradition
for some time. Rather than rehearse them, I want to take up Foucault's
contention that desire was animated by discourses of sexuality and productive of new forms of power. It is a particular wedge of that discourse about
European desire that interests me here—one that divided those Europeans
who embraced European bourgeois respectabilities from those who did not.
I want to look at how asymmetries in the production of the discourse of
desire differed by gender and class, at how effectively these distinctions
affirmed a shared notion of European bourgeois culture and its prescriptions
for white normality.

And finally, in bringing us back to Foucault's claim that desire is not
opposed to the law but produced by it, I want to ask what sorts of desires
were incited by certain colonial discourses on moral reform and sexual regulation. What of those, for example, that spoke incessantly of the subversive
dangers of mixed bloods and their moral perversions? Those that reiterated
the base sexual drives of common European soldiers and their homoerotic
tendencies? Those Protestant dailies and weeklies in the Netherlands that
proliferated in the 1880s, incessantly warning "every Dutch youngster"
against the "indescribable horror and bestiality" that reigned in the Indies
army barracks and the sexual dangers that awaited them (Ming 1983, 79)?
Those that spoke of the sexual precocities of Indies youths and the passions
that the tropics unleashed? These were not only recordings of inappropriate
desire, but discourses that struggled to define what was racially distinctive
about bourgeois sexuality itself. Surely at one level they reaffirmed that the
"truth" of European identity was lodged in self-restraint and self-discipline,
in a managed sexuality that was susceptible and not always under control.[21]
But they also confirmed that if "the colonized" were driven by an insatiable
instinct, certain Europeans were as well.

The point is an important one because colonial enterprises produced discourses that were not only about a racialized sexuality and a sexualized notion of race. These colonial discourses of desire were also productive of, and
produced in, a social field that always specified class and gender locations. It
is the cultural density of these representations that interests me here. The
fact that these discourses do not reduce to racial typologies alone suggests
that the colonial order joined sexuality, class, and racial essence in defining
what it meant to be a productive—and therefore successfully reproductive—member of the nation and its respectable bourgeoisie.

What is striking about the sexual stories that European colonials and their
metropolitan observers told about their own desires and about what distinguished themselves is how boldly they turned on defining and affirming the

bourgeois order in specific ways. Thus European children were said to be susceptible to sexual desires in the tropics at a much earlier age than in Europe. This demanded a vigilance about their rearing, their cordoning off from "precocious Indies youths," repeated enumeration of the sexual dangers posed by servants, and protection from a climate that encouraged "habitual licentiousness" at an early age (Price 1939, 31). Investments in a European-spirited education confirmed how much the European identities of these children had to be protected from the sexualized Other and how much those native adults and children with whom they came in contact had to be monitored and controlled. These discourses on children's sexuality were rooted in a racial grammar, confirming that education was a moral imperative for bourgeois identity and a national investment, designed to domesticate the sexual desire of children and to direct how they would later decide whom to consider eligible recipients of it (Stoler 1995, chapter 5).

A basic tension in the sexual politics of colonial states was created by the promise of new possible objects for desiring male subjects and the implementation of policies that closed those possibilities down. Thus the regulatory policies that first condoned and then condemned concubinary relations between Asian women and European men activated as much discussion about the merits, pleasures, and gratifications of these utilitarian relations as about their morally degraded nature (Stoler 1995). In the name of British, French, and Dutch moralizing missions, colonial authority supposedly rested on administrative efforts to distinguish between desire and reason; native instinct and white self-discipline; native lust and white civility; native sensuality and white morality; subversive, unproductive sexuality and productive, patriotic sex.

But these Manichean lines were not always drawn with racial clarity. The class divisions of colonial discourses of desire distinguished subaltern white men from their middle-class counterparts in fundamental ways. Lower-class European men were repeatedly accused of giving in to their biological drives at the cost of empire—and by more than contemporary colonial apologists. Grenfell Price, in a 1939 publication of the American Geographical Society, attributed the downfall of sixteenth-century Portuguese colonies to the "unbridled passions of the lower types of invaders" (1939, 16). Ballhatchet (1980, 2) notes that in eighteenth-century British India, "special provisions"—not applicable to the "educated English gentleman"—were made "for the sexual satisfaction of British soldiers because they came from the lower classes and so were thought to lack the intellectual and moral resources required for continence." Genovese (1974, 421) similarly notes that lower-class white men invariably were made responsible for the sexual abuses of slavery.

In the Indies, the equation of lower-class origins and unchecked licentiousness was much the same. Here, prostitution was excused on the grounds that a common European soldier had to satisfy his "natural sexual appetites" and "that a woman remains indispensable to him" (Hesselink 1987, 206–7).[22] If prevented from exercising his "natural" sexual urges, he would resort to "unnatural vices"—to masturbation or sexual relations with other men (Weijl and Boogaardt 1917a, 8). Concubinage with native women in the Indies army barracks was justified as preferable to homosexual contacts and social intimacies outside the state's control. Not everyone agreed, however, for the debate about whether it was "healthy" for common soldiers to refrain from indulging their "sexual drive" spoke to other concerns as well. Thus one outspoken critic of the barracks-concubinage system, Dr. J. Kohlbrugge (1901, 33), spoke against an Indies ethic in which the indiscriminate satisfaction of one's sexual tendencies was considered a "right," a "necessity," or even "as in France, a *droit du travail*." In his opinion the serious consequences of such a course were clear; a "paralysis of energy," a "disappearance of self-control," a "dampening of the desire to work"— all characteristics that described the native and were opposed to what was definitively European.

It is difficult to assess the extent to which what Foucault would call the "discursive verbosity" that surrounded the sexual relations between European agents of empire and local women actually animated new sorts of desires for such relations. Whose pleasures and what sorts of desires were produced out of this careful surveillance is hard to tell.[23] What we do know is that because common soldiers were barred from marriage and poor European women were barred from the barracks, sexual accommodations of varied sorts prevailed.[24] Concubinage was condoned as a "necessary evil" by military officials on the grounds that it significantly lowered the subsistence requirements of soldiers without incurring higher wages or the increased medical costs that came with prostitution and a syphilitic rank and file.[25] The availability to European recruits of native women in sexual and domestic service—"living grammar books" (*levende grammaire*) as they were sometimes called—was part of the male "wages of whiteness." This was a set of policies that legitimated the intimate regulation of the lives of European soldiers and those Asian women who came in contact with them. But what is absent from, and usually unspeakable in, this discourse on "evil" is as striking as that which it contained; the dangers of a homosexual European rank and file were implicitly weighed against the medical hazards of rampant heterosexual prostitution: both were condemned as morally pernicious and a threat to racial survival.[26]

While the moral dangers of homosexuality in these debates on concubinage often went unstated, strident moral disparagements were explicitly cast on those of inferior class and race. In this discursive terrain, the eugenic peril of mixing the "lower elements" of Europeans and Asians was supposedly illustrated by the dismal fate of the children of these mixed unions. They were referred to disparagingly as *soldatenkinderen,* a term that implied illegitimate and sordid origins. Here was fertile ground for moral intervention and charitable goodwill, for extended debates about native prostitution and white pauperism, and obvious evidence for why managed sex and a moral upbringing should be the state's concern and under its control. What was animated, however, were not only sexual fantasies and titillations about the barracks underworld, but a set of practical and perceptual "effects" that kept questions of racial mixing and racial clarity in clear view. The desire to know the "truth" of race and sex, to know what caused European men "to go native" and European women to choose a native man, made questions of moral deprivation and the psychological coordinates of racial belonging favored and recurrent themes among the architects of colonial rule.

Thus the discourse that condoned concubinage and assented to the biological drives of common European men did more than justify military policy. It distinguished those middle-class European men who had a right to rule from both those decadent nobles and those class and racial commoners who did not. It identified men who degenerated and left the European camp, and distinguished those betrayed by their desires from those Europeans guided by self-discipline and sexual restraint. It divided "men of character" and reason from men of passion. And as more restrictions were placed on concubinary arrangements for all civil servants and military staff at the turn of the twentieth century, it rehearsed and took solace in a specific narrative that concubinage only remained in those outposts where "cultivated marriageable European young women were scarce."[27]

Within this racialized economy of sex, European women and men won respect by steering their desires to legitimate paternity and maternal care, to family and conjugal love; it was only poor whites, Indies-born Europeans, mixed bloods, and natives who, as I argue in *Race and the Education of Desire* (Stoler 1995), focused just too much on sex. To be truly European was to cultivate a bourgeois self in which familial and national obligations were the priority, and sex was held in check—not by silencing the discussion of sex, but by parceling out demonstrations of excess to different social groups and thereby gradually exorcizing its effects. Desires for opulence and sex, wealth and excess were repeatedly attributed to creole Dutch and lower-class Europeans, to those with culturally hybrid affiliations or those of mixed-blood origin. Once again, persons ruled by their sexual desires were natives and "fictive" Europeans, instantiating their inappropriate dispositions to rule.

Pleasure, Power and the Work of Scientific Pornography

The discourses of desire that surrounded European colonial women reflect some predictable qualities of nineteenth-century gender ideology, but not in all ways. We know the received, official script, that white women were encased in a model of passionless domesticity, mythologized as the desired objects of colonized men, categorically dissociated from the sexual desires of European men, and disallowed from being desiring subjects themselves. As custodians of morality they were poised as the guardians of European civility, moral managers who were to protect child and husband in the home. But clearly some women saw other options and made sexual and conjugal choices that disrupted this neat picture. European women who veered off the respectable course were not only stripped of the European community's protection of their womanhood, but disavowed as good mothers and as true Europeans. Thus the Indies mixed-marriage law of 1898 relegated to native status those European women who chose cohabitation over marriage and chose native men over the European-born, on the argument that if these women were really European, they would never have made such inappropriate choices.

In Dutch colonial novels, women of European status but of Indies birth, or of mixed-blood and common-class origin, appear as sensual, erotically charged beings driven by passion in ways that "pure-blood," middle-class European women supposedly bereft of desire were not.[28] Each of these representations of bourgeois propriety and the social norms prescribed by them hinged on the presence of other actors, on a marking of their sexuality as the essence of what *kinds* of human beings they were, as an index of the social category to which they truly belonged. These discourses of sexuality could tell not only the *truth* about individual persons, but about racial and national identity as well. They linked subversion to perversion, racial purity to conjugal white endogamy, and thus colonial politics to the management of sex.

The production of new sites and strategies of colonial control that the discourse on sexuality engendered is easier to identify than the production of the "incessant spirals" of pleasure and power that Foucault would suggest it allowed. For the "talking cure" about sex in the colonies was voyeuristic and visual as well as discursive, and not primarily in the confessional mode. It addressed less directly the "truth" of one's own desires, than a phantasmic litany of sexual specifications and excesses that distinguished these Others from European bourgeois selves.

A "gynecological study," *Women on Java,* published simultaneously in Semarang and Amsterdam by a Dr. C. H. Stratz in 1897, exemplifies that mode.[29] Here the sexual pleasures of scientific knowledge join with the pornographic aesthetics of race. The "pleasures" infused in Stratz's study (1897) derive only in part from its full-front illustrations of naked nubile women's bodies with their arms raised and hands clasped behind their heads; for this quintessential example of "scientia sexualis" is a guide to racial taxonomies and racially attributed psychological and physiological characteristics as well.

What does this pornographic racial taxonomy entail? Preceding the photos, the study is introduced with an analysis of different races, of those "colored" who morally "lag behind those of the pure race," and of the Javanese who are "very indolent, fearful, without initiative and who have an entirely different understanding of lying and cheating than do Europeans" (Stratz 1897, 5). Gynecologically speaking, these might seem superfluous observations. But this is more than a sexual treatise on women; it is a "scientific" treatise on the aesthetics of race, on the erotics of the exotic, on Javanese women as prototypes of what makes their bodies desirable to Europeans, and their bodies and minds so different from theirs. Stratz's description of Javanese women attends closely to skin shade and to color and quantity of body hair as he moves down from "their sleek dark [head] hair," to the "dark dusky eyes," to the nearly hairless armpits, and to the "thick-haired mons veneris" (6, 8).

The titillations that this passage may provoke are not unrelated to the particular kind of knowledge it holds in store. First, it celebrates the beauty of *all* Javanese women's bodies as a generic type. Second, in asserting that Javanese women of the "Hindu and Malay type . . . share many common characteristics," it underscores that whatever differences might exist among Asian bodies, what is more marked (and significant) is how they differ from those of Europeans and how much, among them, they are the same.

But what stands out in Stratz's account is how clearly internal and skeletal body form reveal a woman's hidden racial characteristics even when her physical appearance is that of a European. The case in point that Stratz provides is that of the distinctively Javanese pelvic shape of "a young woman, who was a fifth generation descendant of a Javanese mother and who distinguished herself by a conspicuously white, soft skin and pretty blonde hair" (14). Outward similarity masks essential difference. The contrast with European women's bodies is shown by the "more spherical" shape of the skull and (in a "cursory inspection" of some twenty-five women housed in Soerabaja's women's hospital) by the measurements of the pelvis which (like the skull) is "rounder." This holds too, Stratz notes, for the "colored of all racial types," who share this "round form." The pelvis tells the inner "truth" of race and identity in ways that could not otherwise be visually observed.

Following a centimeter-fine comparison of pelvic measurements, Stratz turns back to his aesthetic concerns. He counts the "fine modelling of the trunk, shown especially in the delicate line of the dorsal muscle" as being "one of the great beauties of the Javanese female body." This he notes is less a "racial characteristic" than one due to the "total absence of a corset in the Javanese women's dress" (14–15).[30] Thus, despite their small size, they can be "very elegant," and Stratz points the reader to the frontal and profile photographs of two nude young women, one only adorned with an ankle bracelet, her body positioned in a languid pose, her arms lifted and curved away from the photographer, wrapped around her neck.

Stratz confirms that "this fine modelling of the trunk" is not a "racial characteristic," noting that many European women on Java wear no corsets or do so only in the afternoons, and "therefore one finds among them as well many more beauties and also more well-kept up figures at a later age than in the high gloss (*geverniste*) fashion world of Europe" (15). This is a dissonant passage on several counts: first because the dress codes of European women would seem to be beside the point, and second because few texts attribute any beauty to European women in the tropics and certainly none that might derive from their physical form. More commonly underscored is the aesthetic and emotional price that European women pay to live indolently in the tropics—the ravaging of their bodies by inactivity, cumbersome and dangerous pregnancies, and rash-producing heat. It is the tropics that bring all women closer to (their) nature.

But Stratz does not dwell on these climatic levelings. He turns back to racial characteristics, to those "finely built limbs," to the "hyperextension of the elbow joints" that one often sees in the "engravings at Borobodur," to the shape of the fingers, legs, feet, and toes, and to the "extremely limited development of the calves," a "characteristic [that Javanese] share with all Oriental peoples" (16). Again he returns to color, to the skin tone of Javanese women, to the "blue spot" at the base of the spine, and finally to a studied description of the vagina's pigment variations from the outer labia to those "smaller pigment spots lying scattered high in the vagina." Nowhere is Stratz on, as it were, more firmly pleasurable and knowing ground.

While chromatics and other sensory modes reign supreme in his classifactory scheme, in fact it is the *hidden* features of racialized sexuality—and

Stratz's expert gaze—to which the reader is asked to attend. Differences found on the outer surface of the body are confirmed by the special and privileged knowledge and view he shares of the deep and unique markings within it. Commenting again on the lack of hair around the clitoris, he instructs his readership to the "particularly clear" view of this in figure 7. But there is nothing clear in the figure at all. And this is just the point. The reader's gaze must be intense because there is little to see in this profile picture. We must rely on Stratz's privileged view. Our gaze is pointed inward, to that which is not visible but—with Stratz's expert help—easily imagined.

The meticulous attention paid to detail in the preceding descriptions contrasts sharply with the section that follows on gynecological illnesses among European women. There is no symmetry in form or content: no detailed descriptions of bodies here, no pictures, no European women sub-jected to view. There is no nuanced discussion of the European women's sexual organs, no lingering over their texture and gradated hue. In this con-text, talking about and looking for the truth of identity in sexual organs is reserved for nonwhites. For European women, there is only a list of geni-tal pathologies, and a note that despite his meager sample in comparison to European statistics, noteworthy differences are evident deriving from a tropical way of life. Rather than discussing physical form, Stratz describes what he sees as more relevant, a colonial lifestyle for European women that compares "with [that of] the most comfortable classes in Europe" (20). Their distinctions are not defined by vaginal coloring: matters of leisure, power, and privilege determine where the difference rests. He notes that white women are surrounded by a bevy of servants who spare them diffi-cult physical labor, outside the home and within it. They have, he notes, the time to keep themselves pure and clean, bathing at least twice a day in cool water, lathering the whole body. And lest we think these purifying ceremonies are confined to grown women, he notes that "daily vaginal douches . . . to children are an integral part of daily bodily cleansing."

Here the aesthetics is, if anything, of race, and the pleasures are of purifi-cation. In contrast to Stratz's earlier allusion to the beauty of some European women in the tropics, here he returns to a more conventional portrayal, of colorless bodies, cleansed of dirt, devoid of sex. The discourse is one of physical inactivity and vigilant hygiene for women and children as well. He notes that this "hygienic way of life" seems to contrast sharply with the striking "paleness of all European women living in the tropics," which even experts attribute to a so-called tropical anemia. But Stratz dismisses the ill-ness as bogus. His antiseptic ethnographic account ends with approval of a dress code that affords European children in the Indies freedom of movement and adult women freedom from the restricting undergarments of Europe that press on stomach and breasts (22).

While it would be disingenuous to take Stratz's study as representative of what preoccupied all Dutch colonial medical practitioners, the aestheticization of race and the distributions of sexual desire that it invoked were neither confined to the Indies, unique to the Dutch, nor unusual among them. In fact Stratz's discourse is part of a well-honed tradition in the science of race. Mosse (1985) dates the aestheticization of race from the late 1700s; the eroticization of race is a much earlier discourse of the Renaissance. Gilman (1986) documents such scientific study of the unique sexuality of different races from the early 1800s; others, such as Freyre, continued to produce such discourses well into the twentieth century. But the "standard of beauty as a criterion of racial classification" did not produce as neat a correlation between beauty and desire, between aesthetically pleasing and racially superior populations as Mosse and others would lead one to expect (Mosse 1985, 23). Javanese women could be considered both "beautiful" and "lazy," "elegant" and "deceitful," "finely-modelled" and intellectually lacking at the same time. To be physically "underdeveloped" and libidinally "oversexed" was not an oxymoron, for this was a discourse and a domain of knowledge that was productive of and responsive to taxonomies of power and a range of desires that articulated unevenly with the multiple hierarchies of class, nation, gender, and race.

It is significant, for example, that this "gynecological study" of women on Java eroticizes some women and not others and that the section on obstetrics contains no photographs. Sexuality is the stronger marker of difference, and it is what Stratz knows about. He writes that both native and European women unwisely consulted poorly trained native and European midwives rather than doctors like himself. As he puts it, "the white woman on Java" was "very far behind her European sisters." In the domain of reproduction Javanese and European women would seem to be similar, but this too is not the case. The discourse on respectable European women in the Indies is almost exclusively framed by their functional roles as mothers and wives in contrast to that on native and mixed-blood women, which is certainly not.

Stratz's text is blatantly salacious, deceptively straightforward—and misleading. From that text alone one might conclude that discourses on sexuality always took a predictable form, in which colonial knowledge and power were invariably produced from the prurient sexual pleasures bestowed on those who recorded, read, and vicariously participated in them. It demands that we rivet our attention on genitalia in the defining of race, confirming the story that colonialism was that quintessential project in which desire was always about sex, that sex was always about racial power, and that both were contingent upon a particular representation of nonwhite women's bodies. In short it rehearses the now well-honed story that native women were the object of the white male gaze and white women were assiduously protected from it. Even from a critical vantage point, we are caught within its frame. It is a story about powerful subjects looking upon sexual objects, one in which sex was about power, and other desires were merely deflections and projections of both.

While we should attend to such accounts, they have their limitations. As I have argued elsewhere (Stoler 1995), the discourse of sexuality tied truth claims about persons to the truth about sex in more nuanced ways. That discourse embraced a range of other desires between mothers and children, nursemaids and their charges, European men and their Asian housemaids, and between European men that spoke to a broader set of sentiments. If we want to understand the production of desire, then it is neither to Stratz's aestheticized prurience nor to the greedy gaze of French colonial postcards that we need to turn. We need to situate these discourses in a wider frame where desire itself is the subject; where its relationship to the colonial order of things was sometimes askew, sometimes opaque; where desire and race were mediated through other sentiments by which they were more insidiously bound.

Of Desire and Other Sentiments

We can follow Foucault in arguing that these discourses on sexuality had concrete effects that in turn intensified the microcenters of colonial control: a strict control of servants, a protracted discourse on and investments in the education and rearing of European children, a century-long debate over poor white welfare, and increasingly tighter restrictions on which Europeans could immigrate to the colonies and on moral standards and domestic arrangements. Cultivation of the bourgeois self depended on a catalogue of sexual dispositions about different human kinds. This sexual taxonomy was paired with a wider set of psychological and invisible characteristics that glossed the categories of bourgeois respectability, whiteness, and true Europeans.

But sexual desires were structured by desires and discourses that were never about sex alone. Desires to "pass" as white, to have one's progeny be eligible for higher education, or the sentiment that Frantz Fanon attributes to the man of color who desires "to marry white culture . . . to grasp white civilization and dignity and make them mine" all suggest that sexual desire in colonial and postcolonial contexts has been a crucial transfer point of power, tangled with racial exclusions in complicated ways (Fanon 1967, 63). Such desires may use sex as a vehicle to master a practical world (privileged schooling, well-paying jobs in the civil service, access to certain residential quarters), which was in part what being colonial and privileged was all about.

How do we untangle what is about sex and what is not? Foucault's starting point in some ways facilitates that task, for *The History of Sexuality* is not a history of Western desire but a history of how sexual desire came to be the test of the way we distinguish the interior Other and know our true selves. From this perspective, the protracted colonial discourses that linked sexual passion to political subversion and managed sexuality to patriotic priorities make sense. These were discourses that secured the distinctions of individual white bodies and the privileges of a white body politic at the same time. But Foucault's account in volume 1 of *The History of Sexuality* assumes that sexuality was the dominant, principal mode in which the truth of the self was expressed—a claim on which his later volumes were to cast some doubt.

What is so striking in the discourse on the sexuality of masturbating children, servants, degenerate white men, and intruders in the bourgeois home is what constitutes the threat in these transgressive moments. Sometimes sexual intimacy and precocity were at issue, but it was rarely just these. Evidence of affective ties, affective kinship, confusions of blood and milk, and sentiments of cultural belonging and longing were as dangerous as carnal knowledge. Nor can those other sentiments be reduced to other ways of talking about sexual contagion.[31] Subversions to the bourgeois order were those that threatened the cultivation of personality, what Weber once called "a certain internal and external deportment in life," that repertoire of sensibilities that were glossed as "personal character" and that carefully marked the boundaries of class and race (1948, 426).[32] It is these alienations of affection, these moments of "cultural contagion" that cut across the dichotomies of ruler and ruled, that clarified and confused what being respectable and colonial was about. Control and release of sexual desire was one of the leitmotifs of that story, but it embodied other themes as well that at once defined the interior landscapes of "true" Europeans and the interior frontiers of the superior polities to which they were constantly reminded that they rightfully belonged.

Foucault's equation of desire and power poses a problem for our view of the psychological ambivalences that colonial discourse invoked, for it suggests that desire and power were always bound. Is it only an "illusion" and "vanity," as Foucault claims, to ask whether there were no desires that stood to the side of colonial power or beyond it? Were there no desires that evaded the grip of power and escaped subsumption? Or would these retreats from the norm only further substantiate a normalizing process by which all those with claims to civility—and those who rejected it—were bound? We have evidence of some such possible evasions, but not enough: accounts of European men and native women who cohabited in ways that went beyond the utilitarian sexual economy of concubinage, of European men who relinquished their claims to privilege and chose liminal lives on the outskirts of European society, of native mothers whose desires to stay close to their children and not give them "up" to European schools may have expressed a bold rejection of the bourgeois European scales of merit.

While it is clear that the production of these desires was not indifferent to the taxonomies of rule, the desires produced did not always help fortify the categories of control. We may reject, with Foucault, a notion of primordial drive but still explore a space for individual affect that may have been structured by power but not wholly subsumed by it. Thinking about the "education of desire" more broadly frees us from another Foucauldian quandary; by avoiding such an intense focus on sexuality, we can avoid reproducing the very terms of the nineteenth-century imperial discourse that reduced and read all desires as sexual ones.[33] This is not to suggest that an obsession with sexuality does not underwrite colonial discourses, but to acknowledge that a wider range of transgressive sentiments and cultural blurrings informed what was unspeakable and what was said.

If a desiring subject, as Judith Butler writes (1987, ix–x), has the philosophical aim of discovering the "entire domain of alterity," of finding "within the confines of this self the entirety of the external world," then the imagined and practical world of empire must be seen as one of the most strategic sites for realizing that aim. If desire is about both externalization and mimesis, as so much of the philosophical literature on desire suggests, then no political story is more relevant to the production of Western desire than colonialism, itself the quintessence of a process in which the mirroring of bourgeois priorities and the mimetic subversion of them played a defining role. Affirmation of the bourgeois self entailed an overlapping series of discursive displacements and distinctions on which its cultivation rested. There was no bourgeois identity that was not contingent on a changing set of Others who were at once desired and repugnant, forbidden and subservient, cast as wholly different but also the same.

That "enemy within" that Foucault traced to the defense of society and the one that Freud traced to the defense of the self may have more in common when the issue of racism is in clearer view. In an imperial frame the psychological and political anxieties attributed to European bourgeois society draw on a common vocabulary in some striking ways—that European bourgeois self defined by its interior Other, those European nation-states built on their individuated and collective "interior frontiers," and those colonial empires that were the exteriorized sites where these internal borders were threatened and clarified are not part of a different order of things. Together they articulate what has made racial discourse so central—and resilient—in defining what being bourgeois and European were all about.

Truth claims made in the discourse on European sexuality can only appear as part of the deep genealogy of a European confessional mode when the imperial coordinates of the nineteenth century are out of view. But even for Europe that genealogy is doubtful. For if we take our cue from Foucault's lectures on race, rather than from volume 1 of *The History of Sexuality,* Foucault himself alerts us to look at a set of already racialized relations. The nineteenth-century discourse on bourgeois sexuality may be better understood as deriving from the recuperation of a protracted discourse on race that provided the discourse on sexuality with many of its most salient elements. That discourse on sexuality was binary and contrastive; its nineteenth-century variant always posed middle-class respectable sexuality as a defense against an internal and external Other that was at once essentially different but uncomfortably the same. The tropes of contamination and contagion in twentieth-century sexual discourse were not new: they recalled and recuperated a discourse that focused on defensive techniques for "constant purification."[34]

Foucault might be right that the explanatory *scientific* weight accorded to sexual instinct only emerged in Freud's psychoanalytic theory of the nineteenth century, but its genealogical antecedents go back much further still.[35] Assessments of sexual proclivity and racial membership were joined much earlier in a discourse that conferred the right to live in a certain way on those with the cultural competencies to exercise freedom, the cultivated sensibilities to understand the limits of liberty, and the moral strength to be untempted by lust and leisure. Sexual excess and misguided sentiments characterized those who were more fit to be slaves, indentured workers, and the laboring underclass or, like creoles and Indos in the Indies, unfit to rule an imperial world; domesticated sexuality and managed sensibilities were endowments of those who were not.

The point is not to reduce the entire discourse that coupled the truth of the self and the truth about one's sexual desire to a discursive variation on the discourse of race, but to suggest that the production and distribution of desires in the nineteenth-century discourse on sexuality were filtered through and perhaps even patterned by an earlier set of discourses and practices that figured prominently in imperial technologies of rule. Civilization could be defended against trangressions by invoking the reasoned logic of race. The general point is one with which Foucault would agree: there was no unitary bourgeois self already formed, no core to secure, no "truth" lodged in one's sexual identity. That "self," that "core," that "moral essence" that Fichte and colonial lawyers like Nederburgh sought to identify, was one that Europe's external and internal Others played a major part in making.

In locating the power of the discourse of sexuality in the affirmation of the bourgeois self, Foucault short-circuited the discursive and practical field of empire in which Western notions of self and other had been worked out for centuries and continue to form. Race comes late into Foucault's story in *The History of Sexuality;* race is not fundamental to the making of bourgeois sensibilities, where in the lectures he seems to suggest questions of race belonged. One could argue that the history of Western sexuality must be located in the production of historical Others, in the broader force field of empire where technologies of sex, self, and power were defined as "European" and "Western" as they were refracted and remade.

CHAPTER TWO

Contested Images and Common Strategies:
Early Colonial Sexual Politics in the Massim

ADAM REED

Malinowski's work on the sexual life of Trobriand Islanders still pervades our view of indigenous sexuality in the Massim. He represented these people as "extremely lax" (Malinowski 1922, 37) inhabitants of a land where "chastity is an unknown virtue" (53). Twenty-two years before the ethnographer arrived in the region, a Reverend Field,[1] stationed in 1892 on Panaeati, reported that "among the young men and women . . . as far as I have found out, there is no practical knowledge of the word chastity" (Australasian Wesleyan Methodist Church 1892, 1: 6). Malinowski's image of the licentious indigene therefore developed in conjunction with those images put forward by Field, other missionaries, and local administrators. Yet by contrasting it with what he saw as repressive European attitudes to sex, he hoped to provide a critique of sexuality in his own society. Unlike his colonial contemporaries, he argued that "as is probably the case in many communities where sex morals are lax, there is a complete absence of unnatural practices and sex perversions" (Malinowski 1922, 38). Missionaries and officials did not share his evaluation of indigenous sexuality, but they concurred with his image of the unchaste Massim Islander. Like him, these colonial pioneers assigned a sexual body to the indigene. This chapter examines the attributes they gave that sexual body and the strategies by which they intended to make it a target for intervention.

The Massim region (the southeastern peninsula of mainland Papua and offshore outlying islands) was annexed as part of British New Guinea in 1888 and then, as part of the Territory of Papua, came under Australian rule in 1906. Its administrative centre was Samarai, but there were government and mission stations in Milne Bay, the D'Entrecasteaux Islands, Goodenough Bay, the Trobriand Islands, Woodlark Island, and Misima. Samarai was the second-largest town in Papua, and the Milne Bay coast had one of the fastest-growing European populations (Wetherell 1977, 244–45). Throughout the Massim there were many Europeans; in 1910 there were around 268, out of a total in the Territory of 775 (Papua 1911, 49).[2] Outside of Samarai, missionaries exerted the most influence. The greater part of the region was apportioned to the Methodists. In 1914 they had sixty-one churches dotted across the islands (Colwell 1914, 554).[3] The London Missionary Society established a presence around Kwato Island,[4] while the Melanesian Anglican Mission was located at Dogura,[5] on a part of the mainland. This chapter covers the early years of the colonial regime from annexation to the outbreak of the Second World War in the Pacific. In that period, between 1888 and 1942, Massim Islanders experienced intense proselytism. They encountered not only missionaries but also magistrates and settlers to a degree unknown outside the state capital of Port Moresby.

Contested Images of Indigenous Sexuality

Europeans stationed in Papua offered a relatively uniform image of indigenous sexuality.[6] They portrayed the Massim Islander as possessing a sexual body whose unbridled energies encouraged licentious behaviour from an early age.

In these images the sexuality of the Massim Islander appeared unrestrained and dangerous in contrast to the controlled sexuality of the civilized white. Sir Hubert Murray, the governor of the Territory from 1906 to 1940, in comparing the Papuan to the European, declared that "self restraint has not been developed to anything like the same extent, and sexual matters loom very large in their lives" (Papua 1928, 123). Missionaries and colonial officials argued that Papuans were uninhibited and aggressive in their behavior precisely because they were not conscious of their sexual bodies—savage because they were unrepressed. Whites therefore privileged themselves on the basis of their own sexual repression. In their eyes sexuality was a defining quality of the individual, something mysterious, potent, and essential that affected all behavior and lay at the root of being. Desires emanated from deep inside and, if left unchecked, could reduce a person to savagery; thus there was a need to channel these potentially dangerous energies: "I realise that purity in deeds depends on purity of thoughts and I resolve to watch myself right down to the deepest instincts" (Malinowski 1967, 181). This privileged sexual anxiety left Europeans unable to enjoy the same sensual pleasures as the Massim Islanders. Instead it compelled them to survey these desires and thereby check what they termed *sexual excess*.

Europeans sometimes provided ambiguous images of indigenous sexuality. While they represented the Massim Islander as prone to excess, they also recognized that savage ignorance to a certain extent mitigated such behavior. Colonial officals were fond of quoting Kipling's famous description of the native as "half-devil and half-child" (Monckton 1921, 139). Missionaries too enjoyed pointing out that

the Papuan[s], like all primitive people, are curiously unbalanced in
character. They have some qualities which are admirable, and yet side
by side with these are the most abominable vices and the grossest cru-
elty. It is hard to think that these merry-eyed people can become, on
occasion, such monsters of fiendish barbarity; that these easy-going
men and women can delight in causing the most awful suffering; that
these children of nature can become devils of horrible sensuality. (Burton 1926, 25–26)

They believed that the Massim Islander was closer to nature, possessing both
an animal sensuality and a childlike innocence. The implication was that
any excess caused by the indigenes'primitive sexuality could be discussed on
the basis of their infantility.

This ambiguity allowed Europeans to present multiple, and often con-
flicting, sexual images. Representations of the Massim Islander alternated
between devil or child, aggressor or victim. Each figure implied the other;
these fluctuations often manifest as a cross-cutting relationship between
male and female, black and white. While white males produced the dominant sexual images in Papua, they did not always reach a consensus. Those
images that were in conflict usually dealt with representations of sexual acts
across race lines.

Missionaries portrayed white males who participated in sexual relations
with black women as "low whites," sexually aggressive, and potential ex-
ploiters of the indigenous woman's childlike vulnerability (Burton 1926,
109). Reports from across the Territory enforced the impression that traders,
planters, miners, labor recruiters, and even resident magistrates regularly
"interfered" with indigenous women. Some missionaries initiated a campaign against this "low-white" abuse. In 1901, the Anglican mission in the
Massim helped a girl bring charges of sexual assault against a patrol officer
called Yaldwyn—the first case directly against a European. The court in
Samarai acquitted the officer, but he was dismissed from government service
(Monckton 1921, 264–66). Missionaries portrayed such white men as members of some kind of sexual cabal, in league against Christianity. They held
them responsible for spreading European habits of vice and exacerbating
the indigene's own inclination to licentious behavior. Burton regretted that

we have sad examples of the debasing effect of the evil lives of some of
our own colour. . . . The girl could resist the ordinary and frequent
temptations of the village, but she could not oppose the command of
her father, brought by the stick of tobacco of the white man. . . . [S]uch
a man undoes in months more than a missionary can do in years, and

lowers the standard of life among a people where it is already far too low. (1926, 109–10)

Other Europeans contested this image of white male sexuality. They offered excuses for low-white behavior. Many believed that the Papuan climate induced excess and nervous exhaustion in its white residents. Byam and Archibald, the authors of a popular manual on tropical medicine, warned their readers that "both in male and female there is greater generative vigour in the tropics, but excess in venery is more speedily followed by an exhaustion and neurasthenia than is the case in temperate climates" (1921, 12; see also Stoler, chap. 1 in this volume; Manderson 1996). Beyond this climatic challenge, colonial officials and settlers claimed that indigenous women deliberately titillated their nervous sexual potential. Malinowski (1967, 225) referred to the "perennial whorish expression" of the women; resident magistrates played down the missionary's image of the sexually aggressive white male and emphasized instead the woman's consenting role. If, in Murray's words, Papua was a "land of sin, sweat and sorrow" (West 1970, 138), then the white male could not be held entirely responsible for his sexual conduct. Monckton, who led the government inquiry into the Yaldwyn incident, believed the girl involved had consented to the liasion of "her own will and accord," and blamed the Anglican mission for bringing the charge (Monckton 1921, 266). Murray too suggested that white men rarely had to force their attentions upon indigenous women, claiming that "there has, so far as I am aware, never been a case of the rape of a native woman by a White man in Papua" (Papua 1927, 10; but see Inglis 1974).

When it came to representing sexual relations between Papuan men and European women, the images were less contested. Government employees and settlers adopted an almost hysterical attitude to the possibility of such an encounter. From the 1920s onwards, as wives and children began to accompany white men to the territory, the image of the dangerous, sexually aggressive, black male emerged. The victim was not the promiscuous black female, but the pure, sexually sublimated white woman. Murray made this point explicit: "[D]oubtless there are native women who set the highest value on their chastity, but they are the exception; and the rape of an ordinary native woman does not present any element of comparison with the rape of a respectable White woman" (Inglis 1974, 72). In 1925 this distinction was sanctioned in law with the introduction of the White Woman's Protection Ordinance, which introduced the death penalty for those Papuan men found guilty of rape or attempted rape of European women (Papua 1927, 9). Colonial officials justified the punishment on the grounds that it was the only punitive measure the male indigene understood. Members of the Government's Legislative Council in 1926 claimed that "none of us like the idea of capital punishment, but we are all agreed that even capital punishment . . . is preferable to the greater horror of White women and young children being violated by natives" (Inglis 1974, 75–76).

Missionaries shared this sense of horror but concerned themselves more with white violation of black women. They suggested that the ordinance be extended to protect these women (Wetherell 1977, 268). It wasn't. Outside the capital, settlers and officials displayed far less fear of white women being sexually assaulted by black men. Wetherell claims that "there is a strong suggestion, in the nonchalant and relaxed way in which women embarked on medical patrols with Papuan males, of a distinct cleavage between the type of sexual attitudes in white men's towns and those in bush missions" (1977, 267). With the exception of the commercial settlement at Samarai, missionaries provided the pervasive images of indigenous sexuality for the Massim. The aggressive black male was therefore not a key sexual figure.

White interests in Papua were not homogenous; missionaries and colonial officials had different agendas. Sexual images therefore had to be negotiated and were often left open to dispute. In what follows, the differences between missionary and magistrate are clarified, but at the same time shown to be subsumed in a number of wider agendas or sexual strategies.

Strategies of Sexuality

Underlying the images of indigenous sexuality lay a wider concern with "life": the biological or natural processes of human existence. Foucault (1978, 139) stated that in Europe this existence was manifest in two basic forms: the body of the individual and the body of the population. Europeans believed that each individual and demos owned or possessed a life with a unique organic history. Growth characterized the living body, which was bounded in a finite manner by birth and death. This construct was the object underlying discourse about indigenous sexuality and the subject of colonial mechanisms of power. Missionaries, pedagogues, magistrates, and medical officers, both at home and abroad, engaged in relations of force with these bodies, aiming to take charge of them as living beings and thereby exercise a control at the level of life itself. This dominion targeted the body of each person through the introduction of anatomical disciplines, and the body of people as a whole by regulating them as a population.

In Papua, the agents of colonialism christened their project "peaceful penetration" (Lett 1945, 126). They presented their mission as the "spread of civilisation and education over the whole of Papua . . . to make the wel-

fare of the native population paramount over every other consideration"
(99). In doing so, they perceived themselves as dealing not simply with
savages, but with a unit of life or population. The supervision of these living
bodies was centered around a debate over depopulation. For the first fifty
years of colonization fears abounded that the Papuan was a dying race. Sol-
emn warnings were frequently given by missionaries that "if things are allowed to go on as they are at present there is nothing but extinction ahead
of these people" (Abel 1934, 143). Many believed that evolution towards
civilization inevitably led to the demise of primitive races. Others took a
more optimistic view. In 1885 Sir William McGregor, who three years later
became the governor of British New Guinea, addressed a meeting of Fijian
chiefs. He explained that the high number of deaths resulted from poor,
unhygenic housing, an insufficient food supply, and a general disregard for
the health of women and children (Roberts 1927, 252). Depopulation began to be seen as a medical problem, in which endemic disease, the limitation of the food supply, and infant mortality were all contributing factors.
The latter was perceived as causing an especially "serious leakage of life"
(Williams 1932–33, 224–5). A growing awareness developed that the encounter with European civilization need not necessarily entail depopulation. Colonial figures like Sir Hubert Murray felt able to offer a less negative
picture of the demographic effects of colonization. At the 1923 Pan-Pacific
Conference in Melbourne, he asserted that

> the establishment of peace in place of the tribal warfare that prevailed
> in old days, the suppression of sorcery, improved sanitation in native
> villages, medical treatment, improved transport and the consequent re-
> striction of drought and famine areas—all these tend towards the pres-
> ervation of life and the increase of population; while the introduction
> of new diseases, the use of European clothing, alcohol, opium, and
> other more subtle and even more deadly influences have a contrary
> effect. (Papua 1925, 14)

While Murray believed that evidence existed to suggest that the Papuan
population was either stationary or slowly increasing, he conceded that a
decline continued in certain areas. The most obvious and dramatic example
was seen to be the Massim (Papua 1925, 6).

Europeans perceived sex as being at the center of the problem of depopulation in the Massim. As in Europe, they saw intersecting in sexuality the
life of the human body and the life of the population; sexuality was essential
to the preservation of both (Foucault 1978, 145). Colonial officials and missionaries chose to intervene at different levels, however. The former tended
to focus their attention on the social body of the indigene and the regulation

of the population, while the latter concentrated on disciplining the individual body. These different approaches mirrored the different agendas behind state and missionary intervention.

Resident magistrates and patrol officers primarily concerned themselves with pacifying the Massim Islanders as a whole and exercising an ordered control over their lives. Bushell, an officer in the D'Entrecasteaux Islands, reported that while on patrol he always ensured that "careful enquiries were made in every village concerning such fundamental matters as birth and death rates during the past twelve moons" (Bushell 1936, 240). Although he monitored the sexual variables of the population, Bushell and other colonial officials only interfered with what they saw as indigenous sexuality when it affected this pacification process. So, according to Sir Hubert Murray, adultery became an offense in the Territory "not from any scrupulous care for native morality, but in order to prevent the social disorganisation and the quarrelling which its commission is likely to cause in a native community" (Murray 1925, 70). Government officers became interested in venereal disease, contraceptive, and abortive practices for the same reason. In such areas they held the sexual behavior of the indigene responsible for contributing to a population decrease, thereby affecting the state's ability to govern this unit of life.

Indigenous sexuality fascinated missionaries because of its perceived influence on their efforts to proselytize the Massim Islander. They saw the indigene's licentious behavior as an obstacle to conversion, contradicting their own practice of monogamy and conjugal virtue. Missionaries therefore worried over the sexual behavior of individuals. They hoped to prevent transgressions by making them aware and accountable for their inner desiring selves. To ensure that the indigene developed this Christian self-mastery, the ability to abstain from sexual activities and thwart desires, they could not rely on the implementation of general measures against the population. They had to "introduce a system of self-discipline" (Bromilow 1929, 216) to attack sin on a person-by-person basis. Sister Edith Lloyd, stationed in the region in 1902, stressed "the necessity of watching the inner rather than the outer life" (Australasian Wesleyan Methodist Church 1902, 11: 11). Missionaries therefore instructed the Massim Islanders that their future and fortune as a social body was tied to the development of Christian interiority, to the manner in which the individual disciplined desires and made productive use of sex.

Despite their different agendas, the issue of depopulation in the Massim generally brought missionaries and colonial officials together. For a while they shared interest in matters such as abortion, monogamy, venereal disease, and adultery. In each case they campaigned for or against a specific kind of sexual behavior, out of concern for the preservation of indigenous life. Beyond these concerns, their motivations for action were often markedly different: missionaries opposed adultery because it was a sin, colonial officials because it disrupted the social fabric. Although this alliance was sometimes tenuous, it did enable wider European sexual agendas to develop in the Massim. From this temporary alignment of interests, strategies arose which took the sexual conduct of the population and individual as objects of analysis and targets for intervention. In the eyes of Europeans every member of the Massim population had a sexual body which needed to be controlled.

Foucault posited the existence in Europe of "four great strategic unities which . . . formed specific mechanisms of knowledge and power centering on sex" (1978, 103). These were "a hysterization of women's bodies," "a pedagogization of children's sex," "a socialization of procreative behavior," and "a psychiatrization of perverse pleasure" (104–5). None of the strategies could be said to fit neatly into the sexual projects of Europeans in the Massim. Yet of these four the last appears least appropriate, for among missionaries and colonial officals there was little discussion of indigenous perversions. However, Foucault's other three strategic unities have some relation to the colonial project in the Massim. They resonate with the sexual figures put forward for the Massim, which in this chapter will be recognized as the procreative couple, the precocious child, and the irresponsible mother. None of these three figures is exclusively distinguished from the others; they frequently overlap and at times even appear to fuse. They also have their own strategic complexion, distinct from that identified by Foucault for sexual figures in Europe. They differ for several reasons: the pervasive influence of the Christian church, the racial dimension, and the issue of depopulation.

What follows is an account of the colonial program of sexualization, by which indigenes were informed that they owned a sexual body and were instructed in its proper control and use. This program encouraged them to confront European images of sexuality, but one cannot assume the indigenous response. No claims are made that the Massim Islander was sexualized by these attentions. They did not immediately identify with European representations of sexuality. Behind these figures lay Western assumptions about individuality and the self which the indigene is unlikely to have shared. This chapter does not attempt to provide a Massim Islander's interpretation of sexual strategies. Where possible, however, I problematize the sexualization program by noting discrepancies in the colonial texts.

The Procreative Couple

The perceived need to confront the depopulation crisis and address the native's low fertility led colonial officials to intervene in the sexual lives of the marital couple. Matrimonial relations became the object of discussion and the subject of regulations, concerned less with sexual restraint and more with encouraging procreative behavior in the legitimate couple. Europeans identified this couple as the primary unit of reproduction and life, essential to raising the birth rate of the struggling Massim population.

A consensus emerged among missionaries and officials that Massim Islanders were generally unwilling to have large families. In 1925 the Anglican mission held formal talks on the causes of this "limitation of families among Papuans" (Papua 1927, 10). They concluded that indigenes, especially women, viewed large families as disgraceful (11). Atkinson, an assistant resident magistrate at Baniara in Goodenough Bay, confirmed this point. In that year he reported that "a woman who has a number of children over and above what is usual is scoffed at by the other village people, and referred to as a dog" (Papua 1926, 40). All agreed that the indigenous couple needed to be taught their responsibilities with regard to the social body as a whole.

The mission played an important role in encouraging married couples to perform their procreative duties. Both Anglican and Methodist missionaries saw the institution of marriage and the practice of monogamy as the ultimate confirmation of conversion. They presented this ideal as a significant achievement, given that "Christian marriage involves a standard of life so high that the native is slow to get a true conception of it" (Melanesian Mission 1904, 9). Legitimate couples were expected to identify themselves as subjects of desire and sin. It was not just acts or behavior that indicated sin, but thoughts and feelings. Transgression was apparent whenever the native experienced pleasure, which suggested illicit or unproductive sex. Missionaries urged converts to make explicit their efforts to resist infidelity, and thereby share the burden. William E. Bromilow, Chairman of the Methodist District from 1891 to 1908 and from 1920 to 1924, described this struggle as expressed by Sailosi, a Dobuan convert: "I found higher desires in my heart. . . . I had many temptations to do wrong before marriage and after it; but whenever I felt temptation I flew to prayer, and God kept me from falling" (Bromilow 1929, 228).

Given what was seen as a past history of sexual license and uncontrolled acquiescence to desire, such confessions appeared to be a breakthrough. The missions hoped to produce legitimate (i.e., Christian) indigenous couples, who practiced monogamy, professed faith in God, and reproduced at a prodigious rate. From an early age, station-school girls and boys were groomed to this end. Whether they eventually became native teachers or returned to their villages, as converts and spouses they constituted exemplary Christians. Part of their Christian responsibility was to have a large family, and in mission centers, where there were many such married couples, the population appeared to increase noticeably. A census taken in 1924 by one of Abel's indigenous converts illustrated the point. The convert, called Apolo, noted that on the islands of Sariba and Wagawaga it took 119 couples to produce 130 children, whereas on Kwato 70 couples produced the same number of offspring (Wetherell 1977, 228). In the same year Murray noted that "the families of Christian natives appear to be consistently larger than those of non-Christian" (Papua 1925, 7). While the missions—those "little depots of civilisation" (Bushell 1936, 242)—surveyed their compounds for sexual license and heard confessions of sins, they also turned their gaze to the monogamous Christian couple and urged them to procreate.

The colonial administration reinforced this message by introducing fiscal incentives for the legitimate couple to reproduce. In 1918 officials started to enforce an indigenous taxation scheme. Among those exempt from this scheme were couples with at least four living children (Papua 1920, 5). Each of these families was given a bonus card, which entitled them to a yearly payment. The amount of their "baby bonus" increased with every child born over the threshold of four (Papua 1924, 16). In 1922 the state paid out a total of £902 to Papuan couples (Papua 1923, 22). Murray asserted that "the object of the bonus is to mark the Government approval of large families, and to make large families the fashion; and there is evidence that it is having this effect" (Papua 1924, 16). Magistrates who administered the measure claimed that indigenes viewed it favorably, treating bonus days as holidays. Champion, the Director of Native Taxation, reported that crowds surrounded the recipients, public applause increasing in volume as those with the largest families stepped forward. Officials presented the baby bonus as part of their campaign against depopulation. Humphries, a resident magistrate in 1925, reported that "the natives are finding through tax and the family bonus a new interest in life" (Papua 1926, 32). The introduction of this bonus assumed that the colonial state could materially manipulate the sexual behavior of the marital couple and thereby increase the fertility of the Massim population.

Many believed that a rise in European trade, commerce, and industry contributed to the contraction of indigenous families. Missionaries in particular emphasized the role of indentured labor in reducing the birth rate (Wetherell 1977, 228). They claimed that fewer children were born because husbands were so often away, working as labor recruits on plantations or mines. In 1911 government medical officers warned against separating spouses for long periods of time. Fears arose that adultery, prostitution, and other abuses could result, and even more seriously the fertility of the population could be threatened (Papua 1911, 124). Europeans recognized that indentured labor could encourage nonreproductive sexual behavior in men. A colonial official stated "we were told that homosexuality was rife at places of employment, and that the practice is carried to villages with harmful results to the native population. The birth rate is affected by the absence of the labourers from their wives" (Burton 1949, 58–59). However, homosexuality was never more than a minor theme in the wider discourse on indigenous sexuality, and those who discussed it focused, as did Burton, upon the procreative consequences of such behavior for the legitimate couple.

Missionaries saw extramarital sexual behavior as a special threat to the stability of the monogamous and fecund couple. In the sermons of Reverend Abel of Kwato mission, there were explicit assertions that depopulation was a punishment for such behavior: "Putting the matter in a nutshell the Papuan is dying through persistent sin" (Wetherell 1977, 226–27). Many considered that infidelity among indigenes was rampant: "owing to the circumscribed choice, to the extreme fickleness of the Papuan heart, and to the little exalted state of morality generally, adultery is far from uncommon" (Great Britain 1893, 15). Such widespread beliefs contributed to adultery becoming an offense within the Native Regulations. The colonial government first constituted these regulations in 1890 as a set of rules designed to bear upon native custom, justice, and welfare (Great Britain 1891, 12). They restricted the definition of adultery, as a legal term, to infidelities committed against a man; hence the only possible offenders were married women and their lovers. The maximum sentence was six months imprisonment. Adultery was a common offense and featured strongly in conviction statistics; in 1909, 34 of the 47 cases brought before the resident magistrate in Papua's eastern division were for adultery (Papua 1909, 68).

The law offered other incentives for fidelity and monogamous sexual practice. A Native Regulation for "deserted wives and children" ensured that a husband who had deserted his wife and child could be made to pay for their continued maintenance (Papua 1922, 66). Missionaries too expended a lot of energy in attempts to prevent marital separation or divorce (White 1929, 32), and all these measures targeted the sexual conduct of spouses and reminded them that they had a responsibility to use sex productively for the sake of the population as a whole.

Discourse on and interventions against venereal disease closely linked the bodies of the procreative couple and the life of the population. The Massim was perceived as Papua's venereal province. In 1906 the Territory's annual report stated that venereal diseases "in all the complexity of forms in which they are presented, have undoubtedly been the plague spot of this island group" (Papua 1908a, 109). Europeans believed that gonorrhoea, chancroids, ulcerating granuloma, and syphilis were rife. The sexual license of the indigene appeared to corroborate this belief. Colonial officials claimed that despite the "immodesty of natives," they had no knowledge of how venereal disease was spread. The first medical task was therefore to instruct the islanders on the connection between sexual behavior and disease. Dr. Bellamy, Papua's first special venereal medical officer, initiated this education program in the Trobriands. He stated "the first thing a patient was taught on coming in was, if a male, that he had contracted the disease from a woman, and, if a woman, from a man. This was such a novel view that it was received incredulously on all sides. It was drilled into their ears day after day" (Papua 1908a, 110). Missionaries also contributed to the discourse on venereal disease, but they encouraged Islanders to see it as a "White man's disease," the result of European traders' and planters' licentious activities (Wetherell 1977, 225). When Malinowski arrived in the Trobriands in 1914, he reported that the indigenous people were openly blaming Europeans for its introduction (Malinowski 1929, 473). However not all Massim Islanders accepted the illness's sexual origin, and in 1911 Dr. Fleming Jones, stationed near Samarai, maintained that "many patients even now do not realise that the maladies from which they are suffering . . . are venereal diseases" (Papua 1911, 149). Nevertheless the missionary and the medical officer continued to stress the links between promiscuity and disease, and disease and depopulation, presenting monogamy as the only prophylactic.

Venereal disease fostered discussions about sex, in which health administrators analyzed the sexual habits of the population and encouraged native patients to confess their sexual histories. The venereal clause in the Native Regulations sanctioned this (Papua 1922, 17, 9, 70–71), stating that natives who believed they had a disease were to notify a village constable immediately. Upon receiving such notification, the constable would take them to the nearest magistrate or doctor. If natives suspected others of suffering from the disease, they had to report them to the constable too. The clause asserted that a native "who has, or thinks he has, venereal disease must abstain from all sexual intercourse while so diseased." Dr. Bellamy in the Trobriands sought to rigorously enforce these prescriptions. Bellamy aimed annually to examine all Trobrianders, and under his direction regular medical patrols systematically investigated and recorded cases of infection, names, and results in a "venereal register" (Black 1957, 234). By this method, which treated every native as a "venereal suspect" (Papua 1908b, 90), he inspected most of the island's population, 4,976 of a total of 8,500 natives in the first six months of 1908 (Black 1957, 234). On average, he diagnosed 5–10 percent of these as suffering from venereal disease. By 1912 there were 7,097 natives on the venereal register (Papua 1912, 169).

Success convinced Bellamy of the need to expand his project to other islands in the Massim. He believed that "the only method which will reduce this menace to reasonable proportions is for a census to be taken house by house, village by village, of every man, woman and child, and for every man, woman and child to be inspected by a qualified medical man at least once in every twelve months" (Papua 1920, 92). This venereal census soon included a record of births and deaths by months, and in effect it became the first annual census taken in Papua. By the outbreak of the Second World War, the indigenous legitimate couple had received forty years of instruction on the pathogenic consequences of sexual license. Yet medical officers frequently expressed doubts over the exact status of venereal diseases. Dr. Fleming Jones emphasized the problems of securing a reliable medical history and claimed that attempts to determine the subjective symptoms of a patient usually ended in "diagnostic disaster" (Papua 1911, 147). When Dr. Lambert arrived in Papua in 1920, he reported that traders and missionaries regularly mistook yaws for syphilis (Lambert 1941, 30–32), and Dr. Strong, the acting chief medical officer for Papua, acknowledged that many of the diseases diagnosed as sexually transmitted were in fact nonvenereal ulcers (Papua 1921, 101). However, the venereal campaign continued with both colonial officials and missionaries repeating their claims about the links between sexual behavior, disease, and sin.

The Precocious Child

Europeans also targeted what they saw as the sexualized body of the Massim child. They presented the child's sexual behavior as expected and inevitable, yet also unnatural and premature. In 1902 Abel noted that "the Papuan child . . . pleases himself. He is savage, in thought and vice, before he is ten years of age" (Abel 1902, 43). Malinowski, too, sanctioned the image of a "premature amorous existence" (Malinowski 1929, 55), and estimated that Trobriand girls engaged in sexual behavior from as early as age six and boys from age ten. Missionaries and colonial officials feared the consequences of this precocious activity.

Administrators represented early coitus as unproductive and degenerate behavior, affecting disease and infertility in the collective social body. Missionaries expressed concerns not only for the population, but for the development of each individual. Precocious sexual activity was to them a sin, which, if not addressed, could leave the Massim Islander stunted both spiritually and corporally. Just as parents, educators, and doctors in nineteenth-century Europe began to concern themselves with the sexual behavior of the young, so these fears prompted missionaries to guard the indigenous child's "precious and perilous, dangerous and endangered sexual potential" (Foucault 1978, 104; Stoler 1995).

The missions portrayed all native villages as centers of vice and sexual depravity. Missionaries thus had grave concerns for the moral welfare of children brought up in the contaminating atmosphere of village life. Sister Tinney, who joined the 1892 Methodist mission, spoke of this concern: "[T]he longer I stay here the more I see of the dense, dense darkness where Christ is not known. And the children are being brought up with a knowledge of all that is going on" (Tinney n.d., 25). In response, missionaries initiated a program to uproot children from villages and raise them within the relative safety of the mission compound (Colwell 1914, 556; cf. Young 1989). To many, the hopes of Christianity rested on its ability to relocate young minds before they became saturated with vice, for "no boy could be brought up in the evil atmosphere of a Papuan village without becoming a heathen like his parents" (Abel 1902, 192). Missionaries believed that the compound provided native children with an opportunity to grow normally in character and health of mind, supported at all times by the constant gaze and surveillance of the staff. The introduction in 1890 of a government ordinance allowing resident magistrates to place children convicted of an offense, orphaned, or deserted by their parents in mission hands made this endeavor easier (Great Britain 1892, 10). Those placed in the care of Europeans were known as "mandated children."[7] The Native Regulations also gave magistrates the power to take children from a native village and detain them in hospital for medical treatment (Papua 1922, 71). Often the nearest medical facility was at the mission station. The most important custodial duty of the mission, however, was education. The introduction of compulsory education brought many children to the compound, since nearly all schools were run by the missions.[8] Until 1945 the colonial administration chose to subsidize these operations, rather than fund an expensive government education program. Each mission compound contained a mission house, native nursery, orphanage, and boarding school. In Christian eyes these settlements represented a refuge for children, a haven for their vulnerable sexual potential.

All who held a measure of authority in the mission station were perpetually alert to any behavior that might be deemed sexual. They monitored prepubescent and adolescent development, and those activities they saw as having sexual associations. Missionaries placed great emphasis on the "unremitting attention [to] and care" of native children (Hurst 1938, 60), in the belief that each child "needs all the help we can give him, by preaching, by schools, by industrial training, by constant watching and advising" (Dauncey 1913, 183–84). Reverend Abel took exceptional measures to ensure this constant surveillance, always bringing his mission children with him on his trips to other islands and, while he was overseas, appointing older native inhabitants as overseers (Abel 1934, 101). Methodists divided their indigenous girls into groups and assigned them to live with members of the sisterhood. According to Sister Tinney, stationed at Dobu from 1892 to 1902, this was a considerable responsibility: "Even with five we are almost worried out of our lives sometimes. They are very raw material. It is one's work to watch them and do nothing else" (Tinney n.d., 39). Surveillance was also inscribed in the architecture and spatial arrangements of the mission settlement. At Dobu station two separate compounds were established: one for girls and one for boys. The mission house stood between them, allowing Bromilow and his colleagues to observe any trespass (Bromilow 1929, 214).

Malinowski commented that indigenous parents were completely indifferent to infantile sexual indulgence (Malinowski 1929, 56). Missionaries wanted them to change and to take charge of their children's sexual potential. Converts and church-goers heard the message regularly. S. B. Fellows in the Trobriands "preached on the flood—and speaking of impurity I spoke of the unrestrained sexual connection of the young people and asked the elders to help me to stop it" (Fellows n.d.).[9] Missionary agents often appropriated the role of parental surveillance for themselves. The mission children on Dobu called Dr. and Mrs. Bromilow father and mother, while they addressed the other missionaries as elder brothers or sisters. At Kwato Mission, Abel was very much conscious of his adopted role and parental obligation:

> We put ourselves in the place of Christian parents to them, and just as
> your father and mother would prevent you from going where you
> would get harm, and would shield you from mixing with evil com-
> panions before you were old enough to judge rightly for yourselves,
> so we acted towards our large Papuan family. (Abel 1902, 193)

The metaphor of parental scrutiny used by Abel illustrates the role of "watching" which missionaries assigned to themselves. As guardians of these native children, they believed it was their responsibility to intervene when the immature sexual body displayed signs of unwarranted activity.

Mission station rules were largely based upon the assumption that childhood sexuality was precocious, active, and ever present. A rigid code of behavior stipulated that boys could not visit the girls' workshop, that messages could not be passed from one to the other, that neither sex could marry outside the mission community, and that girls were not to present boys with gifts of cooked food (Wetherell 1977, 123). If a child breached these rules, the staff immediately assumed a sexual liaison, and suspected sexual transgression between mission boys and girls led them to be expelled from the station to avoid contamination of the other children. Missionaries reported these incidents with great expressions of disappointment: "We had very sad news this morning. Watisoni, one of Mrs. Bromilow's best boys, and Alomita fell into sin last night, and had to be sent back to their villages" (Tinney n.d., 123). Those who subsequently redeemed themselves by regular attendance at church and school had the opportunity to return. Less serious breaches of the rules resulted in private interviews with the head missionary, who encouraged children to assess their actions and suggest their own punishment. Bromilow expected this process to awaken what he saw as the dormant conscience of the Massim child (Bromilow 1929, 216). Yet missionaries realized that to most children Christianity appeared as a negative prescription. The hope was that as "they are laying to heart the 'shall nots', doubtless in time they will rise to the level of the 'Thou shalts'" (London Missionary Society n.d.).[10]

The Methodist mission taught its European recruits that "the real secret of stabilizing Christian life is to give it something to do, and when emotion is thus harnessed to service a true character is more likely to be formed" (Burton 1926, 75). Missionaries aimed to make every hour of the native child's day full, industrious and disciplined; otherwise the consequences for the immature sexual body would be catastrophic. Boarding pupils led a highly ordered existence. From sunrise to 8 A.M. they worked around the station. Then they had breakfast, which they cooked themselves. Before school commenced, they had to clean out their dormitory and bathe in the sea. Classes ran until midday; students were free for the afternoon. Yet their time was nearly always occupied in sport, technical training, or other recreational exercises. From 3 P.M. till 5 P.M. they were assigned more work around the station. At 7 P.M. dinner was served, followed by evening worship and then bed (Chignell 1911, 132–37). Lights were out by 9 P.M. There was no school on Saturday, but the morning was devoted to outdoor work and the afternoon to supervised recreation. Sunday was a rest day, but was taken up by church, Sunday school, and class meetings. At the heart of this routine lay an attempt to instill a sense of self-discipline in the students and thereby check childhood sexual indulgence. Discipline and obedience were perceived as the most important elements in education, which Abel believed met an essential Papuan need: "Add to the lack of discipline the fact that the child gains his knowledge from what he hears and sees where license is unbridled, and the result is a savage" (Abel 1934, 51). Habits of reliability were patiently and persistently drilled into pupils; punctuality was vital. The inculcation of these qualities had priority over academic learning. In 1895 Sister Billing, teaching at Dobu station, claimed that "however much or little knowledge they may gain, from an educational stand-point, the benefit of the discipline and regular routine on the moral part of their natures is incalculable" (Australasian Wesleyan Methodist Church 1895, 4: 3).[11] Missionaries recognized that this routine did not ensure a permanent end to sexual precociousness. Children often abandoned the rules of the mission station and the lessons of school upon returning to their village. Reverend Chignell, an Anglican missionary posted to the Massim in 1907, saw this as somehow inevitable: "Some day, they will go back to their wallowing, but it is good for them to have been trim and well disciplined even for a part of their lives" (Chignell 1911, 108).

Missionaries believed that sport strengthened moral character, and their desire to dissipate the child's sexual energies by instilling self-discipline led to recreational sport and physical drill becoming important parts of the school syllabus. Abel at Kwato mission was the chief apostle of "muscular Christianity"; his compound boys played cricket and football, while his girls played badminton, croquet, and tennis (Wetherell 1977, 212). On Kwato the children strictly adhered to the rules of these games. This was not the case in the Trobriands, where Reverend Gilmour introduced cricket in 1903. At first young converts obeyed the formal rules, but gradually they began to introduce more unorthodox elements. Cricketing teams challenged boys and men from different villages and would field sometimes as many as fifty players. Young men and women prepared themselves by decorating their bodies, hoping to appear attractive, and even erotic dances and chants entered the games. Ironically, then, sport became a forum for what the missionaries would have termed sexual titillation. By their own admission Trobrianders had "rubbished white man's cricket," thereby defeating its repressive agenda (see the film *Trobriand Cricket* 1975). However, the arrival in 1926 of Guides and Scouts reinforced this colonial agenda in most other islands of the Massim. The movement instructed young girls and boys in physical drills and exercises, and encouraged them to express athleticism. Hurst, a London Missionary Society agent who visited the region in 1936, reported that through strenuous training, girls and boys "are finding new interests and new joys with which to fill up what used to be unprofitable and dangerous leisure hours" (Hurst 1938, 76–77). Indigenous youths also filled these hours with industrial training: boys were instructed in boat-building, carpentry, and agricultural cultivation; girls in domestic arts and hygiene (Burton 1926, 83). Schools in the Massim devoted any remaining hours in the day to instruction in personal hygiene and cleanliness. Hurst proclaimed "a healthy and well-developed personality in a clean and healthy body seems to be the aim of the school" (1938, 75).

To many the success of this routine could be measured by a visit to the mission station. Sir Hubert Murray described his inspection, in 1926, of the Wesleyan station at Salamo in these terms:[12]

> This is a recently established station and is a model of neatness, order, discipline, and efficiency. All hands turned out to meet the visitors, and we passed through a double row of bright smiling boys and girls, their clean brown skins glistening in the sun, and all of them obviously well and happy . . . one does not require to be an expert to appreciate the almost military order and precision of the whole station and the good appearance of the natives who are being trained there. (Papua 1927, 14)

Colonial officials praised such an ordered, well-disciplined regime as evidence of progress. They believed these "smiling boys and girls" had succeeded in checking the temptations of sexual license.

Missionaries did more than censure or silence Massim children. They attempted to introduce them to the concept of interiority, for they believed that young converts could not repress their sexuality until they recognized and made explicit the presence within them of sex and desire. This meant encouraging them to uncover desires, to confess them, and thereby subject them to a constant watch. Missionaries did not want mute converts. At prescribed gatherings they asked children to talk about their sexual bodies and the desires that stirred inside them. Each week after Sunday service girls and boys participated in separate class meetings, where they were encouraged to confess their sins and urged to survey their inner selves: "At prayers in the evening Sister Eleanor gave the girls two texts to repeat after her: 'Watch and pray lest ye enter into temptation' and 'If sinners entice thee consent thou not,' and in her prayer made special mention of those who had not been good during the day" (Tinney n.d., 104). Some missionaries required their converts to make public confession of their struggles with sin. The Methodist Williams described an occasion in 1911 in which "four young men at the call of the minister in the middle of the sermon stand up, walk up to the front of the church, face a congregation of say 250 people, to every one of whom they are well known, and there make confession of their sin" (Australasian Wesleyan Methodist Church 1911, 20: 17). He depicted this as a spiritual catharsis, claiming that "their voices choked, they broke down completely, but began again bravely, and continued to the end" (18). Missionaries expected indigenous children to reveal everything.

Through confession and surveillance they hoped to induce them to transform what they saw as their "desire" into speech.

This ambition was not immediately achieved. Massim children may have been induced to talk about sexuality, but there is no evidence that they discovered an inner desiring self. Indeed missionaries cast doubt on their own ability to instill a sense of sinfulness. Reverend Copland King, who established the Anglican head station at Dogura in 1891, recognized that this would be the last aspect of Christianity the indigene would grasp (White 1929, 68). Abel too accepted that to the native "it is a transgression if detected, but being detected is the calamity, not the sin" (Abel 1934, 166). He wanted Massim Islanders to understand their inner sexuality and feel guilt, rather than just shame at public revelation of any indiscretion.

The Irresponsible Mother

Missionaries and colonial officials portrayed all Massim Islanders as sexually saturated, but the most visible and important figure was the irresponsible mother. They assumed that indigenous women were the sexual protagonists in the village. In their eyes the Massim woman was the temptress, someone who "nearly always tempts the man" (Great Britain 1904, 25) and leads him into infidelity. The image was reinforced by missionaries, who often reported the prevalence of harlotry (Bromilow 1909, 484), as well as any other example of what they saw as female wayward behavior. Bromilow commented that "up to the time of marriage the women are undisguisedly unmoral, and afterwards the restraints are doubtfully observed" (1929, 98). According to many, this sexual behavior engendered an indifference to family obligations, which posed a serious threat to the survival of the social body. They held the Massim woman's lack of responsibility to be the basis of depopulation in the region.

A discursive explosion surrounding the subject of abortion and contraceptive practices epitomized this concern with feminine irresponsibility. Missionaries in Papua regularly stated that young native women mixed, cooked, and ate preventatives, consisting of powdered obsidian and vegetable products, in order to restrict the frequency of childbirth and allow their licentious behavior free rein (Papua 1927, 11). Resident magistrates condemned what they saw as low maternal instinct. Both shared a belief in the prevalence of abortive techniques. Bromilow (1909, 483) claimed to know of four common methods: abortion by jumping from a height, by massage, by lifting a heavy weight, and finally by "playing games boisterously so as to fall heavily." Austen, a resident magistrate in the Trobriands, reported abortive practices such as eating charmed leaves or drinking boiled salt water (1934–35, 106). Nearly all medical, mission, and administrative reports mention abortion, representing it as some kind of hidden explanation for the low birth rate. Sometimes even more strange, clandestine contraceptive measures were suggested. Rentoul, a district patrol officer in the Massim, stated,

> I have been informed by many independent and intelligent natives that the female of the species is specially endowed or gifted with ejaculatory powers, which may be called upon after an act of coition to expel the male seed. It is understandable that such powers might be increased by use and practice, and I am satisfied that such a method does exist. (1931, 153)

These discussions always focused on the indigenous mother, who was expected to give birth and avoid fertility preventatives.

Indigenous women were important targets of missionary attentions. In 1892 the first members of the Methodist Sisterhood arrived in the Massim. Their assigned role was to challenge and transform female sexual behavior. Bromilow stated that "we saw in the higher status of Dobuan women on the one side a medium through which we might redeem it from its debasement on the other, and make it a purifying influence in Dobuan life at its very source. The agency needed for this was an order of missionary sisters" (1929, 212). The first members, Sister Eleanor Walker, Sister Minnie Billing, and Sister Jeannie Tinney, began by organizing schooling for girls (213). Sister Elizabeth Tomlinson of the Anglican mission at Dogura (Wetherell 1977, 86) and Beatrice Abel at Kwato soon followed their lead. They all saw education and the regularity of station life as the best means of transforming woman's sexual body. Sister Billing believed that "the comparison between the girls living on the mission station and those in the villages shows how much the latter are improved by leaving their sinful surroundings, and although many of the girls in the school go back to their villages when school is over, still the influence on their lives must tell" (Australasian Wesleyan Methodist Church 1895, 4: 3). The sisters instructed their pupils in hygiene, cleanliness, sewing, and ideals of personal purity (Burton 1926, 119). In much the same way that sport became a measure to occupy "unprofitable and dangerous leisure hours," so domestic arts became a conduit through which they hoped girls could safely divert their enormous sexual energy.

The Christian missions hoped that the "influence of pure womanhood" (Australasian Wesleyan Methodist Church 1892, 1: 3) might inspire a sexual transformation in girls. Some looked to the missionary sisters to provide this inspiration; others to movements like the Girl Guides. The latter presented

its arrival in the region as "the beginning of a new girlhood and womanhood in Papua . . . part of a new way of life which, as it helps to lift the
women of Papua, is going to do more than any other thing to lift the whole
level of life" (Hurst 1938, 51). Fellows held up the native teacher's wife as
an example of female purity: "[I]t is by her personal touch as she moves
among the women and girls that the greatest influence is exercised. Her
house is in a prominent place in the village, is cleaner and better kept than
the surrounding houses, an atmosphere of friendliness and help radiates
from this centre" (n.d.).[13] Missionaries wanted to impose this level of womanhood by restoring what they saw as the mother's organic communication
with her children, family, and wider social body. To arouse the "mother-
heart" in the Massim woman (Bromilow 1929, 312), the missions experi-
mented with placing girls in charge of the station nursery. Here they had to
care for alien children and infants. Mrs. Bromilow believed that the nursery
provided "a continual object lesson on the sanctity of infant life, far more
effective than spoken words could be, so obvious that it could not be missed.
This happy band of children, rescued and cared for, set in their midst, before
their very eyes, was a settled challenge" (207–8). Through the use of such
tactics, missionaries claimed to have taught indigenous women to be responsible wives and mothers (Burton 1949, 104; cf. essays in Ram and
Jolly forthcoming).

The findings of the 1896 commission "appointed to enquire into the
decrease of the native population, colony of Fiji" sanctioned the idea that
indigenous women needed to be made aware of their procreative responsibilities and familial duties. Although the commission focused on Fiji, Papuan administrators took up many of its recommendations. These included
measures like the "prevention of neglect of children," "improvement of
women's condition," "better care of pregnant, lying-in and suckling
women," and "hygienic missions by European women" (Fiji 1896, 184–
88). In the late 1930s colonial officials also encouraged the establishment of
Village Women's Committees, which they hoped would occupy the attentions of indigenous women by inducing them to fulfil mothering tasks.
Members were expected to raise the quality and range of food crops, maintain domestic hygiene, beautify villages, care for the old and infirm, send
children regularly to school, and generally to work towards raising the standard of living (Spencer 1964, 166).

To arrest depopulation, missionaries believed it necessary to revolution-
ize the standards of health care and morality in village life. They targeted
women as the agents of this revolution, for "it is only as the prospective
mothers of the race are familiarised with the principles of health and with

the contemplated and necessary changes in the social structure that the success of the village—the real unit of all native life—can be assured" (Burton 1949, 145). Married women living on the mission station and Girl Guides received regular lectures on childbirth and infant care (Papua 1934–35, 20). Both Methodists and Anglicans introduced qualified health staff to the Massim in the 1920s, and many of the missionary sisterhood's new members were certified nurses or welfare workers. They initiated health instruction programs for indigenous women in the belief that "if a mother has been taught the cause of disease on a simple scientific basis, and has been instructed to use her knowledge and reason in the prevention and treatment of them, there comes not only better health, but also a great liberation of mind" (Burton 1949, 146; see also Fildes, Marks, and Marland 1992).

Colonial medical officers also began to concentrate their attentions on the surveillance and treatment of women's health. The special venereal hospitals in the Massim opened obstetrics wards, while new hospitals, all focused upon maternity care, were established at Salamo, Kwato, and Dogura. In 1935 the secure hospital at Samarai still took in 272 venereal patients a year (Papua 1936–37, 8), but the disease no longer dominated medical discussion. Instead attention shifted to other diseases,[14] and to the care of child-bearing women. In the 1930s, government and mission hospitals established prenatal clinics to monitor and care for expectant mothers, informed each pregnant woman of the approximate time of parturition, and gave advice on correct dietary measures and realistic work loads. Postnatal clinics provided continued advice and observation for at least a year after childbirth. They required mother and infant to present themselves at the hospital for regular examination and weighing (Papua 1934–35, 20). Clinics also organized wet nurses and set up village maternity centers in more inaccessible areas. Medical staff trained and utilized indigenous nurses, who provided a local contribution to the reduction of maternal and infant mortality and thereby to the sustainment of viable life in the Massim (cf. colonial Malaya, Manderson 1992a, 1996).

By filling their idle hours with mothercraft, missionaries intended to divert the sexual energies of indigenous women. In this manner they believed that the temptress could become the paragon of Christian womanhood; the licentious influence she was said to have exercised over the Massim family would be replaced by the equally powerful example of conjugal virtue. Where she had once been deemed responsible for the degradation of the Massim population, now she could act as a guarantor for the sanctity of life. The missionaries believed they could thus refigure the female sexual body, containing its energies in a monogamous sexual practice. In the space of fifty years they had identified the Massim woman as possessing a sexual body, targeted that body as a site for intervention, and then asserted that they had removed from the woman's body the worst of its sexual excesses.

Conclusion

Before Sir William McGregor left the Territory in 1898, he reported on the transformation the Methodists had wrought in parts of the Massim: "Mr. Bromilow has reduced Dobu and its neighbourhood to a decently-behaved community, who keep Sabbath, go to school, attend church, and conduct themselves like an ordinary Christian parish" (Brown 1904, 15–16). To McGregor's list of pastoral achievements one might add the establishment of the confessing device, of a general incitement to talk about sex. Foucault saw the device as involved in the Christian "task of passing everything having to do with sex through the endless mill of speech" (1978, 21). Missionaries encouraged their converts to perform this task, to reveal inner desires and confess transgressions. And they did; mission reports were full of these accounts. But there is no evidence that converts adopted a Christian sense of interiority or an awareness of sex as something hidden inside them. Colonial officials repeatedly stated that indigenes failed to understand the precepts of European civilization, such as criminal responsibility or individual culpability. In 1912 Murray commented on their ignorance of court-pleading procedures. He complained that both the accused and witnesses tended to say what they felt would please the magistrates, rather than present an accurate description of events (1912, 226–28). It seems plausible that indigenous converts were doing the same thing, confessing sins in order to meet mission expectations.

The basis for the strategic union between magistrate and missionary was a shared fear of depopulation. This concern propelled the construction of sexual figures—the procreative couple, the precocious child, and the irresponsible mother—and subjected those figures to a considered supervision.

From 1888 to 1942 mission and state worried incessantly about the preservation of life in the Massim. In that period missionaries exerted greater influence over local people. Foucault claimed that in Europe the uniformity of purpose provided by the Christian church until the eighteenth century was broken up and dispersed by the arrival of new disciplines interested in the sexual body. He argued that demography, biology, medicine, psychiatry, psychology, ethics, pedagogy, and political criticism all allowed sexual strategies to spread out and multiply (Foucault 1978, 33). Massim Islanders encountered few of these disciplines, and those that they experienced entered the region under missionary sponsorships. The missions ran all schools and often hospitals and field clinics as well. This affected the trajectory of sexual strategies. As a discipline, these strategies tended to focus more on the individual, rather than the wider social body. Confession remained a spiritual rather than secular device for inciting people to talk about sex. Missionaries encouraged the indigene to make sexual associations with sin and evil. They presented monogamy as the sexual norm, the only legitimate avenue for satiating desires, preventing venereal disease, and raising the birth rate. For the indigenous child, mother, and couple to become responsible owners of their sexual bodies, they had to accept this outcome.

Until new disciplines emerged independently of the mission, little directional change could occur. Jolly suggests that in colonial Fiji and Vanuatu, "it was the influence of missionary persuasion rather than the efforts of state coercion which [was] crucial" (1992, 29). At least until 1942 this was the case in the Massim also. However, it seems likely that once the colonial state began to invest more heavily in the region, sexual strategies branched out, and new sexual figures emerged. After the Second World War, missionaries themselves started to question their role. Burton, in reassessing the Methodist performance in Papua, critiqued their prohibition of polygamy. He claimed that "where monogamy became the recognised practice, child bearing was much too frequent in the condition of society, and there came about an alarming death rate of infants under twelve months of age" (1949, 49). In the years following 1945 Massim Islanders encountered a wider variety of disciplinary experts and had to respond to far less uniform sexual strategies.

Acknowledgments

This chapter emerges from my thesis, completed in 1993 for an M. A. at the University of Otago in New Zealand. I would like to express my thanks to Ian Frazer, Ilana Gershon, Margaret Jolly, Lenore Manderson, Barbara Placido, and Annalise Riles for their advice and their critiques of this paper.

CHAPTER THREE

Gaze and Grasp: Plantations, Desires, Indentured Indians, and Colonial Law in Fiji

JOHN D. KELLY

Adolph Brewster Joske was the stipendiary magistrate in a remote court-house at Nadarivatu in Colo North, a hinterland province of the largest island of the Fiji group. His station had originally been set up to monitor and, if necessary, intervene in what the British called "the Tuka cult," a hinterland religious complex that the British regarded as intrinsically disorderly. By the time that Joske took up his station, Tuka had been officially suppressed. The prophet-priest Navosavakadua and hundreds of his followers were in exile on distant islands, officially designated as "dangerous and disaffected natives" in need of rehabilitation.[1] In fact Joske's court had little Tuka business over the years. Relations between the colonial government and the hinterland Fijians at last grew more routine. But like most magistrate's courts in the indenture period in Fiji, his was overwhelmed with criminal cases emerging out of the plantation "lines" housing South Asians brought to Fiji people committed by contract to five years of labor.

In 1915, the Fiji government proscribed official use of the word *coolie,* part of a reform effort designed to impress India. Until then (and indeed, for quite a while after) the Indians were generally called and imagined to be "coolies," and the rural magistrate's courts in cane-growing areas came to be known as the "coolie courts." These courts were a focus of indenture-contract discipline, the site where fines were levied and indenture times extended for violations of the labor contract such as failing to complete tasks, insolence, refusing to work, absence from the "estates" without permission, and other violations of labor law carrying penal sanctions. These courts were also the sites of charges laid for extraordinary numbers of violent crimes, crimes also emerging from the plantations and "free" Indian settlements nearby.

Among all the magistrates of these courts, Joske kept by far the clearest and most detailed records. He was unique among his peers for the meticulously typed documentation of all testimony that he presented to the Supreme Court.[2] His records will lead us into the world of law, order, and violence in indenture Fiji, and his very specific juridical gaze will help us to clarify, and complicate, general questions about the constitutive powers of colonial gazes.

In Joske's Court

Supreme Court case #12 of 1907 began in Joske's court. An indentured man named Surajvali was charged with a brutal assault on a woman who had been living with him. According to police testimony, the police found the weapon, the scene of the crime, and, in a distant hut, the victim, because the accused brought the constables to them. An Indian constable testified, "The accused came to the police station. He said I have cut my woman. . . . I have offended against the Government. Arrest me." The investigation then commenced.

I have often wondered, when examining the records of this typical sort of case, whether these police narratives of confession were sheer fiction. The eerie story, repeatedly represented in Fiji's court records, is of indentured immigrant men launching brutal public attacks, and then immediately seeking out the police to confess. Was this story merely the constabulary's efficient means of shaping the necessary evidence, or was it a report of surrenders and confessions that actually occurred? Joske's records, here, are very helpful. We can track, through the clear detailing of Surajvali's interventions in court, something of what he did and did not care to make clear about his own actions. Surajvali, present for all the testimony against him, cross-examined no one but the victim, Jaine. Jaine testified from her hospital bed, describing her jewelry and its origins, and describing the attack on her. He asked her, "Did I ever neglect to feed you or take care of you, or do anything to pain you?" She replied, "I am too weak to answer and my mouth is sore and I cannot talk." After this, the court asked her a question, not recorded in the documents, to which she replied, "I do not know if I shall recover or not, that God will decide." (I also do not know if she survived.) Surajvali made only one other intervention in his own defense during the evidentiary proceedings. When her jewelry was introduced as evidence, before her testimony, he insisted that the thick silver necklace (Exhibit C) had been given to the woman by Sundar. "Sundar showed her the necklace and she ran away from me." None of her jewelry was given by Surajvali; her other necklace, the small one, she said was a gift from a man "now in Suva gaol."

The overseers, the inspectors of immigrants, the magistrates, and other government officials were well acquainted with this as a type of crime. The Fiji government had decided, after investigations in the 1880s and 1890s, that the cause of crimes such as this was "sexual jealousy," and they ex-

plained it as an Indian racial trait (see Kelly 1991b; Lal 1985a, 1985b). Surajvali confessed in court: "It is the fault of the woman. It is true that I beat
her. Had she not gone to the house of Sundar I should not have struck her.
That is all." Sundar did not testify, and not surprisingly, Surajvali was found
guilty by the Supreme Court and was sentenced to seven years and 24 lashes.
This is what makes this case typical: a hopeless, self-justifying confession
publicizing a never concealed, extraordinary act of violence by a man
against a woman with whom he once had a sexual relationship, leading to
severe punishment by court, generally death if the victim also had died. As
in this case, there was often at least one male rival involved; sometimes the
rival was the victim of the violence. As in roughly half the cases, in this case
no "European"[3] man was alleged to have been involved, either as a sex
partner or as an assigner of rights to women.

The Sexual Violence of Indenture in Fiji

From 1879 through 1920, over 60,000 people were recruited in South Asia
and brought to Fiji to work as plantation laborers, under five-year indenture
contracts with penal sanctions. Violence was fundamental to the indentured
labor system and plantation life in Fiji (Kelly 1990, 1991a, 1991b, 1992).
Scholars such as Ali (1980), who frame the struggles of the Indians in Fiji
within the boundaries of political economy, explain violence as a response
to labor exploitation, focusing on rare labor gang riots and attacks on overseers, and they have often repeated the colonial explanation of men's frequent attacks on women and on other indentured men, and the frequent
suicides, as products of "sexual jealousy." To the colonials, the whole explanation for the violence lay in this terrible "jealousy," a package of racial traits
thought to include violent temper and a cool willingness to die, unleashed
by the lack of "traditional" restraints of caste and village in Fiji, and exacer-
bated by the fact that indenture brought over only 40 women per 100 men.

   Here I will reject the racist story of an instinctual unreason, this jealousy
narrative, but I will accept the colonial designation of the violence as sexual,
although this latter choice is problematic. This violence obviously has other
dimensions as well, even if our conceptions of sex and sexuality are broad.
As I have argued earlier (Kelly 1991a), indentured men found it harder
to establish marriages and households—in effect, to constitute patriarchal
domestic places privileging themselves (cf. Beall 1990 on indenture in South
Africa)—than they did to find sex partners. We could seek a nonsexual
center to the facts here, and emphasize the degree to which the real story
was one of gender domination and a broader struggle over domestic rules.

But accounts of pure reason, clean reconstructions of measured utilities and interested calculations, are not really more plausible than stories of constituting instincts. Despite the danger of colonial stereotypes of animalistic lust creeping back into our accounts, I think we should seek more than an antidote depiction that makes the agency of these indentured men seem reasonable—especially agency that is so deliberately destructive of others and self.

In any case we cannot follow colonial accounts. The ruling colonials were astonishingly unable or unwilling to generalize about their own role in the violence, no matter how often white overseers were implicated in the stories told of men fighting over rights to have women. Fiji "European" accounts varied by genre and distance from the lines. Europeans with personal experience of the plantations seem generally to have been aware not only of the alleged Indian instinct for "sexual jealousy," but also of frequent sexual liaisons, paid for and otherwise, between European men and Indian women. Walter Gill, in his memoir of his years as an overseer in Fiji, provides ample evidence of this awareness.[4] But the formalities of the courts became mechanisms for bureaucratic repression and denial. When European overseers were snarled in the circumstances of a violent crime, the courts generally ignored those aspects of defense evidence (but see note 7 below). In egregious cases, especially when the European was losing control over the Indians, court cases were avoided altogether, and the European was transferred or resigned, and not infrequently was sent back to Australia. But when general accounting for the violence was called for, the European authorities (including Gill)[5] reproduced the narrative of "sexual jealousy." When Europeans were involved, blame was laid almost always at the feet of the Asian siren, to whose wiles the European had succumbed. Gill provides a window into the fantasies of European men on plantations, mixing imagery of nature, primitivism, and the Oriental exotic in his extensive descriptions of Indian women in indenture Fiji. Life in the lines, to them, was dangerous but exciting for those who could maintain control. The fantasies of the plantation Europeans about the Indian women gained far greater social extension than did news of their own actions. How, exactly, did this happen?

To understand these facts, we need more than a science of political economy or any other method for reconstructing "practical rationality" (cf. Obeyesekere 1992, 19). Can we capture the contours of this reality, instead, as the history of some sort of gaze? We can identify various kinds of colonial gaze operating in the stories, from these fantasies of the plantation whites to the formalities of the judges examining witnesses. But which gazes had what effects? What was made real, if we "deploy" a bit more contemporary vocabulary, when which gazes "inscribed" what, where?

Gaze Powers

Attention to the colonial gaze has done much to open studies of colonial power to relations and effects that do not follow mechanically from production or other pragmatic exigencies. However, exclusive inquiry into gaze has had the unintended consequence of presuming too much about the powers of the gazer. This essay will join inquiry about the colonial gaze with inquiry about the colonial grasp, especially regarding the constitutive powers and limits of both in relation to the sexual bodies of indentured Indian women in Fiji. Court records, especially those of A. B. Joske, provide a window into the ambiguities of official attempts to investigate and regulate. Questions will also be raised about Indian resistance and also Indian initiatives in the constitution of their own and colonizers' bodies, but my main focus here will be the powers, modes, and limits of colonial agency.

Critical scholarly inquiry into powerful gazes can be found in many disciplines. Much could be said about the complex trajectories of critical psychoanalytic reformations of the scientific self and its positively empirical gaze—from Freud to Lacan, Kristeva, and others. More influential in current scholarship on colonial culture and history are Foucault's magisterial syntheses, especially his crystallization of a distinction between a modern, panoptic mode of discipline, in which a dominated body is incited to interiorize the disciplinary gaze in a self-disciplining subjectivity, and (allegedly) all earlier forms of discipline, wherein spectacles of punishment were arranged instead to produce fear and submission to specific external authorities (1977). I will return both to Foucauldian scholarship on colonial culture and history, and to nineteenth-century positivism. But let me start with an art-historical touchstone of gaze theory from John Berger's *Ways of Seeing,* where he suggests problematic conventions that entail the following:

> *Men act* and *women appear.* Men look at women. Women watch themselves being looked at. This determines not only most relations between men and women but also the relation of women to themselves. The surveyor of woman in herself is male: the surveyed female. Thus she turns herself into an object—and most particularly an object of vision: a sight. (1972, 47)

As he criticizes artistic representations of nude women, Berger distinguishes a European tradition with roots in Christian conceptions of shame from the tradition of nakedness in Indian, Persian, African, and pre-Colombian art, where "nakedness is never supine," and which is more likely to show "active sexual love as between two people, the woman as active as the man" (53).

Thus, Berger finds a sexual gaze at the core of a Christian tradition of gender difference, men surveying and objectifying women, and women interiorizing their own surveillance, and he gives us a brief glimpse of a vast, lost Garden of Eden beyond the West, in which genders were equal and sex was free and active.

Foucault and Berger deliver us two different versions of the social history of the powerful, other-transforming gaze. To simplify, let us call them *modernization* versus *original sin*—a story of an axial modernity of overwhelmingly different and new powers versus a story of a Christian-European long run of moral inscription. When we take up problems of sex and gender in colonial culture and history, however, the larger patterning of agency stays the same whether we bring with us a story of European culture as original sin, a story of modernization, or a synthesis of the two: we script the colonized from the outset in the position of patient and victim, and tend to grant the colonizer all active powers.

Consider Timothy Mitchell's *Colonising Eygpt* (1988). Mitchell tells us that Egypt's modern colonizers had novel powers to "enframe," a uniquely envisioning and vision-insistent way of ordering space, time, and people which enabled the colonial agents to remake the place in their own image of it, a kind of power that only a postmodern and postcolonial consciousness like Mitchell's own could actively understand and confront.[6] In contrast, Michael Taussig (1987), in inquiring into the space of death on the colonial frontier, argues that the "good speech" of the colonizer was deformed, the efforts of even the most critical of colonial observers to depict the real scene generally failed, and visualizing faculties were taken over by cascading fantasies of evil and violence that overcame other ordering schemata. But again one might synthesize and fit Mitchell's and Taussig's accounts into a story of colonial ordering: at the beginning, and on the edge, there are failures and deformation, but eventually and centrally the colonial gaze will reshape its world and inscribe even the subjectivity of the colonized. A counterpoint to this resolution, then, is Ranajit Guha's argument (1989) against the idea that colonial regimes, and that of the Raj in India in particular, were ever actually hegemonic. Guha argues forcefully that the British in India never succeeded in constituting a civil order that made their domination seem unquestionably natural, inevitable, necessary, or even simply good for India. The colonial projects failed to establish a rule of law that actually constituted citizens, law with consent and collaboration of the governed. By Guha's argument, European "bourgeois culture hit its historical limits in colonialism" (277), as its willed self-alienation from the colonized contradicted its promise to lead, rather than simply dominate, people it regarded as Others. Precisely as they reorganized towns and gridded out new, antiseptic cantonments or quarters exclusively for the ruling whites (cf. Mitchell 1988, 178–79), and made their "modern" vision real, in Guha's view the European colonial states ensured that they would not achieve the hegemonic ordering powers found, for example, in the nation-states of Europe.

We are already far from Berger, and from gazes that are frankly sexual. Let us return to Gill, the *randi-wallah,* or overseer, and his gang of indentured women workers:

> As a gang they gave a minimum of trouble. It was as if they wanted me as part of their strange coolie lives. When we squatted together on a headland at midday, one or another of them would shyly offer me a "roti" or "chupatti" from her meagre ration of thin unleavened bread. And they would discuss themselves and me, bawdily, yet naturally, shrilling like starlings at their own crude humour. Though still "The Sahib," I was their particular sahib; part of them and of their lives.
>
> The routine seldom altered. To them the act was fresh each time they went into it.
>
> "How old is he?" Chini would ask in the vernacular, peering at me from the fringe of her sari.
>
> "Old enough." The girl who said it would giggle and wriggle her hips.
>
> Muniamma's snicker was contagious. Invariably we heard it before she asked, "Do you think he's a virgin?" And because opinion was divided, and none of them could prove I was not, they would argue among themselves. Then a long, skinny Tamil, with an unprintable nickname, would wonder what I would be like in bed. This was their chance to cackle over individual fantasies. It was erotica uninhibited, and because it was also part of them, something to be revelled in. And because nobody knew what I was like physically, there would be a shaking of cloth-covered heads and a cracking of knuckles in long, brown fingers, until one of them would tell a fantastically intimate story of an experience all of us knew never happened. And then at last old Latchmi would wrap it up, saying, "Arre! He'd be just like the rest of the sahibs," and she would look over her shoulder and down her back with a surprised expression. "Two shoves like a rooster, and the hen left without a tail-feather ruffled."
>
> I have been told I should have got up and walked away—there was something about my dignity and the prestige of the white man—yet I could never understand why (Gill 1970, 39–40).

In his fantasy that he was experiencing "erotica uninhibited . . . something to be revelled in," women speaking "bawdily, yet naturally," Gill, like

Berger, imagined an Eden of active eroticism beyond the strictures of European morality. Later, Gill did arrange a regular sexual liaison for himself with an indentured woman, as discussed below. Here, I suggest we attend to the gazes, not only to Gill's image of these women, their natural, Oriental eroticism in his gaze, but to their active gaze on him.

Even if this active, speculative female testing and imagining of his sexuality occurred partly in Gill's imagination, I doubt that he wholly invents it. I suspect that the women did playfully test which sexual rules, plans, and taboos would emanate from their young sahib. They could not address it or approach him directly. They certainly could not grasp him or even touch him on their own initiative. Later in his text, Gill described being grabbed by an indentured woman shocked by nearby lightening in a storm: "Her action confirmed her fear. To have touched me, unless stimulated by something uncontrollable, would have been impossible for her as an Indian" (1970, 78). It was difficult even for them to address him directly. Note the shyness when he was addressed directly, or when food was proffered, food being highly significant in South Asian cultural marking of rank and social boundary. Trapping his attention with their "act" and watching his reactions, trapping him in their gaze by putting on a theater for him, may well have been both their tactic and their pleasure.

But I want to keep hold of something else here too: Gill's internalized sense of being observed. Women watch themselves being looked at, but what of white men? George Orwell, in his essay "Shooting an Elephant," tells of his duty to act, as a police officer in Burma, once trapped in the gaze of a crowd of "natives" who had called him forth to see an elephant on rampage:

> A sahib has got to act like a sahib; he has got to appear resolute, to
> know his own mind and do definite things. To come all that way, rifle
> in hand, with two thousand people marching at my heels, and then to
> trail feebly away, having done nothing—no, that was impossible. The
> crowd would laugh at me. And my whole life, every white man's life
> in the East, was one long struggle not to be laughed at. (1950, 7)

Gill's account of his raucous luncheons, in contrast to Orwell's of his grim march, suggests what might have made Gill an interesting puzzle to the women in his gang: his resistance to a "duty" not to see or hear such things as he did, the duty that made being *randi-wallah* the job for the most junior man, "something about my dignity and the prestige of the white man." Gill claims not to have understood this, but in fact he knew that he "should have got up and walked away" if he wanted to appear respectable. Who and what was at risk in the sexual joking of the women's gang?

According to Berger, a woman's every action "is also read as an indication of how she would like to be treated. . . . Only a man can make a good joke for its own sake" (1972, 46–47). British colonial men, so possessive of their own "prestige" and "dignity," could not tell a good joke for its own sake except in the confines of their own race, class, and gender, at their clubs or military camps, and some could not even do so there. We need not doubt that self-surveying was a crucial matter for Indian women who wished to appear respectable and good in character to Fiji Europeans. But let us also notice more than the transforming power of Gill's colonizing gaze, as he monitored his prestige, dignity, and authority (risking all to pursue his own pleasure, but aware of the precariousness of his position) while his gang made up, and frequently reenacted, good jokes about his body and sex life in a vernacular he could not always follow, and laughed about him in his presence.

Sexual Violence and the End of Indenture in Fiji

The sexual exploitation and violence endemic in the lines played a role in the demise of the system. As the best historians (see for example Lal 1985a, 1985b) make clear, not all plantations in Fiji were the same. They varied in the frequency, stability, and degree of permitted coerciveness in the sexual liaisons between European men and indentured women, and the prevalence and top-down tolerance, support, and investment in open prostitution in the lines. Gill's gang did have consequential things to learn about him, as well as a chance for pleasure at his risk. The greater risks were those faced by the women, especially when the Europeans' interests extended beyond gazing and joking. The scenarios alleged in court testimony strongly suggest that the violence—brutal assaults, murders, rapes, and suicides—can be connected to the plantations where the European planters and overseers were living out the vision of exotic sensuality and predatory promiscuity intrinsic to the nature of the "indentured" women.

Gandhian nationalists in India told a story about Fiji quite different from any told by Fiji Europeans. The Gandhians told stories of virtuous women struggling to protect their chastity in an atmosphere of coercive evil. With evidence from supporters in Fiji and research expeditions, they were able by the 1910s to marshall overwhelming anecdotal and medical evidence of real evil there. Faced with outraged public opinion in India, Gandhi called India's first national *satyagraha*—insistence on the truth campaign—and the colonial government of India put an end to indenture and to all labor migration to Fiji.

A crucial part of this story, the collapse of a very profitable labor regime, was the official reluctance to look. For decades, protests about abuse of Indian women were directed at the colonial government of Fiji both from within Fiji and from India, even from official India. By the 1910s, the inquiries from official India were frequent and increasingly insistent. But official Fiji never took new initiative to look into what it generally saw as the sordid business of Indian "sexual jealousy" (see Kelly 1991b). When forced to, it conducted cursory investigations only, mainly to prove that complainants were of low moral character, untrustworthy as witnesses, and unworthy of sympathy.

This reluctance to look is all the more odd when we juxtapose it with the willingness to inquire minutely into the details of employment—something more like the "panoptic" or "enframing" colonial state now familiar to us in the literature on colonial power. By the late 1900s and the 1910s, Fiji's Immigration Department was issuing very detailed annual reports on Indian labor immigration and work practices on each plantation (held in the National Archives). Wading into the vast table that is Appendix D to the report for 1909, for example, we learn that 1.75 (mean number) female immigrants worked on the tiny Lau "plantation" in Rewa, working 86.98 percent of the days, missing 0.68 percent for Unlawful Absence, 0.26 percent Absent with a Pass, 0 percent in Court or Gaol, 11.41 percent for Sickness, 0.45 percent for Bad Weather, and 0.22 percent for Holidays. They (the 1.75 of them) earned 7.42 pence per working day, or 8.53 pence per days actually worked. Summarizing for all plantations, the report concluded happily,

> The various returns comprised in this Report support the view that the general condition of indentured immigrants in the Colony is in the main satisfactory and one of gradual improvement. Comparing 1899 with 1909 the following figures show that the average number of days worked upon and the daily wages earned are higher than in 1899, and that the improvement during the past few years has been constant and progressive.

In the course of delineating both immigrant mortality and immigrant crime, the reports do include data about violence. By 1914 this included a ten-year murder rate summary; the general murder rate (actually, murdered rate) from 1905 to 1914 varied from 0.006 percent in 1911 to a high of 0.066 percent in 1908. Yet they saw no need to figure the percentages specifically of adult women killed (between 1905 and 1914, 29 women as against 12 men, despite the reverse sex ratio of 2.7 men to 1 woman in this period). They do not calculate, as I have from their data for 1905 to 1918, when the lines were emptying, that (in their terms) 0.11 percent of adult indentured women were murdered each year (this leaves out those "grievously wounded," and "free" women wounded or killed)—in effect that one out of 185 women was killed during a five-year indenture in this period. But the reports do show that an extraordinary number of indentured laborers, especially men, commited suicide (at least 62 indentured men and 5 indentured women between 1909 and 1914, for example—and I am missing the report of 1911—while over these six years 20 women were murdered). Using the report statistics for the period between 1909 and 1914 (not including 1911), 79 indentured men were either murdered, executed for homicide, or committed suicide, a rate of roughly 1 per 115 over a five-year period of indenture.

These rates are extraordinarily high, and the Fiji government knew it. Its reluctance to generate more illuminating summary statistics was no doubt partly strategic. Indenture was under a cloud, and officials sought to write reports with conclusions like the one above: news about rising incomes was definitely putting their best foot forward. But there was more to this. They knew that indentured Indian men were killing Indian women, other Indian men, and especially themselves, at extraordinary rates. And they didn't need to investigate because they already knew why: "sexual jealousy." The 1909 annual report of the Immigration Department gave two-sentence summaries of its ten suicides. It found one case of "home-sickness"—Sambhar, register number 39803, committed suicide two days after arriving at his plantation—one case of derangement, three cases cause unknown, and five which were, one way or another, matters of "sexual jealousy." "Shankar . . . had previously threatened to kill his woman or to take his own life"; "Murari . . . Evidence pointed to jealousy of his woman"; "Ganganna . . . Depression of mind owing to desertion of her husband was proved"; "Goviden . . . had quarrelled with and been deserted by his woman"; "Ramadhin . . . clearly due to the conduct of his woman who had been enticed away by another man." The report summarized as follows:

> The number of cases in which the cause of suicide appears to be attributable to sexual jealousy and disappointment is as usual large. It is connected with the disproportion of the sexes at present existing on most plantations, and the consequent facility with which women abandon the partners to whom they are bound by no legal ties for others who offer a better inducement. Among the "free" Indian population, where the disproportion of sex is becoming obliterated, cases of suicide from this cause are comparatively few.

The theory of sexual jealousy was a routinized, bureaucratic alibi. It filled the space of explanation. Opprobrious about women making choices ("abandoning partners"), and generally silent about top-down involvement in the cases,[7] the reports depicted a sad reality governed by Indian racial natures, about which little could be done—when they offered an account at all. The report for 1910 made no general comment on suicides. The last to explicitly mention "sexual jealousy," the report for 1912—"it is probable that in the majority of cases sexual jealousy was the principal factor"—also introduced a new generalization into suicide reporting: "In the remaining cases owing to lapse of time or other reason, the cause for the act could not be clearly ascertained, but no evidence as to ill-treatment of any individual immigrant as the cause for suicide was either proved or alleged at the inquiry." As criticism mounted in India and official Fiji was pressured for explanations of this violence in its system, the reports stopped commenting about "sexual jealousy" or other causes; after 1912, the reports either made no general comments about suicide, or repeated a version of the "no evidence of ill-treatment" sentence. Evidence was getting to be a dangerous thing for official Fiji in these cases, but the government had begun long before to resist the responsibility for gathering it.

Respectability, Dignity, and Responsibility

A dynamic of distinction between an ordinary Indian of suspect motives and the extraordinary Indian of demonstrated "good character" was in place very early in indenture Fiji. Only the latter was thought by most Europeans to be worthy of their recognition or compassion—thus the curious official tendency to pursue evidence first of all about the character of a complainant, not an accused, in most official allegations of sexual abuse. But distinguishing among the Indians was a real problem.

Europeans like Gill, as we already know, were much more willing to involve themselves with all manner of Indians than were their more squeamish seniors. Gill did not restrict himself to respectable people and situations. At one point, he claims, vague guilt almost led him to cut off a chance conversation with a shy young *ayah* (nanny), who appeared to be interested in him. But "then it seemed to me that if I did, I would be allowing the white women to make an unwarranted intrusion; interfering in a situation beyond their understanding" (1970, 79). Here and elsewhere Gill blamed white women for an impinging moral code that would lay down a sexual color bar (cf. Knapman 1986; Ralston 1988; Stoler 1989, 1991).[8] Gill provides us with a detailed account of his relations with this *ayah*, Appelema, who was not married but lived with a man in the lines.

> It was a strange set-up. I was grateful to her, and because, for her, life was a nightmare of poverty, she eagerly accepted the few shillings I was able to let her have. She never spoke of the man except once, to

assure me that he would do as she told him. From then on she came
on two nights a week, arriving about eight and leaving when it suited
her—invariably before ten. When she came she would go to a mat in
a corner, and sink down on it crossed-legged, with her skirt spread
around her and her hands in her lap. Then we would talk of the little
things in her life, and of the people amongst whom she lived. Soon I
was made to realize that the mat was hers; by the little pat of invitation
if I lingered, and by the strange intimacy of the three folded garments
on its lip when she undressed. (1970, 80)

The image Gill constitutes is of a delicately, mutually negotiated space
and time of sexual exchange, outside of any morality but squarely founded
in the economics of indenture. Europeans gossiped about it, "But the small
islands of resentment, invariably married women, in the end meant nothing." What meant more was Appelema's resentment, when she believed
false gossip in the lines about Gill and another indentured woman and
stopped coming. "In four weeks I only saw her once, but because of a
gaggle of white women on their way to tennis, I shied from speaking." (Gill
1970, 80) And then Gill proved how asymmetric, in many ways, were his
and her powers to control social space and time. Gill's recounting is apologetic, but in an extraordinarily vague and limited way.

For a few more days I held out, and then of all people I must choose
Abdullah Saib to bring her to me. . . . I would have chosen my words
more carefully if I had remembered certain things. . . . It was possibly
the most stupid combination of words I ever uttered. (81)

His *sardar* (Indian work boss) Abdullah Saib, sent to "fetch her here; that's
all," dragged Appelema screaming past the company office and other overseers' bungalows. Gill claims that he was able to restore his relations with
her, especially because of his sexual fidelity, but that he was unable to discipline the sardar.

Next morning Abdulla Saib salaamed and then said, "You want to
speak to me?"
I did, but I knew the answer. "Remember what you said about carrying out orders? Was it my fault she wouldn't come? Anyway, that's
what a woman's hair is for. And it's just as well she's a Muslim, or I
would have been rough."
He told the head sirdar that working for me and holding a mongoose
by the tail were the same thing. I got no sympathy from Baili Khan
either. He said there were few Europeans who had a man as faithful as
Abdulla Saib. And I had to agree. (82)

In short, Gill was more constrained and responsible in his relationships with the men of the plantation hierarchy, including the Indian work bosses who were truly "faithful" to him, than he was in his relations with either the white women or his paid lover. He presents himself as if coerced, as if he "had to agree," but it is Gill who plants the misogynistic joke about hair in the sardar's imaginary speech.

Throughout his depictions Gill insisted on the notion that the good overseer was simultaneously careful to learn to know and to distinguish between the different kinds of Indians, and careful to avoid "bringing himself to coolie level" (1970, 51). One new overseer spoke Hindi with actual fluency, but talked "too much. . . . The Indians were getting on top and knew it", and the India-born white man was soon sent off to Australia. Gill moralized, "Perhaps the kindest way of putting it would be that an Australian does not necessarily have a flair for working with Australians" (52). It was no accident that Appelema had not come from Gill's gang, nor that his relations with the sardars were less malleable. Gill loved, hated, and paid women, but gave and took responsibility with men.

If this was how Gill and perhaps many other Europeans made their way in the world of the lines, the situation was different when Indians, especially women, needed to deal with Europeans who were not plantation people. These Europeans needed a simpler, safer code of distinctions, and often dealt with Indian women or men in terms of a simple binary of respectability. Indians, both indentured and "free," frequently sought to use their good reputation with one European as an avenue of mediation in their dealings with another, leading to curious interventions, especially by churchmen, in affairs of business and government.

A particularly elaborate example of this process is provided in Bhagwan Singh's family history and life story, *My Father's Land* (1984). Singh's grandparents, Ram Chander and Padam Kaur, were indentured laborers in Fiji. Twists of fate and the mediation of a Christian education led to a clerical career for their son in Fiji and then in India. Their grandson, Bhagwan Singh, rose bureaucratically in India, and finally became, from 1971 to 1976, India's High Commissioner in Fiji. It is not an average family history, and Singh narrates it with a strong sense of the propriety of distinguishing those worthy of special treatment, especially as he narrates the events that first put his grandmother into contact with the Catholic mission—her struggle for justice for her husband.

The way Bhagwan Singh tells it a century later (all information on the case here is from Singh 1984, 16–25), Ram Chander became embroiled in a feud between two work gangs on his estate, a feud that could be traced in part back to shipboard rivalries, and probably included insults to Padam

Kaur. When the sardar of the rival gang pressured Ram Chander to help suborn perjury to keep members of his gang out of jail, Ram Chander refused, and the men were convicted. A few months later, in June 1890, a fire destroyed this sardar's house, and members of his work gang identified Ram Chander and others of his group as arsonists. Ram Chander was convicted and sentenced to 15 years in prison.

This sardar, Dost Mohammed, and the members of his gang who testified against Ram Chander, were assaulted on their return to Ra province, the site of their plantation. Four men were arrested and brought to A. B. Joske's court, charged with the assault. "For lack of evidence, Joske dismissed the case though he noted on the file that he had no doubt to the moral guilt of Bernard and Budhia in the attack on the complainants." The next month Padam Kaur's indenture contract expired, and she was sent to Suva (Fiji's capital) with a letter, drafted by a literate line-mate, to a Roman Catholic missionary.

The missionary took her in. She converted to Catholicism, changed her name to Parbotti, and began a succession of efforts to secure her husband's release. Her husband's letters, written in "Urdu and a particular dialect of Hindi spoken around Agra," each page topped with "Lord Ram is Ever Helpful," provoked no new inquiries, but her appeals gathered more attention. After living at the mission she was able to arrange to stay at the Immigration Depot, whose superintendent, H. J. Milne, wrote to the Governor that "[s]he appears to be a superior sort of woman, very respectable." She had a European barrister write a formal petition, and the governor ordered an inquiry. "Unfortunately the Magistrate who conducted the enquiry utilized the services of Dost Mohammed as an interpreter. For obvious reasons, nothing new came out."

Parbotti then found a new witness who would testify that Dost Mohammed told him that Ram Chander was innocent, and managed to recruit a new barrister, the influential G. J. Garrick. Garrick wrote in a memo to the Governor,

> I have prepared this petition and am forwarding it not in a professional capacity but from a conviction of the innocence of the prisoner of the crime he was convicted of. I have had considerable experience of the principal witness for the Crown and believe him unworthy of credit. (Quoted in Singh 1984, 24)

Not in twenty years at the bar, he added, was he more convinced of a false conviction. The governor then instructed, "Let the Superintendent of Police make the most careful enquiries and give a report with as little delay as can be."

Back to Joske's Court

Singh then provides us with a fascinating glimpse of the fastidious Joske reversing his previous decision:

> The Superintendent passed on the file to A. D. Joske [*sic*], the Stipendiary Magistrate at Ba, who carried out an extensive enquiry. He visited Penang [the plantation] and interviewed Coster, the Assistant Manager, Birja, the new Head Sardar, and numerous labourers. In his report, he reversed his own previous defence of Dost Mohammed's character and pointed out that the "public Indian opinion at the Estate was that it had been a trumped up charge." He concluded by saying that although in such cases it was nearly impossible to pin down anything positive, particularly at such a late stage, he strongly recommended clemency. (1984, 24)

In May 1893, close to three years after Ram Chander's conviction, the governor pardoned him. He and his wife began new careers as workers at the depot, then as warders in the Suva gaol, and their son received a good Christian education. The Christianity did not stick, but they had become well known as people of good character.

The case gives a strong feeling for the difference made by moral sponsorship, a phenomenon hardly unique to indenture-period Fiji, but perhaps particularly important across the colonial color line. But what interests me most is the powerful, aphoristic line attributed by Singh to Joske, simultaneously an apology for his earlier opinion of Dost Mohammed's evidences, and justification for vast revisions upon learning the governor's leanings: "[I]n such cases it was nearly impossible to pin down anything positive."

A very interesting aphorism, not only for its invocation of the "positive," a sign of extraordinary power in European epistemology of the nineteenth and early twentieth centuries, but also for its verb. The positive facts, here, are not known by sight, but have to be pinned down, not a visual but a tactile metaphor. Not a matter of gaze, but of grasp. How could court officers constitute the facts in these matters of arson, grievous wounding, and murder? How, indeed, was one to constitute positive information out of the testimony of the people denigrated as "coolies," who surely hated the courts more than they were hated? Testimony sometimes conflicted wildly, other times seemed arranged in lock-step, because it was. Was it more suspicious when all witnesses agreed or when they disagreed? How could one monitor even the translation process? Who or what was worthy of trust?

We proceed now to the case that motivated this essay, another charge of violent crime passed on to Fiji's Supreme Court by Joske in 1907. It is the case from Fiji that I find most unforgettable, although I still am uncertain what to say. Unlike most of the cases I have addressed here and elsewhere, no one died or was hanged, but the form of injustice involved has bothered me more than that in any of the other cases. It is a story of the power of European sexual fantasies, but also of the limits and powers of gazes quite different from those of the lascivious European overseers—the magistrate's gaze of meticulous A. B. Joske and the medical gaze of Hospital Superintendent G. F. Dunckley. It is a case about the power, the limits, and the will of scientific and legal authorities to resolve the facts.

Almost everything I know about the case, and all of the testimony I quote below, comes from the record assembled by Joske for the Supreme Court (Supreme Court #24 of 1907). The case was also mentioned in the *Fiji Times,* Fiji's main newspaper, on 7 December 1907. In the local news column, much space was taken by the story of a drunk indigenous Fijian "roosting" on a Suva rooftop. This story was followed by the news that Hon. D. and Mrs. Robbie had returned from their trip to Europe. "Both are looking well." Then came the paragraph about the Supreme Court sitting, then news that Messrs. A. M. Brodziak and Co. were the successful tenders of the native tax on kava (*yaqona*) for 1908, and the news that at the first meeting of the newly constituted Suva Town Board, "His Worship the Warden suitably welcomed Mr. R. Crompton as the newly elected Councillor." In the midst of these more detailed items was the court summary:

> The criminal sessions of the Supreme Court continued on Wednesday, Thursday and Friday during which time five cases were heard, viz., a charge of rape (discharged), horsestealing for which an Indian was found guilty and sentenced to two years hard labour, arson, by two Indians, (5 years), wounding (18 months and 24 lashes) and wounding (2 years and 24 lashes).

We turn to the charge of rape, prepared by A. B. Joske against Ramdial and Kurkut, and a trial that passed through colonial Fiji's public culture leaving barely a ripple.

An Indeterminate and Ugly Story

Let us begin, as Joske's proceeding did, with the testimony of the complainant, Janka:

> I am an Indentured Indian woman under agreement with the Colonial Sugar Refining Coy., at Tavua. I know the defendants here present before the Court. Their names are Ramdial & Kurkut. They raped me Wednesday of last week 19 June. It happened on the Company's Estate

at Tavua. I went about 2 or 3 chains from where we women were working to the river's edge to stool. I did that, washed myself & returned to work. As I returned I saw Ramdial & Kurkut. Ramdial lifted me up & carried me into the acacia scrub I cried out & Kurkut shut my mouth with a cloth. Ramdial had connection with me first & penetrated me. Then Kurkut had me. He penetrated me also. Patun & Sertaji saw Ramdial seize me by the hand. They ran away. I went home at five o'clock & I then told my husband. He went to the Sirdar who told us to go to the Manager, Mr. Thomas. It was 10 A.M. when these men raped me. I went to the Hospital Superintendent & was examined by him. The only part that I was bruised on externally was one of my toes.

Defendants did not cross-examine, but the court did. The woman's testimony went on as follows:

> Defendants did not pay me anything. I made no assignation with the men. Ori is the woman's sirdar. I did not go & tell him as on a previous occasion he had beaten me for going to stool without telling him. I was afraid of the Sirdar. Cheddi heard Sertaji & Patun tell the Manager that they had seen Ramdial take me by the hand. That is why I have mentioned him as a witness lest those two should go back on me.

In her answers we can hear something of Joske's questions, and in the questions, the stipendiary magistrate's lines of doubt. Indian witnesses were widely accused of lying, frequently disparaged, and harshly cross-examined in Fiji's courts. As Janka demonstrates here, she too seeks to foreclose the options of those whose testimony can help her, fearing that they would "go back on her" in the hostile courts of colonial Fiji. There were other lines of doubt: Was she a prostitute? Was her story coherent? Why didn't she tell the authorities sooner? Her answer, that she was afraid of her sardar, suggests how little space and time she could control, if her story is true: she was unable to report a rape because she would have to admit to leaving work to stool. "The Sirdar beats us if we go away to stool," noted another witness, one of the few uncontested claims in the evidence of the case.

Patun and Sertaji, the other women, testified and backed up Janka's story. Sertaji testified unambiguously that "[h]e seized her forcibly." Patun was more ambiguous: "I heard Janka say that she would tell about it." "Whether he was going to force her or whether she was willing I know not." Ramdial cross-examined; the question was not reported. Answer: "I did not hear you arrange with Janka to meet her on the river bank at 10 A.M. as we went to work at 5 A.M." The only other Indian, apart from the defendants, to testify was Mullu, Janka's husband, who told the story of hearing about the rape from his wife and then going to the authorities—testimony entirely supportive of Janka's own.

Both Ramdial and Kurkut testified in their own defense. Ramdial told a story of simple prostitution, with a prepayment of four shillings, that was complicated when Patun and Sertaji saw Janka at work and announced their intention to gossip about it. Kurkut told an incoherent story, perhaps because he sought to agree both with Ramdial's testimony and with the testimony of the manager, Harold James Thomas. Thomas had already reported that on the night of the event, once confronted with news of medical evidence, Kurkut confessed to having forced sex with Janka "because Ramdial told him to." Kurkut claimed in court that Ramdial had told him beforehand of a sex-for-money arrangement, then admitted confessing to Thomas, and then claimed that Ramdial had forced Janka but that she had invited him to sex.

This case, Supreme Court Case #24 of 1907, is unusual in the Fiji archives, not least for the fact that the Supreme Court found the Indian defendants not guilty. I have little doubt—though I must admit, no positive proof—that the most important testimony was that of George Frederick Dunckley. What, indeed, did he see?

Positivism

Before delivering Dunckley's version of the truth, I want to delve more deeply into the background to the questions I have raised here about gazes, grasps, and quotidian colonial knowledge and power. In particular, remembering Joske's reported aphorism—"in such cases it was nearly impossible to pin down anything positive"—I seek a better feel for the very idea of "positive knowledge," an idea credited with vast and general influence in nineteenth-century Europe.

Let me explore further the differences between Joske and Dunckley, the magistrate and the doctor, in their forms of surveillance and truth-telling. What happened to the positive knowledge of the doctor, the knowledge that enabled the plantation manager Thomas to obtain a confession, when it was examined in the court? This requires some retelling of the stormy history of relations between positive procedures in science and positive procedures in law.

Law involves different challenges than does science, many authorities tell us (see Turner and Factor 1994). Whereas a positive science can aspire to eventual clarity, unity, and completion, positive law must be capable of adequate adjudication, which is to say consistent and predictable application with respect to both the facts of real cases and the code of the law. The law courts cannot, especially in the lower rungs, choose which matters to attend to in what order, and must render judgments on all matters. The legal positivists led by John Austin had to add a clear and unambiguous definition of what law was to the positively seen and known universe. Law was not only a product of reason but evidence of will. Austin argued that for law to exist, it had to be, in the first instance, the command of a sovereign power.

Both scientific and legal positivism sought to banish all theology and metaphysics, to scrub away all the murk at their foundations. They could recognize in each other a kindred spirit; each descended from August Comte's quest to cease all argumentation and conflict caused by metaphysical vagaries in depiction and explanation. But there was lots of room for misunderstanding and arguments at cross-purposes between these two vast developments of "the positive philosophy." Legal positivism found doctrines of natural law (as well as unwritten constitutions and doctrines of equity, fairness, and customary rights) themselves to be metaphysical. To be positive, the law required dogmatic categories, provided by sovereign will; thus, for example, so-called customary law could be properly, positively adjudicated only after it had been codified. In short, while scientific positivism sought to erase mistaken doctrines imposed upon nature by human will and to reveal pure order in nature, legal positivism sought to erase mistaken doctrines of nature imposed onto human will, to enable pure ordering by will.

From this complex history, the point can now be made to seem very simple. Recent scholarship from the social sciences has tended to treat the modalities of colonial power as if they were a *scientific* monolith. But an enormous amount of crucial work in the ordering and reordering of colonies was done by professional lawyers. In the social sciences, we think about law and order far too reflexively to gain a really clear understanding of what went on in the European colonial empires.[9]

I think it is time that scholars of colonial societies stopped being satisfied with their discovery of such a will to order in colonial legal codifications, as if it were a secret (or the bedrock of a Nietzschean, Foucauldian human nature). We need to pay more attention to the political wills in plain view, to official, especially legal, decisions about where and how to to apply sovereign will so positively, and contrarily, to various kinds of denial, to where and when colonial sovereigns refused to act or even to look. As Kaplan (1989) has argued, invention of disorder was as crucial as invention of tradition in colonial "constituting moments," as in refusals to see law, order, or preexisting sovereign power in the institutions of the colonized. Here, we track the exercise of judicial will in the microcosm of individual cases, as courts in quotidian operation ponder what they do and do not, can and cannot know about the morals and motives of witnesses across a colonial color line. What do judges and other government officials do when "it [is] nearly impossible to pin down anything positive"?

I find more than one "gaze" operating—we have clearly tracked four: the Gill-style overseers' moral-sexual fantasies, the gaze pressure felt by the dignity-preserving colonials, the codifying but also sometimes refusing-to-look gaze of legal and other official reporting, and Dunckley's allegedly expert eyes of science. But I also want to test whether we might be better served by supplementing theorized "gaze" powers with other metaphors of power. The gaze might be the phallic, leering, vital vehicle for the ramification of desire, or the vehicle of a claim to transcendence and virtual omniscience, but in all modes it flies through space, too ambiguous in its attachments to handle all the transactions and transcursions of real power.

I suggest then that grasps are at least as well worth thinking about as gazes, as we try to write about power. Equally and more viscerally embodied than gazing, grasp is nevertheless neither more nor less intrinsically material. It is, like gaze, yet in a different way, another vehicle for inscription, embodiment, and objectification, for realization of representations in self and world. As the Indian intellectual tradition has been more keenly aware, it is equally capable of empowering abstract application.[10]

Thinking about gaze as a modality of grasp, or about legal positivism as a gaze-theory solution to a grasp problem—the maintenance and extension of effective sovereignty—might lead us to reconsider a great deal. As Hackshaw points out, Austin's definition of law was "inherently circular, in that 'law' could only exist by the will of a supreme and unaccountable sovereign, who governed an independent political society," while such a body politic could exist only if it recognized a sovereign and laws (1989, 100). Dogmatic insistence on that circularity was what cleansed positive law from muddier grounding, made it nothing other than what it said it was, and enabled it to define or inscribe every entity into its terms—whatever things and people found their way into legal proceedings. In democratic nation-states, such legal inscription might to varying degrees inform the subjectivity of citizens, make more and more modes of action into matters of rights, law, and order, with increasing participation of a wider field of agents in the mechanisms of law.

But what of a colonial social field, with its Others? There, as Guha (1989) already alerts us, a contradiction was sharply revealed. The promise of positive, productive, extending circularity could only be realized at the cost of inviting into legal agency the colonial subjects, even the colonized subjects. The oxymoron of the democratic state, constituted in the metropolis as the powers of grasp were made to seem a mere consequence of the powers of gaze, was not felt to be possible in the European colonial world, where the grasp increasingly held others down and out, where cleanliness, of law as much as of household, seemed to depend upon limiting "their" access.

Finally, we also might want to take very seriously the unevenness of talent, training, and intention that was part of the actual gazing and grasping of the colonial state. On the one hand, the colonized world included modes of knowledge and order beyond the ken of the Europeans—leading among other things to the various legal efforts to codify "customary" or "personal" law (for Fiji, see especially France 1969; Kaplan 1989; Kelly 1989). On the other hand, the colonizers were nowhere all masters of the arts and sciences of their own civilizations. I would not suggest that in the Fiji courtroom, Janka or Kurkut were particularly empowered by the philosophical discourses of South Asia, any more than Dunckley can be expected to have benefited from Renaissance artwork. Consider the problem that arose with one peripheral witness in the first case discussed above: "Sanicheri the next witness cannot be sworn as she does not know whether she is a Musulamani or a Hindu & does not know the meaning of religion having been born in Fiji." (She was cautioned to tell the truth and warned of the consequences of giving false evidence.) Dunckley will show more mastery of both medical and courtroom techniques, more control of his own role. But from this we shouldn't generalize too hastily. If we are to believe Fijian Indian accounts, and I do, it wasn't only the lack of typewriters, but also because some of the European magistrates could barely read and write, that several of Fiji's district courts left behind little or no written trace. Remembering this, let us return to colonialism as it actually existed, to the long arm of the law and the manners of its grasp, in the Magistrate's Court of A. B. Joske, in Colo North in 1907.

Dunckley's Grasp of the Facts

What did Dunckley do on the night of the incident? What did he see, and how did he understand it? How was it that his inquiry was powerful enough, via the Estate Manager Thomas, to impel Kurkut to confess at least partially, and then, in court, powerful enough to negate the confession? Here is his evidence in its entirety, as recorded by A. B. Joske:

> Am Hospital Superintendent on the Colonial Sugar Refining Company's Estate at Tavua. At the request of the Manager Mr. Thomas I medically examined the woman Janka on Wednesday last the 19 June. It was in the evening. I discovered an internal wound in the lower part of the vagina. It looked very much like a tear as if a portion had been torn away. I then called Mr. Thomas to see it also. The tear was certainly due to violence. There was a distinct tear & clot of blood on it.

I do not think the tear was due to excessive copulation. By all appearances it was due to violence. I could not say whether the wound was self-inflicted, but it was fresh made within twenty hours.

The unstoppable, privileged gaze of power: the hospital superintendent, investigating the vagina of the possible rape victim, decides to call in the Estate Manager to see the evidence also. Horrible enough. But they were investigating violent crime, and no doubt felt justified, especially when they found what they were looking for. One story was consensual sex. The other was rape. Call in science: was there evidence of violence? Science triumphed; reasonable men concurred on the evidence (cf. Shapin 1994), a wound that was fresh. There was violence, "by all appearances." Something positive was pinned down. But it was not enough evidence to finally vindicate the complainant. Why not? The law was not only long-armed and beyond common decency; it was also, sometimes, incapable of resolving the facts, even when it was in complete control of both the means of measure and the terms of reference.

On the Wednesday night the evidence of violence seemed compelling enough to pressure a confession out of the weaker of the accused. But in the court, alternative narratives each strove for momentum. Lawyers and judges have no option but to play speculatively with stories of motive, as they "engage in the activity of placing the already described act into legally relevant categories," especially "categories of culpability" (Turner and Factor 1994, 168).

> Even in the face of uncertainty about motivation, the lawyer nevertheless must provide reasons for deciding cases one way or another, and must do so within the framework of these categories. In doing so, the lawyer may need to construct a "theory" or narrative of the case which accords with the evidence and provides an explanation of the intentions of the persons involved which can be used as the basis of a classification in terms of the "dogmatic" legal categories of culpable action. (Turner and Factor 1994, 169)

Joske brought the charges and sent the case up the line to the cool, comfortable chambers of the Supreme Court in Suva. Without records of events or deliberations there, we cannot speculate too much, but it seems very likely that the court had to decide whether there was sufficient plausibility to the accused's narrative—the story of prostitution—to create doubt that rape actually occurred. Science had spoken. Clearly, there had been violence. Yet Dunckley had added, "I could not say whether the wound was self-inflicted, but it was fresh made."

What could make reasonable the bizarre speculation that lay behind this line of inquiry? By Janka's story, she was raped, feared to complain all day, was forced to complain and then to endure colonial examination in order to save her marriage, and then saw the assailants go unpunished. The other story is that she sold sex for money, was discovered, and then did violence to herself to dazzle the gaze of science, to save her marriage, and to protect herself. Here, precisely, is where the legal gaze must look beyond science. Here is the kind of problem of order that science does not solve: the immediate duty of a judge to render a consequential judgment. A judge cannot view ambiguity benignly and look forward to further research, but has to decide what to reach and grasp with the law's long arm.

The agents of law have no choice but to impose their own categories; they must not only gaze, but grasp. But which categories, in the specification of motive? Aggressive courts that force a lattice of economic reason, "rational choice" and its interests and responsibilities, onto all parties, courts that look for contracts and ignore ignorance, can make people live and act by their terms, can call their categories into being. But a very different social synergy required the Fiji courts for its maintenance and extension. In operations from the enforcement of penal labor laws, to hostile encounters with witnesses, to cases in which violence is measured, the Fiji courts found, made judgments about, and sought, in effect, to will into being a lattice of premises about what was conceivable as motive and action in otherwise unknown indentured Indians. The world of Gill's "animalistic" Indians, the world of "sexual jealousy," violent passions, and female promiscuity, needed the support of the courts to go from fantasy to legal presumption, the basis for law and order.

On the plantations themselves, the indentured Indian women in Fiji were the object of pernicious, denigrating, lascivious gazing. But these gazes did not simply create their truths across clean, open, unbridged spaces, virtual or real. There were also real struggles between strong and weak, in public and private, grasps taking possession, taking pleasure, seeking embodied facts and leaving their figurative and all too literal marks and scars. Gazes can inscribe, say scholars insisting on the constitutive powers of representation. But I am not so sure that gazes, by their nature, can generate the finality that the metaphor of inscription suggests. Gazes don't scar. It is grasps, from the furtive to the righteous, to the dispassionate and scientific, to the willful, official and legal, that cut and leave the deepest marks on real bodies, as in the typical indenture horror story, in its movement from jewelry, to a knife attack, to a noose.

Gazes and Laughter

We cannot win with our words battles that are mainly lost by exploited people in the real world. But the indentured laborers had other weapons with which to fight rape than reliance on the constabulary and courts. As I have described in more detail elsewhere (Kelly 1992), the archives provide several accounts of very visceral public humiliation of targeted, abusive European overseers—attacks that, perhaps deliberately, reduced the prestige and dignity of a European overseer and certainly demonstrated his loss of control. As far as I can tell, from admittedly scanty and anecdotal materials, overseers bombarded with shit, or held down and pissed on, were invariably transferred or sent back to Sydney. And I have never seen a record of anyone charged in court for such an attack.

There were also friendlier transactions between Indians and Europeans. After retiring as magistrate and later district commissioner, A. B. Joske became A. B. Brewster, amateur ethnographer and memoirist, often invoking Kipling (see Kaplan n.d.). The Indians basically fell out of the stories he told of the Fiji of his memory, but some do appear once in a while in his most famous book, *The Hill Tribes of Fiji*. One was Joske's cook for thirteen years, "the faithful Ferdinand" with his "great culinary skill" (Brewster 1922, 302). Otherwise, Joske's first mention of the Indians is as the source of Fiji's only real crime.[11] But he also remembers how frequently he assisted the Indians in obtaining land leases, "many of which I pegged out myself . . . on account of the scarcity of duly qualified surveyors" (299). Indian hands prepared his food; his hands pegged out their land. "I left Fiji in May, 1910, and it seemed to me then that our settlers from Hindustan were the happiest of people . . . the proof of their contentment was that ninety-nine percent of them elected to remain." Actually 40 percent went back to India, even though they had to stay in Fiji ten years to be eligible for free return passage, but the point here is Joske's moment of nostalgia. When Joske himself prepared to depart from Colo North, a delegation from the local Indian community presented him with a silver tea set, a token, they said, of appreciation for his service as their magistrate, "a very great tribute of their affection as I was leaving them for good, and they could have no hope of any favour from me in the future" (300). Lots of sinister political things can be said about tea in the maintenance of British bodies (see, for example, Sahlins 1988, or Mintz 1985 on sugar) and about this sort of gift within the body politic, but not in comparison to the things we have been considering.

Remembering, then, that there was terrible violence, some limited but successful resistance, and a social field with more benign relations as well, I finish with another look at an official gaze and some laughter.

In Fiji the highest-ranking government officer with specific responsibility for the welfare of the immigrants was called the agent-general of immigration. In late 1910 or early 1911, the colonial secretary received a letter in Tamil (dated 23 September) from "the Madrasi Coolies of Wainunu Tea

Estate."[12] The letter was successfully translated in late January, 1911, and sent to the agent-general of immigration for investigation. The writers alleged that a "Jiroj," as it came through in the translation, was abusing workers and raping indentured women: "Our females are compelled to be victims to his debaucherous character." This complaint itself, about "our females," concerned both rape and medical exams, and was a patriarchal objection to science as well as crime: "We haven't married our wives to be so disgracefully treated in allowing a male, to examine females right through."

P. R. Backhouse, Labasa inspector of immigrants, was sent to the remote plantation to investigate, and found that George High, the overseer accused, had been dismissed in December for drunkenness. Noting that "his past record is far from clean," Backhouse recommended that High be watched if employed elsewhere. But it was not necessary to proceed further with these charges, because "everything seems to be running smoothly" on the estate. Backhouse also reported, with evident satisfaction, that the letter was "very exaggerated." He had mustered the women and then all the laborers, and asked which of them had a complaint to make. Only one woman made a public complaint, "and she had not any witnesses to support her statement." Two men complained about conditions on the estate, but they had just served prison time, "and their manner and bearing did not at all influence me in their favor." Otherwise "the appearance of the labor at the muster was quite satisfactory."

On his way back to Labasa from this estate, Backhouse was laid up for a week at Levuka, where, on his own initiative, he held a muster of "all the time expired immigrants on Ovalau" Island. He found that many of them could not produce their C.C.D. or C.I.R. documents, the documents that would certify that they had completed terms of indenture. He "left all particulars" with the local constables, to inquire further and arrest all suspected deserters. His own unfounded suspicions, but not repeated allegations by indentured Indians, merited and received further action.

The uncorroborated complaint of the woman never became a charge of rape in court. In his report, Backhouse rendered his own judgment: "That High had illicit relations with the woman, I think there is little doubt, but I am inclined to believe that the woman was a willing party." We know that Backhouse was not out of step with the rules, written and unwritten, of the Immigration Office. By 1919 he had been promoted to agent-general. And we may never know any of the judgments or other comments rendered about Backhouse by the workers of the Wainunu Tea Estate, and especially by the indentured women. Backhouse, very much the colonial official, observed the scene at the estate, but maintained a far greater distance than did Walter Gill:

The appearance of the muster was quite satisfactory & they seemed very happy and contented. When I was leaving the estate I noticed them laughing amongst themselves. The people were well and cleanly dressed.

He was too much the inspector ever to know what, or whom, they were laughing about.

Acknowledgments

I acknowledge permission from the Commonwealth Government of Fiji to conduct research there in 1984–85 and 1986, and from the Republic of Fiji in 1991. I thank S. T. Tuinaceva, archivist, for permission to use the records of the National Archives of Fiji, and I greatly appreciate the assistance of the staff at the Fiji Archives. An early version of this paper was read at the annual meetings of the Association for Social Anthropology of Oceania in Kailua-Kona, Hawaii on 26 March 1993. Thanks to Margaret Jolly for criticism and advice. As usual, the paper owes a great deal to Martha Kaplan, and I should get all the blame.

CHAPTER FOUR

From Point Venus to Bali Ha'i: Eroticism and Exoticism in Representations of the Pacific

MARGARET JOLLY

In a recent paper Teresia Teaiwa considers the relation between the two *bikinis*—the daring new swimsuit of 1946 and the atoll after which it was named, on which the Americans dropped twenty-five nuclear bombs between 1946 and 1958. For her the connection of the two bikinis is not contingent. She argues that "the bikini bathing suit is testament to the recurring tourist trivialization of Pacific Islanders' experience and existence. By drawing attention to a sexualized and supposedly depoliticized female body, the bikini distracts from the colonial and highly political origins of its name" (1994, 87).

Here I explore some earlier manifestations of connections between bodily revelation and imperial might in the Pacific, and ponder if and how we can posit such a close connection between eroticism, exoticism, and political and military colonization. I focus not on Micronesia, where Bikini Atoll is,[1] nor on Melanesia, where rather different conventions of viewing pertain (see Jolly 1993a), but on Polynesia. As most of these texts and images do, I focus on the sexually saturated figure of the Polynesian woman and the way in which she is represented in successive European visions. But I also draw into the frame women of the western Pacific, Indochinese women, and white women. I consider travel texts and images—from the first writings, drawings, and engravings deriving from the Cook voyages, through the texts and photographs of an early-twentieth-century lady traveler, Beatrice Grimshaw, to some of the more recent images of Hollywood cinema, and especially the hit musical *South Pacific* (1958). This is a very promiscuous scope—from the eighteenth to the twentieth centuries, including both texts and images—a promiscuity which my rather breezy title renders as a journey—from . . . to . . . But these places—Point Venus in Tahiti and Bali Ha'i—are imagined places rather than mere loci on the map. Given this traveling in time and space, I will fix my coordinates by posing four basic questions.

First, what is the relationship between the constitution of the exotic and the erotic? That is, how and when does the creation of the distance of difference stimulate desire, and how might this relate to sexual or political possession? Second, how do these several texts and images work in terms of the gendered and sexualized ethnicity of both the subjects imaged and the imagined reader/viewer? Third, how does the consistency of the trope in European visions of the beautiful, partially clad, usually Polynesian woman relate to the shifting character of colonial and strategic relations in the region? Fourth, how have Pacific peoples, and especially Polynesian women, negotiated such alluring objectifications, which connect the bounty and the beauty of their islands with the beauty and sexuality of their bodies?

Allow me some preliminary caveats. Although eroticism has pervaded European visions of the Pacific (and especially Polynesia), Polynesian eroticism was not a figment of the European imagination. But in the ancestral cultures of the islands of Hawaii and Tahiti (as in much of the eastern Pacific) sexuality was not so much "free" as celebrated and sacralized.[2] Indigenous eroticism was remolded through relations with Europeans. European representations both reflected and inflected actual sexual liaisons between Pacific women and European men. The liaisons which transpired from the first European voyages in the region generated not only romances but many children of mixed ancestry, and occasioned massive infertility and depopulation from venereal disease.[3] My stress on the erotics of the exotic may offend many Pacific people who are committed Christians and who lament this emphasis on Island sexuality and deplore the contemporary sexual freedoms of visiting tourists. But the erotics of the exotic are so pervasive in contemporary representations of the Pacific, especially those for tourist consumption, that they deserve a critical history. This is a summary first attempt.

At Point Venus with Cook

I start in 1769 at Point Venus, a place so named because it was from this site in Tahiti that the astronomers on Cook's first voyage were to witness the transit of Venus. The observation of this heavenly body proved rather difficult, but there were other heavenly bodies which were more proximate and seemingly more accessible—those of Tahitian women. The textual and visual materials of Cook's three voyages in the Pacific are replete with images of Polynesian women.[4] Many of these images are eroticized—beautiful women gazing at the artist and the viewer, the body draped but breasts revealed, or women bathing in the luminous pink light of William Hodges's painting *Tahiti Revisited* (plate 4.1). These visual images accompanied texts which not only reported but evoked a state of sexual excitation. Hawaiian and Tahitian women are constantly referred to as alluring: "a beautifully proportioned shape, an irresistible smile, and eyes full of sweetness and spar-

Figure 4.1. *Tahiti Revisited,* by William Hodges, 1776. Oil on canvas, 36 ½ in. x 54 ½ in. National Maritime Museum, London.

kling with fire," combined with a "charming frankness" (Forster 1778, 421) and eagerness to engage in sexual commerce with foreign men (see Jolly 1993a):[5] "The view of several of these nymphs swimming nimbly all around the sloop, such as nature had formed them was perhaps more than sufficient entirely to subvert the little reason which a mariner might have left to govern his passions" (G. Forster 1968 [1777], 161).

These are the words of George Forster, who traveled with his father Johann Reinhold Forster, the German naturalist, on Cook's second voyage. They both consistently castigated the common sailors for succumbing to the beauties of Tahiti. But, as I suggest elsewhere (Jolly 1993a), their texts lurch between haughty moralizing and titillating voyeurism. For them only textual seduction was legitimate. Yet, although the gentlemen and the scientists attempted to distinguish themselves from those common sailors on board who engaged lustily in both sexual and material commerce, there were suspicions, contemporaneously and since, that scientific curiosity could not be so readily dissociated from sexual interest (see Thomas 1994a). Sir Joseph Bank's sexual liaisons at the court of the Tahitian "Queen" Oberea were flagrantly satirized in a ballad of 1788 called *Transmigration* and, as Bernard Smith ironically notes, the suspicion arose that Banks was "more interested in exotic women than in exotic plants" (1985 [1960], 46).[6]

It is worthwhile pausing a little to reflect on how such a slippage in exotic interest was possible. How was the exotic constituted by these eighteenth-century Europeans? How was the exotic rendered erotic?[7] Let us revisit Tahiti (see plate 4.1). At first blush, it fulfills what Smith describes as Hodges's alternative dream of Tahiti as "a tropical paradise of sunshine and sensuous liberated women—even more beautiful, more tempting than Italy" (1992, 132). But Tahiti encoded aesthetic ambiguity. Her beauty was marked by distantiating signs—the tattoo on the bared buttock, the image of the *tii* looming above the naked women, in the distance a corpse shrouded with drapery which connects it back to the foreground, to the body both of the god (*tii*) and the woman whose back is bared to us. But do these ethnographic marks temper the lasciviousness of the viewer, as Smith suggests, warning him (or perhaps her) of enigmatic mysteries, connecting desire with death and the transience of the flesh? (1992, 132–33, plate 140). Perhaps such marks of an inscrutable difference—the tattoo, the statue, even the shrouded corpse—might rather enhance desire, combining the half-revealed bodies of beautiful women with other elements which render them remote and dangerous.[8]

Other images from the Cook voyages portray Polynesian women, some in less lascivious ways. There are many named portraits of men and women, most of which cast Hawaiians and Tahitians in Orientalist or classical forms. Few eroticize the male body in the same way.[9] There are certainly pictures which show men half naked in their canoes, as shown in *The Resolution and the Adventure in Matavai Bay* (see Smith 1992, 127, plate 131), boxing, or in the midst of vigorous dancing (e.g., John Webber's *A Man of Hawaii Dancing*, in Smith 1992, 185, plate 164). But male bodies are usually not displayed to the viewer, nor painted in the voyeuristic manner of *Tahiti Revisited*. Although there are suggestions of same-sex interest on the Cook voyages (Hawaiian men propositioned Lieutenant King in particular; see Wallace 1993), there are few traces of this in the visual material. Indeed when male and female bodies are portrayed as part of the same ensemble, men are often more fully draped, and they are gazing at the exposed breasts of the women as the viewer is also invited to do (as in Cipriani's *A Dance in Raiatea*, Smith 1992, 172, plate 150).

Is it then that these pictures imagine a viewer who is male, heterosexual, European, and wealthy? Not quite, for when these images first circulated in England and beyond in Europe, many of the consumers were female, and this fact was central to the debate about their circulation (see note 5), which by the 1780s was very wide. I now focus on another famous image, which does suggest (like the bikini) an intimate connection between colonial power and the revealed female body. This is John Webber's portrait of *Poedua*—a beautiful young Polynesian woman (plate 4.2). Her hair is dark

Figure 4.2. *Poedua,* by John Webber, 1777. Oil on canvas, 57 in. x 37 in. National Library of Australia, London.

and flowing, she has flowers behind both ears, her features are delicate, her smile winsome, one hand holds a fly whisk, and the other—draped across her body—is tattooed, though the marks are barely visible. Her canonical Polynesian beauty is enhanced by her drapery, in George Forster's admiring depiction "a fine white cloth like muslin, falling a little below the breast" (Forster 1968 [1777], 156). She stands exposed to artist and viewer. Smith suggests that this is an image of the Pacific itself as "young, feminine, desirable and vulnerable" (1992, 210).

But who was Poedua? She was the daughter of Orio, the chief of Raiatea in the Society Islands, part of what is now called French Polynesia. It was Cook's last port of call in Tahiti on the third voyage before he sailed to colder climates further north and to Hawaii, where he died. Cook seems to have engaged in far more violence on his last voyage—both against members of his own crew and Pacific Islanders (see Obeyesekere 1992; Smith

1992, 202–9; cf. Sahlins 1995). The violence on the boat and on the beach were here, as elsewhere, often connected. Two sailors, "enchanted by the island life" (Smith 1992, 210), decided to desert. In order to get them back, Cook took hostages—Orio, his daughter Poedua, and her husband. They were enticed on board the *Discovery,* locked in a cabin, and kept imprisoned until Orio secured the return of the deserters. This took five days, and it was probably during this time that Webber painted Poedua's portrait (Smith 1992, 210).

The connection between colonial power and the revealed female body here is very close. This impression is strengthened when we situate this image in the broader aestheticization of a pacific Pacific, which is the signature of Webber's corpus from the third voyage. Webber was enjoined on this voyage not to represent the violence of contact (as Hodges had done on the second voyage; witness the violent landing scenes at Erromanga, Vanuatu),[10] but rather to confine himself to scenes of "joyful reception"— showing Cook exchanging handshakes in New Zealand; trading wood, water, and fresh food for axes, chisels, saws, and buttons in Nomuka, Tonga; or enjoying the boxing at Lifuka. Smith rightly suggests that Webber's corpus is full of silences and elisions, dedicated as it is to presenting Cook as the peacemaker, "the friendly voyager."[11] The image of Poedua is an intrinsic part of this process, of the aestheticization of the violence of Cook's voyages (Smith 1992; Hoorn 1993). But why is this most pervasively and powerfully effected through a partially revealed female body? Let me return to what happened after Poedua's capture. Says Captain Clerke,

> I order'd some Centinels at the Cabin Door, and the Windows to be strongly barred, then told them, we would certainly all go to England together, if their friends did not procure their release by bringing back the 2 Deserters. My poor friends at first were a good deal struck with surprize and fear, but they soon recollected themselves, got the better of their apprehensions & were perfectly reconciled to their Situation. . . . The News of their Confinement of course was blazed instantaneously throughout the Isle; old Oreo was half mad, and within an hour afterwards we had a most numerous congregation of Women under the Stern cutting their Heads with Sharks teeth and lamenting the Fate of the Prisoners, in so melancholy a howl, as render'd the Ship while it lasted, which was 2 or 3 Hours, a most wretched Habitation; nobody could help in some measure being affected by it; it destroyed the Spirits of the Prisoners altogether, who lost all their Chearfulness and joined in this cursed dismal Howl, I made use of every method I could suggest to get them away, but all to no purpose, there they

would stand and bleed and cry, till their Strength was exhausted and they could act the farce no longer. When we got rid of these Tragedians, I soon recover'd my Friends and we set down to Dinner together very chearfully. (Cook 1967 3:1317–18, cited in Smith 1992, 210)

Clerke wants to dismiss this as performance, albeit farce or tragedy, and although hardly endorsing such colonialist cynicism, Smith also detaches himself from the events as distant spectacle—"it is not difficult to imagine how the camera crew of a not particularly friendly nation might have recorded the scene" (1992, 210). Hoorn has analyzed this incident but has declined to discuss the meaning of the women's weeping, not wanting to speak for "Pacific women" (1993). But a Maori woman, rewitnessing this event through recirculated texts and images at a Summer School at the Australian National University in 1993, had no doubts as to what the women's howling portended.[12] It was, she thought, as if Poedua, her father, and her husband were already dead. To be kidnapped and taken in the *Discovery* to England was to be lost to the world of the living. The women were weeping and slashing themselves with shark's teeth in a conventional style of Polynesian lamentation.

I relish this concluding detail in the story of this image of Poedua and its reinterpretation through its recirculation. Perhaps I have an investment in an alternative image of Raiatean women not as vulnerable and pacific, but as howling mourners, evincing rage and culturally constituted lamentation at the kidnap of their kin. Perhaps I am succumbing to an alternative "romance of resistance" (see Abu-Lughod 1990). More of that later.

In the Strange South Seas with Beatrice Grimshaw

I now sail into a later epoch in the history of exoticism and eroticism in the eastern Pacific—the travel writings and photographs of Beatrice Grimshaw. Born in Northern Ireland into a middle-class family, she was well educated there and in England, and exemplified the "liberated woman" of the 1890s. She worked as a journalist in Dublin and London before embarking on a career as a travel writer. In return for writing promotional literature and travelers' tales for *The London Graphic*, Cunard, and the Union Steamship Company rag *The Red Funnel*, she received travel vouchers and tickets. From 1904 she sailed extensively in the South Seas and wrote prodigously about them in factual and fictional genres (including about thirty novels with titles like *When the Red Gods Call*, *Sorcerer's Stone*, *Beach of Terror*, *South Sea Sarah*, *Murder in Paradise*, and *The Adorable Outcaste*, which was made into a movie). She became a publicist for government and commercial interests through newspaper articles for *The Sydney Morning Herald*, *The Daily*

Graphic, and *Pearson's Magazine.* A trip to Papua in 1909 turned into a twenty-seven-year sojourn. Here she became an intimate friend (though not a lover) of Sir Hubert Murray, the lieutenant governor, and a frequent visitor to Government House. Not only did she appear to wield some influence with both Murray and Australia's Prime Minister Deakin, but she had a wide popular audience for her novels, especially among white women in the colonies. She has been much written about of late, partly as a result of feminist reassessments of colonizing women, and not least because of how she authors herself through both positive and negative objectifications of Pacific women (see Gardner 1977; Laracy and Laracy 1977; Gardner 1987–88; Branigan 1993; Grimshaw 1907a; Evans 1993; Jolly 1993b).[13]

I focus here on one text, *In the Strange South Seas* (Grimshaw, 1907a), a record of Grimshaw's travels through Tahiti, the Cook Islands, Niue, Tonga, and Samoa to New Zealand, where her writing and photographs collude to create, yet again, an image of exotic Polynesian beauty (see plate 4.3). There are discursive, genealogical connections between these and the Cook voyage texts and images to which she often alludes. But there are also important differences—she is a female not a male voyager, and her travel writings and romances date from a far later period, the early twentieth century, when colonization of the Pacific islands was ongoing rather than in prospect, and when Christian conversion had successfully enjoined most Polynesian women to cover up.

This does not prevent Grimshaw from eroticization; in particular, she associates their beauty and their languidness with the beauties of nature. Here is how she describes her experience of the Sunday morning market in Papeete, Tahiti:

> The native beauties are here in a merry crowd. . . . Scarcely one but wears a flower behind her hair . . . all are so wreathed, and crowned and necklaced with woven blossoms, the air is heavy with scent. . . . One exceedingly pretty girl, with a perfect cataract of black hair overflowing her pale green gown, and a pair of sparkling dark eyes that could never be matched outside the magic lines of Cancer and Capricorn, is making and frying pancakes with something fruity . . . inside them. She has half a dozen French officers about her, enjoying breakfast and flirtation. (1907a, 17)

The association between women and waterfalls or the lushness of local vegetation is a constant trope in her purple prose. Later in Rarotonga she writes of a "drooping veil of leafage fine as a mermaid's hair" and "that lovely ironwood, a tree with leaves like maiden's locks, and the voice of a mermaid's song in its whispering boughs" (1907a, 74–75).

Figure 4.3. Tahitian Beauty. Photograph by Beatrice
Grimshaw, from *In the Strange South Seas* (1907).

In her romantic depictions of the beauty of Polynesian women, she constantly associates free-flowing hair and free-flowing garments. The fact that
most women are encased in long coveralls—Mother Hubbards—introduced by missionaries is no impediment. She constantly typifies these as
"night gowns" (cf. Branigan 1993, 41) and aestheticizes them as flowing
and loose as against the tightly belted and corseted garments of the resident
white women, who refuse to divest themselves and "go native," for fear of
others "saying things" (Grimshaw 1907a, 103). She betrays an attraction to
the "graceful robe of the native," however, and even allows her hostess
in Tahiti to adorn her with long necklaces of sweet, white blossoms and a
heavy crown of woven gardenias in lieu of her straw hat: "She wants to pull
my hair down as well, but in a temperature of eighty degrees, the idea does
not sound tempting, so I decline to follow Tahitian custom further. Besides
there is no knowing where she would stop!" (1907a, 15). There is even a
photograph of Beatrice herself in a Mother Hubbard, with the caption
"Mamee-Apple Fruit and Tree" (1907a, 57).
    Although Grimshaw sexualizes Polynesian women, she does not com-

pletely disempower them in her depictions. There are several points in this narrative where she celebrates the power, the dignity, and what she calls the *mana* of older Polynesian women, like Queen Makea or Princess Tinomana of Rarotonga and the Chieftainess of Atiu (1907a, 68–85, 162–63 and plates opposite 72 and 162). But this is usually linked to a nostalgia about their past romances and a lament about their faded beauty, as in this description and her accompanying photograph of Makea (see plate 4.4):

> Makea, since the death of her husband, Prince Ngamaru, . . . has laid aside all vanities of dress, and wears only the simplest of black robes, made loose and flowing from the neck in island fashion. She is supposed to be at least seventy years of age, and she is extremely stout, even for her height, which is well over six feet. Yet a more impressive figure than this aged, deposed, uncrowned sovereign, in her robe of shabby black, I have never seen. Wisdom, kindliness, and dignity are written large on her fine old face, which has more than a touch of resemblance to the late Queen Victoria. And oh, the shrewdness, the ability, the keen judgement of men and things, that look out from those brown, deep-set eyes, handsome enough, even in old age, to hint at the queen-like beauty that once belonged to this island queen. (1907a, 70)

Although compared favorably with Queen Victoria, Makea is portrayed as recumbent on her ironwood sofa, patting her pet turtle, and the pervasive depiction of Polynesian habit is of laziness, languidness, and sleepiness verging on torpor.

Her evocation of the beauty and the laziness of Polynesian women is, however, constantly and blatantly contrasted with her denigrations of the ugliness of Melanesian women and depictions of them as "beasts of burden," especially in her accompanying volume *From Fiji to the Cannibal Islands* (Grimshaw 1907b; see Jolly 1993b). This dichotomous contrast also has a long discursive genealogy and echoes the racial typifications and hierarchizations which emerged from Cook's and other "Enlightenment" voyages (see Branigan 1993; Jolly 1993a), but the contrast is more pronounced and strenuous in Grimshaw's writing, both factual and fictional. Branigan (1993, 32) has argued that it corresponds with and derives from her divergent stress on promoting tourism in the East and settlement in the West. My sense is that there is something less conscious, deeper, and far nastier at work here and that, as Evans (1993) has argued for Grimshaw's novels, the very region of Melanesia comes to stand for darkness, danger, evil, and cannibalism (and perhaps the darkest menace of all—the sexuality of the black man).[14]

But as well as this local contrast with islands to the west, there is also the

Figure 4.4. Queen Makea of Rarotonga. Photograph by Beatrice Grimshaw, from *In the Strange South Seas* (1907).

stereotypical contrast between "the islands" and "civilization," that is, life back in England or Australia. The book starts with her Pacific voyage as a rupture in the austerity of an English winter: "[A] Cunard liner bore me away from the streets and shops and drab-coloured, huddled houses of Liverpool, down the muddy Mersey—off round the world" (1907a, 5). She regularly addresses her imagined reader as a man trapped back in an office in E. C. in London, or Pitt Street in Sydney, the "Left Behind" or "The Man Who Could Not Go." Her travel writing is in many ways, often explicitly, a solicitation to white (or rather British/Australian) settlement,[15] through a seduction to the South Seas. "The British Pacific Islands need settlers" (53), but the problem is to realize the dream and the masculine adventure which is the South Seas:

> I can see the Left Behind in the office raise his head at this, and look
> through the muddy panes of the counting-house window, or across
> the piles of summer goods on the shop counters, out beyond the clang-

ing street, and right through the whole round world to the far-away
Pacific lands. He wants to get away so very badly, that poor Left Behind, and he does not quite see his way to do it. (54–55)

The colonies do not need wastrels, the ne'er-do-wells, she insists, but
decent Englishman, preferably with capital. She offers advice about travel
and settlement costs, pontificates about which are the most suitable crops
for plantation and export, and gives prospective white female settlers advice
about how to concoct dishes out of local produce, deal with the lack of
fresh meat, handle the domestic servants, and combat invasions of mos-
quitos, crabs, and spiders (1907a, 56–65). This practical advice to colonists
is insinuated along with romantic depictions and celebrations of place eroticized through women's bodies.

Like the Cook voyage texts and images of the eastern Pacific, *In the
Strange South Seas* is pervaded by the language of seduction and of voyeurism. Grimshaw writes as a woman, a New Woman who is free to travel.
She constantly reminds us of her own female body in exotic places, in her
muslin nightdress, under the mosquito net, undoing her plaits. Evans (1993)
notes that in her novels, as well as her travel writings, the white woman as
heroine is often in a state of arousal as she lies awake listening to the sound
of the sea. Dara, the white heroine of *My South Sea Sweetheart,* lies "watching the lace rising and falling on the breast of her sea-blue gown" as she
hears the water lapping on the reef, "[c]alling—calling. The call of the sea!
The call of the wild sea life and of the wild souls who lived it" (Grimshaw
1921, 131; cited in Evans 1993, 61). Grimshaw frequently portrays herself
not just as a "wild soul," a woman of adventure climbing mountains or
undertaking perilous sea journeys; when the day is done, we find her lying
awake exhausted listening to the sound of the "far-off creaming of the
breakers" (1907a, 31), of the surf crashing on the shore.

Constantly her eye returns to the bodies of Polynesian women. One
wonders about her own romantic life, and despite her express pursuit of the
path of true heterosexual love for her white heroines, her authorial voice
also talks of the "slip-knotted noose which is marriage" (Grimshaw 1922,
29).[16] I am not imputing lesbian desire, repressed or otherwise, so much as
an extreme objectification of Polynesian women through which she both
authors her own superiority as a white woman and assumes the gaze of a
heterosexual male voyeur-cum-lover (see Kelly, chap. 3 in this volume). In
her textual construction, Polynesian women invite the white, preferably the
adventurous British boy, to colonize. Her romances about Polynesians, as
much as her denigrations of Melanesians, are a blatant part of her projects
of colonial promotion. The deeper racial and sexual tensions are murky in

her travel writing, but exposed in her novels, in whose repetitive plots inter-racial romances are doomed by death or eclipsed by the true romance of love and marriage between white man and white woman.

South Pacific: **The Aesthetics of American Presence**

Finally, I arrive with the American fleet at the moving pictures and the (in)famous *South Pacific,* typifying what I dub the aesthetics of American presence. This is a cinematic adaptation of the Rodgers and Hammerstein musical, produced first on Broadway in the 1950s and then directed as a film by Joshua Logan in 1958. One commentator opines that the film shows "that Joshua Logan and Broadway musicals belong on Broadway" (Bergan 1982, 82). But it is not the aesthetic merits of the movie so much as its World War Two setting and the erotic exotics of American military presence which concern me here.

This cinematic representation of romance in the context of American military campaigns in World War Two is based on some vignettes in *Tales of the South Pacific* by James Michener (1947).[17] In this transformation the original settings, which were situated around the major American staging bases in Vanuatu, and various battlegrounds in the Solomons, and Papua New Guinea, have become rather more vague. There is a mélange of im-ages from Fiji and the spectacularly beautiful Hanalei coast of Kauai in Hawaii where the film was shot (Reyes 1995, 107).

Exoticization in *South Pacific* tends to collapse and dissolve the differences between East and West, which were so central to the images of the Cook voyages and the later representations of Beatrice Grimshaw. This is a generic Pacific, which is conjured by the dreamy image of Bali Ha'i—remote, in-accessible, and draped in vaporous clouds (its true geographic location mys-terious). This island is a paradise of lush, dripping foliage, with drooping bougainvillea and ferns, and erect, multicoloured crotons. It is a landscape saturated with watercourses and waterfalls. It is down these waterfalls, slid-ing on slippery, mossy, rocks that we witness Polynesian beauties—women and men—cavorting in the water and swimming sinuously, as they have done in most movies about Polynesia since the silent films of the 1920s.[18]

But Bali Ha'i is not just inhabited by Polynesian beauties. When the navy comes to call, they find an extraordinary retinue of women living there—not just Polynesian women draped lasciviously in sarongs and wreathed in flowers as of old, but Tonkinese women, like Bloody Mary and her beautiful daughter Liat, and a platoon of white women, presumably daughters of the French planters, sequestered there during the war, attired in frothy dresses and sunhats or hiding beneath huge umbrellas. There are even a few French nuns in dramatic black-and-white habit. But this is not just an erotic theme park of women's variety; there is also an equally polymorphous collection of Pacific men.

The creation of a generic, spectacular Pacific is probably most flagrant in the extraordinary representations of ritual on Bali Ha'i. Loosely derived from Michener's satiric allusions to the ritual slaughter of tusked boars in Vanuatu (1947, 205 ff.) the ceremony has been aestheticized, sanitized, even anaesthetized, as if it were an act of dentistry to remove the tusk rather than an act of sacrifice to the ancestors through porcine slaughter. The accompanying dance is performed to drums which sound African rather than Pacific and choreographed with masked men from New Guinea, Rapanui bird men, Fijian firewalkers, and Polynesian hula dancers. There are a few darker men in laplaps, with shells or pigs' tusks on their breasts, who are played not by ni-Vanuatu, but by whites blacked up, who bear names in the credits like "Chief—Archie Savage."

And so the Pacific is rendered as a kind of ethnographic flotsam and jetsam, drifting pieces on a sea, where all marks of cultural diversity and difference can be retrieved as spectacle for the American presence and our view. Equally interesting is how the film constructs the space of "back home." Instead of the fields of England, or the flurry of Pitt Street in Sydney, "back home" has become Little Rock, Arkansas, or Philadephia, PA (Pennsylvania). The American home with which the exotic is contrasted is no longer so confidently a site of colonial or racial superiority, however. There are those small-town (or even big-town) American values of 1950s coziness and clichés—as "normal as blueberry pie," as "gay as a daisy in May," as "high as the flag on the Fourth of July."[19] But the homey American values of secure heterosexual domesticity, of innocent springtime pleasures, and of patriotism are challenged and confounded by the exotic locales, the enticing prospects of different bodies, and the heightened passions of heterosexual romance in the midst of war.[20]

The desire at the heart of the two central heterosexual romances is the desire of difference. The first is that between Lieutenant Joseph Cabel of Philadelphia (played by John Kerr) and Liat—the daughter of Bloody Mary, a French-speaking woman from Tonkin (France Nuyen).[21] The second is between Ensign Nellie Forbush, officer-nurse from Little Rock (Mitzi Gaynor) and Emile de Becque, the island planter who is a fugitive from France (Rossano Brazzi).

The erotics of the exotic here work through a series of displacements and fugitive transformations. It is not the old story of white man desires and wins Polynesian/Pacific woman. Rather, Lieutenant Cabel is linked not to a woman of the place, Melanesian or Polynesian, but the daughter of a

Tonkinese migrant woman, Bloody Mary. When this handsome marine flies into the base, already populated by hunky but not so suave ordinary sailors, Bloody Mary tries to seduce him. "You sexy man," she proclaims. "You're looking pretty fit yourself," is his embarrassed response. She entices him in song—"Bali Ha'i"—whose plaintive tones merge the body of a singing woman with the vaporous island, "Where the sky meets the sea. Here am I, your special island. Come to me, come to me." He finally succumbs and visits her island, although fearful of the eager embrace of this older, experienced woman.

But she summons him there on behalf of her daughter, the beautiful Liat, who is an incarnation of the inscrutable, passive Oriental woman (unlike her forward mother). The lovers speak together falteringly in French, and Liat and her mother perform a strange bowdlerization of Polynesian hand-dance movements to "Happy Talk" (see plate 4.5), but the bodies of the young lovers find each other in easy and passionate communication (even underwater). He must forsake their passion, not so much for his "girl back home" as for the fear that death probably awaits him. His special secret mission is behind enemy lines as a coastwatcher, attempting to turn back the tide of Japanese invasion. Bloody Mary plays her last card, threatening to marry the forlorn Liat to a wealthy old French planter. This fails, and the beautiful Lieutenant goes off to spy on the movement of the Japanese fleet, air force, and infantry, dying heroically in action somewhere in the Solomons (probably Guadalcanal).[22] His corpse is shrouded in leaves by two "local" men (one of whom looks like Archie Savage).

What intrigues me about this film is that indigenous Pacific women are a chorus, a beautiful backdrop, part of the lush scenery of Bali Ha'i, but not the subjects of interracial romance, which is enacted elsewhere. It is the migrant Oriental woman, not a Polynesian woman, who is the lover of the beautiful American. Polynesian women, listed as a chorus at the end of the credits, are thus a sort of generic, insular enticement rather than differentiated subjects of passion. Apart from their collective choric presence, Polynesian women also figure as an absence in the second romance—between Nellie Forbush and Emile de Becque, the French planter.

Again their desire is constituted through difference, not the difference between the "West" and the islands, but rather between America and Europe.[23] Nellie is portrayed—indeed authors herself in song—as a green, jejune, small-town gal, a cockeyed optimist, "a dope with hope," "Knuckle-Headed Nellie." Emile de Becque is, by contrast, the epitome of French sophistication—a suave, older man, his library is stocked with Marcel Proust and Anatole France. He drinks cognac out of the right glasses, not coconut liquor out of shells. His plantation sits at the top of the hill, with panoptical

Figure 4.5. Liat, Bloody Mary, and Joe Cabel making "Happy Talk" in *South Pacific*. Courtesy of Film Stills Archives, Museum of Modern Art, New York.

views over the ocean, and gardens beautifully manicured by his Tonkinese staff. This mature, civilized, very Mediterranean man is hiding a deep, dark secret—indeed two deep, dark secrets. The first is that he killed a man, when young, by accident—in the name of liberty and equality if not fraternity—but killed him nevertheless. He is thus a fugitive from France. He peremptorily confesses this secret early in his romance with Nellie, but she manages, also rather peremptorily, to forgive him.

The darker, obdurate secret remains—that he had been married to a woman of the islands, a Polynesian woman who bore him two exquisite children, who spoke French fluently, and even had good table manners. Nellie is charmed (thinking they are the children of his Tonkinese servant), but then discovers they are his own children (see plate 4.6). The thought of his previous Polynesian wife is too awful to contemplate; she breaks off their romance. She can only take him back after bitter self-reflection on her own racism, forged in the heat of battle and Emile's reincarnation as a war hero. Though first refusing the dangers of the coastwatching mission, after Nellie's rejection he decides to proffer his intimate knowledge of the islands and join forces with the Americans against the Japanese. He and his buddy Lieutenant Joe Cabel are dropped together behind enemy lines. Liberty, equality, and fraternity acquire an American uniform, but his Yankee brother dies and he survives. Through the heightened, fearful passions prior to Cabel's death in the eventual military action, Nellie finds it within herself to forgive de Becque his first wife. And this moment of cathartic transformation, effected through the spirit of the dead Joe Cabel, reveals that her racism is not in her, but taught to her. Prior to his death, in accounting for Nellie's racism to Emile, Joe Cabel coins a hymn to cultural construction. He chants "[Y]ou've got to be taught to be afraid of people whose eyes are oddly made, and people whose skin is a different shade."[24]

Despite its pretensions to racial tolerance, the film can hardly be read as

Figure 4.6. The plantation site of Emile de Becque in *South Pacific*. Nellie Forebush greets the children, whom she first believes are those of his servant. Courtesy of Film Stills Archives, Museum of Modern Art, New York.

avowing equality of race, sex, or class. There is not only the extraordinary absence of Islanders, except as a part of the lush backdrop, but one of the singular features of the Pacific war—the large number of black American soldiers—who figure prominently in Islanders' memories and myths—are virtually absent (see White and Lindstrom 1989; Lindstrom and White 1990). There is one lonely black American soldier. The class differentiations between the officers and the common sailors are represented rather more palpably, particularly in the persona of Luther Billis, with his big, exposed belly inscribed with a tattoo of a sailing ship, heaving around the navel. Indeed Luther, like Baines in *The Piano* (1993) signifies the lower-class white man who is on the verge of "going native," but in feminized fashion. He is the one most desperate to get to Bali Ha'i, to taste some of that coconut liquor and see bare-breasted women in grass skirts, but he also shows Bloody Mary how to make grass skirts with greater rationality and capitalist economy, and ultimately cross-dresses as an Island woman for the Thanksgiving burlesque.[25]

The cross-dressing codes displayed by both Luther and Nellie at this performance are quite telling. For most of the film Nellie is in states of revealing undress—in a gorgeous, low-cut evening gown which sculpts her bosom; in a red bikini, with a revealing tanned midriff; in very short white shorts (while the male officers wear pants), in a kind of cavegirl outfit on the beach as she "washes that man right out of [her] hair." But for Thanksgiving she dresses up as a man—not an officer but a common sailor in a voluminous white and blue sailor suit. The cross-dressing does not negate the female body within, but rather emphasizes its hidden curves, especially as she authors and objectifies her hips as Twirly and Whirly. Luther meanwhile is downstage, with a coconut-shell bra, a long wig, and a net skirt adorned with leaves and shells. His wriggling hips are safely confined in board shorts.

Cross-dressing here thus breaches the racial, class, and gender lines. But does this also imply a cross-looking, a subversion of the hierarchical codes of the gaze, or merely a reinscription of them? Men look at women, perhaps with more perverse interest, when they are dressed as men. But white male bodies are also flagrantly sexualized and on display, with lots of bared sailor chests and beautiful officers in uniform. Bloody Mary seems to subvert the codes of gendered spectatorship when she pants, "You sexy man"—but ultimately colludes in the hypersexualization and objectification of her daughter Liat. And although Nellie gazes as longingly at Emile as he at her, she is enjoined to objectify her allure in ways that he does not. It is hard to imagine the greying, statuesque Rossano Brazzi, rather than the blonde, lithe Mitzi Gaynor, performing Twirly and Whirly. But what we never see here are beautiful Pacific men or women whom we are invited to identify with or even gaze upon, except as a chorus of singers and dancers. This eroticization of the islands but not of individual Islanders is perhaps symptomatic—the presence of beautiful Americans has eclipsed the beautiful indigenes. Is this a final colonial culmination of the erotics of the exotic?

Conclusion

In conclusion, I return to what Teresia Teaiwa (1994) has said about the two bikinis. Her thesis is both serious and shocking—namely, that the eroticized female body distracts from and obscures the violence of colonial occupation and especially of American military presence and nuclear testing in Micronesia. There is no doubt, as she attests, that the two are connected. The bikini, launched by French designer Louis Reard to celebrate Allied efforts in World War Two, was named after the atoll. Sexual imagery also pervaded the nuclear detonations on Bikini; the first device exploded there was nicknamed Gilda, and painted with an image of Rita Hayworth. For her, the "generic female body" disguises the horror of the bomb; the excessive visibility of flesh renders the politics of colonialism and anticolonialism invisible. She further claims that the bikini and the female body divert attention from indigenous decolonization movements and the realities of Islanders' resistance to their place being made a nuclear playground (see Firth 1987). She perceives the bikini and semi-nude bodies on the beach as more about European and American sex/gender constructs than about Pacific Islanders. Although she makes extensive use of Marxist, Freudian, and Western feminist theories of the commodity and the fetish in her analysis of both bomb and bikini, she also acknowledges that such largely "Eurocentric theories must remain ornamental to narratives that interrupt dominant historical and cultural constructions of the islands as miltary bases and tourist sites" (1994, 102). But her own paper is an interruption—a deployment of Eurocentric theories perhaps, a different form of politics from the Movement for a Nuclear Free and Independent Pacific no doubt, yet nevertheless a politically charged interruption of the dominant colonialist and masculinist scripts which have dominated Pacific history. In the rewriting of these narratives, it is probably as important to subvert European voices (as I have tried to do here) as it is to reinsert Islanders' voices. My argument is complementary— apropos the ethnic character of the female body, male bodies, the posited relation between hypervisible bodies and invisible politics, and finally how we might imagine regional relations which transcend the active subjects and passive objects of colonialist spectatorship.

First, I suggest that the ethnic character of women's bodies is as important as the fact that they are female. Teaiwa talks of the "generic female body," by which she signals femaleness and heterosexuality, regardless of other specific social identities (1994, 93). Yet, as is clear from the several stages of her argument, the ethnic character of the female body also matters. The eighteenth-century images of the Pacific as inhabited by noble savages and people akin to Greek gods or goddesses were about Polynesians and especially about Tahitian women.[26] And although romantic images of the South Seas and classical allusions may have also been adduced for the bikini, it was primarily for European and American women to wear at the beach (as she notes, in contrast, Islanders today, on the beach and swimming with few exceptions, are well covered). A rather more differentiated code of gender, sexuality, and ethnicity is at work. It matters whether the body being revealed is that of a Polynesian princess, a ni-Vanuatu woman, a Tonkinese migrant, or a white woman. Gazing at women's bodies is structured by ethnicity and by epoch.

In the Cook voyage images it is the bodies of Island, or more especially Polynesian, women which are constructed as alluring and inviting. They are opposed to very negative images of Melanesian women as ugly and as sexually sequestered. But Tahitian or Hawaiian women are also simultaneously differentiated from Englishwomen, beautiful in terms of classical form and familiarity. The Englishwoman, moreover, was stereotypically represented as chaste: less inviting, accessible, or eager (with the exception of prostitute women in Drury Lane).

Significantly this kind of masculinist voyeurism about women's bodies as desirable and available is not just the preserve of male writers and artists but is present in the work of female travelers in the Pacific, as in Grimshaw's texts and photographs. Here, although we are often reminded of her female body in the text, we rarely see it; rather, she invites us to gaze on other women. The objectification of Pacific women is as pronounced in those alluring romantic images of the East as it is in the appalling denigrations of women in the West. In so objectifying them, she not only authors herself as superior to Pacific women, but assumes a white male gaze. By contrast she rarely objectifies Island men, and secretes the beautiful body of the white woman, except in her novels. Ultimately, although the body of the Polynesian woman seduces the white man to the islands, the white man will "go native" if he stays with her too long—lapse into a torpor of freedom and lazy sensuality. Many of her novels are about white women arriving in the colonies to rescue men from the ruin of marriages to local women. Melanesian women in such plots are depicted most negatively. But even the most romantic liaisons of white men and Polynesian women are often doomed to end in death in her fictions. True romance is not just cross-sex but same-race.

Transcending the dark past of interracial marriage is also what Nellie must do in *South Pacific*. Emile's Island wife is already dead, and he is also subtly differentiated from her by nation.[27] The other romance, between the Oriental woman and the American man, is doomed by his heroic death. And whereas Nellie Forbush is constantly revealed, her body typically flaunted in states of undress, Liat in contrast is (at first) well covered and inaccessible. The exposed white woman and the draped Oriental woman are joined by a bevy of Island women, but although they are portrayed as sexually untrameled, the eye of the viewer is not invited to rest on them. Polynesian women's bodies are revealed, but they are backgrounded rather than foregrounded. It is rather the exposed body of the white woman which is up front.

Men's sexualized bodies are perhaps not totally out of the picture in these several examples. Indeed in Bougainville's reference to Tahitians, which Teaiwa quotes for his classical allusions, both the bodies of men and of women are celebrated as Mars and Venus. The first signifies masculine activity and athleticism to be admired; the second rather signifies the naked, passive female form. Island men, naked or partially clad, are present in some of the eighteenth-century images, but they are usually active and engaged rather than displayed to the gaze. Sometimes this naked activity is a mark of resistance to or aggression against the incursions of white men, most palpably in representations of the western Pacific, where the nakedness of men was not just a sign of savagery but of their virility and aggression as warriors. When Polynesian men are represented as warriors, some of this naked defiance is evoked (as in Webber's portraits of Tahitian men in helmets), but more often their bodies are encased in drapery and, if they are naked, the marks of their warriorhood are elided (as in Webber's reworking of a sketch of a chief of Bora Bora, where the man is drawn first with a lance, which is removed in the final version; see Smith 1992, 211, plates 189, 190).

The photographs which illustrate Grimshaw's *In the Strange South Seas* include some benign images of Island men—at a native picnic in Tahiti (frontispiece) or dancing in Samoa (1907a, facing 332)—but they are not singled out for their bodily beauty in the way women are, and her texts have no eroticized pen portraits of Polynesian men that are akin to those of women. She sometimes alludes to a Polynesian male presence in a slightly suggestive way, but in both her novels and her travel writing set in Melanesia, men's bodies rather epitomize dark terror and sexual menace.

In *South Pacific,* the excess of eroticized male flesh is embodied by Rossano Brazzi and, of course, American men in uniform. As earlier noted, this has a class code—from the bared bellies and chests of the common sailors to the dashing cut of the officers in pants (especially Joe Cabel). The aesthetics of American men in uniforms and their propensity to break out in song, surely does distract us from the violence of their military mission. Island men, in varied states of dress and undress, are not eroticized and are in no way cast as a threat. The only Island men who are more than a choric background are two Solomon Islanders, who true to history, assist de Becque and Cabel in coastwatching and attend to the corpse of the dead marine. It is significant that this film was produced during the period of American military involvment in Asia as well as in the Pacific (cf. Manderson, chap. 5 in this volume, on *The King and I*), and the American presence is portrayed not just as benign but as morally justifiable and as welcomed by Island men. Thus while earlier European images may have distracted from colonial violence in the Pacific by revealing the bodies of Pacific women, *South Pacific* adopts a divergent tactic of distraction, revealing the bodies of American women and of men. It not only aestheticizes the violence of the war while insisting on its moral and political justification, but it also elides Pacific peoples, "tastefully" removing them from their own islands.

I want to pursue further this idea of "distraction" or "diversion" and the language of visibility and invisibility. Teaiwa (1994) connects the bomb and the bikini ultimately by a theory of repression—that the horror of the first is so great that it requires repression, effected by the fetished female form. Perhaps this psychoanalytic argument is appropriate to the bizarre psychology of Oppenheimer and the way that he conceived of his creation of weapons of mass destruction as "fathering" children and named them as girls or boys. Moreover the use of images of Rita Hayworth in the sexualization of the nuclear devices detonated on Bikini Atoll continues a Euro-American genealogy of domesticating destruction through the use of female names or forms on fighting planes and miltary vessels. But I question the broader applicability of such a theory of hypervisible bodies and invisible politics. In the representations from the Cook voyages, the colonial purposes are blatantly acknowledged, if contested. Even if the violence of the voyages were criticized contemporaneously by some (like George Forster; see Jolly 1992) and Cook was instructed to avoid violent encounters, violence was expected and to a large extent justified rather than repressed or silenced in this period. Similarly, in Grimshaw's texts, colonialism is not something to hide—she espouses settlers' and planters' interests, especially if they are British, and her use of the trope of "the native beauty" is a blatant part of her seductive promotion of the Pacific.

There were, no doubt, blatant celebrants of the bomb, as well as those who opposed it. But what is distinctive about the period from the 1950s to the present is that such confidence in racial and colonial superiority is receding. This is not just a matter of self-criticism but of political resistance. Paradoxically, as the Americans invaded the Pacific during World War Two, and subsequently claimed as the spoils of victory significant parts of Micronesia as U.S. Trust Territory, the American presence also helped to generate independence and anticolonial movements in many of the countries of the southwest Pacific. Thus, without denying the horror of American military colonization and especially of nuclear testing, we probably have to admit that their presence in the Pacific, like that of Christianity, has had both colonizing and decolonizing effects. Independence movements in the southwest Pacific have drawn on American notions of "freedom" and images of American soldiers or presidents at the same time as others have opposed American occupation or neocolonial influence.

Finally, I turn to the relation between these Euro-American fantasies and Islanders' lives. Are these mere foreign fictions which bear no relation to the realities of Island life? Unfortunately not. They surely distort the lived reality—as Lutz and Collins (1993) point out, we see few poor or hungry people in the pages of *The National Geographic*. These representations are not inconsequential, precisely because they are an intimate part of the processes of colonization, militarization, and neocolonial dependency. Islanders might laugh them off as silly or fantastic,[28] or might subvert them by movements of anticolonial resistance, which often challenge the very concept of "Pacific paradise." As Teaiwa demonstrates, anticolonial, nationalist, and antinuclear movements, especially in Micronesia and Polynesia, have often opposed the trivialization and depoliticization of such edenic, erotic images.

But these alluring objectifications have also become a part of Pacific realities, most palpably in the processes and images of the tourist industry. Tourism is a billion-dollar industry in the Pacific, and although Island governments are often ambivalent about such alluring images of their islands, about the potential sexual expectations and depredations of tourists, and wary about the spread of HIV/AIDS, the lure of the islands is still often promoted as sun, surf, and sex. There are other forms of tourism which try to entice on the basis of wilderness, or on the basis of exotic rites or ways of life. But in an era of rapacious logging companies and of predominant patterns of Christian commitment and development (moderated by tradition), these other objectifications also have their problems. I turn to my local newspaper, *The Canberra Times,* to discover that the main attractions for a tourist in the South Pacific this year are still the stunning scenery of the islands, the friendliness of the people, and a series of beauty contests. In this new circuit of "transmigration," can the politics of colonialist and masculinist spectatorship never be transcended?[29]

Acknowledgments

I must acknowledge the excellent assistance of Annegret Schemberg in the research for this paper. I am also grateful for comments and conversation to Chris Ballard, Sandra Buckley, Michel Dominy, Barbara Holloway, Christine and Stephen Hugh-Jones, Ian Keen, Lenore Manderson, Alison Murray, Tom Ryan, Nicholas Thomas, Andrew Walker, and other commentators and critics at seminars at the Australian National University, Griffith University, and the Museum of Sydney. Special thanks also to Harriet Guest, Jonathan Lamb, and Bridgett Orr for their inspiring work on the eighteenth century and the Pacific voyages. My greatest debts, however, are to Bernard Smith, whose work continues to inspire and challenge me and to whom I dedicate this paper, and to Nicholas Thomas for domestic and intellectual support and inspiration, in his own work as much as in his commentaries on my own. All errors and deficiencies, of course, are mine.

CHAPTER FIVE

Parables of Imperialism and Fantasies of the Exotic: Western Representations of Thailand—Place and Sex

LENORE MANDERSON

Occidental Texts

Analyses of Orientalism have focused particularly on the written rather than the visual or performance text. However, the elements of myth-making, stereotype, and elision of nation and sex, and of sex with race are common to a range of media—artistic, scientific, and popular—and various art forms (Gilman 1986; Broinowski 1992). In this chapter, I focus on three popular films, *The King and I* (1956), *Emmanuelle* (1974), and *The Good Woman of Bangkok* (1991), and their representation of nation, sex, race, and raced desire. The films are, in the terms of de Lauretis (1987), technologies of race (and empire) as well as gender.

This work draws on that of Edward Said (1978) and his argument that European creation of the Orient as an object of discourse, scholarly endeavor, and institutional containment was both produced and sustained by the structures of imperialism. While Said's Orient was largely the Middle East ("Far West," in fact, for many of us), his arguments generalize to countries in Asia and the Pacific. The Orient was an imagined geographic and cultural entity (an invented place, *pace* de Certeau [1984] and Noyes [1992]) that shaped tangible political, economic, and social relations between colonizing states and the territories over which they established hegemony.

The Orient, in Said's terms, was and is a product of intellectual endeavor, but its impact was expansive and flowed into all aspects of popular culture: from early imperialist encounters to traveler's tales and romances; visual representations, including museum collections and displays; architecture and interior design; the performing and visual arts; and in the twentieth century, film. The representation of the Orient in film, the subject of this chapter, is but one example therefore of the Orient as part of Occidental popular culture and imagination. This representation informed and shaped Western perceptions and understandings of other places, and the Thailand portrayed in artistic modes and the media is part of a "real" Thailand both for its audience and for many tourists.

As noted, the study of representation has focused particularly on the written text—the novels of Flaubert, Forster, Haggard, and Kipling, for example, along with travel diaries and the like (e.g., see Said 1978; Kabbani 1986; Viswanathan 1990; Pratt 1992; Suleri 1992). In the second half of the twentieth century, however, despite the orientalist debts to the written text, film is often more accessible and its representations more familiar to most people. The relationship of the individual to the text (book compared with film) is, however, a questionable one. De Certeau (1984) differentiates the written from the viewed text (television, in his example) in terms of the ability of the reader/viewer to transform the text to his or her own ends. The reader can appropriate the text literally, annotating the surface and manipulating meaning, although without the freedom to re-create that is afforded in an oral tradition. With televized text, de Certeau suggests, the viewer is "dislodged from the product . . . and becomes, or so it seems, a pure receiver" (1984, 31). One could argue this passivity with respect to any film text. But this is an illusion, for images and filmed narrative can be read very differently according to the viewer's own positioning with respect to the politics of the film and his or her identification with its characters. The debates that have developed around *The Good Woman of Bangkok* (see Berry 1994, 24–32) illustrate the potential for a film as well as a printed text to take on, after production, a life of its own. But *The Good Woman of Bangkok* also exemplifies the power of film to be both manipulative of and able to be manipulated by the viewer: the "readable"—in the widest meaning of this word—"transforms itself into the memorable" (de Certeau 1984, xxi). This is my fascination with all three films examined in this chapter, and indeed with the genres they exemplify.

The films are Western products (of the United States, France, and Australia) and tell stories that have been shown primarily to Western audiences. They are about Europeans *in* Thailand, not about Thailand. The location in Thailand, not "at home," allows the viewer to appropriate and manipulate place and hence to invent space, or "practiced place" (de Certeau 1984, 107, 117–18). Indeed each film commences with an arrival scene that establishes the invented place, or what Nichols (1994, 64, 67) refers to as "imaginary geography," with a claim to establishing authority and, to varying degrees, the illusion of "truth" (see Nichols 1994, 64). The act of travel and the arrival scenes, Nichols argues, differentiate between "here" and "there," us and other, establishing distance between the other, and the person behind the lens—and the viewer who shares/interprets his or her gaze.

The films prescribe the space within which action takes place; in establishing the boundaries of action, they define the mythic Orient for the viewer. There is "off-camera" space, but its complexity is dependent upon the viewers' prior knowledge, and this is limited when such films are screened in the West for Western audiences.

The films raise the question of how raced desire is produced (Shrage 1992), and the degree to which ideas of race and gender are manipulated in the context of sexual consumption. Shrage suggests that "the actions of sex customers epitomize beliefs and values about race and gender" that are oppressively sexist and racist. She analyzes Asian sex tourism not in terms of political economy (i.e., women's poverty is for her an insufficient explanation of their commoditization) but in terms of the structure of the market in accordance with consumer "tastes and preferences" shaped by popular images of Asian (and black) women in Western culture (44–45). Asian women are constructed as superfeminine, submissive, mysterious, desirable, and docile. These are stereotypes recounted by men in screen documentaries and films like *The Good Woman of Bangkok*. In this constitution of Asian woman, the Orient itself is feminized (and can be raped). Films about Asia and Asian women perpetuate both myths of the nature of the Oriental woman and effect the alignment of race, sex, and place (Broinowski 1992, Jiwani 1992)—a generic representation parallel to that of the muscular, white, American male which Hollywood has explored (Tasker 1993).

Within and beyond Occidental film texts, including the films discussed in this chapter, and in both contemporary Thai society and fictional representations of it (see Hamilton, chap. 6 in this volume), the intersections of race, sex, and class are multiple and many-layered. These intersections— economic, political, and social—include those among Thais, between Thais and Europeans (that is, people from Europe, the United States, and Australia), and between Thais and other Asians (Japanese tourists especially). The live sex acts of Patpong highlight this layering. Here women (and some men) perform in ways that are expected to capture the erotic imaginations of other (foreign) men, or perform in ways that they or the bar managers or owners, many of whom are European, consider to be "what men want" (Manderson 1992b). Elsewhere, in Bangkok and Pattaya, in transvestite/ transsexual shows such as *Calypso,* Thai transvestites, cross-dressed actors, and transsexuals—all with different notions of their own sexuality or gender identity (Manderson 1995; Jackson, chap. 7 in this volume)—similarly perform in ways that reflect their (Thai) perceptions of the feminine, or their perceptions of Western notions of the feminine; often they parody both. In the texts discussed here, the intersections of race and sex are explicit and constraining. Thai sex, but not sexuality—that is, sexual practice rather than identity or the interrelationship of the two—is defined and given a purpose as a vehicle for Western libidinal fantasy and the enactment of power. Most often, Thai sexuality is invisible and faceless; so too are Thai citizens invisible as people.[1] As Tasker argues of Hollywood films and the construction of masculinity, "power is written differently over the black, white and Asian bodies of its heros and heroines." Film inflects and redefines "already existing cinematic and cultural discourses of race, class and sexuality" (1993, 5). Thus the boundaries of intercultural connections are defined, and the "nature" of Thai sexuality presented, if at all, as essentialist and homogenous.

Notes on Musical Genealogy

The King and I, Emmanuelle, and *The Good Woman of Bangkok* are, as already suggested, part of a continuing popular rendering of an Orientalist tradition: modern versions of travelers' tales, early ethnographies, and collections of exotic erotica, as well as the visual and performing arts. The earliest of the films examined here, *The King and I,* was first a theatrical musical, and so shares with nineteenth-and twentieth-century opera the use of the "Orient" as an elaborate and fantastic dramatic backdrop for European music. *Les Pecheurs de perles* (Bizet 1863, "Ancient Ceylon"), *Aida* (Verdi 1871, Egypt in the age of the Pharaohs), *Lakme* (Delibes 1883, mid-nineteenth-century India), *The Mikado* (Gilbert and Sullivan 1885, Imperial Japan), *Madama Butterfly* (Puccini 1904, early-twentieth-century Nagasaki), and *Turandot* (Puccini 1926, legendary Peking) are all famous examples of operatic Orientalism and fantasies of political intrigue and sexual mores.[2] Arguably, the difference between film and opera is one of form, partly because each director and actor can manipulate textual meaning in stage performance, in contrast to the fixed nature of film (once produced and released, that is; this is not to deny multiple readings of a film, of course), and partly because the immediacy of film—its apparent "realism"—sustains a suspension of disbelief such that its audience is more likely than the audience of an opera to accept that "what they see" is "how things really are." At the same time, of course, films vary in their insistence on analogue, fantasy, and veracity. The films discussed below fall into rather different categories: *The King and I* is a musical romance, but based on diaries of an historic personage and hence has certain claims to "truth"; *Emmanuelle* is pornographic fantasy, yet filmed on location, anchored, and hence has certain claims to genuine representation of place and the social actions that occur there; *The Good Woman of Bangkok,* according to the filmmaker, Dennis O'Rourke, is "documentary fiction," but read very much by reviewers as autobiography and largely judged in that light (again, see Berry 1994; see also Berry, Hamilton, and Jayamanne, in press).

Each of the films has its own genealogy. *The King and I,* as Donaldson (1992, 35) documents, has a rich heritage. It dates from Anna Leonowens's diaries from her time at the Bangkok court, published after she had left Thailand (*The English Governess at the Siamese Court* 1870, *The Romance of the Harem* 1873a, *Siamese Harem Life* 1873b).[3] These were, of course, her own accounts of events of politics and sex/gender relations for which there are many different possible accounts, both European and Thai (Morgan 1991, ix–xii). The diaries were adapted by Landon (1944) into a novel, *Anna and the King of Siam,* and then by Jennings and Benson (1945) into a screenplay of the same name; this was in turn adapted by Rodgers and Hammerstein first as the Broadway play, *The King and I* (1951), and then as the film of the same name (1956). The film was exceptionally popular; it was, according to Donaldson (1992, 34), "perhaps the greatest success of all the Rodgers and Hammerstein stage-to-screen productions" and was recently re-released as part of nostalgic "Mothers Day" promotions (in Australia in May 1995; see Jolly, chap. 4 in this volume). There are echoes in turn in later musicals,[4] and the film is sufficiently rich in political and social commentary to be read in very different ways. Donaldson, for example, analyzes it in terms of a feminist critique of Thai court culture and the position of women therein; imperialism; abolitionist views (see the embedded Siamese court version of *Uncle Tom's Cabin*); more global feminist demands (a *house* of her own); *and* the contradictions that emerge in terms of ideology and structure— "the film's stated discourse of liberation" on the one hand and "the unstated discourse that controls its rhetorical systems" on the other (1992, 50).

Emmanuelle's genealogy relates both to its historical positioning in terms of the erotic films that were widely available in the early 1970s and its representation of sexual liberation projects of the time. This visual representation of sex-in-Thailand as part of a burgeoning industry of soft-core and erotic films also occured at a time of liberalization of censorship in a number of countries (Australia included). *Emmanuelle* competed with and sat between such films as the sepia-pedophilia of David Hamilton on the one hand and Warhol's brutal artistic explorations of sex (e.g., *Heat, Flesh, Dracula,* etc.) on the other. This *Emmanuelle* (1974, directed by Jaeckin with Sylvie Kristel in the title role) was followed by a series of other, reminiscently entitled films. *Emmanuelle* (1974) was part of a trilogy with Kristel that included *Goodbye, Emmanuelle* (1975, directed by Francis Giacobetti, set in the Seychelles), and *Emmanuelle L'Antiverge* (1977, directed by Francois LeTerrier and set in Hong Kong and Bali). There were other later Emmanuelle films too, such as *Emmanuelle in Soho,* many of which conflated sex and race, collapsed the categories of exotic and erotic, and argued the potentiality of liberation in such moments of inter-cultural connection. In addition, there were apparently several cuts of the 1974 film, with versions produced for different purposes—for drive-in cinema, for theaters, and a "Collector's Edition" for home video use only. In the theater version discussed here, the central theme is Emmanuelle's liberation under the tutelage of Mario.[5] The setting is Thailand, and therefore a study of the prototypical film provides us with some insight into the way in which Thai sexuality is construed and the exploration of sexuality is argued as possible in Thailand. The two are not the same, of course, although notions of Thai people and Thailand collapse in the crude rendition of sex and nation within the film text.

The Good Woman of Bangkok claims kinship with *The Good Woman of Setzuan* (1941; see Brecht, 1970). However, it also finds kinship with a number of documentary films made since the late 1980s on the traffic in women, in particular sex work and mail-order brides, most of which have been concerned with Thailand and a few with the Philippines (e.g., *Foreign Bodies* 1988, *The AIDS Domino* 1992, *The Thai Sex Industry* 1993, *You Can't Buy a Wife, Can You?* 1993). Newspaper and magazine articles have explored the same theme in very similar ways (e.g., Neumann 1979; *Bangkok Post* 10 April 1992; Eddy and Walden 1992; Kammerer and Symonds 1992; Kempton 1992; Hollington 1993; Cook 1993). *The Good Woman of Bangkok* has been treated rather differently from these other films, as an "art film" as opposed to a conventional television documentary (i.e., it has been reviewed in film journals and has provoked a number of scholarly articles and longer works; see, e.g., Berry 1994, Berry, Hamilton, and Jayamanne, in press). In certain issues of substance, however, including its narrative of the political economy of sex in Thailand, it differs very little from these other films.

The King and I (1956)

For many in the "West," born in the 1940s or 1950s, Rodgers and Hammerstein's musical *The King and I* (1956) was their first exposure to "Thailand."[6] As noted above, it is based, loosely, on Anna Leonowens' autobiographical work and on Margaret Landon's recounting of this in *Anna and the King of Siam* (1944). The film tells of Anna as an English governess in the court of Siam, and with this as foreground, provides an account of Thailand's resistance to the imperializing West, its maintenance of political autonomy ironically by yielding to Western cultural dominance (here personified by Anna as schoolteacher). Thailand is portrayed as naive; Thai perceptions, behav-

iors, and understandings are characterized as childlike. Thus the locally produced classroom map of the world depicts an anthropomorphic masculine
Thailand challenging a naked, unenculture Burma and an insignificant,
ungendered, and unknown Other as the rest of the world. Knowledge is
portrayed as prescientific—the world is flat, biblical tales are read as literal,
political-social relations are feudal, women are items of exchange, the king's
power is absolute, and his appetites and controls over others extrahuman.
Yet even the king is childlike, innocent in his excitement for (Western)
knowledge, playful in his testing of power (for example, in forcing Anna to
lie on the floor to remain lower than him), naive in his embrace of English
accoutrements.

The King and I, despite the constraints of the musical film genre and the
period of its production, addresses both the sexuality of Western women
and of Thai men and women, and uses sexuality as a vehicle to explore
broader issues relating to Thai foreign relations, which include Thailand's
efforts to maintain autonomy from Britain and France and to resist imperialism through a process of self-directed modernization. In pursuing this
theme the film positions Thailand as woman and victim, deserving to be
raped if she fails to act in an appropriate (i.e., Western) manner culturally
and politically. Thailand's "barbarism" is masculinized, however, in the context of its own regional dominance, as represented in the scene related to
the Thai court map and the presentation of a "correct" map by Leonowens
(see plate 5.1), and the presentation of Tuptim to the King of Thailand as a
minor wife from the court of Burma. Tension between Burma and Thailand
was of considerable interest to the British as imperial territorial and colonial
capitalist interests expanded. Hence the suppression and prostitution of Thai
culture to "prove" to the British entourage that Thailand was not "barbar-
ian" and so deserved to maintain political autonomy. The worldliness/West-
ernization of the Thai court is reflected in its adoption—for the purposes
of a special banquet—of European food, music, dress, and assorted para-
phernalia like cutlery, which Anna Leonowens represents to King Mongkut
as symbolic of modernity and civilization. In the context of the banquet,
"traditional Thai culture" reemerges only in the quaint theatrical adaptation
of an American novel ("Small House of Uncle Thomas"); its anti-slavery
stance is not lost on the King, however (see Donaldson 1992). The final
scenes of *The King and I* anticipate the evolution of neocolonialism: the
death of Lun Tha and the impossibility of "true" (bourgeois) love in the
context of the sexual politics of the court of Siam; Mongkut's threat, and in
the face of Anna's disapproval, his inability to follow "tradition" and flog
Tuptim for her perfidy and disobedience; and the transmogrification of the
story line into a modern version of Beauty and the Beast (Mongkut lan-

guishes for love of Anna, and dies at the moment of reconciliation). This all foreshadows the supplication of the Thai nation state to European hegemony and control.

There is a twist. Mongkut, representing Thailand, eager to be enculturated (Westernized), is male; the enculturating/civilizing agent, Anna, is female. In this set of oppositions, the more usual Orient:Occident :: female:male sets are disbanded in favor of Orient:Occident :: child:mother, a rendering that demands that Thailand be feminized in order to be controlled, domesticated, tamed. Anna is the agent who enables the subjugation of Thailand by her male compatriots.

Figure 5.1. Anna (Deborah Kerr) encounters King Mongkut (Yul Brynner) after hanging the "correct" map of the world. Scene from Rodgers and Hammerstein's *The King and I* (20th Century-Fox Production, 1956). Courtesy of Film Stills Archives, Museum of Modern Art, New York.

Despite (or perhaps facilitated by) the frippery of the genre, *The King and I* provides extensive commentary on Thai sexual practices and institutions, European encounters with Thai sexuality, and Western women's sexuality and gender, without the racism that characterized later popular texts on Thai and other Asian sexuality.[7] The film was made in the mid-1950s, during a period in the United States and elsewhere in the industrialized world when women were subject to a rigid, domesticating ideology, penalized for stepping outside of the domain of the home and the institutionalized roles of wife and mother (Friedan 1965), tricked out of the possibility of any independence or autonomy by the cheap lure of vacuum cleaners and washing machines, and harassed by repressive psychologies that blamed any misdemeanor on bad mothering and that normalized women's emotional, economic, and social dependence. The domestic politics of the subjugation of women concurrent with the rise of consumerism took place against a backdrop of the "cold war" and naive anti-Communist sentiment. Americans and others were involved in suppressing anti-imperialism and peasant movements in Indochina, the Philippines, and Malaya; Americans were overtly involved in the Korean War and in undercover politicking elsewhere in Asia and Latin America. Within the United States, there was a suppression of intellectuals, of which the trials under McCarthy were only the most excessive form, and a continued denial of black as well as women's rights.

Against this imperialist, conservative, and anti-intellectual backdrop, the musicals of Rodgers and Hammerstein seem extraordinarily liberal (see also Jolly, chap. 4 in this volume). *The King and I* anticipates Thailand's continued autonomy, although at the same time the cultural adaptations to counter the notions of "barbarism" foreshadow the neocolonialism of the 1960s and 1970s, when Thailand was to be transformed through American involvement in the Vietnam war into a military, political, and recreational base for American forces.[8] Thai sexual institutions and women's sexuality are both depicted liberally. Although the prestation of women and their lack of personal freedom are treated critically, court polygyny as such is not criticized. Mongkut's consort, Madame Thiang, speaks (sings) in support of the institution and of her willingness to operate within it to maintain the monarchy ("he is wonderful"); she is the mediator between the King and other wives, and the King and Anna. The entire narrative is set inside a court that is dominated by "powerful and influential women"—"a female state within the male-dominated state," a "highly ordered society" of women of power and authority (Reynolds 1994, 76).[9] Anna is represented as an independent woman who has traveled to Thailand without a male protector upon widowhood, who rejects male patronage/remarriage, and whose own eulogic representation of monogamous love ("Hello, young lovers") is parodied by her obvious attraction to the King.[10] She is inhibited not by moral objections to his polygyny nor her complicity in it (nor her breach of chaste widowhood), but by her objections to the other manifestations of the power of the court (prostration, slavery, absolute authority).

It is important to note that the film's backdrop of Thai nationalism and resistance to colonialism is not unique; it was explored also in Thai-language performance texts. Reynolds (1994, 65) gives the example of the 1936 Thai musical drama, *Luat Suphan,* which pursues the tensions of gender and race in a narrative of Thai nationalism (it deals with Burma and Thailand—providing a nice comparison to *The King and I* in terms of genre as well as sexual and political relations, e.g., with respect to the gift of Tuptim, the map of the world, etc.). Reynolds also notes relatively early debates (1920s) in the Thai press regarding gender relations with respect to polygamy, prostitution, and pornography (66–67), in which context the treatment in *The King and I* of sexuality, polygyny, and court authority, and Leonowens' discussions of these themes, are especially interesting. In light of these debates, too, the flow of ideas between European and Thai intellectuals during this period and earlier would appear worthy of closer attention.[11]

Emmanuelle (1974)

Emmanuelle (1974) suggests that a marked shift in the representation of Thailand and Thai sexuality had occurred in the two decades since the production of *The King and I,* involving an increasing objectification of women and of Thai people (women and men). The incorporation of Thailand (and other Asian states) into the global economy, the establishment of an American military presence in the region, the use of Thailand as a military base to repress communist insurgency in neighboring states and as a stronghold of capitalism against an encroaching Asian communism, and Thailand's role as a sexual playground for American naval and ground troops led to a pervasive neoimperialism that had cultural as well as economic components (for example, through educational links and the import of American cultural products). In this latter context, go-go bars opened, introducing new elements into a sex industry that already operated to meet both expatriate and local market demands (e.g., Dawson 1988).

The story line of the film is as follows. Emmanuelle joins her French diplomat husband (Jean) in Bangkok, and is encouraged by him to be sexually adventurous. He directs her to let Mario initiate her into the joys of liberated sexuality. She resists his efforts and those of two women—Marie-Ange, a young woman (cast as nymphet), and an older woman (Arianne, husband's lover, seductress also of Emmanuelle). Instead, she commences an affair with and is enamored of an American woman archaeologist, Bee. Bee rejects Emmanuelle, and Emmanuelle, on the rebound, then turns to Mario, who takes her on a journey of sexual liberation. Thailand here is a simple exotic backdrop for primarily European sexual games, although the geographic setting is rendered "authentic" through shots of *klongs,* river markets, crowds of Thai children, bar scenes, and boxing—all familiar scenes because of the commodification of place as a tourist resort. It parallels, too, other cinematic representations of the "Orient" as a space where white men and women "discover" themselves (Tasker 1993, 99; Hamilton, chap. 6 in this volume). Finally, the location and the travel and arrival scenes (from Paris to Bangkok, in this case) conjure associations for viewers and establish a metaphor for "voyages of self-discovery" (Nichols 1994, 64).

In *Rambo III* (1988), self-discovery is effected through immersion in a Buddhist monastery; the "vehicle" is meditation. In *Emmanuelle,* the vehicle is sexual intercourse, cut loose from the ties of conventional, heterosexual monogamy. Within the film, a range of oppositions of intercourse are depicted: lesbian/heterosexual, married/adulterous, Thai/European, naked/clad, indoor/outdoor, watched/private. Certain themes emerge from these congeries of couples. The only sex acts in which participants are fully naked are the "legitimate" married heterosexual coupling of Jean and Emmanuelle and the "illegitimate" and threatening (to Jean, and to heterosexual sex and its institutions) coupling of Emmanuelle and Bee. This latter lovemaking is in turn mimicked by lesbian stage acts of Thai women. Emmanuelle and Bee's coupling stands out as the one romantic/sentimental liaison; the collapse of the relationship results in Jean's commentary to Emmanuelle that "love, the kind of exclusive passion they talk about, is not for us, it's too sad, too humiliating to accept that kind of dependency . . . you'll get revenge in other arms."

Thai male sexuality is in all cases violent or semiviolent. Thai men are always clothed, as are the women they fuck. Apart from an early scene of bourgeois married coupling (Jean and Emmanuelle), all European heterosexual encounters involve men who are fully clothed, with only their penises extruding for the act; in all cases women simply hitch up, or have raised, their skirts (and none appear to wear knickers: in Arianne's pseudo-rape, this is precisely the invitation of conjunction). Jean's quasi rape of Arianne mimics an earlier Thai-Thai rape and is juxtaposed to the sentimental encounter of Bee and Emmanuelle. Finally, Emmanuelle's liberation is a public rape, as she kneels before Mario, raises her skirt up over her back, and is fucked from the rear by the victorious Thai boxer—as his prize for winning—before Mario and the Thai audience (and the viewing audience; see plate 5.2). Through all of this, the only sexualized organs portrayed are breasts, and buttocks in the shot of cigarettes being inserted and "smoked" in the vagina of a woman on stage; even in this, the vulva and pubis are hidden. Anality and sodomic referents are sustained throughout the film, and this cigarette scene ties them to the rear-penetrative sex scenes involving Emmanuelle: both an anonymous airplane sex scene and the final "liberating" encounter. Also worth noting is the absence of what Burgin (1994) characterizes as the "paranoic space" of racism, in which context white women are to be protected and controlled to avoid rape by a black (here, Asian) man. Instead, the "delusional jealousy" is of lesbianism, and Thai men are inserted (literally and metaphorically) to dissolve the emotional investment of Emmanuelle's sexuality.

Thai female sexuality is largely implied. In the early pseudo-rape, the Thai woman is portrayed as animalistic in her erotic response to spying on Jean and Emmanuelle's love-making, in her "teased" resistance to coupling (one of a series of pseudo-rapes), and her orgasm. The Thai women who observe the live sex performances are passive voyeurs; the women on stage anticipate later depictions and popular suppositions that *Thai women will do anything,* and the explicit acts—both the vaginal cigarette "smoking" and the lesbian lovemaking—foreshadow the performances that had come to

Figure 5.2. Emmanuelle (Sylvie Kristel) with Mario (Alain Cuny) at the Thai boxing match. From *Emmanuelle* (Trinarca Films, 1974). Courtesy of Film Stills Archives, Museum of Modern Art, New York.

dominate the stages of Patpong and Pattaya by the early 1990s (Manderson 1992b), although not, as Dawson claims (1988), in the early to middle 1970s when *Emmanuelle* was made. No interaction between Thais and Europeans occurs at all outside of intercourse, and Thais are cast as the house servants of and subservient to Westerners. In each encounter, a new layer of race, sex/gender, and sexuality is underlined: we are led to understand that bourgeois sexuality (marital monogamy) constrains and that liberation is attained through the jettison of sentiment (romantic love) and embrace of anonymity, exploration, and animality. Thai men (or Thai Man) here are encapsulated by the notion of the "animal"; their brutish, penetrative sex allows no room for personal encounters nor the trappings of intimacy that might be implied by foreplay, undressing, or the exchange of words. They are always anonymous.

Emmanuelle is a didactic text, partly articulated by the men (Jean and Mario) in the film (though to a lesser degree also by certain women characters), and partly realized through the filmic narrative effected by the sequence of alternated couplings—framed moments of eroticism—in which the subordination of woman and subsumption of person by the body are the major messages. The argument, sustained through a series of polemic statements, is one of liberation through the rejection of bourgeois sexual relationships. As noted, for Emmanuelle this liberation is effected through the agency of Mario on behalf of Jean, the husband, and facilitated by Marie-Ange, who embodies an innocent, childish/animal sensuality ("She is my professor," says Emmanuelle),[12] and by Jean and Arianne. Each derides romantic love and its appurtenances, and seeks to free Emmanuelle of her naive sentimentality, reflected by her dependence on Jean and her interlude with Bee. Thus Mario postulates that "the road to liberation" is possible: "A life free of moral slavery, of taboos and all those repressive laws created by those who fear life, created by those imprisoned"; later, in the sole direct reference to "Oriental" sexual practice, he says,

> But of course it's true that Orientals consider bodily technique and control can be used to make contact with others, and with ourselves. We must loosen the bonds. We must liberate the screams that have been silenced for centuries. . . . Love to be real has got to be unnatural. The true definition of love is the enactment rather than the orgasm. Love between couples should be outlawed. Yes, every act of love must include a third person.

Emmanuelle finally accepts this ideological twist: of the final, public sexual encounter, she says "I'm a real woman now. I spit on the others, those who think sex is a dirty word, those who laugh in a stupid way."

It is clear from the description above, I hope, that *Emmanuelle* is *not* about Thailand; Thailand is simply the backdrop for a European pornographic fantasy. The film might have been set anywhere, as indeed other Emmanuelle films were. And yet, the film fed into an emerging image of Thailand as sex-haven, and this was not accidental. In many aspects, Thailand is the imagined Orient, "a world elsewhere, apart from the ordinary attachments, sentiments and values of *our* world in the West" (Said 1978, 190), a generic fantasy world of slaves, dancing girls and boys, a place of licentiousness, decadence, experiment, perversion, and satiation.[13] It became, as Said has so eloquently argued, the place "where one could look for sexual experience unobtainable in Europe." In time, for travelers, "oriental sex" was to become "as standard a commodity as any other available in the mass culture, with the result that readers and writers could have it if they wished without necessarily going to the Orient" (190). Hence emerged the novels that perpetuated these myths of licentiousness and liberation, and the performing arts that carried those ideas into different, popular forum: *The Mikado* (Gilbert and Sullivan 1885), *Madama Butterfly* (Puccini 1904), *Miss Saigon* (Boublil and Michel-Schonberg 1989). Thus Rana Kabbani (1986) argues that

> [t]o perceive the East as a sexual domain and to perceive the East as a domain to be colonised were complementary aspirations. This kind of narrative did not only reflect strong "racial" bias—it reflected deep-seated misogyny as well. Eastern women were described as objects which promised endless congress and provoked endless contempt.(59)

The Good Woman of Bangkok (1991)

Nichols (1994, 68) contrasts pornography—"a set of staged representations of desire (for more pornography)"—with ethnographic film—"a set of staged representations of knowledge (by means of more ethnographies)." In the case of *Emmanuelle,* despite the authenticating Bangkok imagery, the two remain largely distinct. In *The Good Woman of Bangkok,* the two merge, and sex is a commodity that is part of the tourist package.

The controversy that surrounds *The Good Woman of Bangkok* indeed relates to its "authenticity," in light of the filmmaker's biographic account in the prologue and his obvious involvement with Aoi in the film (hence Berry's sense of discomfort [1994, 22] upon realizing that part of the price of the ticket to view the film would go to defray O'Rourke's costs in hiring Aoi, the prostitute), compared with his implicit disclaimer in the credits through his description of the film as "documentary fiction." The point that has not been pursued in the critics' arguments about the film—which largely center around the political economy of sex work, heterosexual exploitation, and female agency—is the purpose of O'Rourke's description of the film genre; he does not deny his own involvement.[14]

In *The King and I,* Thai sexuality was represented as male. In *Emmanuelle,* the object focus was male, but moments of the film diverged to provide a summary representation of women's sexuality. Two decades later, the axis had shifted, and Thai men had been displaced almost entirely by Thai women in film, as they had been, it would appear, in practice. Smith (1971) stresses that the earliest model of sexual encounters were the marriages between American women and elite Thai men, but this was inverted with the arrival of American troops in the early 1960s, originally during short periods of leave from Vietnam and then as a result of their continued presence at bases in Thailand (Cohen 1982, 407; Dawson 1988; Pasuk 1982). Increasingly the sexual encounters involved American (and later other European) men and Thai women, although Bamber, Hewison, and Underwood (1993) make clear the historical context of these liaisons and the expansion of sex tourism. This inversion of sexual liaisons marks the evolution of Thai/Western relationships: political, economic, and social relations are symbolized by and mediated through women's bodies and sexual relations.

By the time that *The Good Woman of Bangkok* was made, sex tourism had escalated, and Thai women had become a blatant commodity (Cohen 1982; Wahnschafft 1982; Kleiber 1991; Hawkes and Hart 1993; Manderson 1995). In documentary films, the putative sexuality of Thai women had replaced Thai male sexuality as the cinematic subject, or rather, Thai women's sexuality had been collapsed into commodity sex. Thus O'Rourke explores in *The Good Woman of Bangkok,* as in his earlier films, "the commercialization of the tourist encounter . . . to the point of the commodification not merely of the handicrafts and the photographic image, but to the [indigenous] person" (MacCannell 1994, 102).[15] In *The Good Woman of Bangkok,* Thai male sexual behavior is alluded to in the commentaries of Aoi and her wise village aunt with respect to men's treatment of wives and daughters, and their patronage of bars and brothels also, but Thai men have no voice other than as blind singers and pimps at bar doors. Other films and documentaries—as produced in the West and concerned with commoditized sex—are silent about Thai men too, although by the late 1980s it is also true that Thai women's primary if not only roles in popular film are as objects: their commoditization is nearly absolute.

I have noted that the film has been described as autobiography (of the filmmaker, Dennis O'Rourke); reviews highlight O'Rourke's "emotional entanglement" with the main character, the prostitute Aoi.[16] In the prologic and epilogic texts, and his own vocal interceptions in the film, O'Rourke presents the film as fact, contextualized against the collapse of his marriage:

> The film-maker was forty-three, and his marriage had ended. He was trying to understand how love could be so banal and also profound. He came to Bangkok, the mecca for western men with fantasies of exotic sex and love without pain. He would meet a Thai prostitute and make a film about that.

The filmed stage work of the women of Patpong—Aoi and her friends—documents bar work observable in any bar in Thailand attracting a European or mixed clientele. The erotic dancing, ping-pong, and razor-blade acts are common on the night stages of Bangkok and other tourist centers, their misogyny and the characterization of female sex and desire form the palate of European taste of Thailand. Here, the exotic and erotic are merged; so too are the genres of traveler's film/ethnographic film and pornography. The collapse of nation and bestiality is implicit in behaviors and reported or observable encounters (the snake act in Patpong is the crudest of this kind; see Manderson 1992b), although this imagery draws on a wider repertoire of the Oriental woman's insatiability (see Said 1978; Suleri 1992; Marcus 1992; Broinowski 1992, 35, 39, 105–8), and in a panoply of tales of other sexual encounters with the animal world (dogs for women, sheep and chickens for men) used to ridicule and reduce minority, poor (and presumed mentally deficient) peoples. All of these reflect the crude collapse of a vague geography and moral essentialism into an "Asia" that Broinowski, following Kabbani (1986), refers to as an "illicit space," "an Adventure Zone for adults in which civilized norms of Western male behaviour could be abandoned and taboos breached" (Broinowski 1992, 39).

The films I have considered here evoke certain moral sagas. In *The King and I,* Asian male lust (political, not sexual) is contained (or more correctly, defeated) by the white woman; in *Emmanuelle,* white woman's liberation is effected through the corporeality of Thai men (although through the intellectual will of her own men). In *The Good Woman of Bangkok,* the dilemma is a modern one—alternative stories, contrasting positions—and the moral text is the viewers' (our own). Controversy about the film has been substantial, as noted, centering on voyeurism:[17] Is O'Rourke making a film about himself? Is he the only voyeur/exploiter? Is it a film of all men (or all foreign men), who therefore must share with O'Rourke any disapprobation? Or are we—Western film viewers, or Western consumers of the film and of Thailand as a tourist destination—all equally voyeurs and equally parties to Aoi's demise, poverty, embitterment, and entrapment? (See plate 5.3.)

Categorization of the film as "documentary fiction" implies, however, alternative readings, flagging for viewers (anthropologists, at least) that this is not ethnographic film, at least according to definitions that insist upon minimal distortion of behavior, minimal time distortion and continuity distortion, synchronous sound, cultural and physical contextualization of behaviour, and whole bodies rather than parts (Weinberger 1994, 7). O'Rourke deliberately diverges: the film is edited, its continuity is broken, Aoi's accounts are cut and spliced, the soundtrack is a Mozart aria rather than rowdy traffic sounds of night Bangkok, the body is objectified and compartmentalized.[18] The technique or approach is that of montage (Marcus 1994), allowing the filmmaker to break with a conventional narrative mode and its artificiality. Hence we have O'Rourke's and Aoi's dialogue (his insistence that he will only buy her a farm if she ceases prostitution; her interrogation of his motives), but also his rejection of chronology as well as the cinematographic conventions of ethnographic film. O'Rourke is part of the story, but he de-

Figure 5.3. Aoi's fingers frame her gaze at the filmmaker (O'Rourke) from her blind eye. From *The Good Woman of Bangkok* (O'Rourke and Associates, 1991). Courtesy of Film Stills Archives, Museum of Modern Art, New York.

clares far less innocence than most ethnographic filmmakers, and the discourses of the films are more transparent and contentious as a result.[19]

To some extent, *The Good Woman of Bangkok* offers an analysis similar to those of published sociological studies of prostitution in Thailand (e.g., Khin Thitsa 1980; Muecke 1992; Pasuk 1982; Sukanya 1983, 1984, 1988; Odzer 1994; and for a review of the latter, Rosca 1995) and supplemented by documentaries made about Thai prostitution and related sex work. In general these argue the necessity of understanding Thai sex work in the context of the political economy of the country, although they vary to the extent that they accord women agency also. The film *Slaves of Progress* (1984), for example, speaks of women working in the bars of Patpong from "poverty-stricken villages," picked up by men, held against their will, and sold to the highest bidder. *Foreign Bodies* (1988), along similar lines, argues for a complex set of circumstances that include rural poverty and indebtedness, the importance of the tourist industry, the establishment of a foreign-oriented sex industry as a consequence of the Vietnam war, and the continuing, subsequent American presence, together with—they argue—the subordination of women and their lack of negotiating power within Thai society (women are "chattels under Buddhism"). Several studies emphasize too the cycle in which women are caught. Despite some evidence that women are able to move from prostitution back to conventional village life when their earning potential within the sex industry decreases or other circumstances change (e.g., Embree 1950, 186; Manderson 1992b; Muecke 1992), others are skeptical of this and note the usual downward mobility of women involved in various paying liaisons (Cohen 1982, 424; see also Gray 1990). In *Foreign Bodies,* Bee asks, "What can I do? I can't go back to being a virgin"; in *The Good Woman of Bangkok,* Aoi's aunt says, "She is so damaged now. No man in this village would marry her."

In many respects, *The Good Woman* breaks through the sanitization of prostitution by insisting upon different interpretations, understandings, and responses to sex work not only within Thailand, but also by individual woman at different times (see also Law, chap. 10 in this volume). Aoi is caught in the contradictions of her circumstances:

> Aoi: They're drunkards and morons but we have to go.
> Aunty: Thai men are no different, all the adult men go. Don't think Thai men don't go. Our men know how to go and have fun. Chinese or Thai, it's the same. The politicians also like going to the bars. They all go to the bars.

Later, Aoi says,

> I do not want to be a bad woman. In my conscience, I am not. . . .
> But I am fragile and weak. And I'm very naive. I have to work in the

bar. I am very hurt because I must act against my will. I have to close my eyes and force myself to do it for money. I have to take responsibility for so many things. I go to the temple and pray that the gods will understand and take pity on me.

And about love, she says,

I don't know what's love. What I love, I don't know. I want love but I know me. Me is no good. No people can love me. I don't have anything good . . . only bad. Who can love me? No. Say love me, I don't believe.

Aoi and her fellow workers may be caught in a web of poverty and trickery, indebtedness and fraud. The men in O'Rourke's film are not so complex; their spot interviews offer us stereotypic vignettes of what "European" men are like, while reminding us too of Hwang's comment in *M. Butterfly* (Garber 1992, 127) that "the West has a sort of an international rape mentality towards the East," and of the way in which racism and sexism, and fantasies of imperialism and colonialism, coalesce (see also Kondo 1990). Thus an "Indian" traveler (without stated nationality) compares Thai women favorably to women elsewhere in Asia and his sampling of them; the Dutch tourist comments,

I'm talking in Dutch about the girls, the girls are very friendly and it's very pleasant here . . . with the gorgeous women. Holiday in Thailand is the best way, yeah, I think Thailand holiday is nice, very nice.

The Englishman says,

It's the same in England. You know, you take a lady out, wine her and dine her, you take her home, you pay your money and you take her home, it's the same thing, it's the same everywhere.

The American says,

American women are fucking bitches. You don't want to deal with American women—these women are the best, their minds have the right attitude. There's no girl in the world (other than in Bangkok) that will give you a shower, give you a blow job, fuck your brains out, [and] fold your clothes with a smile on her face.

The Australian says,

They are prostitutes and we feel sorry for them. They're very poor, but we love 'em. I feel sorry for them because they have to resort to what they do. I think that it's best that we do go with them because what we give them . . . it helps them . . . if it helps them, it's not so wrong.

The oldest girl comes to Thailand (i.e., Bangkok), they try to get a job and this is all they can really get because they haven't got an education. So to break a vicious cycle they send the money home to get an education for the younger ones, which is good, because eventually there won't be this, they won't need to do this.

Here O'Rourke uses satire to establish identity, staging national stereotypes—recognizable enough—to mock those who go on sex tours. MacCannell (1994, 104) argues that "[p]arody . . . potentially raises the consciousness of an audience that is the butt of it"; this has clearly been true when the film has been viewed among Australian audiences, where men have been shocked, hurt, and confused about their complicity in international sex tourism as a result.[20]

But the parodist must take risks, as MacCannell (1994) notes. Indeed, as an Australian sex tourist, O'Rourke aligns himself with his compatriots and offers the same logic as the young men in the film—*he* buys Aoi land in an attempt to get her to "break (this) vicious cycle," despite her warning to him not to "help me if you want something in return. I don't need that." The Australian attitude to the women whose sexual services they buy—their apologetic social welfare—fits with a more general minimization of social distance by Australians, and perhaps also captures some recognition of the proximity of Asia to Australia (the Australian men wave "Hello, Mum" into the camera lens) and its permanence. This is a point to which Broinowski (1992, 39) alludes, for while the "Illicit Space of Asia" was an elusive fantasy of abandonment, allure, and repugnance for other Western men, it was proximate and real, hence also more problematic, for Australian men.[21]

Chris Berry (1994) argues this more fully; for him, *The Good Woman of Bangkok* is an exploration of "Australia *in* Asia." Berry argues that the film is a "cautionary metaphor about the bankruptcy of the white savior myth, for it is O'Rourke that [*sic*] is abandoned and left behind by its persistence as much as Aoi" (18), but it is also about the Asian-Pacific region and Australia's role within the region—undermined by sex tourism and rendered as "a dangerous place in which Australians are in danger of being corrupted and/or seduced, frequently through the metaphor of a sexual relationship with a local" (36, 39).

Conclusion

The analysis of representation in the context of this chapter and the treatment of film as text freeze action, since such analysis is unable to explore the consumption of such representation—"what the cultural consumer 'makes' or 'does'" with the images and narrative, as de Certeau (1984, xii) has argued. However, I am suggesting that the representations of sex, sexuality, and race within popular film constitute, or shape, or inform people's expectations of place and interactions with the Other. Since these are Oriental texts, they also reflect contemporary cultural themes at the point of production; that is, they speak of Western—American, French, and Australian—debates about sex and power, and hence are of interest at the level of the articulation of ideology.

The films are historically situated social documents which illustrate a transforming Western commentary on Thailand and Thai sexuality. While the creation of the Orient and its icons has its roots in nineteenth-century imperialism in particular, its appropriation has been pervasive, and the images that stand for "Thailand" have come to be recognized within the country as well as abroad. This is especially so for women, who are used representationally to market food and beverage, clothing, holiday resorts, airline services, business equipment, and so on, leading internally as well as overseas to "the identification of Thai culture itself with certain images of womanhood" (Reynolds 1994, 75; Manderson 1995). Moreover, within Thailand as well as beyond, veracity of race and place is irrelevant. Reynolds notes the preference for "the Eurasian face" in beauty contests and in magazines, representing "a kind of pan-Asian model of beauty that suits the exporters of Thai products to Asian markets" (1994, 75) and reinforces the notion of an Orient that is unattached to any historic/geographic place, culture, or people.

In the films discussed above, the narratives are generic, modern travelers' tales that allow viewers to insinuate themselves (histories or fantasies) into the text. Representations of Thai sexuality within these films, and their collapse of race and sex, facilitate and legitimize sex tourism. The images from these sources—and others of their genre—shape the fantasies and myths of race and sexuality that can then be explored in the liminal spaces of overseas holidays.

Acknowledgments

This chapter evolved from an earlier paper, "Intersections: Western Representations of Thailand and the Commodification of Sex and Race," prepared for and presented at the Wenner-Gren Symposium, "Theorizing Sexuality: Evolution, Culture, and Development," convened by Gilbert Herdt and Paul Abramson and held 19–27 March 1993 at Cascais, Portugal. Versions of this chapter were presented at a conference, "The State, Sexuality and Reproduction in Asia and the Pacific," convened by Margaret Jolly and Kalpana Ram of the Australian National University (July 1993), another conference, "Representations of Culture, Sexuality, and Marginalization," convened by Sandra Gifford of La Trobe University and held in Melbourne (July 1994), and to women's studies classes in 1994 and 1995 at the University of Queensland. I am very grateful to various colleagues and friends, particularly Margaret Jolly, for their comments and suggestions. I also wish to acknowledge the generous assistance of Terry Geesken of the Film Stills Archive, Museum of Modern Art, for her assistance with the plates.

CHAPTER SIX

Primal Dream: Masculinism, Sin, and Salvation in Thailand's Sex Trade

ANNETTE HAMILTON

A Rorschach blot of the map of Thailand can liberate some interesting images in the mind of a westerner: "two legs and the trunk of a headless female; Bangkok the pubic tuft; the Chao Phraya River the fetid entry into that sprawling area of darkness . . ."

John Cadet, *Occidental Adam, Oriental Eve*

Libidinal Thailand

The libidinalization of Thailand has long been recognized by travel agents, journalists, social commentators, and tourists on "holidays." A principal attraction is the availability of sexual liaisons with partners working in the sex industry. These partners might be male (see Jackson, chap. 7 in this volume), female, or some other category, but in public images it is the alluring, very young woman who is the central icon for the quintessential Thai experience.[1] This image is circulated in many forms, including tourist brochures, airline advertisements, guidebooks, elementary conversation handbooks,[2] and, of course, by word of mouth. The extent of the Western[3] identification of Thailand with sex for sale, or "play-for-pay," as it is often referred to in Bangkok, has come as a real shock to many members of Thai middle-class and educated society. The issue was brought to a head in the "Longman's dictionary affair" of 1993, when Bangkok was defined as being "famous for its temples and other beautiful buildings and also often mentioned as a place where there are a lot of prostitutes." Respectable members of Thai society were outraged: the entry was described as "against moral principle," and many letters were published in the local press. All Longman's publications were banned in Thailand until the company "complied with a Government request to 'correct' the entry in its Dictionary of English Language and Culture" (*Bangkok Post* 22 November 1994, 3).

Many Westerners, including residents of Thailand, regard this episode as an example of Thai hypocrisy. There may be some truth to this, but foreign interpretations of "the real Thailand" are in fact insulated from the majority of Thai people, who have no direct contact with the *farang*-oriented flesh trade and no idea of what goes on in the *farang* bars of Patpong, Soi Cowboy, and Pattaya.[4]

Since most of the women working as prostitutes are from poor families in distant areas, or may be ethnically non-Thai (e.g., Chinese, Burmese, hill-tribes), their activities have little relevance to the urban middle or upper classes, and their fates have until recently caused little public concern.[5] Of course it is well-recognized that Thai men frequently visit prostitutes, but this recognition remains within the circuits of the publicly unspoken, like so much else in Thailand (cf. Hamilton 1991). Although there is some uncertainty about the extent to which rural Thai males use the services of sex workers in brothels (e.g., Lyttleton 1994a), there seems to be little doubt that a significant proportion of all Thai men will have at least some experience of commercial sex, and that for many this is a regular and normal aspect of their lives (cf. Fordham 1993a, 1993b). The situation of women in brothels servicing a largely Thai clientele seems to be more characterized by coercion than that of bar-girls and "hostesses" who entertain either foreigners or elite Thai or Sino-Thai, and the working conditions are much worse, with very much lower pay and little or no medical attention. In the far south such brothels primarily service Malaysian "tourists"; these brothels are reputed to be among the worst in the country, with many young girls lured or forced into sex slavery. Thus there is a very wide range of activities and conditions which are lumped together as "prostitution" in Thailand, obscuring the significant differences both for sex workers and clients. However, for many foreigners, residents, or visitors, the sexually focused bar scene in Bangkok or other major tourist destinations is central to the imagining and experience of Thailand (Manderson 1992b, 1995), although this fact has not been widely known among "respectable" Thais.[6]

Moreover, "commercialized" sexual relationships are pervasive in Thailand. Exclusive bars for women, for example, provide contacts with attractive young men; middle-aged women often "patronize" young male performers in traditional theatre arts. Many Western female tourists engage in liaisons with Thai men which inevitably have a commercial or financial aspect. It is assumed that anybody, male or female, young or old, will prefer to have a "companion" than otherwise, and it is also assumed that the worth of such companionship should be recognized financially. The deep cultural relationship between money and love in Thailand has hardly been explored, but it affects all aspects of human exchange, including parent-child ties. This indeed is one reason that young women give for assenting to work in the sex trade: their narratives inevitably refer to their obligations to support their parents, specifically their mothers. This is not necessarily because the parents are "poor," but because the parents have spent money bringing up the daughter, and it is her duty to repay the debt (cf. Muecke 1992; Whittaker 1994).

The money-love relation becomes particularly problematic in sexual transactions between *farang* and bar girl. As in the Philippines (see Neumann 1979; Law, chap. 10 in this volume), many girls spend periods in and out of the bar trade according to the state of their current relations with a *farang* who has become a "boyfriend" rather than a client. Dr. Yos Santasombat, associate professor in anthropology and sociology at Thammasat University, has touched on these issues. He describes the process whereby girls may enter into relations with men for purely financial reasons, but they nonetheless may go on to form more or less lasting attachments. While maintenance of the relationship is contingent on adequate financial support, emotional attachments and desires may play an important role, and marriage remains a potential outcome in many cases (see Krich 1989).

> The line between money and love becomes very fuzzy, because the money itself cannot be distinguished between signs of affection, tender caring and love itself. Mutual or material dependence frequently engenders some sort of an emotional attachment on the part of the girl herself.
>
> So, what starts out as a money-oriented transactional arrangement becomes a mixed involvement, a more complicated relationship . . . it somehow gradually detaches itself from the material aspects or the money. . . .
>
> The farang's sense of the world, his cognitive map, is thrown into chaos because he cannot make sense of what is going on in this deal. He cannot apply his concept of prostitution to the Thai situation. And he somehow would feel very uncertain whether a girl is with him for love or for money. (Yos Santasombat, in Walker and Ehrlich 1992, 15–17)

The global HIV/AIDS crisis has prompted foreign scholars to recognize the importance of Thai sexual practices and the prevalence of commercial sexual relations. As in Africa, the pattern of rapid spread of infection through multiple channels, notably heterosexual intercourse, has made Thailand an important site for examining the relations between cultural, social, and economic parameters implicated in the spread of the disease. Some of these are only now beginning to be understood: for example, the organization of the trade in girls, which spreads far beyond the boundaries of the country (Gray 1993); the attitudes to commercial sex among young males in the provinces (Fordham 1993a, 1993b); attitudes to prostitution in the context of mother-daughter relations (Muecke 1992); responses to the anti-HIV/AIDS public education campaign (Lyttleton 1994a); and Buddhist accounts of AIDS and attitudes towards homosexuality (Jackson 1993). There is also an extensive Thai literature, largely from a medical and epidemiological standpoint (but see also Sukanya 1988). While these works are concerned with Thai sociocultural factors in commercial sex, relatively few studies have focused on various aspects of the interactions between Westerners and Thai women. Among these are Cohen 1982, 1986, and 1988, and Manderson 1992b, 1995, and her chapter in this volume. Considerably more attention to the topic is apparent in films, both documentary and popular/sensational, and in magazine articles (see references and discussion in Manderson 1995 and chap. 5 in this volume).

Although there is a substantial level of voluntarism in women's participation in the *farang*-oriented sex trade, from an economic point of view each sexual transaction is the end-point of a highly organized market that is oriented largely toward heterosexual white males. The Bangkok experience provides substantial profits for those in the tourist, bar, and restaurant trades, as well as those supplying and managing the sex industry. Many foreigners manage bars and restaurants, in conjunction with Thai wives or partners, and hence provide conditions which will attract their compatriots. Thus some bars are known for their Australian clientele; others attract Germans, French, and so on. This pattern has a long history in Bangkok especially.

The tourism boom began in 1987 as a result of government policies signaled by the "1987 Visit Thailand Year" campaign, which clearly targeted the traveler interested in sexual experience. Even today, promotional videos designed to lure tourists, slickly produced in the latest video-clip style, include images of beautiful young women, rural and urban, as central elements of Thailand's essential character.

Tourist agencies provide prospective male visitors with photograph albums containing pictures of attractive ladies who will act as escorts or girlfriends. This has been particularly well organized in Germany; the affluent tourist can select his preferred partner through file photos or videos without having to undergo the potentially humiliating experience of making direct connections with women in bars and hotels. Escort services are widely available from hotel front desks, and even in respectable or family-oriented hotels it is possible to summon a girl to a guest's room with very little fuss or notice. Hotels have contract arrangements with providers of services, and the girls must comply with standards of behavior and appearance. Girls are required to hand in their identity cards at the front desk and to collect them again as they leave. In major hotels these activities are carried on with discretion, and seldom is it apparent to the casual visitor that the girl going up or down in the lift is a sex worker on her way to or from a "house-call."[7] Most provincial hotels have coffee shops, nightclubs, or "Karaoke Bars" where arrangements can be made between customers and girls. In such hotels the lower floors are reserved for people engaging in sexual trans-actions, the upper floors for "respectable" guests. In addition there are the ubiquitous "curtain hotels," which provide privacy for the patron's car and cater largely to a local clientele.

It is also well known that many companies and industries with large single-male workforces, especially in difficult and isolated areas, provide holidays in Thailand as part of their "rest and recreation" conditions. In the stories to be discussed here, the worker on the off-shore oil rig is a frequent character.[8] The reason for choosing Bangkok is obvious: the worker on leave can have limitless access to sex, alcohol, more alcohol, and more sex. Many tourists return to Thailand frequently as a result of the sexual experi-ences found there, and because of relationships with one or more girl-friends. Some seek a means to become more permanent residents, as is the case with the many *farang* bar owners. One lovelorn swain from Finland even proposed to become a *tuk-tuk* driver (Walker and Ehrlich 1992, 109).[9]

It is commonly thought that the fundamental attraction of the Thai woman arises from her apparent willingness to satisfy conventional male desires: not merely sexually, but in terms of her willingness to carry out tasks associated with nurture and caring behavior. The example of the drunken American tourist who praises the Thai prostitute for not only having sex with him but folding up his pants afterwards, is mentioned in Manderson (chap. 5 in this volume). The inherently confusing and ambiguous nature of these relationships provides an experience which is reflected upon by the *farang* community at many levels, not least in writing.

Bangkok by Text

The Bangkok experience is written about in a variety of ways. The "Trink Page," a feature published every Saturday in the *Bangkok Post* (the principal English-language newspaper for the expatriate community in Thailand) is possibly the best known. Bernard Trink, a long-term resident and expert in the bar scene, provides "exemplary tales," reporting in detail what is going on in the various bars and clubs around town and in Pattaya, where a new batch of girls is to be found, which foreign bar-owners have sold out or started up new businesses, which strip-joints overcharge for "entertain-ment" or harass the casual visitor, where the live sex shows may be found and under what conditions, which bar owner or female Thai partner is putting on a birthday party with free drinks or food. He also provides tips on how to deal with the manifold infuriating aspects of expatriate life in Bangkok, the latest scams and rip-offs, and the eternal "visa problems." His page is rounded off with some rather curious tale, perhaps drawn from recent scientific research or some philosophical quirk, and then the signature phrase in capital letters appears: "BUT I DON'T GIVE A HOOT." The "Trink Page" and its many years of publication are a testament to the centrality of the Bangkok bar scene to the expatriate community, and the degree to which this aspect of Bangkok life is simply taken for granted.[10]

A different sense, one of pathos mixed with banality, can be gained from reading the letters which pass between *farang* and their girlfriends. Most letters are written in English, and since few Thai girls can read or write English, it often happens that any long-term resident with both Thai and English is called upon to read and interpret the letters, and to send replies. Some of the insights available from this textualization have been discussed by Cohen (1986). A collection of letters between bar girls and their foreign boyfriends, under the title "Hello My Big Big Honey!" (Walker and Ehrlich 1992), presents the letters together with interviews with the bar girls who receive them.

A large number of texts dealing with the *farang*—Thai woman connection are less well-known.[11] These are novels and collections of short stories, written generally from the perspective of the foreign male resident in Thailand. Published in limited paperback editions, in Bangkok or Chiangmai, they are sold in bookshops with an English-language clientele.[12] There seem to be no comparable works by Europeans (French, Germans, Italians, etc.) on sale in Bangkok, although they may well exist in their home countries. Likewise I am not aware of comparable works by Japanese, Middle Easterners, or others frequenting the Thai sex trade, although they could of course exist.

A number of the authors referred to here are well known in other fields, being long-term residents of Thailand, with extensive experience of the country from a number of points of view, as expressed in their stories. Some write of everyday life in Thailand, largely from a Thai point of view (e.g., Smithies 1993), but the majority concentrate on themes arising from expatriate life in the Bangkok demimonde. Among these are Hinds 1989; Cadet 1981, 1987; and Piprell 1989, 1991, 1993. Some are thrillers or adventure stories with a Thai setting (e.g., Moore 1993; Haylock 1990); others are comic tales drawn from the author's life (e.g., Eckhardt 1991) or dealing with imagined Thai characters (Kuaytaek 1993).

Stories of the demimonde have an extraordinary sameness to them. The typical story is usually written as a third-person narrative constructed around a male subject who "centers" the story. He is almost always depicted as a

Bangkok Old Hand, the exile or expatriate habitué of the bars of the capital, a man of the world who finds an addictive pleasure in the hotbeds of sin where he spends his free time and an awareness of a heightened form of "being alive" unavailable elsewhere. In spite of this "low-life" quality, the central figure is an educated middle-class person, making his way (usually for unstated reasons) in the strange and exotic milieu of Bangkok. He moves in a world of like-minded peers, an exclusively male group which meets regularly in certain bars where much of the action takes place. These groups have a shifting membership, as one or another associate leaves Bangkok, often after trouble with police or bar girls, or as a result of death in ludicrous circumstances, as happens to Sid, squashed to death by a bar girl after their *tuk-tuk* overturns (*Sid's Wake*, in Piprell 1991). The central character offers a philosophical approach to life in Bangkok. Sometimes he engages in moral discourses against which other expatriates are judged too low, such as the leering pedophile Bill in *Tukataa* (in Hinds 1989). The Bangkok Old Hand, unlike other visitors and more "respectable" expatriates, truly understands "real life" in Thailand.[13] Whatever his origins, he feels alienated from them. The impossibility of "going back" is stressed, in spite of the difficulties of staying in Thailand. Repeatedly it is stated, or implied, that the experience of this kind of life has been transformative, opening up a register of truth for the male subject; in this place he was able to become himself, to realize himself, to express fully his deepest desires, and to discover the primal pleasures which only untrammeled access to feminine sexuality, as well as uncomplicated male companionship of like-minded peers, could offer him. Of course the other side of this is the likelihood that many such men are in fact "losers," men who couldn't make it in their home environments, but this perspective is suppressed in favor of the idea of a kind of moral and transcendent self-discovery. Thus, a central motif of these narratives, whether they are merely a set of stories reflecting "real life" or more extended inventions with plots, characters, and denouement, or even "comedy" tales of the perils of being a *farang* in Thailand, is the sustaining masculine identity available in this world, which contrasts, implicitly or explicitly, with the lack of a similar sense of being "at home," that is, in "the West."

This masculinity may be marked by a profound misogyny expressed towards the "Western" woman in particular, who appears sometimes at the edge of the Bangkok world; for example, there is the English girl Daphne who persistently believes Frank will marry her, since he has told his mother he leads a bachelor life in Bangkok (*Mother Makes a Match*, in Piprell 1991). More direct misogyny may be introduced through a character who expresses extreme views to some ambivalent acclaim from the group of male peers. For example, "Dexy" is "a beer-bellied, bandy-legged, foul-mouthed

whoremaster and offshore oil platform manager" (Piprell 1991, 46). He has
a distinctive philosophy with respect to marriage:

> Don't marry nobody. . . . A woman ain't nothing but a life-support
> system for a pussy, anyhow. Yuh know what I mean? And what do
> you want to buy a cow for, anyways, when milk's so cheap? (49)

Many stories seek to persuade the reader that the narrator or central character is not such a bad person; on the contrary, he is actually a very good
person. The reader is led to understand that the Thai woman too is a good
person, sadly misunderstood and mistreated by her own family, her own
society, her own social milieu, and indeed by everyone but the narrator.

The Essential Woman

Central to these narratives is the desire and expectation of true love, constantly expressed, which the narrator or another character hopes to find
with one or another Thai woman, his struggles to obtain and keep that love,
his puzzlement at the incomprehensible responses of the woman, and finally
his despair at being unable to "rescue" his love object from the life to which
she seems to have consigned herself. The Thai woman is constructed as "the
essential woman"—possessing an essence which women in the West have
long forgotten, if in fact they ever really had it. Hence the frequent references to "Eve," against which the male character is "Adam." This woman
is young, slender, beautiful, delicate; her legs, and hair, and breasts are described in repetitive detail; she is kind and loving, and exciting in a way
Western women simply could not be; she may know sexual tricks which
bring a man to heights of delight. She is not interested in his appearance:
he can be bald, paunchy, thin, bearded, aging, but the Thai woman as constructed in these narratives pays no attention to this. On the other hand, she
does pay attention to the man's financial abilities: but because of the differential between her needs and his abilities to pay, almost any foreign man is
a "rich" man and therefore a "powerful" man. It is inevitably because of
his wealth that he is able to launch himself into campaigns of "salvation" of
the woman. He can buy her or her family property such as rice-fields (as
did Dennis O'Rourke for Aoi, in *The Good Woman of Bangkok* [1991]); he
can pay her family's debts and expenses, and her siblings' educational costs
(which protects them from having to work in Bangkok bars for their future
living); he can buy her presents, such as gold chains, which give her some
financial security; he can pay for her to be educated in a trade or profession,
or he can simply provide her with a regular sum of money to get her out
of the bar scene and thus free her from the life of sordid bondage which
otherwise would remain her lot.

In these respects, the ideal woman can call forth an ideal man. The man's self-esteem is immensely enhanced, within the conventional Western masculinist imaginary, by being able to engage in these relationships. He can have a younger, beautiful woman, or as many of them as he wants. He is certain of being able to have sex with them because that is what the relationship is all about. He is able to experience a full range of unusual sexual pleasures, because the woman is skilled in providing them, offering proof of her genuine femininity. Furthermore, he is able to adopt a position of superiority both to the woman concerned and to the society which has produced her. Unlike her family and compatriots, he does not want to see her remain in the flesh trade: he can be a Sir Galahad, rescuing her from her degradation, replacing the stream of drunken customers with an exclusive fidelity to himself. Even if relatively poor by Western standards, he is rich by her standards, and so he has the financial ability to play the rescuer role, to offer the Thai woman a salvation which she so sorely needs. The perils of life for women in these situations are often referred to in episodes of violence and degradation. Frequently the male narrator or central character is called upon to perform some sustaining favor for one of his ex-girlfriends who has got into difficulties with another client, a pimp, the police, or some other threatening person. He willingly performs these services when he can, taking pity on her suffering while recognizing his inability to really bring about any transformation in her experiences, although he still aspires to bring about such transformations for his current girlfriend. The decent central characters are shown as sensitive and polite, more concerned for the dignity of the bar girls than are other men (such as the drunken German in the story Nit, in Hinds 1989). Germans come in for a particularly strong negative depiction in these stories: their English is parodied, their physical characteristics lampooned, and their behavior depicted as disgusting in the extreme. Rudi, the German in Nit, teases the new seventeen-year old bar girl by placing one hundred baht notes in his shirt and pants pockets, daring her to extract them with her teeth. Since his clothes are dirty and he smells, this is particularly cruel. When Rudi is reprimanded by the American Jim for his poor behavior, he repeatedly remarks that he is on vacation. Finally Jim loses patience and punches him in his huge belly. He vomits everywhere, and the bar girl stoops down to wipe him clean (Hinds 1989, 49–56). Thus the Anglo customers are depicted as a positive benefit to the social scene, as against others who do not know how to conduct themselves in these circumstances. On the other hand, it never seems to occur to them that they are engaged in anything sordid, or that their own presence contributes in any way to the victimhood of the girls. On the contrary, the views expressed are often similar to those of the young Australians in *The Good Woman of Bangkok*—views that suggest they are doing the girls a favor by patronizing them, for example, because it helps out their families and means that others will not have to enter the trade (see Manderson, chap. 5 in this volume for these remarks).

Speech and Desire

The preceding aspects are predictable enough within masculinist imaginary. However what also emerges is the strange way in which this ideal "feminine" woman nonetheless resists a man's desires, manifested through her speech, which is "not-speech," or not the speech of his desire. The great majority of women are depicted as speaking only "bar-girl" English, which means that they are unable to converse with foreigners except in a most limited, stilted, and stereotypical fashion. This matters profoundly, because, unable to speak, they cannot reveal their true selves. Many men in the stories pay substantial sums to have their girlfriends study to learn English. Similarly, numerous letter-writers in Walker and Ehrlich (1992) say that the money they are sending to their girlfriends is for this purpose. Although many of the male characters state that, unlike male tourists and new-chums, they can indeed speak Thai, it is clear that their capability is extremely limited. Thus, the normal framework of intimate human communication is rendered impossible, and the *farang*-Thai relation is marked by the absence or impossibility of "intimate speech." Yet, the difficulties of speaking in these relationships involve more than just an inability to "speak the same language." The Thai woman is depicted as avoiding conversation, more importantly avoiding questions and answers. The insistent Western lover plies her with questions about where she has been, what she has done, what she intends—but she avoids answering, turns away, changes the subject. The dominating interrogative power of the male is undercut by the avoidance of speech by the woman.[14] Where the woman is depicted as able to speak good English (as well as German, Japanese, or whatever), there is a twist to the tale. Pawn, for example, has had a university education but is unable to find work that pays as well as the flesh trade. The foreigner Chet is falling in love with her, meeting her at bookshops, sharing a taste for literature, but she puts him off time after time. One night he goes into her bar and is told she has killed herself. When he asks why, he is told she was tired of being a "lady-man." Thus he discovers that his literary love was a transvestite, or *kathoey*.

The avoidance of speech by the "essential woman" adds to her allure and mystery. She is not devoted to the ceaseless round of rational discussion, demand, insistence, requirement, justification, and so on which is taken to characterize relationships with Western women. On the other hand, the male subject never knows what is going on, and this, in another way, creates an insoluble dilemma for his projects. His mere bodily pleasure is readily available, but the final, triumphant moral pleasure of enforcing the woman's salvation is refused him. Furthermore, the longer he stays in Bangkok and the more deeply he engages with this underworld, the more he becomes aware that, far from being the passive figures of his desire, these women have intentions of their own. They lie: the narrators or central characters discover quickly enough that the ailing mother and the seven siblings don't exist, or don't exist in the way they have been depicted. The ceaseless demands for money, the sob stories on which these demands are based, the insistence that the man is a kind loving man with a good heart, come to be seen as a ruse for the continued extraction of financial benefits from him (see Odzer 1994).

Yet even this does not seem to undercut the virtues of these women; perhaps in this respect, it merely confirms the masculinist understanding of what women, all women, after all are "really" like. Seldom are any strong protestations or recriminations expressed when it becomes apparent that the stream of financial support has not gone where it was supposed to go, and above all that the woman has returned again to the bar life from which the central character has done everything to rescue her—as in *The Good Woman of Bangkok*. Rather there is a kind of weary disappointment, a bemusement: this woman is not the perfect woman, after all. Let's go to the bar, and see if we can find another woman who is.

The repetitive patterns of these relationships, far more than the usual prostitute-client encounters in the West, seemingly establish a set of paradigms around masculinity, identity, and experience from which the male subject is unable to extricate himself. This life expresses at once an absolute promise of liberation and an inevitable context of failure: failure to achieve the "rescue" of the woman, and finally failure of the self. Hidden behind these narratives is always the awareness that the final fate of the Bangkok Old Hand is to sink into a delirium of alcoholism, to spend the last of his days propping up a dismal bar and being fleeced by the next generation or two of bar girls, still able to stir the fantasy of his masculinity into life.

Man Writes Woman

The refusal of speech by the woman leads to another odd textual maneuver. Narratives often present the "female" perspective, that is, the purported view of the woman engaged in these transactions. The position of the male author is submerged within another voice, one which appears to provide the "explanations" for the incomprehensible behavior of the women. In this effort to subsume himself into the feminine position, the male author turns his view around onto himself, and onto how he (and other *farang* males) might appear to the women they are involved with. This is very reminiscent of the strategy used in *The Good Woman of Bangkok,* where Aoi is made to give her account of how she sees her life and the men who occupy it, while the filmmaker hovers out of sight at the edge of the frame. I have suggested elsewhere that this idea of the man entering the persona of the "fallen woman" has a long genealogy in Western literature—for example, in Flaubert's presentation of Madame Bovary *as if* he were part of her being—and may well be understood as the adoption of a position of masochism normally associated with femininity (see Hamilton, in press). The extent of this textual maneuver varies among the works being considered here; it is central to some and virtually absent in others. However it creates an odd and disturbing counterpoint to the assertive masculinism of the genre. The demand for comprehensibility, for making sense of the way these relationships develop and are curtailed, forces the author into giving what he understands to be a woman's explanation—into thinking like a woman.

The basis on which these authors write is very interesting. Recall that one of the principal issues in the debate around O'Rourke's *The Good Woman of Bangkok* concerned the question of whether he was "telling the truth" or not. The expectation that a film dealing with such a touchy subject should be ethnographic and therefore true was undercut by the filmmaker's description of the film as "documentary fiction." On the other hand, Thai viewers interpreted the whole film as a fiction and refused to believe it was based on a real situation at all (see Hamilton, in press). In constructing the relationship between *farang* man and Thai woman, the "real" position of the writer or narrator is seldom made clear. Rather, there is the same kind of slippage between "real" first-hand experience and claims of a fictional imagination. It is not immediately apparent why this situation calls forth these reactions. Obviously the authors must have spent some time in bars and in relations with bar girls to have had the knowledge to write in the way they do. Yet they disguise their own participation in some way: sometimes by creating a central character, presented in the third person, but assumed by the reader to be the author; sometimes by presenting the narratives from a kind of "distance" which does nothing to disguise the autobiographical quality of much of the story. For example, in the preface to the second edition of *Faces of the Night* (1989), which is entirely devoted to depictions of the intimate lives of a series of Thai bar girls, John Hinds explicitly addresses the nature of his writing, but not his position as author:

This book is not a novel. . . . The stories do have a few male foils who reappear, but that does not make it a novel. Jim, the character who most frequently allows the development of the female personality, appears as a central character in nine of the original fifteen stories, but in only one of the additional four. . . . The stories may be read in any order, and the plots do not carry over from one to another. The stories in this book combine fiction and fact. This means that some of the stories are based on experiences, though these experiences are not necessarily mine. (Hinds 1989, iii)

He explains that his moral intention in writing the stories is to provide the reader with an understanding of the essential humanity of the "prostitutes" of Thailand. The individuality of each female character is stressed: the appeal is to the reader to "Give her the dignity to select her own path through the shadow world, and give her her voice" (iv). This latter remark is particularly odd, since in fact the voice we are receiving is not hers at all, but that of the male author. Many feminist critics of *The Good Woman of Bangkok* demanded that the camera be given to the woman, so she could speak—but really this is just another demand from the West that the woman *must* speak and thus present herself for assessment and evaluation (cf. Spivak 1988).

Another Woman of Bangkok

Commercialized sex between Thai woman and *farang* man is often regarded as a relatively recent phenomenon, as is the depiction of Thailand as the privileged site of erotic truth. The spread of this reputation is often traced back to the years of the Vietnam war, when the presence of thousands of U.S. and other troops on leave is said to have resulted in the boom in brothels and organized prostitution. However a novel published in 1956, *A Woman of Bangkok,* by Jack Reynolds, certainly suggests that the Western masculinist imaginary, with Thailand as its privileged site, was already fully established at that time. It depicts, in dramatic and fascinating detail, the way in which a repressed Englishman encounters himself and assumes his manhood through the agency of sex in Thailand. This book was published originally in England and reprinted there four times, and then published and reprinted several times in Bangkok by Editions Duang Kamol between 1985 and 1992. The latter edition is for sale only in Southeast Asia. There is no introduction or preface by the author; hence the reader is not able to decide whether the tale of the awakening of Reggie Joyce, vicar's son, from Malderbury, is to be identified with the life of "Jack Reynolds," if indeed this is the real name of the author. The fact that the book is written largely as a first-person narrative makes the identification extremely difficult to resist.

Reggie is a virgin at the age of 27 and is reeling from the impact of his erstwhile girlfriend Sheila's marriage to his elder brother, in whose shadow he has been forced to live most of his life. Although he is a keen amateur poet, who has had all his experiences from books, he nonetheless was a failure at school and a disgrace to his father. Employed as a commercial salesman, he is sent by his firm to work in Bangkok, about which he knows nothing. Reggie is hesitant, clumsy, uncomfortable, and constantly afraid of making a fool of himself or expressing any emotions openly. Early in the story Sheila's behavior and attitudes are revealed as typical of those of English women, and Reggie reveals his fundamental rage at all of them. He is hoping Sheila will at least be there to see him off at the airport:

> And if she isn't what matter? Half the human beings in the world are female. The breed is produced by the busload. Billions of the bitches. And every one stamped in the same press. Rigged on the same jibs. That sounds slightly suggestive . . . (Reynolds 1992, 15)

The key moment in the failure of his relationship with Sheila took place when they were alone together and he tried to make love to her. At the crucial moment she cried out "No Reggie, no. Don't do anything we'll regret—please" (15).

Sheila is there at the airport, but Reggie discovers she is pregnant by his brother. His dismay knows no bounds. They have an argument, in which Sheila describes to Reggie's landlady what it was like when they were lovers. He was "the most spineless goddam lover. If I snapped his head off he'd slink away all sorrowful and apologetic like a puppy that's wetted the floor. Next day he'd be back with some horrible poem about my right eyebrow or my left breast or something" (20–21). In the same conversation Sheila reveals that she gave up Reggie for Andy because Andy "never wrote a poem in his life. He did what a lover should do—he made love to me" (21). Reggie protests that he too made love to her, but she stopped him. She replies that this was true, but this was not what he should have done. "So you walked away and after a bit you came back looking all noble like Sir Galahad and no doubt with a new poem in your head." "WHAT DID YOU EXPECT ME TO DO—RAPE YOU?"

> Why not? . . . It's a pity you don't understand women, Reggie. . . . No young girl wants to lose her virginity—that's instinct— . . . but how can a young girl know what's best for her? Maybe it would have done

me good to be raped. Anyway you ought to have gone ahead, Reggie. I'd put myself in your power. But—you backed off. (21)

Thus Reggie's imminent departure is framed within the context of a woman's desire for rape and contempt for a man who treats her respectfully and writes her poetry. It is clear that Reggie is ripe for a transformative experience, which of course he gets very quickly in Thailand. He remains a virgin for only a short time, being taken to a brothel by his Thai workmates while up-country in Korat on business. He also starts to drink heavily, and to eat Thai dishes, and to learn some Thai, immediately marking him off as an "insider," one of those who increasingly belong in Thailand. He has always believed there were no "bad women," but now his view is changing; or rather, he identifies the women who make themselves sexually available to men such as himself as having positive agency in this, and sees them no longer merely as victims. After his sexual initiation up-country, he muses on the changes to himself. He contrasts the way in which the old Reggie Joyce (who is now renamed Rejoice by one of his close colleagues) would have thought he was having a good time if he had seen picturesque views, photographed temples, and visited interesting places. But now he is able to live in the moment; at the same time he begins "to feel less alien in Thailand than I used to feel in Islington" (73). Moreover, he has a new confidence in himself.

> For the first time in my life I don't feel apologetic to the porter. Heretofore I have always suspected in him a person superior to myself but forced by unkind circumstances to act as my minion. Now I ask myself, "Has *he* had seventeen different women in six weeks, and one of them half-a-dozen times?" (74)

The stories of his sexual exploits have already reached the capital, and on his return, he is hailed by his fellow workers, both *farang* and Thai. But almost at once he becomes embroiled in a passionate obsession with a dancer at the Bolero nightclub, Vilai, who is known as "The White Leopard." She is the most famous "Bad Girl of Bangkok." At the end of part 1 we leave Reggie hopelessly drunk in a *samlor* (bicycle-rickshaw) declaiming his undying love for Vilai while taking her home for a very expensive sexual encounter.

With part 2, the narrative is up-turned. Reggie is replaced by Vilai as the focus of the story. The reader is introduced to the most intimate aspects of her everyday life: the way she plucks the hairs from her underarms, her food preferences, her worries over her weight and approaching middle-age (she is 27), her love for her twelve-year-old son and anger at his rejection of her occupation. This section is written in a staccato style, quite different from the leisurely and cultivated sentences of Reggie's narration. The narrative is in the third person, but it is clear that we have now entered Vilai's mind and her understandings.

Now we are permitted to share her views about taking money for sex. She describes her disappointment in Dick, a man she has slept with seven or eight times. She believes he has insulted her, because he asked her to sleep with him for nothing "[a]s if she were a very low girl with no self-respect at all. Only the lowest girls slept with men for nothing—for love, as the foreigners said—but she was a very high girl, she had a price, and if a man liked her he would show his respect by paying that price" (127). She believes that Dick's plea for a free fuck is evidence that he despises her. "Would he have spoken to one of his own white women like that? No, of course not. He would never have dreamed of insulting a white girl so badly" (128). Indeed, this kind of behavior is common among white men. "She despised all men. And especially she despised white men because they despised her own race. There was only one good thing about white men: they had more money than any one else. And it was her duty to get as much of that money off them as she could" (128).

When her son is injured in a car accident, Reggie (whom she calls "Wretch") happens to be nearby. He offers to take the child to hospital and agrees to pay his medical bills. Before he can do this, however, there is a strange altercation between them. Vilai insists that they should take the injured boy home; otherwise she will be late for work at the Bolero. Reggie is shocked and horrified that she can think of going to the Bolero at a time like this. At his insistence they take the boy to the hospital, but she rushes off to go to work. In spite of his disappointment, he is overwhelmed by his love and desire for her, and begs her to come to see him at his hotel, since he cannot any longer bear to see her at the Bolero, flirting with other men. He knows he loves her, and he wants her to renounce her life.

She takes her time going to his hotel, and then helps herself to a large sum of money from his wallet. He is past caring, and only wants to make love to her. She is "famous around the world" largely because of her skill in simulating sexual pleasure. However, we are told that with Reggie she does not need to simulate; she experiences the real thing. She also realizes that Reggie might be worth more than he seems. She asks him for money, so that she needn't return to the Bolero and can instead go the hospital to be with her son. Reggie is delighted with this evidence of decent maternal instincts and gives her a check for half of his savings.

With part 3, "The Slaughter," the narrative shifts back to Reggie's first-person voice. He both despises and admires himself for the amount of money he has spent on Vilai. "'At last I'm out of my adolescence,'" he says to himself; "'At last I'm man-size.' My muscles automatically flexed themselves. My body had come into its own. I could face adults now eye-to-eye" (211). Almost immediately Vilai bursts into his room to announce that her son is dead, and she blames him for it entirely. He expresses sorrow for the child, but she remonstrates that she is the one to be pitied. Shortly afterwards she lies down on the bed and tries to entice him to join her. He is horrified: he says it is like "murder in a cathedral" (214). Nevertheless he cannot resist, and when he sees her again a few days later, he again gives her a large sum of money. She tells him something about her life, but he knows it does not tally: she is not telling the "truth." All the same, he begins thinking he might marry her. He asks her to come and live with him, but she laughs this off, saying he doesn't have enough money; she can earn twice his salary at the Bolero. And besides, if she did, she'd have nothing to do all day, and would get fat. Her words to him are irresistible: "Wretch, you good boy to me. I like very mutss. I sink no one good more batter than you. Sometime I sink you like the God. I sink I want you to wiss me to country, see my Mama. I sink, if Udom [her son] had liff, I want he like you in everysing . . ." (221).

Her words make his heart "swell with pride." No other women, including his mother, his ex-sweetheart, and his landlady, have been able to praise him like this and make him feel so significant. He goes to Chiangmai on business again, and confides his love to his Thai partner. This man scoffs at him, saying such women are only after a man's money, and are good just for one or two times only. He rejects this idea. "I had an indestructible belief in the essential goodness of human beings, especially the female sort; and an impulse to 'save' those who according to my judgment had temporarily strayed from the right path would flare up in me quite as fiercely as in a missionary . . ." (226).

He recollects the girl he had had in Korat, believing only that she was unfortunate: "All she'd needed . . . was to be shown the way out of the hell she'd got into and she'd take it" (227). However, he is unable to get over his passion for Vilai. He takes her to Chiangmai on a "moneymoon," where she extracts the last of his savings. She ditches him at the end of the week to go off with an American. He is shocked into realizing the peril he is in, in every respect. He goes off on another business trip, believing he is over his infatuation. But he tells her before he goes that if she is ever in any real trouble she should call him: right to the last moment he still wants to be the knight in shining armor. Needless to say, she does. He endangers his life and his job by taking the company jeep to drive directly to Bangkok to save her, but he wrecks the car, and when he finally gets there, he discovers she wants 10,000 *baht* urgently but won't tell him what it's for. She convinces him that he should try to rob his employer's wife of her jewelry in order to raise the money. He goes along with the plan, to his own astonishment, but botches it. She then disappears, and he realizes he must renounce the East and seek to live more like his own father, whose virtues he reevaluates.

The novel ends with a letter from the American with whom Vilai had left Chiangmai. He and she are in the far south, where he is raising money to run a leper colony, and she is "managing" it for him.[15] We leave Reggie Joyce in the plane, taking off for the return journey to England.

Love and Marriage

This saga of the early fifties already includes the framework of the *farang*— Thai woman relationship as it is repeated in stories and novels into the 1990s. The patterns arising in these relationships emerge from the codes of masculinity underlying the common form of heterosexual relations in the West. The Western male believes in love, and believes that he can and must find love. The easiest women to love are bar girls— they are always more than this. Thai bar girls do not view themselves as purely commercial prostitutes; they believe they do have choices, and they also seek the possibility of a closer relationship with the *farang* male. As is evident from many of the interviews in Walker and Ehrlich (1992), the prospect of marriage is strong in many of the women's minds. They are deeply hurt if and when the boyfriend drops the relationship; they do not seem to understand the man's disappointment when the girl goes back to the bar, no matter how much money he sends her. Of course, much of this is pretence. As is clear from many sources, including the interviews published in Walker and Ehrlich, experienced bar girls know pretty much what they are doing and what they can expect. Yet there is still the sense of hope, of possibility, of something better around the corner.

In the case of longer-term expatriate residents, many of whom do marry Thai girls legally or have long-term relationships with them, some kind of accommodation across the cultural divide must be made. The "essential woman," it should be noted, may become very difficult as a wife. Most notable is their supposed proclivity for castration. As Eckhardt reports,

> A Thai wife will wait till her unfaithful husband is asleep, castrate him, then chuck the offending member to whatever pig or dog or duck that happens to amble along. This quaint custom prevents doctors from performing "penile reattachment"—an operation for which Thai surgeons have gained international fame in medical journals. . . . [S]pousal

castrations are *not* all that common. Two or three monthly in a kingdom of 50 million. Thai wives, though, would have you believe the
Knife falls routinely and the next victim could be you. (1991, 7)

Apart from the nightmare of imminent physical castration, there are
ceaseless demands for financial support for the family on the one hand, and
on the other, the lack of basic communicative intimacy which sustains most
long-term relationships in Western society.[16] Failure in one relationship,
however, simply leads to the pursuit of another in the hope that it will be
more successful. The series of relationships between *farang* men and Thai
women thus seems interminable.

In spite of recent efforts by the authorities in Thailand to clean up the
sex trade, there is little evidence of change. The trade in women continues,
and men, both Thai and *farang,* continue to patronize prostitutes and to
resist safe sex practices. Fordham (1993a, 1993b) suggests that central elements of Thai masculine culture, at least in provincial regions, have effectively subverted the intention of safe-sex education programs. The extent
to which the same might be said for Western males at this time (1995) is
unknown, but it is certainly the case that, well into the 1990s, the men
who engaged in commercial sex with Thai women also resisted the safe-
sex message by means of a number of denials, many examples of which
appear in the books and stories under consideration here.

For example, in *Child of the Enlightenment* (in Piprell 1991), Ernest is con-
fronted by his Thai girlfriend's fear of AIDS. She arranges to go for a test.
The narrator asks Ernest, "Are you going for a test as well?" He replies:
"Hell no! There's no reason at all to think I might have AIDS. . . . Christ!
I'm not a homosexual. I'm not a haemophiliac, a heroin addict, or a Haitian. . . . Anyway, what good would it do to have a test supposing you did
have AIDS? Like I told you, we've been together almost a year now, and if
I've got it, then she's got it" (126). He suggests that even her belief that she
could have it is just superstition: "I'm a *farang* and us *farang* brought the
disease to Thailand. The government has called it a foreigner's disease, and
Noi has been sleeping with a foreigner. . . . It's nothing but some kind of
guilt trip" (127).

Defiance and denial are likely to be as prevalent among Western males as
among Thai males, and for similar reasons. Sex with attractive young
women is evidence of "real" manhood, which must be demonstrated not
only to the subject himself but to the group of peers within which competition inevitably exists. For the Thai male, sex with prostitutes becomes an
element of his display of masculinity. However, he can also undertake socially desired proofs of masculinity by marrying a "respectable" girl. Even

if the young Thai male cannot yet afford to do this, he has a reasonable expectation of doing so at some future time.

For the Western male in Thailand this strategy is not available. Many men have rejected women from their own backgrounds, have had unsatisfactory relations, been divorced, or have been unable to find a partner. They often attribute this to the lack of "femininity" in Western women. While respectable Thai women are unlikely to accept a Western male as a marriage partner, since they would lose social status and possibly be rejected by their families, there are thousands of Thai girls of lower social status, already compromised by working in the sex trade, for whom a *farang* is an excellent husband or long-term partner (cf. Krich 1989).

From the man's point of view this requires that he secure the woman's sexual fidelity and rescue her from her occupation. But this involves him in providing lavish financial support to her and to her family, on whose behalf she says she is working in the first place. The consequences are well recognized in the expatriate literature:

> Anyway, the hard fact remained—marry one of the local girls, and you assumed responsibility for her whole family unto the *n*th generation or probably even further. With some of these upcountry families, that could add up to a number that should entitle you to U. N. aid. And there was nothing like a *farang* in the family, sometimes, to raise the general level of expectations up to brand-new heights, so far as life prospects went. (Piprell 1991, 45)

Even where no long-term partnership is envisaged, there is still the question of "love." In Western thought, love must be noncommercial; the fine line between prostitution and marriage must be marked by the deferral or disguise of financial transactions. Self-esteem is enhanced by the generosity a man can display to his girlfriend or wife. However, ceaseless demands for jewelry, money, and other tangible gifts suggest to him that the woman is not sincere in her affections: she does not love him. This dilemma lies at the heart of the misrecognition which characterizes Thai-*farang* sexual relationships (Krich 1989). In the stories considered here, the tenacity of the desire for and belief in the possibility of love forms the leitmotif, disappointment and confusion the counterpoint, and cynicism the coda.

Thus, while some modes of sexual transaction differentiate the position of the girl in the bar from that of the girl in the brothel, there seems to be a common element among the men who form the clientele, whether *farang* or Thai, at least in terms of the expression of a defiant masculinist culture marked by excessive alcohol consumption and frequent change of sex partners. What differentiates the men, however, is the commonly expressed quest for love and the hope of a gallant rescue on the part of the Western male. The disregard for common sense and self-preservation in the context of HIV/AIDS has only brought into focus elements of behavior with a very long history. While the repetitive elements common in these relationships suggest a profound misfit between *farang* and Thai, there may in another register be a kind of true satisfaction for both: the masochistic male who identifies with the abused woman, the "good woman" who sadistically revenges herself through a clever masquerade of passivity and obedience. In this sense their projects are meshed, sustained by their mutual disguises.[17]

CHAPTER SEVEN

Kathoey >< Gay >< Man: The Historical Emergence of Gay Male Identity in Thailand

PETER A. JACKSON

Introduction

Parallel with Thailand's economic boom, Thai gay subculture has bloomed in the past decade. In 1977 John Stamford's *Spartacus International Gay Guide* listed ten gay venues in Thailand, all in Bangkok, at which time the English term *gay* was most likely to connote a cross-dressing or effeminate homosexual male. Just over a decade later Eric Allyn (1991) listed over one hundred gay bars, saunas, restaurants, and discos around the country. Until 1983 there were no Thai-language magazines published by and for Thai gay men. In 1993 nine monthly Thai-language gay magazines competed on the newsstands. In the 1990s, the Thai image of "gay" is increasingly masculine—gym-enlarged biceps and pectoral muscles, accentuated body and facial hair—and the Thai gay male is likely to confidently proclaim, "I'm gay and I'm a man."

In this chapter I consider the rapid historical transformation in Thai conceptions of male homosexuality and theorize the relationship between the emerging masculine definition of gayness in Thailand and the preexisting male sex/gender categories of the gender-normative "man" (*phu-chai*)[1] and the transgender *kathoey*.[2] In studying the history of gay identity in Thailand, a number of questions arise. For example, is Thai gayness a Western borrowing that has been imposed upon traditional sexual and gender norms, or does this new formulation of male homosexual identity have an indigenous history that locates it within the Thai sex/gender system as a distinctively Thai cultural phenomenon? Does the genealogy of Thai gayness position it closer to the transgender category, *kathoey,* or to the predominantly heterosexual gender-normative masculine category, *phu-chai*? What is stigmatized more strongly in Thai culture, effeminacy or male homoeroticism? To answer questions such as these and to develop an understanding of the character of gay identity in Thailand requires an analysis combining historical and ethnographic perspectives.

In previous work (P. Jackson 1989, 1995) I analyzed letters to a homosexual advice column published in a popular Thai fortnightly magazine, *Plaek*

(*Strange*), together with the replies given by the column's "agony uncle," who writes under the pseudonym of Uncle Go Pak-nam. The primary objectives of that work were to document the lives of Thai homosexual men in the early 1980s and to describe the sanctions against male homosexuality within Thai culture. In this chapter I reflect upon my earlier study, incorporate more recent data, and respond to Rosalind Morris's (1994) theorization of the emergence of modern categories of sexuality in Thailand. I also expand and refine Gayle Rubin's (1975) notion of the sex/gender system as an analytical framework for cross-cultural studies of gender and sexuality.

In conclusion I suggest that gay male identity in Thailand represents the emergence of a ternary term in the previously binary structure of Thai male sex/gender categories, and that gayness renders explicit a previously unlexicalized domain between the poles of the Thai "complete man" and the demasculinized *kathoey*. I argue that while gayness in Thailand has drawn selectively on Western models, it has emerged from a Thai cultural foundation as the result of efforts by Thai homosexual men to resolve tensions within the structure of masculinity in their society. Given this, the proposition that gayness in Thailand is a "Western borrowing" is misplaced and overlooks the internal structuring of Thai masculinity, from which Thai gay male identity has emerged as a largely continuous development.

Understanding Thai Sex/Gender Categories

In tracing the history of sex and gender categories in Thailand, it is important to note that, even in the modern Thai language, the domains of biological sex, culturally ascribed gender, and sexuality are not clearly distinguished. All three concepts are commonly rendered by the same term, *phet,* used either alone or in compounds: for example, *phet-seuksa,* "sexology"; *phet-chai,* "male," less commonly "masculine gender"; *phet-ying,* "female," less commonly "feminine gender"; *ruam-phet,* "to have sexual intercourse"; *rak-ruam-phet,* "homosexuality" (literally, "love of the same sex/gender"); *rak-tang-phet,* "heterosexuality" (literally, "love of the opposite/different sex/gender"). While uncommon, the term *phet-gay* has recently been coined. This last expression cannot be translated by any single English term and combines the three notions of gayness as including different biological sex, a distinctive form of gendered existence, and a sexuality. Other Thai sex and gender terms also have a range of nuances that cross more than one domain. For example, both the binary pairs *chai/ying* (roughly, "male"/"female") and *phu-chai/phu-ying* (roughly, "man"/"woman") denote the domains of biology and culturally ascribed gender. Distinctions such as those between the English terms *man/woman* (denoting sex and/or gender), *male/*

female (denoting only biological sex), and *masculine/feminine* (denoting only gender) are not easily made in Thai, with all three of these English binaries commonly being rendered by one or other of the Thai couplets *chai/ying* or *phu-chai/phu-ying.*

Given this, it is clear that Thai categories cannot be contained within any one of the domains of biology, gender, or sexuality, and that an analysis which imposed these divisions arbitrarily would reflect the structure of Western discourses rather than the cultural patterns of sex and gender in Thailand. For this reason, Gayle Rubin's (1975) coinage of the compound expression *sex/gender* in her notion of sex/gender systems appears especially useful. Following Rubin, Julia Epstein and Kristina Straub (1991, 3) have defined sex/gender systems as historically and culturally specific arrogations of the human body for ideological purposes. In sex/gender systems, physiology, anatomy, and body codes (clothing, cosmetics, behaviors, miens, and affective and object choices) are taken over by institutions that use bodily difference to define and coerce gender identity.

In the Thai case I think it is useful to extend this definition and to conceive of a sex/gender system as being constituted by a range of sex/gender categories that combine and cut across the domains of biology, gender, and sexuality (cf. the introduction to this volume). In this chapter I regard the Thai sex/gender system as combining first the limited number of sex/gender categories that are linguistically recognized in Thai culture, and second the pattern of moral and other sanctions that coerce individuals to assume a valorized combination and desist from assuming a stigmatized combination, and which structure sex/gender categories into distinctive hierarchical patterns.

A Preliminary History of Thai Sex/Gender Categories

The history of Thai sex/gender categories is yet to be written, and the task will not be easy, because the limited sources we have are scattered and largely fragmentary. As Craig Reynolds (1994, 64) has remarked, to a large extent gender and sexuality have been elided from Thai historical records and neglected by scholarly research. The paucity of historical data in some measure results from more benign legal and religious attitudes towards homoeroticism throughout Thai history compared to those of Western societies. Much of the early history of homosexuality in Western societies has been reconstructed from criminal legal records and condemnatory religious discourse. However, male homoeroticism is not proscribed in Thailand and, being invisible to Thai law, is absent from the legal records. Similarly, while the sexual behavior of Buddhist monks is closely monitored, the sexuality of lay people has historically not been a concern of the Thai Buddhist clergy, with the exceptions of prohibitions against rape and adultery.

While homoeroticism has a cultural history in Thailand, by and large it lacks an institutional history; falling outside the interests of the Thai state, it has remained largely undocumented. It is only since the mid-1960s that taboos surrounding the discussion of non-normative gender and sexuality have lifted sufficiently in Thailand to permit public discussion of transgenderism and homoeroticism in the Thai press and media. In researching the history of prostitution and attitudes towards women in Thailand, Scot Barmé (personal communication) reports an almost complete absence of references to homoeroticism in Thai newspapers and popular magazines from the 1920s and 1930s. This contrasts with the voluminous press reportage of heterosexual prostitution and the changing roles of women at the time, and the existence of a thriving underground industry in heterosexual pornography. The history of homoeroticism in Thailand before the contemporary period must therefore rely primarily on ethnographic and linguistic data, with only occasional support from rare references in documentary sources.

Thus, almost anything one says stands to be countered by the recovery of previously overlooked fragments of this unspoken history. There is significant room for error in interpreting the synchronic patterns of gender and sexuality in Thailand, and in tracing the diachronic movements of those patterns, and not merely because of poor data. I concur with Morris's (1994, 18) reflection upon the experience of conducting research on sexuality in Thailand when she says, "I have often found myself astounded by the plasticity of Thai gender and sexual identity." In our astonishment, the analyses we develop are often limited by our preconceptions, and coming to an accurate understanding requires as much an unlearning of such preconceptions as the application of interpretative frameworks to Thai gender and sexuality.

While historical data on homoeroticism and transgender phenomena in Thailand are limited, it is nevertheless suggestive that northern Thai and Mon (Central Thailand) Buddhist origin myths (see Guillon 1991; Peltier 1991) appear to describe three original human sexes—male, female, and hermaphrodite. Morris (1994) variously calls this mythic pattern the "system of three sexes" or the "system of the third gender." In the Central Thai dialect a biological hermaphrodite is called a *kathoey*.[3] In its idealized expression in myth, the hermaphrodite category is not identified as a variant of either male or female but as an independently existing third sex. This notion of three human sexes appears to have remained prevalent in Thailand up until this century and is reflected in the early twentieth-century Central Thai colloquial expression for *kathoeys* as *phet-thi-sam*, "the third sex."

The linguistic condensation of the domains of biology, gender, and sexuality in Thai leads to a common tendency to "naturalize" both ascribed gender and sexuality to biology. For example, in Thai discourses on gender and sexuality the categories *chai, ying,* and *kathoey* are typically conceived in terms of the performance of masculine, feminine, and transgender roles, respectively, which in turn are believed to be biologically based in maleness, femaleness, and hermaphroditism. Within this traditional discursive context, male and female homoeroticism are conceived in terms of sex/gender inversion. While the homosexuality of a *kathoey* is assumed to derive from biological hermaphroditism, a same-sex erotic preference among masculine-identified men is explained in terms of psychological hermaphroditism, that is, having a woman's mind in a man's body. A similar logic is applied in accounting for female transvestism and homoeroticism. That is, a woman's interest in cross-dressing is commonly put down to biological hermaphroditism, while a same-sex erotic preference among feminine-identified women is explained in terms of having a man's mind in a woman's body.

Historically, the importance of sexuality in the construction of Thai sex/gender has varied from category to category. Until the last couple of decades, Thai culture and language have not recognized distinctive homosexual or heterosexual identities for those males and females who adhered respectively to normative masculine and feminine gender roles. Homosexual and heterosexual behaviors were recognized in Thai verbs,[4] but not in any Thai nouns that denoted homosexual and heterosexual types of gender-normative males and females. In the case of the Thai sex/gender categories "woman" (*phu-ying*) and "man" (*phu-chai*) we should conceive of sexuality,[5] whether homosexual or heterosexual, as a zone of slippage that may move across these two categories without necessarily disrupting their core identities. Nevertheless, as described below, both male and female homoeroticism are variously subjected to restrictive sanctions in Thailand.

Unlike its role in the Thai categories "man" and "woman," sexuality has been central to the construction of the *kathoey* category in recent Thai cultural history. It is appropriate to refer to the *kathoey*, which is a noun not a verb, as a type of male homosexual identity, not simply a form of homoerotic behavior. While originally denoting hermaphroditism, the denotation of *kathoey* now extends beyond the domain of biology to culturally ascribed gender, and the term is generally regarded as describing a deficient variety of masculine gender, rarely of feminine. Thai now distinguishes between "genuine *kathoeys*" (*kathoey thae*), or hermaphrodites, and "artificial *ka-*

thoeys" (*kathoey thiam*), or males (rarely females) who exhibit cross-gender characteristics. In recent years the denotation of the term *kathoey* has extended yet further to include the domain of sexuality. *Kathoey* is now also a derogatory term used by some heterosexuals to refer to homosexual men, whether or not they exhibit cross-gender behavior. In this usage *kathoey* has a similar force to derogatory English terms such as *poofter* (Australia, United Kingdom) and *faggot* (United States)

Morris (1994, 24) makes the important point that, while the definition of *kathoey* as still found in Thai dictionaries acknowledges both male and female cross-dressers,⁶ the popular stereotype of the term is now of a male who makes himself up as a woman, not a female who makes herself up as a man. Some contemporary emic Thai accounts of *kathoeys,* that is, descriptions of *kathoeys* in terms of Thai cultural conceptions, continue to describe such people as a distinctive third sex/gender who occupy a middle ground between male/masculine and female/feminine. The name of one of Thailand's most successful gay magazines, *Midway,* indicates that the conception of *kathoey*/gayness as a condition of "in-betweenness" is also held by some Thai homosexual men. However, in developing an etic, or external, account of *kathoeys,* it is necessary to recognize that such people are in fact overwhelmingly considered to be a variety of male, not female, and so are not a genuine intermediate category. From a theoretical perspective, the *kathoey* and "man" should be considered to be alternate categories of Thai maleness. Nevertheless, the term *kathoey* is still occasionally used to refer to female cross-dressers in the Thai press (e.g., Jackson 1995, 130), although female cross-dressers are now usually called *tom* (from the English "*tomboy*"), while feminine-identified lesbians are called *di* (from the English "la*dy*").

The historical shift in the use of *kathoey* to refer only to transgender males is reflected in the contemporary Thai colloquial description of *kathoey* males as *phu-ying praphet sorng,* "a second type of woman." Thai does not possess a parallel expression "second type of man" to describe transgender females. Morris (1994, 24) remarks that this shift represents an appropriation of the mythical Thai androgynous category to the structures of masculinity, in which even femininity is rendered as a domain accessible to males. This may be the case, but it would be a mistake to think that both feminine (*kathoey*) and masculine ("man") categories of maleness have equal status within the Thai sex/gender system. Male appropriation of femininity is associated with stigmatization of the *kathoey* relative to the valorized position of the "man." And within the dominant heterosexual construction of Thai sex/gender categories, the feminization of the *kathoey* also defines him as a male who in sexual terms relates exclusively to other males. The notion of a heterosexual cross-dressing male has only a muted presence in the contemporary Thai conception of the *kathoey,* which is overwhelmingly regarded as denoting a homosexual male.

Thus while sexuality was to some degree a variable in the traditional construction of the normative Thai "man" and "woman" (although heterosexuality was structurally dominant and homosexuality subordinate), it was integral to the construction of the stereotype of the *kathoey.* In linguistic terms, homosexuality was a verb for Thai "men" in the traditional Thai sex/gender system; that is, it was an activity they might engage in but which did not determine their sex/gender identity, provided certain conditions were met. (Differing attitudes to "masculine" and "feminine" forms of male homoeroticism in Thailand are described below.) On the other hand, homosexuality was a noun for *kathoeys,* that is, a sexual object choice which, together with their feminine behavior, speech, and dress, defined their identity as sexual beings.

The Place of *Kathoeys* in Traditional Thai Society

The roles of the Thai "man" and *kathoey* are polar opposites, nuclei for two constellations of sexual norms and gender characteristics regarded as being mutually exclusive and as constituting a male's sex/gender identity. That is, a Thai male has traditionally been regarded and has regarded himself as either a "man" or a *kathoey.* The complementarity of the cultural opposition between the "man" and the *kathoey* is shown by, among other things, the common designation of *kathoeys* as being a "second type of woman" who can relate sexually with a "man," and also by the fact that a *kathoey's* ideal sexual partner is almost universally a heterosexual "man."

The valorized status of being a Thai "man" and the stigmatized status of being a *kathoey* are respectively formed at the conjuncture and disjuncture of three sets of behavioral, sexual, and social norms. The Thai male who dresses, talks, and acts in ways expected of a Thai man, who takes a dominant position in sex, and who fulfils his social obligations by marrying and fathering a family is honored by being considered to be a "man"—*phu-chai.* In contrast, the *kathoey* represents the negation of manhood. He is the Thai "un-man." A *kathoey* is not a man in dress, speech, or demeanor; he is subordinate to another man in sex, and he rejects the sanctioned expectation that all men other than Buddhist monks should marry and become fathers.[7]

In practice, not all Thai "men" or *kathoeys* abide by all of the norms usually expected of their sex/gender category. There are, for example, Thai *kathoeys* who are married and have children, and there are Thai "men" whose sexual preference is to engage in receptive anal sex with a *kathoey.* However, as historically dominant cultural stereotypes, these two male categories are recognized explicitly in language and play a pivotal role in the construction of male sex/gender identities, including newly emergent identities such as gayness.

While *kathoeys* are generally derided and, like women, may be subject to sexual attack and rape (see Jackson 1989, 227 ff.), they are much more visible in Thailand than male transvestites and transsexuals are in Western societies; they live and work openly even in villages and country towns. But in the absence of comparative ethnographic studies, it is not possible to say whether *kathoeys* represent a larger proportion of the male population in Thailand than transvestites and transsexuals do in Western societies. Greater visibility does not necessarily imply greater numbers, but may reflect weaker sanctions against the public expression of male transgenderism in Thailand. Class and generational factors do not appear to be significant in influencing *kathoey* identification. *Kathoeys* are found in all social strata except the highest ranks of the Thai nobility, and in both urban and rural areas. Furthermore, a large number of young *kathoeys* in the 1990s perform in transvestite revues at Thailand's plethora of gay bars and other venues, indicating that many young Thai men continue to assume this role after gayness has been widely established as an alternative identity for homosexual men.

The *kathoey* occupies a marginal but recognized position in Thai society in some ways comparable to that of a "man's" minor wife or a female prostitute. *Kathoeys* are popularly stereotyped in the Thai press and media as sexual libertines and prostitutes, but while many *kathoeys* do work as prostitutes, large numbers work in ordinary jobs or run their own businesses. From anecdotal reports, it appears that in some situations *kathoeys* play the role of sexual initiators of young men. In a society in which premarital sexual relations (apart from men's relations with prostitutes) have traditionally been tabooed, and in which it has been customary for young men and women to socialize in same-sex groups, a local *kathoey* sometimes appears to have provided an alternative sexual outlet for unmarried young men. The expression "a second type of woman" appears to reflect this. Perhaps one reason *kathoeys* are more accepted in Thailand than transvestites and transsexuals are in the West is that historically they have provided a ritually "safe" sexual outlet for unmarried youths. From the standpoint of traditional ritual sanctions, it would have been more acceptable for an unmarried youth to visit a *kathoey* than to have sex with an unmarried young woman, whose reputation would be sullied were she discovered. Visiting a *kathoey* would also have been a safe sexual option for a village youth who wanted to avoid the ire of a young woman's family if discovered. However, a man who visited *kathoeys* as a youth would be expected to abandon homosexuality after he married. Should this speculation on the historical role of the *kathoey* in rural Thai society be accurate, then the contemporary stereotype of the *kathoey* as a prostitute may be based on more than misogynistic prejudice.

Echoes of a possible historical role for the *kathoey* in rural Thai society may perhaps be found in the *kathoey* beauty contests that are now regularly staged as attractions at Thai up-country fairs, and in the popular *kathoey* revues at tourist venues in Chiangmai, Bangkok, Pattaya, and Phuket. Thai men and women demonstrate an unabashed fascination with *kathoeys* and openly express admiration for how well a particularly feminine or graceful *kathoey* passes for a woman. This admiration of *kathoeys* is perhaps related to the importance attached to image (*phap-phot*) and presentation (*kan-sadaeng*) in Thailand. In any event, *kathoey* beauty contests at country fairs are immensely popular among rural men, and not only because of their novelty. It is generally known that many *kathoeys* competing in these contests are sexually available, although not necessarily for financial exchange, as reflected in a recent BBC documentary, *Lady Boys* (1992), which followed the lives of two teenage *kathoeys* from northern Thailand in the early 1990s. In years past, traveling *likay,* or folk opera troupes, may also have provided career opportunities for *kathoeys* as well as chances for village men to meet them (Schneider 1992).

A recurring theme in Thai literary and filmic representations of *kathoeys* portrays the *kathoey* as falling in love with a handsome "man" who initially shows interest but ultimately abandons her for the love of a "real woman" (*phu-ying thae*). The first Thai film to have a *kathoey* protagonist, *Phleng Sutthai* (*The Final Song*), released in the mid-1980s, followed just such a theme and concluded with a dramatic suicide-scene as the jilted *kathoey* took her life on stage at a Pattaya transvestite revue. This recurring theme perhaps reflects the cultural history of the *kathoey* role in Thailand, namely, to provide a transitional sexual outlet for young, unmarried, heterosexual males. Thai critics of *kathoeys* and homosexual men commonly cite the "suffering" (*khwam-thuk*) endured by such people as an argument against leading a homosexual lifestyle. Thai *kathoeys* themselves commonly lament the difficulty of finding "true love" (*khwam-rak jing*) from a "man." If the *kathoey's* historical role in Thailand has been to provide men with a transitional sexual outlet until they marry, then the "suffering" of living with a broken heart and the impossibility of finding lasting true love would appear to be the culturally ordained fate of *kathoeys* in traditional Thai society.

Eric Allyn (personal communication) suggests that an additional factor in many Thai men's sexual interest in *kathoeys* is a widespread fascination, even festishization, of anal sex. Many heterosexual Thai men regard anal intercourse (*tham khang-lang*—"doing it behind") as an exciting sexual variation. Heterosexual brothels commonly recognize the special attraction of anal sex through differential pricing of sexual services, offering their clients "three kinds of chicken" (*kai sam yang*), that is, vaginal, oral, and anal sex. This fascination is perhaps further reflected in a common derogatory term for *kathoeys*, *tut* (short vowel, high tone), which is phonemically close to the colloquial term for "backside" or "anus," *tut* (long vowel, low tone).

David Buchbinder (1993) observes that within a patriarchal culture, males play a more important role than females in conferring masculinity or manhood upon other males. A male is recognized as being a "man" when he is so regarded by other males who have already achieved the status of manhood. That masculinity is a currency exchanged between males is seen in the fact that in many traditional and contemporary societies, including Thailand and the modern West, a young male's rites of passage to manhood are largely enacted before other males for the purpose of eliciting their acknowledgement of his masculine status. For example, in Thailand visiting female prostitutes is a common signifier of masculine status and is often practiced as a group activity. While the sex act remains private, a bout of drinking, carousing, and sexual banter followed by a collective departure to a brothel is extremely common for vast numbers of Thai males from all socioeconomic strata. In this cultural context, the *kathoey*, or unmasculine homosexual male, stands as a symbol of failure to achieve masculine status, providing an image with which Thai males contrast themselves in the effort to define their masculinity: "I am not a *kathoey;* therefore I am a 'man'."

We can therefore understand the *kathoey's* structural importance in the Thai sex/gender system. If within patriarchal cultures a male's masculinity is defined relationally with respect to other males, rather than with respect to females, then we can see that the *kathoey* is pivotal to the construction of Thai masculinity. The *kathoey* represents all that a masculine Thai "man" is not. In this situation, the *kathoey* is not constructed on the model of a genuine femininity, but rather as a stereotype of unmasculinity.

Sanctions against Male Homosexuality in Thailand

While tolerated in certain contexts, homosexuality remains unacceptable male behavior in Thailand. My previous work (1989, 1995) described the psychological, interpersonal, and social difficulties faced by Thai homosexual men and developed a preliminary account of antihomosexual sanctions in Thailand. In summary, these are not based on explicitly defined legal or religious interdictions, as in the West,[8] but on cultural norms of appropriate and inappropriate male behavior. Thai sanctions concerning male homosexuality are generally noninterventionist, more often involving the withholding of approval rather than active attempts to force a male to desist from what is considered to be inappropriate behavior. But even these sanctions, mild by Western standards, usually only come into play when inappropriate sexual behavior becomes publicly visible or explicitly referred to in discourse. So long as a Thai homosexual "man" maintains a public face of conforming to normative patterns of masculinity, he will largely escape sanctions.

There is comparatively little pressure for integrating one's public and private lives in Thailand. Historically, religious interdictions against homosexuality and antisodomy laws in the West have constructed private sexual practice as an object of surveillance that is subject to legal intervention and penalty (see Foucault 1980, 38 ff.). In contrast, Morris (1994, 27) observes that in Thailand power, including sexual power, is structured "as a regime in which the maintenance of form is a social imperative but . . . the invisible deed is still considered beyond jural control." Private homosexuality, even when generally suspected, is considered a separate realm that does not affect a "man's" public performance of his civic duties.

For example, it is widely rumored in Thailand that several recent Prime Ministers have been homosexual. One of these former Prime Ministers was a member of the Thai nobility. Another was head of the Thai army before entering politics, never married, and is now a member of the Privy Council, the elite body that advises H. M. King Bhumibol Adulyadej.[9] The sexuality of these men has occasionally been raised as a political issue by critics and parliamentary opponents,[10] and gossip and apocryphal anecdotes about them also circulate widely. However, while the political decisions and the legacies of these men's respective periods of political leadership are publicly debated in Thailand, their sexuality is not.

Attitudes would be vastly different, however, if a Thai Prime Minister were a *kathoey,* that is, visibly breaching gender norms as well as privately breaching sexual norms. Given prevailing attitudes in Thailand, it is almost inconceivable that a *kathoey* could hold public office. *Kathoeys* confront significantly greater sanctions against their unconventional gender status than performatively masculine homosexual males do against their sexuality. This is because the *kathoey's* deviance is publicly visible, while that of the homosexual male, even where suspected or known, generally remains hidden. Those who criticize *kathoeys* in Thailand commonly focus on four main points: gender-inappropriate behavior, abnormal sexuality, social irresponsibility or selfishness for not marrying, and the inherent suffering of leading such a life. A Thai male who wishes to be a *kathoey* is free to do so, but he may become a focus of criticism, gossip, and other displays of disapproval, and he will be denied the forms of approval and respect that usually affirm a Thai male's identity as a "man." It is important, however, not to overstate the extent and intensity of the sanctions experienced by *kathoeys*. Some of the strongest criticisms commonly leveled against *kathoeys* both by hetero-sexuals and masculine-identified homosexual men are unrelated to gender deviance; for example, *kathoeys* are commonly criticized for "un-Thai" be-havior such as being loud, vulgar, or lewd.

An example of the noninterventionist character of sanctions that encour-age gender-normative behavior in Thailand was provided in a May 1994 episode of Thai television's family drama *Ban Taek* (*Broken Home*). A Thai informant reports that in the episode a young twelve-or thirteen-year-old girl announced to her family that she was in love with a well-known female model. The young girl began dressing as a boy and told her younger brother that she wanted to be a boy. While her family became concerned, no one intervened or chastised the girl; instead they advised her to give up her boyish behavior and concentrate on school to prepare for a proper life of job and family. However, the young girl persisted, meeting the model and declaring her love to her directly. The model accepted the girl's declara-tion but neither encouraged nor discouraged her young admirer's attentions. The episode concluded when the girl came home from school to find her mother, sister, and the maid dressed as men, and her father and two brothers dressed in drag. The girl stamped her feet, said she wanted her normal family back again, and vowed to become a girl once more. The scene ended as family members hugged each other and gender normality was resumed.

This television drama is instructive in several respects. It demonstrates the comparatively mild nature of Thai families' concern about non-normative gender behavior and the often indirect ways in which pressure to resume a normative gender role is applied. The episode also suggests a relaxed attitude to adolescent homoeroticism, provided that it is ultimately channeled to-wards adult heterosexuality. It is interesting to speculate on whether the family would have responded similarly if one of the sons had declared his love for a male model, dressed as a girl, and said he wanted to be a girl. In some contexts female homosexuality appears to be taken less seriously in Thailand than male homosexuality, being regarded as more of a passing phe-nomenon.

It would be a mistake, however, to think that the comparatively mild nature of sanctions against homosexuality in Thailand leads to a greater level of openness in that country. Apart from *kathoeys,* who cannot conceal their non-normative behavior, Thai homosexual men are in general extremely reluctant to reveal their sexual preference. "Coming out" is often no easier for Thai gay men than for their Western fellows, and publicly acknowledg-ing one's homosexuality is in general not regarded as an important or "polit-ically correct" activity in the Thai gay subculture. To be publicly identified as homosexual or gay remains a source of considerable shame involving "loss of face" (*sia na*) and "damage to one's image" (*sia phap-phot*). This shame largely stems from a persistent stereotyping of homosexual men as unmasculine. However, it also stems from a broader Thai reluctance to talk about one's sex life in public, except perhaps among same-sex friends in one's "drinking circle."

Sexual practice and representing sexuality in discourse or other media are inversely valued in traditional Western and Thai sexual cultures. In recent Western history it has been possible to talk about non-normative sexuality but not to practice it, even in private. Many Christian churches preach compassion for the homosexual sinner who admits his love of men but vehemently condemn his sexual activity. This attitude has been carried over into law in many Western countries: while having sex with men has at times been a crime, admitting homosexual feelings has rarely been so. In contrast, in Thailand private sexual practice evades cultural and legal sanction, but publicly proclaiming one's sexual preferences is regarded as highly inappropriate. Thus a homosexual Prime Minister can be widely rumored to have affairs with military aides and will not be criticized, provided neither he nor anyone else talks about it in public.

The Feminine and Masculine Homosexuality of *Kathoeys* and "Men"

Male homosexuality is present in the traditional Thai sex/gender system as a dominant feature in the construction of the *kathoey* and as a subordinate and often ignored variation in the sexuality of the "man." The homosexualities of *kathoeys* and of "men" are thus distinct phenomena, subject to different cultural constructions and sanctions, and it is therefore necessary to talk of homosexualities in the traditional Thai sex/gender system, not of a single form of male homoeroticism.

A Thai "man's" homosexuality is largely ignored so long as it remains private; if it becomes visible or is explicitly named in public, it is assimilated within a discourse that defines different male homosexual acts in gender terms and ranks them accordingly. "Masculine" homosexual acts are less damaging to a male's masculinity, and include insertive anal sex and playing the fellatee role in oral sex. In contrast, "feminine" homosexual acts are stigmatized, and include receptive anal sex and the fellator role in oral sex. However, the different roles in anal sex are much more strongly gendered in Thailand than the roles in oral sex between men, with much weaker masculine and feminine labeling of the fellatee and fellator roles, respectively. The identification of sexual role in anal sex is important in the traditional sex/gender system because a male who is performatively "masculine," that is, the inserter in anal sex, is categorized as a potentially normative heterosexual man. In contrast, a male who is performatively "feminine," that is, engages in receptive anal sex, is regarded as being less than a "complete man," or even a *kathoey*. Many Thai gay men continue to regard sexual role as being important, as indicated by their distinction between *gay kings* (insertive role) and *gay queens* (receptive role).

Go Pak-nam (Jackson 1989, 73, 80, 83) reflects this differential valuing of "masculine" and "feminine" male homosexuality in response to his correspondents' frequent enquiries about what "type" (*praphet*) of homosexual they are, whether "king" or "queen," terms which denote a sexual preference for the insertive and receptive role respectively in anal sex. Many of Go's correspondents describe their sexual encounters with other men in considerable detail in the hope of receiving an authoritative diagnosis of their sexual condition. In his responses Go places considerable emphasis on whether a correspondent has ever engaged in receptive anal sex, even if unwillingly. In this sex/gender system a man who has engaged in receptive anal sex has been feminized and lost something of his masculinity. Go commonly advises such men to come to terms with their stigmatized condition, even as he provides the opposite advice to "gay kings," namely, to assume a normative male heterosexual role and marry. "Masculine" homosexual acts are often viewed in terms of a "man" enjoying sexual variety, a "new taste" or "new flavor" (*rot-chat mai*) of sexual experience that does not detract from his masculine status. Indeed, the Thai cultural valuing of variety in food, sex, and other sensory experiences can itself be used to justify experimenting with homosexuality. "I'd like to give it a try" (*yak lorng du*) is a common justification for having sex with another man, just as "Do you want to give it a try?" (*yak lorng du mai*) can be used as a nonthreatening sexual request between masculine-identified males who do not consider themselves to be predominantly homosexual.

The Historical Emergence of Gay Male Identity in Thailand

The English-derived term *gay* was first used to refer to male homosexual identity in Thailand in the 1960s. The word is now generally known and used in Thailand, and is well established as a term of self-reference among educated and middle-class Thai male homosexuals, although many less-educated Thais and those outside the urban information networks often remain confused about what the term means.[11] The integration of the term *gay* into Thai homosexual parlance is indicated by the fact that the newsletter of the Fraternity for AIDS Cessation in Thailand (FACT), an organization devoted to safe-sex education among gay men and male and female sex workers, is called *Kunla-gay.* This name has been coined on the model of a Pali loan word in Thai, *kunla-but,* which denotes a son of a noble or illustrious family. The term *kunla-gay* implies not only that gay men are respectable in the sense of being from good backgrounds but also that, like decent sons of noble families, they uphold traditional values.

Generational factors appear to be important in influencing identification as gay, with more gay-identified men among those under forty years of age than among older Thai homosexual men. Until the late 1980s most gay-identified men were urban-dwelling, educated members of the middle or upper class. In the 1990s, however, class factors appear to be declining in importance as determinants of gay identity in Thailand. It is increasingly common to find younger, working-class men in towns as well as the countryside who identify as gay. While most men who place classified advertisements in Thai gay magazines list a Bangkok address, up-country addresses are also common, with many advertisers stating openly that they are from a village or working-class background.[12] This expansion of Thai gay identity outwards from its original location among Bangkok's middle class has paralleled the dissemination of masculine representations of gayness in nationally distributed gay magazines. Thai gay magazines are now sold openly from newsstands around the country, and cheap, second-hand copies that low-paid, unskilled workers can afford are commonly displayed for sale at rural fairs and at streetside hawkers' stalls in Bangkok and country towns.

The notion of "being gay" (Thai: *pen gay*)[13] offers a new sex/gender alternative to Thai homosexual "men." The recent rapid growth of gay subcultures in Bangkok, and less obviously in other major urban centres in Thailand, indicates that this nontraditional male sex/gender category fulfills the needs for identity and self-esteem felt by significant numbers of Thai homosexual males. Gayness separates exclusive male homosexuality from an imputed feminine status, permitting it to be linked with masculinity. In other words, gayness represents a claim, first, for exclusive homosexuality to be recognized as a form of masculinity and, second, for a Thai "man" to be able to place homoerotic relations at the center of his sexual and social life. The Thai term *gay* can be regarded as representing a claim for recognizing the existence of a differentiation within Thai masculinity—that manhood is not unitary in its construction but is open to diverse modes of expression.

A comprehensive account of the origins of gayness in Thailand would need to trace the processes that led to the historical transformation of a homoerotic behavioral preference within the category of "man" into a distinctive sexual identity. Even in the absence of such a study, however, it is apparent that the origins of gay identity in Thailand are primarily to be found in the transformation of the sex/gender category of "man," and only secondarily in the history of the *kathoey*. Thai gays are a variety of "man" or masculine-identified male, *not* a permutation of a *kathoey* in which there has been a reversal of gender identity from feminine to masculine.

That gayness in Thailand is primarily a phenomenon within the sex/gender category of "man" is indicated by the fact that its emergence is not displacing the *kathoey* model of exclusive homosexuality. While the number of Thai men who identify as being gay continues to grow, there are no signs that there are any fewer *kathoeys* in Thailand today than in the past. A further indicator that gayness has emerged as a division within the category of "man" rather than as an historical successor to the *kathoey* is shown by the fact that the stigma attached to being identified as a *kathoey* remains as strong after the development of gayness in Thailand as before. Because gayness represents a claim within the order of masculinity in Thailand, its development has had little impact on the low social standing of the *kathoey*. Indeed, Eric Allyn (personal communication) suggests that the emergence of masculine-identified gayness in Thailand parallels an increasing stigmatization of *kathoeys* in recent years. This development is understandable in terms of the valorization of masculinity and the devaluing of femininity in Thailand. As a "more acceptable" model of exclusive male homosexuality emerges, those homosexual males who remain within the traditional feminine model are typed as the "unacceptable" old face of homosexuality in Thailand.

The masculine gender identification of Thai gay men is apparent in personal classified advertisements placed in Thai gay magazines. I summarize six such advertisements from two issues of the monthly gay magazine *Mithuna*. Phat, twenty-one years old from Pathumthani, just north of Bangkok, says he is a "straight acting" (*mai sadaeng ork*—literally "not expressing [effeminacy]") *man-king*[14] who wants to meet a *man-queen* who is sincere and also straight acting (*Mithuna* 9 [1992]: 105). Kung, eighteen years old from Bangkok, says he is a straight acting *queen* with the "demeanor of a man" (*nai mat maen*) who is only interested in meeting a *man-king* (106). Prayuth, twenty-four years old from Nonthaburi, immediately north of Bangkok, describes himself as "a real man but I'm not interested in women" (109). He also says, "I'm a real man and anyone who wants to come and be my friend must also be a man." Kung, thirty-two years old from Cholburi, east of Bangkok, says he wants to meet a *king* or *bai* (i.e., bisexual man) but "won't take effeminates" (112). Suchart, eighteen years old from Songkhla in the far south of Thailand, is even stronger in his language and says he "detests effeminates" (*kliat phuak tung-ting*) (107), while twenty-five-year-old Worawit from Chiangrai in the country's far north describes himself as someone who has "chosen to serve his country" and who is only interested in replies from "soldiers, policemen, or men in uniform" (115).

The distinctive histories of the sex/gender categories gay and *kathoey* are indicated by the fact that large numbers of Thai male homosexuals who now identify as being gay resisted assuming the role of a *kathoey* before the emergence of gay identities in Thailand. For many Thai gay men, the *kathoey* presents a negative image from which they distance themselves, and the gay/*kathoey* opposition, not the gay/"man" opposition, is dominant in the construction of gay identity in Thailand. This is because the masculine/unmasculine opposition remains focal in the construction of all male sex/gender identities in Thailand. Thai gay men are as concerned about being considered masculine as their heterosexual compatriots. Furthermore, Thai gay and heterosexual males have considerably fewer points of difference than Western gay and heterosexual men. Historically, the Western homosexual male has been distinguished from the heterosexual male by having his sexuality defined as illegal by the state and as sinful by the dominant religion, and he has been subjected to homophobic violence and discrimination in everyday life. The Thai homosexual male, in contrast has no history of living with legal or religious sanctions against his sexuality nor, for the most part, with the danger of homophobic violence. For these reasons the Thai gay man regards himself as being more different from a *kathoey* than from a heterosexual "man."

The lack of intensity in the gay/straight binary in Thailand is also indicated by the fact that most Thai gay men's "opposition" to heterosexual norms takes the form of evasion rather than direct confrontation. This evasive opposition is encapsulated in the modern Thai expression *phom mai khae sangkhom*, "I don't care about society (or society's attitudes to me)," where the term *khae* is borrowed from the English "care" in the sense of being concerned about something. The attitude of *mai khae*, "not caring," common among heterosexual and homosexual urban youth as well as *kathoeys* and gay men, denotes a cultivated indifference to pressures to conform to social norms. Because Thai sanctions against male homosexuality are noninterventionist, Thai gays rarely need to be vociferously rebellious; they show their opposition to restrictive social norms by simply ignoring them.

In this context, it is significant that while Thai has borrowed much of its modern gay and lesbian terminology from English, it has not borrowed the term *straight*, the heterosexual opposite of *gay* in English. Apart from semantically diffuse expressions such as "the usual man" (*phu-chai thammada*) or "the general man" (*phu-chai thua-pai),* the concept of "straight" (heterosexual) is poorly developed in Thai, and the straight/gay binary is compara-

tively weak. In Thailand the divide is not between gay and straight, where
straight by definition excludes homoeroticism. Rather, the male sexual divide in Thailand, now as in the past, continues to be between "man" and
kathoey, where a "man" may engage in either heterosexual or homosexual
sex. The Thai gay man is not predominantly preoccupied with fending off
homophobic interventions in his life. Rather, in the formation of his sexual
identity he is primarily concerned to distance himself from *kathoeys* and
ensure recognition of his masculinity.

However, we must be careful in characterizing the Thai gay man's opposition to the *kathoey,* for it is of an altogether different character from the
opposition that often exists between gay and straight men in the West. This
latter opposition has historically been characterized by intense negative
emotions—hatred, disgust, vituperation—and by physical violence, both
within and outside the law, even to the point of death. The gay/*kathoey*
opposition in Thailand has none of this intensity. Relations between Thai
gay men and *kathoeys* are rarely hateful. On the contrary, as in the West, the
two groups regularly socialize. The gay/*kathoey* opposition is constructed
more by a process of distancing or slippage away from the negative pole of
the *kathoey* rather than by an abrupt movement of expulsion or denial. This
slippage occurs along a continuum where the boundaries of sex/gender
categories are indistinct and often overlap. The slippage from gay to *kathoey,*
or conversely from *kathoey* to gay, is of a quite different character from
the often angst-filled crossing of the line that separates homosexuality from
homophobic heterosexuality in the West. Not all cultural binaries are constructed with the same intensity of oppositional force. It is perhaps instructive to compare the Western gay/straight binary to the opposition of solids
and the Thai gay/*kathoey* and gay/"man" binaries to the opposition of fluids. While counterposed solids remain fixed at their points of contact, fluids
that flow in opposing currents diffuse along lines of contact that often interact to form backflows and eddies.

The *kathoey* remains an integral part of the modern Thai sex/gender system because he is the negative "other" against which the masculine identities of both gays and "men" are defined. Gay will not replace *kathoey* in
Thailand, because it is a bifurcation within the category of "man," a rendering explicit of a previously unnamed liminal or interstitial zone in the structure of Thai male sexuality. Thai gay identity draws its constituency only
minimally from *kathoeys,* and only a small number of Thai gay men are
reconstructed *kathoeys.* In other words, *kathoeys* have a future in Thailand as
well as a past, because together with gays and "men" they form structurally
related components of the emerging Thai sex/gender system, with each

component defining and supporting the construction of the other. Rather than superseding the old system, the emergence of gayness in fact reinforces the polar opposites of "man" and *kathoey* in the old sex/gender system.

It is noteworthy that while the sex/gender categories of homosexual and heterosexual "men" are now lexicalized in Thai (i.e., gay, *phu-chai*), there is still no lexical differentiation between heterosexual and homosexual *kathoeys*. That is, Thai has no notion of a heterosexual male transvestite. Perhaps homosexual and heterosexual types of *kathoeys* have not been constructed to parallel homosexual and heterosexual "men" because the sexuality of the *kathoey* is of only marginal relevance to the construction of the positionally dominant masculine homosexual and heterosexual identities in the emerging Thai sex/gender system. Both gays and "men" are defined as being masculine in opposition to the femininity of the *kathoey*. In other words, after the emergence of gayness as a masculine form of male homosexuality, it is the *kathoey's* feminine gender identity that is of paramount structural importance in the Thai sex/gender system, not his sexuality.

Stephen Murray (1992, xxv ff.) has remarked on an apparently common direction of historical shifts in the dominant construction of male homosexuality within diverse societies, both in Asia and the West. This common direction of change has been, first, from age-structured to gender-structured homosexuality and, more recently, to egalitarian male homosexual relationships. Age-structured homosexuality (e.g., ancient Greece, New Guinea) denotes a cultural acceptance of male homoeroticism when there is a marked age difference between the partners. Gender-structured homosexuality (e.g., Thailand) denotes the definition of male homoeroticism in feminine terms, while egalitarian male homosexuality (e.g., gay identity) denotes a pattern in which the partners are both constructed as mature "men."

The diverse historical and ethnographic data that Murray cites suggest that male homoeroticism tends not to be stigmatized in societies in which the dominant pattern of male homosexuality is age-structured. Indeed, male homosexual sex within this framework tends to be regarded as enhancing masculinity or even, in the case of the Sambia of New Guinea (Herdt 1981, 1992), as a *sine qua non* of the achievement of adult masculine status. It is more common, historically and cross-culturally, for male homosexuality to be stigmatized in those societies in which the dominant pattern of homoeroticism is gender-structured, that is, when homosexuality is regarded as demasculinizing a man. In other words, in those societies, including Western societies since the Middle Ages and contemporary Thailand, where homosexual males are regarded as being like women, they suffer some of the same stigma that attaches to women in a masculine-dominated culture.

This suggests that in these societies it is not homosexuality *per se* which is stigmatized, but the mark of femininity/unmasculinity. The preoccupation of many contemporary gay men, Thai and Western, with achieving recognized masculine status is therefore comprehensible as a distancing from the stigma of feminization in order to establish male homoeroticism as a form of desire that enhances masculine status. The formation of gay identity in Thailand consequently focuses on affirming exclusive homosexuality by simultaneously attempting to exclude the demasculinized model of the *kathoey* and to affirm links with the masculinity of the "man." Male homoeroticism in the traditional Thai sex/gender system was a split phenomenon, with different homosexual behaviors being assigned to different sex/gender identities. Stereotypically, the Thai "man" penetrated the *kathoey*, never the reverse. Thai gay identity integrates these previously divided masculine and feminine homosexual behaviors into a single sexual identity, resolving the contradiction between a Thai homosexual man's self-perceived masculine gender identity and his culturally ascribed feminine status. In particular, in Thai gayness, insertive and receptive anal sex are reduced from defining markers of sex/gender identity to mere personal preferences between which an individual man may alternate with different partners or with the same partner. In other words, Thai gay identity is defined by homoeroticism *per se,* not by any one of its behavioral permutations.

Gayness can be considered a third term in the Thai structure of male sex/gender categories; a gay male is neither "man" nor *kathoey* but combines elements of both. The Thai gay man defines himself positively with respect to the "man," identifying with all the "man's" masculine attributes except his heterosexuality. In contrast, the Thai gay man defines himself negatively with respect to the *kathoey*, rejecting all of the *kathoey*'s feminine attributes except his exclusive homosexuality. Within this ternary model of male sex/gender categories, gayness can be defined in terms of dual forces of repulsion from and attraction to the two poles of the *kathoey* and the "man"; that is, *Kathoey* >< Gay >< Man. This ternary model retains and expands the hierarchical ranking of male sex/gender categories that characterized the earlier Thai sex/gender system. To the extent that a Thai gay man resists and successfully avoids being placed in an imputed feminine position, he assumes a higher position than the *kathoey* in the Thai hierarchy of sexual power. Nevertheless, in failing to fulfil the father-husband role, the Thai gay man still does not match the standing accorded the heterosexual man in terms of popular perceptions of sexual hierarchy.

However, the term *gay* should not be considered to denote a singular midpoint between the polar extremes of the masculine "man" and the feminized *kathoey*. In the construction of their sexual identities, different Thai gay men appropriate and exclude varying elements of the "man" and the *kathoey*. Some gay men are more *kathoey* than "man," while others are more "man" than *kathoey*. Gayness in Thailand denotes the domain that exists between the "man" and the *kathoey*, and naming this domain shows that the "man" and the *kathoey* are not separated by a void but rather by a genuine realm of male psychosocial existence. In fact, the cultural space between "man" and *kathoey* has never been empty. Historically it has been populated by "men" who engaged in homoerotic activity but did not consider themselves any different from any other "men." Until the emergence of the masculine category of gay, much homoerotic activity between Thai "men" tended either to be overlooked or, if observed, not to be acknowledged.

Thai gayness also shows how a "man" can be transformed into a *kathoey* and, conversely, how a *kathoey* can become a "man." As a conceptualization of the idea of slippage, Thai gayness is informed by the widespread Thai view that sex/gender categories are not fixed.[15] In Thailand a "man" may slip and become gay, and a gay man may slip and become a *kathoey*. It is significant, however, that there is now also a growing recognition of the possibility of movement in the opposite direction, that is, that a *kathoey* may become gay, and a gay may become a "man." As Rosalind Morris (1994, 28) remarks, *kathoeys* "are now [as] likely to be 'passing' for gay men as for women, and they frequently move back and forth between these systems of identification on a daily basis." And the slippage from gay to "man" is also possible. Go Pak-nam regularly advises men he regards to be "gay-kings" to become heterosexual and marry.

If we are prepared to suspend the law of the excluded middle, we may conceive of a ternary logic of male sex/gender categories in contemporary Thailand. This ternary logic is constituted not by the conflict of two opposing and invariable identities, but rather by transformation and interchange among a range of terms that are themselves unstable. Thai gayness reaffirms the traditional man/*kathoey* binary as end points of its own movement in two different directions, but it also demonstrates the nonfixed and nonintegral nature of those two end points by showing that one can be transformed into the other.

Thai Gay Male Identity—Indigenous, or a Western Import?

Rosalind Morris (1994, 19) describes the domains of sexuality and gender in contemporary Thailand as "a social landscape inhabited by two radically different sex/gender systems, one a trinity of sexes, the other a system of four sexualities." The older "system of three sexes"—male, female, *kathoey*—has been outlined above. The more recent system of four sexualities that Morris refers to includes the various combinations of male and female, homosexual and heterosexual. Morris represents the systems of three sexes and four sexualities as distinct and mutually irreconcilable sets of discourses and practices that "cohabit in a single social field." Focusing on the supposed rupture between the systems of three sexes and four sexualities, she conceives of the two sex/gender regimes as "independent" and "unrationalized," and represents the latter as "an importation from the West" that sits uneasily as a cultural overlay on top of the former.

However, a detailed understanding of the historical structure of masculinity in Thailand reveals considerable continuity between the older and newer sexual orders in that country. As described above, Thai gay identity does not effect a complete break from the older system of three sexes, for the patterns that now structure the contemporary model of gayness existed as an overlooked "little tradition" of masculine homosexuality within the context of the explicitly recognized "great tradition" of Thai male sex/gender categories. The radical nature of Thai gayness is not that it breaches the old sex/gender system but that it renders explicit what was previously implicit, and transforms into an identity what was previously a behavior. Thai gayness has emerged from within the traditional sex/gender system and challenges that system by making public what was previously private and by seeking general approval for the conferral of masculine status upon exclusive male homosexuality.[16]

Morris (1994, 29) supports her claim that contemporary Thai gay male identities are imported from the West by pointing to the fact "that the first truly politicized gay community to arise in Thailand emerged in response to the AIDS crisis." This is true, but it is Eurocentric to regard politicization as a necessary prerequisite for the emergence of gay identity and to think that there was no "true" (i.e., Western-modeled) gay identity in Thailand before homosexual men mobilized around issues concerning HIV/AIDS. Rather than hindering the emergence of a true gay identity in Thailand, the historical absence of legal sanctions against homosexuality and the consequent lack of a need for political mobilization to achieve homosexual law reform have led to the development of a distinctly different mode of gay identity in that country. Discussing the system of sanctions against homosexuality in Thailand, Morris comments, "[B]y the traditional Thai logic of visibility and invisibility . . . virtually any act is acceptable if it neither injures another person nor offends others through inappropriate self-disclosure. As one of the country's more prominent *kathoeys* remarks about being gay in Thailand, 'There is no problem . . . providing you don't ripple the surface calm'" (32). I question the general applicability of the comment by one of Thailand's "more prominent *kathoeys*." Similar comments—that life for male homosexuals in Western countries was satisfactory provided they were not "blatant"—were commonly made by conservative homosexual critics of the political gay movement in the 1970s. These comments ignored the fact that when a homosexual man's sexuality was revealed, such as through an inadvertent slip in his public performance of heterosexual masculinity, he was immediately subjected to the full force of his society's sanctions. My work (Jackson 1989, 1995) has shown that the traditional sex/gender system presents many problems for Thai homosexual "men" and *kathoeys*, especially those from Sino-Thai and middle-and upper-class backgrounds, whose lives are often riven by considerable tensions and stresses.

Nevertheless, many ethnic Thai *kathoeys* and gay men lead well-adjusted, happy lives by following the cultural maxim that you can do almost anything you want in Thailand, provided you do not call attention to it and present yourself well in public. From a Western gay political perspective this attitude would be considered an accommodation to an inherently antigay society that denies one the right to publicly express one's "true self." However, if leading a "double life" is a generally accepted feature of Thai cultural life, then it is unlikely that Thai gay men will feel deeply dissatisfied with their lives. Few Thai gay men, except those from a Sino-Thai background, feel a great need to "come out," that is, to resolve the tension of living a heterosexual public life and a private homosexual life by publicly affirming one's sexuality. In Thailand, leading a double life is not necessarily equated with duplicity or deception, as it is in the West, and integrating one's diverse public and private personae into a single "identity" for all occasions is not a strong cultural value. For this reason alone, Thai gayness must be considered a cultural phenomenon distinct from its Western namesake, and Western observers are likely to continue to look in vain for signs of the emergence of a politically or culturally radical gay movement in Thailand, except perhaps among Sino-Thai gay men.

It is obvious that the term *gay* in the Thai language and the notion of "being gay" within Thai sexual culture have been borrowed from the West. It is also undeniable that many aspects of the contemporary gay subculture in Thailand have a Western provenance: for example, the emphasis on masculine body images, the rise of a gay "gym culture," and the deemphasis on sexual role as a determinant of identity. Middle-class homosexual men, the first section of the Thai population to assume the gay model of sexuality, are also among the best educated and most traveled Thais, and are part of Thailand's "globalizing sector," intimately linked with international communications and trading networks. Thai gay men participate in what Dennis Altman (1995) has called "the invention of 'gay' as a global category," a phenomenon which often leads to gay men from diverse backgrounds having as much in common with each other as with people from their own cultural group.

However, these global linkages and transnational gay parallels should not be overemphasized. Simply because the same word occurs in different languages does not mean it has the same meaning in all situations. Indeed, I have referred above to the distinctive history of the term *gay* in Thailand, which was subsumed within the traditional Thai sex/gender system when first borrowed. Furthermore, the term *gay* and the notion of "being gay" have not found fertile ground among Thai homosexual men because they represent the borrowing of a foreign form of sexual existence or the creation of something entirely new in the Thai sex/gender system. Gayness is a marking of what has always existed in Thailand but was previously overlooked. What is new is not the existence of this form of male sexuality but the *acknowledgement* of exclusive male homosexuality without necessary demasculinization. To describe Thai male homosexuals as having "borrowed" their gay identity from the West is to remain within a Eurocentric framework. To interpret Thai gayness as being a Western borrowing is to overlook the social forces operating within Thailand and to erroneously think that Asian social movements that appear similar to those in the West lack their own dynamic and exist only as superficial mimickings of "genuine" Western originals.

In the context of his study of age-structured homosexuality in New Guinea, Gilbert Herdt (1992, 35) warns against the cultural relativism of ascribing ego-syntonic value to non-Western cultural systems. As he forcefully demonstrates, it is not only Western cultures that produce ego-dystonic consequences for their members in the domain of sexuality. The emergence of gayness in Thailand represents an attempt by a section of homoerotically inclined men to resolve ego-dystonic contradictions of sex/gender identity within the Thai cultural order. The Thai term *gay* marks a continuing process of redressing the failure of preexisting ways of managing the tensions that the traditional framework of masculinity in Thailand produced in the lives of many homosexual "men." In this process Thai gay men draw as much from their own cultural traditions as from the West.

Thai and Western gay identities are constructed from distinctive cultural elements. Both possess a similar dynamism of resisting the ascribed inferior status of male homoeroticism in their respective cultures, but each grows from its own cultural source. The emergence of gay identity in Thailand has certainly been influenced by Western models, but gayness in Thailand cannot be reduced to a mere "borrowing" of foreign sex/gender roles. Rather, it is a psychosocial potential that has been enthusiastically taken up by large numbers of Thai homosexual men acting *against* the norms of their own society but for reasons wholly endogenous to that system of norms. Gayness in Thailand is therefore as much Thai as it is Western, and as much indigenous as borrowed.

Acknowledgments

I wish to thank the editors of this volume, Scot Barmé (Australian National University, Canberra), David Buchbinder (Curtin University of Technology, Perth), Craig Reynolds (Australian National University, Canberra), and especially Eric Allyn (Bangkok) for their valuable comments on earlier versions of this chapter. Eric Allyn is an independent writer and researcher who has lived in Thailand for over a decade and has authored and edited several books dealing with male homosexuality in that country, notably the following: *Trees in the Same Forest* (1991), *The Dove Coos* (*Nok Kao Kan*) (1992), and *The Dove Coos II* (1994).

CHAPTER EIGHT

State of Desire: Transformations in Huli Sexuality

JEFFREY CLARK

Introduction

In the mid-1940s, during a period of prolonged drought and introduced epidemics, a millenial cult swept through parts of the Tari basin in what is now the Southern Highlands Province of Papua New Guinea. The Huli people who were influenced by the cult renounced the taboos on separation between the sexes as well as those surrounding sexual intercourse, and the bachelor cult was abandoned (Frankel 1986, 29). The Huli make a strong connection between entropy and sexuality, and have a history of ritual inno-vation (Ballard 1994) such that a suspension of practices related to sexuality makes cultural sense of the Huli desire for the millenium. Beliefs in the cult's promises of imminent prosperity and fertility, connected to the recent arrival of European patrols and their encompassment into an indigenous chiliasm, soon diminished.[1]

Although the previous taboos were reinvoked soon after the cult's de-cline, this early, relatively brief "experiment" inaugurating millenial change through transformations in sexuality (amongst other things) presaged the more gradual if equally dramatic changes regarding gender and sexuality which accompanied colonialism. These derived from Huli expectations and experiences of development, as well as from their encounters with forms of state power. Previously, Tari was a region considered "puritanical" in comparative overviews of male-female relationships in the Highlands (Meg-gitt 1964). The bachelor cult, *ibagiya*,[2] provided the institutional and ideo-logical locus for interactions between men and women, particularly inscrib-ing pervasive beliefs in the polluting power of women and their menstrual blood. These aspects of Huli society, gender, and sexuality have been trans-formed through engagement with state power and constituted in con-temporary times through the *bisnis pati* (business party, Melanesian pidgin [MP]). Before examining this transformation in more detail, we need to briefly consider the Huli and the way that notions of "sexuality" apply to them.

A Brief History of the Huli

The Huli are horticulturalists and pig-raisers occupying a basin and plateau at the western end of the Southern Highlands Province of Papua New Guinea; their staple crop is sweet potato. The first European patrols to what became Tari district occurred in the 1930s, but World War Two and various administrative problems delayed the establishment of a patrol station in Tari until the 1950s. Christian missions started operating in the area soon after, spreading their influence outwards from the station as clan parishes were gradually pacified and derestricted by Australian patrol officers. Tari remained unconnected by all-weather roads to the rest of the Highlands until 1980, five years after independence from Australia was achieved, when the Highlands Highway finally extended to Tari station and beyond. The lack of a vehicular connection meant that development and cash cropping were minimal in Tari in comparison with much of the Highlands, and money is most often earned by laborers who migrate to plantations and the larger towns. Many Huli relate increases in such things as "tribal" fighting and male drunkenness to the increased mobility of people and readier access to beer and prostitutes. Such notions fit readily with Huli concerns about the end of the world, which much of their ritual was concerned to avert or control. The extraction of gold and gas from the Huli region is associated with these millenial beliefs, even though it allows some Huli access to large quantities of cash in compensation for land or through sale of gold: it is thought that the earth will dry up and blow away as its substances are removed (Clark 1993).

Much of Huli public ritual had disappeared by the 1960s, particularly the rituals staged to assuage spirits connected to the fertility of the ground. Huli are well known in the anthropological literature for the extent of separation between men and women, who lived in different houses and sometimes harvested and cooked their own crops separately from spouses. Underlying this separation were pervasive beliefs about female pollution, particularly from a woman's menstrual blood. One way in which men learned to deal with their fears of pollution was through the voluntary bachelor cult, *iba-giya,* or "water given." The name indicates the importance of water in Huli thought as a purificatory liquid, associated with the renewal and fertility of the ground as well as of people. In the bachelor cult men learned spells and behavior to protect themselves from women's polluting power. Although the cult was secular and unconnected to spirits, the missions discouraged its practice as heathen, even though, given Hulu "puritanism," the sexuality of their converts did not lend itself to evangelical control in creating Christians from sinful savages (cf. Reed, chap. 2 in this volume). Instead, attention was paid to constituting a Christian family household. Many older men and women fervently wish for the return of *ibagiya,* as the breakdown of sexual morality is invariably blamed for the extent of the social problems faced by the Huli today.[3]

The Concept of Sexuality

Anthropologists may no longer be able to make statements such as the following: "Even when we remember the very free standard of sex morals in the Melanesian tribes of New Guinea . . . we still find these natives exceedingly loose in such matters. . . . As is probably the case in many communities where sex morals are lax, there is a complete absence of unnatural practices and sex perversions." (Malinowski 1961, 37–38). Nor, in a section entitled "Perversion," could a female anthropologist make the claim that "I am not sure of the degree to which masculine masturbation exists. I never witnessed it." (Powdermaker 1933, 277). Yet, with few exceptions (see, for example, Herdt and Stoller 1990; Leavitt 1991), there has been little advance in the sophistication of anthropological analyses of sexuality in Melanesia, nor much consideration of its constitution in relation to the state nor to European histories of sexuality. The ethnocentric and judgmental tone of statements by Malinowski and other anthropologists begs the question of what or who constitutes the categories of "unnatural practices" or "perversion," and masks the ways in which non-Western sexualities are given cultural expression and meaning.

One of the earliest articles to address the topic of "sexuality" in Highlands New Guinea, Heider's account of the Grand Valley Dani, defines sexuality as "both sexual behavior and sexual attitudes" (1976, 189). At first sight such a definition seems reasonable, yet it betrays a Western preoccupation with "attitudes and behaviors" having to do with the act of sexual intercourse itself, particularly coitus. Commentators on sexuality point out that as a category term it is a relatively recent invention (Allen 1992, 9), coming into existence with capitalism and modern forms of society (Caplan 1987, 2). As an area of investigation, sexuality—like madness—was created conceptually by an emergent discourse about the state's control of bodies from the eighteenth century onwards (Foucault 1973b, 1981; Stoler, chap. 1 in this volume). A definition such as Heider's is problematic in its assumption that, despite cultural variability in sexuality, a universal phenomenon exists. What if Dani notions of sexuality do not revolve around penile penetration? Heider (1976, 188, 193) describes Dani sexuality as a "low-energy system," basically because the sex act is apparently infrequent, particularly after childbirth, with a postpartum abstinence period of four to six years; adultery is also uncommon. To understand Dani sexuality, we would need much more information about their notions of aesthetics, erotics, pollution, pleasure, and fantasy. To state that "sex does not have much interest for them" (189) is not the same thing as suggesting that the Dani have little interest in sexuality, "which is always more than one can or would wish to imagine, because it exists in the confluence of unconscious desire and the vagaries of social relations" (Matthews 1992, 124).

The Huli had a postpartum taboo on sexual intercourse similar to that of the Dani, related to notions of female pollution and the danger for the mother of carrying two infants in case of flight; contemporary birth-spacing statistics suggest that this taboo still has some force or that other reasons, possibly financial, now exist for spacing children (see Clark and Hughes 1995). Unlike the Dani, however, the Huli surrounded sexuality with an elaborate cosmology and belief system, although it would be meaningless to describe it as a "high-energy sexual system" by comparison; in fact the latter would once also have been characterized as a "low-energy sexual system" if frequency of intercourse were taken as a measure of sexuality (the Huli put a lot of energy into regulating coitus to avoid contamination, whereas the Dani apparently experienced little stress by not engaging in coitus; Heider 1976, 192). Female sexuality, in particular, was subject to extensive male ritual control, and bachelors were to avoid women. The absurdity, then, of assessing levels of sexuality against a crude tally of coitus is revealed. Huli men were preoccupied, if to varying degrees, with issues of sexuality and its control, while the Dani seem unconcerned with such issues; yet both have lengthy postpartum taboo periods and relatively low frequencies of sexual intercourse.

The problem of a suitable conception of sexuality remains, although a universal definition seems untenable if we reject the notion of a basic human sexuality modified by culture (see Vance 1991). For the purposes of this chapter, sexuality provides a framework for interpreting experience based on notions of the body and related to sexual behaviors and attitudes. Each cultural form of sexuality must be treated on its own terms to avoid ethnocentrism and the imposition of Western assumptions, which treat sexuality as a biological phenomenon subject to empirical, indeed mechanical, measurement; or as a manifestation of libidinous forces, located or repressed in the unconscious, which must be controlled for society (civilization) to prosper; or as a separate category of attitudes and behaviors which can be studied in isolation from other aspects of social life (see the introduction to this volume).

The first assumption reveals positivistic biases about the nature of knowledge, treating the methods and reasons for scientific observation as nonproblematic and value-free, as if sexuality was an instinctive drive and not a social construction. "Measuring" approaches appear to deny the link between knowledge and power while promoting this link as a technique for the surveillance and control of bodies (for example, on the part of the state in its interventions into people's lives, particularly in instances when "primitive" people are seen as "oversexed"; see Reed, chap. 2 in this volume). Clearly, this behaviorist approach is not feasible nor desirable in Tari, where quantifying people's sexuality would tell us little about its cultural specifics or its relationship to politics and history (cf. Altman 1992, 34). An examination of Huli narratives would reveal more than a behaviorist study of sexual practices—as novels often tell us more than sexological research.

The second assumption treats sexuality as a property of the individual and the unconscious, and does not address the cultural context in which sexualities are generated and made meaningful. Paradoxically, it is the control and redirection of sexual energy which is seen to provide the impetus and energy for the (male) creation of culture. The third assumption is that sexuality can be treated as a "thing in itself." While this may be true in Western society with its separation of sex from reproduction (Caplan 1987, 2, 16–17), such an assumption would for Huli society reify sexuality, divorce it from other features of social life, and impede an understanding of the moral dimension of sexuality and the way in which it is ontologically grounded in relations of power and gender.

The last point raises a number of interesting questions. Was it always the case that (Huli) sexuality existed, waiting for the analyst to give it a name (cf. Foucault 1981, 105), or is the outside observer imposing Western concepts on a non-Western society? If the latter, is it still possible that the Huli may have their own concept of sexuality? Given that the invention of sexuality as a concept emerged, for Foucault (1981) out of a changing discourse about the body and its control and productivity under state systems, do Huli notions of sexuality (if they exist) relate to the exercise of power and, today, to the state? To answer the first question, clearly "sexuality" as an area of study imposes a Western framework of beliefs and analysis, which assumes that a category exists "out there" but does not ask whether this is also a category for non-Western peoples like the Huli. Granted that sexuality is an undifferentiated experience for the Huli, it seems undeniable that there is a Huli discourse about sexual practices and the body. If "sexuality" is not (just) a private affair but a set of public beliefs about the practice and consequences of sexual behavior—and for the Huli these beliefs are based in and not separate from a cosmology which equates sociomoral relations with states of health—then the Huli could be said to have a concept of sexuality.

As a concept, it is a reasonably systematic set of beliefs about relations among the body, coitus, and power/knowledge, most marked in the bachelor cult.[4] In support of this claim for an indigenous "sexuality," I suggest similarities with Foucault's argument about the emergence of sexuality as a differentiated form of knowledge accompanying state development. Huli sexuality, while not created as a differentiated subject of study, did have connections with knowledge/power and the control of bodies. In particular it controlled young men, children, and women, not through punishment or incarceration but through concepts of pollution and, to some extent, surveillance. Huli sexuality is tied up with reproduction and its conflicts with a morality of aesthetics and pleasure, whereas Western notions separate "sexuality" from "reproduction" and practice, although a connection with morality and regulation also prevails. My exploratory argument is more concerned with assessing the usefulness of Foucault in writing about "savage" sexualities than with presenting a comparison of a Foucauldian history of European sexuality with divergent postcolonial trajectories (but see Stoler, chap. 1 in this volume).

If sexuality is one mode through which power is constituted, then the project is to discover the "semiotics of sexuality" (Connell and Dowsett 1992, 68), particularly with reference to colonialism. Furthermore, if sexuality is to some extent constitutive of history and society as well as constituted by them (71), then it is as much a product as a producer of postcolonialism, providing a framework for emergent power relations and "new" bodies. The sexualized "tribal" body was once invested with notions of power which did not depend on the state. Transformed sexualities come into being in the boundary zones between the "tribe" and the state, and there were different modes of resistance to the latter than would be found in the West. This helps to explain why it is that the Huli, in their engagement with the *nambis* (seaboard), sometimes couch their experiences in the idiom of unregulated coitus and pollution (Clark 1993; 1995). While the colonial state often surveyed and controlled subject populations through its constructions of an indigenous sexuality, the Huli, in their confrontation with a weak, independent state, use the decline of a highly controlled sexuality as a metacommentary on what has happened to them since incorporation into the *nambis*.

Huli Sexuality and Social Change

Sexually transmitted diseases (STD) are often constructed, from a male perspective, as pollution illnesses in some way connected to Europeans, and provide a metaphor for understanding aspects of transformations in sexuality. STDs are all known by the one term, which is the same term for pollution illness (AIDS is too novel to be yet a stable category. It may eventually be classified as a similar illness). It is crucial, then, to investigate not only the manner in which people construct illness but also their gender identities (see Clark and Hughes 1995).

The Huli understanding of sexuality, prior to this inserted link with illness, would once have been circumscribed by the dominance of the bachelor cult as a site in which, *pace* Foucault (1981), a particular discourse about gender and sexuality was produced.[5] The self, gendered male or female, a particular kind of subject, was produced by experiencing a time and space structured by the moral and behavioral precepts of the cult, which were in turn validated mythologically. There was no monolithic form of "traditional" Huli sexuality, but rather a continuum whose variations related to the discourse and practice of the cult—as evinced in everyday life. The discipline of the everyday created particular knowledges which empowered men and women in different ways. For example, women derived power from their ability to menstruate, while men believed that "women have no *mana* ('knowledge/custom/talk') and so they are precluded from participation in decision-making" (Goldman 1983, 99).

The importance of gender as a structuring principle in Huli society has been considered by a number of authors (Frankel 1986; Goldman 1983, 1988; Clark and Hughes 1995), but only Frankel has specifically considered indigenous constructions of sexuality, mostly in relation to "traditional" forms of pollution illness.[6] Frankel (1986, 97) maintains that "fertility and the control of sexuality are central concerns in Huli religion . . . (and) their view of these issues guides much everyday behavior." Do these concerns still preoccupy the Huli in 1995, or are "modern" forms of sexuality being constructed in a space where the state occupies an "amorphous zone of power" (Taussig 1992) within Huli cosmology?[7] Huli understandings of sexuality are related to notions of "good" and "bad" blood and their consequences for growth and health (Frankel 1986, 99–100). Female sexuality and menstruation were, according to myth, created by the deception of men; Huli cosmology is substance-driven. A central concept by which sexuality is regulated is glossed by Frankel as "desire," or *hame*, raising the question of how Huli think about and regulate states of desire today (*hame*, depending on context, spans emotions from "like" to "lust"). Desire in this instance is a cultural construct, not a biological urge. Given the demise of the bachelor cult,[8] do Huli continue to construct notions of sexuality around blood, or around more modern substances such as money?

Do Christian teaching and an imposed morality enforced by the legal system of the state provide a modern equivalent to the rules and mythology of the bachelor cult? If so, this still does not help explain the supposedly dramatic increase in STD in Tari since 1980, when the Highlands Highway arrived. Do Huli, like Western youngsters, now become socialized as sexual beings in a discontinuous manner, learning about sexuality not in a structured way from the myths and practices of *ibagiya* but from a haphazard array of sources, including Christian discourse on sex and sin, gossip and rumor, videos presenting images of romantic love and violence, outright misinformation, and personal observation and experience in Tari and elsewhere? To answer these questions, we need to posit sexuality as a social construction and not as a type of behavior reducible to biological imperatives and functions. Sexuality is not separate from politics or history. Foucault argues that a change in discourse (a particular combination of power/ knowledge) produces different subjectivities, a different awareness of the body as a site for the experience and production of consciousness. In this chapter the change from the discourse and practice of the bachelor cult, foreshadowed by the millenial cult, to discourse(s) and practice(s) in the time and space of the state, will be discussed as creating "sexualities."

Sexual intercourse among the Huli was meant to be engaged in and enjoyed for the purposes of reproduction only, and male and female sexualities were both created and regulated through the operation of the bachelor cult. Huli sexualities were related to particular constructions of power and knowledge which revolved around notions of "blood." Power/knowledge was displayed through the beauty and decoration of male bodies, associated with birds of the forest and wildness/purity, and assured through the cult control of primordial female blood and through women's bodies, which were made beautiful and "ripe" through menstruation, the elimination of "bad" blood. Male maturation was related to cult knowledge and display (Goldman 1983, 239–240). Goldman (280) argues for a connection between the term for decoration, *yari,* and the tonally different term for cassowary, *yari,* suggesting that the qualities of aggression and autonomy perceived in the bird were valued in men. A woman's maturation continues to be related to her physiology; the onset of menstruation was when a girl turned into a woman. Women's attractiveness was diminished by reproduction if not sexual contact; men's vigor and beauty were diminished by their contact with women and loss of vital substance, semen, in coitus. Fatherhood marked the confirmation and decline of masculinity.

The argument here is that it is no longer the bachelor cult but the *dawanda* or *bisnis pati* (business party, MP), where entrance is for a fee and alcohol and illicit sex can be purchased, which articulates desire and creates Huli sexualities. The *dawanda* contextualizes, and is perhaps an indigenous commentary upon, experiences of the state—through its churches, plantations, mining companies, and so on—which construct contemporary Huli bodies. A particular Huli logic links coitus, cosmology, and entropy, in such a way that transforming sexualities—related to beliefs, for example, that men are like dogs in having sex by the roadside with prostitutes—suggest a world in moral as well as physical decline. To act like a dog is not to be human and denotes a state of illness. Sexual intercourse is no longer only for reproduction but for pleasure and monetary gain. Central to this is how the Huli connect beauty, display, and knowledge, as well as a consideration of the ways in which this triumvirate has been influenced by Christianity, development, tourism, and alcohol.

If Western notions of sexuality are inextricably bound up with rationality, so that masculinity is aligned with reason and femininity with the passions (Seidler 1987), then to what logic is Huli sexuality bound? And can transformations in the latter be historically traced to colonialism, for instance, as they can for Europe since the Enlightenment? Huli male sexuality was strongly connected to notions of beauty and knowledge, and self-decoration was thus a display of ability and power. Goldman (1983, 117–118) suggests that the male body, with its cane girdle and snake headband, is a microcosm of the Huli world, a landscape in which a mythical snake encircled with cane lay coiled under the earth, connecting up the sacred sites which were ritually induced to release the powers of fertility (cf. Frankel 1986; Clark 1993). How is the postcolonial Huli male body constituted, now that power is also identified with the state and its icons, such as money, and not just based in religio-mythic forms? Huli men now rarely grow their hair or wear the wig which symbolizes manhood, knowledge, and control over women (Goldman [1983, 280] again suggests a semantic connection between "wig/hair," *manda,* and the tonally different *manda,* "knowledge"). Today, instead, hair is kept short and Western-style clothes encompass the body, leading some older men to claim the young are dirty, with dull, flaky skin (an idiom of deviance); senseless (like pigs and dogs); and small like insects (shrinking, related to smaller heads of hair/knowledge). This new male body evokes a different cosmology of power and fertility, which is located within the *nambis* and not amenable to local ritual control (Clark 1995). Men are not as beautiful or knowledgeable as they once were; their sense of themselves as sexual beings has changed.

I have noted above that the Huli inhabit a different time and space through their experiences of the state. Time and space were previously constituted by a discourse of the body which relates to the domains of *anda* and *hama,* "house/private" and "open space/public display," respectively (Goldman 1983, 102). Yet knowledge is not as codified nor behavior as regulated as they once were; men are not confined to *anda* and *hama* and can travel to the *nambis* and experience events and things not before imaginable. Social and self-regulation has changed because moral precepts are no longer learned so formally or totally. Young men are accused of practicing sex like dogs in the road, confusing the boundaries between the private and the public. Men, as women say, now *kalapim banis/baret* or jump fences/ditches, crossing boundaries (including that of the *nambis*) where once they were confined to parish areas, and boundary crossing is a mark of deviance implying a breach of norms and resultant pollution illnesses (Goldman 1983, 91, 100).[9]

Sexuality is today not only controlled or constructed by managing the tension between *anda* and *hama,* but also by negotiating a further tension between these domains and the state. If social order was maintained by confining sexual intercourse to purposes of reproduction/fertility, then an increasing emphasis on sex for pleasure, both inside and outside of marriage, suggests a further tension. The connection between disorder and sexual promiscuity is a cause for Huli concern, although the level of anxiety over the STD rate may derive more from cultural construction than epidemiological fact. Indeed, it is the promiscuity of the young which is most often cited by older Huli as a major reason for the decline of the social and moral order. "Modern" forms of sexuality are no longer confined by notions of blood as it affects growth and health and associated in myth with a primordial female power of fertility. Women accuse men of doglike behavior in their increasing demands for sex, resulting in too many pregnancies. Uncontrolled sexuality leads to more pregnancies, which "thin" the blood and may "finish" it; the postpartum taboo by contrast allows for a woman's blood to replenish.

Contemporary sexualities are, then, inextricably related to the exogenous discourse of the state and its institutions, whose power/knowledge is associated with money, not blood. But money cannot be controlled like blood; men state that they only "play" with money and do not fully understand it. Premarital and extramarital sex are commonly described as "play" (cf. Goldman 1983, 98), and money is sometimes referred to as a *pamuk* ("prostitute"; another common pidgin term for "prostitute" is *pasindia meri,* or "passenger woman"), because it is used for brief and nonreproductive pleasure. This metaphor derives its meaning from the equation between the desire for sex and the desire for money, which is believed to motivate some women to become *pamuks*. Sexuality transforms as the context of desire changes. Different forms of power, accessed through new kinds of knowledge, entail different kinds of sexuality. "Modern" forms of sexuality cannot, like money, be controlled, and it is the exchange of money and gifts for sex which comes to define the Huli male experience of their own bodies as dirty and shrinking in the postcolonial world.

Men's attitudes to female sexuality are in many respects unchanged. Basically, women's sexuality is associated with deviance and illness (cf. Goldman 1983, 279). Although women continue to be characterized as lacking willpower and the knowledge and ability to make decisions, men's ability to control and regulate female sexuality has diminished. This is attributed by Huli to the decline of parental control over daughters, to education, and to the lapse of proper *mana* for behavior. Despite the ignorance of many men concerning women's sexual pleasure, my interviews revealed that women are often thought to enjoy sex more than men. This was not related to any physical display of passion during coitus, but to the ability of women to have almost "continual" intercourse, while men can only manage ejaculation once or twice in an encounter. A *capacity* of women, not their actual behavior, was equated with desire and used to explain their moral failings as creatures with a sexual appetite far exceeding that of men. It is thought that married women, even though they want sex as much as, if not more than, their husbands, control their desires because of a fear of pregnancy (some women did divorce husbands because of their sexual reticence). Yet many women can now indulge this appetite to a greater extent, as they are no longer "locked up" but "free." Women no longer "wear grass skirts' (that is, follow custom), and some say that they can now "test" different men, different styles of sex, and different penis sizes. Indeed, this is why men believe women become *pamuks,* as they give in to an irresistible sexual desire; they are "too hot for sex." This insatiable appetite may help to explain a connection between *pamuks,* who covet money and sex, and greedy witches. Women's sexual desire or "heat," *pobo,* is destructive of men's health and bodies. The vagina of a *pamuk* was not only described as "like fire" but "like coffee"; that is, it was on sale for money, confirming a connection between money, female sexuality, and deviance.

The *pamuk* plies her trade at the *bisnis pati,* known more usually as *dawanda,* previously a courting party where married men went in search of unmarried women to sit close to, and sing to, and whisper in their ears, with the supposed intention of finding another wife. A *pamuk* who persists in a relationship with a married man is often referred to as his "wife." It is no accident that the *dawanda* provides a context for the emergence of "new" sexualities, because before colonialism it apparently allowed married men, and to some extent single women, to explore and perhaps experiment with aspects of their sexuality. I do not know if the Huli make any connections between *pamuks* and the single women who went to precolonial *dawanda.* It is difficult to trace out the changes over decades in the nature of *dawanda,* but it seems clear that they mark a gradual transition in sexualities rather than the sort of abrupt break that was initiated by the 1940s millenial cult.

The crucial feature of the modern *dawanda* is that the exchange of sex for money has become a diacritical symbol of Huli interaction with the *nambis* and its power/knowledge, which is why the *pamuk* and the *dawanda* occupy such a central place in Huli discourse about the state of the world, including its imminent demise (the Huli connection between entropy and sexuality has previously been remarked upon). *Bisnis* marks out the preeminent domain of European activity, and the Huli identify business companies, like CRA at the Mt. Kare goldmine, with the spread of STD. The *bisnis pati* itself captures the equivocal and possibly ludic sense in which the Huli relate to capitalism—as playful money-making, a mimesis of business activity, something in which Huli cannot seriously engage. Public drunkenness, prostitution, and *dawanda* attendance may even be forms of resistance to the state's attempts to control its populations.

Ibagiya and the bachelors were the focal sites for Huli constructions of the moral community and sexuality within the domain of *anda/hama*. The bachelor cult was where men learned to be afraid of women's menstruation and its disastrous consequences for their skin, hair, and health. Basically, they learned to be wary of being "cooked" by the "fire" in a woman's vagina—but they did not learn the rules of sex. An older, related man (rarely the father, who would be too ashamed) told these rules to the soon-to-be or newly married man, so that a man came to marriage with little knowledge of the sex act itself (techniques used were magical, not erotic; cf. Meggitt 1964, 210). Intercourse may have been delayed for six months or more before the worried husband—often under the prompting of an older man who told him to have sex, produce children, and become a man—stifled his fear and shame long enough to arrange a meeting with his wife in the gardens or bush. He still used much magical protection beforehand.

It is now the *dawanda* and *pamuks* which, within the encompassing context of *nambis,* provide this focus, although perhaps more in reference to the destruction of community, given the connection between coitus, cosmology, and entropy. The *dawanda* provides a template for Huli experiences of new forms of power/knowledge since the advent of colonialism. Men achieved power through the regulation of sexual intercourse (displaying this power through their bodies) by magical spells, *gamu,* and abstinence; semen controls or "cools" female potency in myth (Goldman 1983, 98). They now lose control over their sexuality through engaging in deviant relations with the *nambis* by exchanging money for sex with *pamuks,* who are symbolic of the uncontrolled and external power of the state (Clark 1995). Europeans are sometimes referred to as "money" people in opposition to "garden" people. Women are frequently said to become *pamuks* because of their "hunger" for money. Men's semen, seen to be concentrated in a stinking residue in the vaginas of *pamuks,* is often cited as the source of STD infection. Semen, the life-giving "water" of men, no longer controls or "cools" power associated with women but, like women's heat, results in pollution. This change in beliefs about the properties of semen is linked to epidemic narratives of a "primal" woman who had sex with a European man and traveled throughout the Highlands spreading STD.

Huli men and women trace STD to Europeans, business companies, and to the decline in the moral order which followed soon after pacification. Young people, it was said, finished high school and then had sex on the road like dogs in heat. This is why young people age so quickly, developing grey hair and loose skin before they are really old. Perceived increases in STD rates may be related to local developments, such as the construction of the Nogale BP gas plant and its employment of Europeans and non-Huli people. The extra money which development brings means that more *dawanda* are staged, more beer can be bought and consumed, more *pamuks* are attracted, and more people contract STD. The boundary which Europeans and *pamuks* represent, and which the Huli cross for employment or nonreproductive pleasure, is identified with immorality and illness.

Colonial Man

Port Moresby, for the Huli the symbolic capital of the *nambis,* is often described as hot and dirty, two of the qualities associated with women (it could be argued that Port Moresby stands for the state, except it is not clear to me if the Huli have such a concept beyond that of an amorphous zone of power). Female heat is necessary for fertility, but it has to be controlled; otherwise dirt accumulates, and defilement and ultimately barrenness occur. Port Moresby is also said to be burnt by the sun, treeless, and largely without vegetation. While this connection between the *nambis* and femaleness is mine, many men describe women as having "too high a temperature for sex," which is why some women become *pamuks.* They cannot resist their sexual urges; they are "too sexy" (*wali tanga bubu),* with a "strong feeling" for sex, and want the novelty of "style sex," new variations on position and technique. Younger women supposedly have a preference for relationships with men such as policemen, not just for material advantages—a salaried government job, housing on the station, and so on—but for their relatively greater sexual sophistication, presumed to be attained as a result of their postings throughout the country. Young men as well as women are said to be in a state of *tanga bubu*. Uncontrollable sexual desire, sometimes causing temporary madness, or *lulu*, and which could lead to pollution illness, was blamed by men on the attractiveness of women (Frankel 1986, 110).

Nowadays men blame beer, which makes them *lulu*, for having sex with *pamuks*, who are "too sexy" and who transmit STD, which can lead to sterility. Women become *pamuks* because of a desire for money and spread STD. This belief connects coitus, desire, pleasure, money, madness, barrenness, and pollution through an illness. STD is thus a bodily metaphor for the experience of postcolonial power/knowledge, producing new "truths" about the relationship between sexuality and growth. Men, once associated with birds of the forest, with what is good and true, are now often associated with dogs and falsity. People who don't listen, a common accusation made against the young, are by the same token people who lie (Goldman 1995). Young men can no longer be bachelors and are often described by older Huli as "rubbish men." *Iba*, water or semen, the control and drainage of which is so important in ground-fertility rituals and the regulation of sexuality, has been displaced by *bia* ("beer" in pidgin; *lulu iba*, "mad fluid" in the vernacular). Beer, along with money, is a prime symbol of external power, but in this case, its blockage and flooding reflect Huli interactions with the *nambis*. This is why beer, money, and *pamuk* behavior are inextricably related, through the *dawanda*, in modern constructions of sexuality and illness. At a Huli *singsing* one of the young male dancers collapsed and died, apparently of a heart attack. People referred to this as *mali mindibi*, "black dance," which was not an explanation of the death but a statement about the blackness of the dancer's skin showing through the paint, the implication being that the man was not fit to be decorated (a healthy man's skin is supposed to be pale). The deceased had recently returned from Port Moresby, and many blamed coastal sorcery for his death. The man's body was said to have decomposed and been very smelly only a day after his death. The link between the state, dirt/smell, and pollution (a strong smell is associated with femaleness), danger, and death, is very clear in this instance.

If the domestic arena was a "zone of primordial [female] power" (Goldman 1983, 103), the *nambis* is a zone of contemporary power from which impurity and contamination can also emanate. Men are sometimes described as ill-featured and having dirty skins, perhaps a reflection of the way in which men are as much compromised and threatened by the power of the state as they are by "female" powers of reproduction and fertility. The epitome of disorder, drunks, are sometimes described as *iba tiri* (water fool). This is also the term for a mythical trickster spirit, or *dama*, who engaged in illicit sex and with whom the Huli interact along "symmetrical lines of deceit," (Goldman 1983, 224, 223), and who is a symbol of boundaries

(Goldman 1995). The classification of drunks as *iba tiri*, however, is a commentary on the asymmetrical and nonreciprocal nature of Huli interaction with the new zone of the *nambis*, the source of beer and money, which deceives them and denies them egalitarian access to resources.[10] The *nambis* is too "hot" to control; it has the potential to make men drunk/*lulu*.[11] Politicians "trick" and lie to those who vote them into power; the state "plays" with the Huli and provides them with money, just as Huli "play" the game of (illicit) sex with the same stakes, and consequently suffer illnesses of contamination. According to Goldman (1983, 103), the *hama* is a place where men's exchange activities, using the media of "pigs, paint, and parlance," minimize the risk of pollution and impurity. It is in the public domain, *hama*, that men appropriate the products of female labor (104, 290), yet the public space in which men operate today is also controlled by the media of money, beer, and (non-Huli) discourse. It is the state which appropriates the products of Huli male labor in an exchange which is largely unmediated and disordered (cf. M. Strathern, in press). Thus pollution is not minimized, and men's display of their beauty and knowledge, the power they obtain through their sexuality, becomes compromised and articulated by the events which take place in the *dawanda*.

If men once "sought their identity deep in the forest" (Glasse 1992, 232), confirming it through the discursive practices of the bachelor cult which linked beauty and knowledge to wildness/purity—the forest was where men could talk to birds and "count" trees, where they could be good, *baya*—they now seek it through the *bisnis pati*. Here appearance and power are linked to the male identities constructed through the *nambis*/contamination. *Dawanda*, sites for beer drinking, the exchange of money for sex, and dancing to the music of string bands, are frequently built close to roads. These are spaces in which experiences of the state/*nambis* are linked to an emergent discourse of sexuality, marked by male perceptions of female sexuality as deviant and associated with violence, illness, and emotions such as anger and shame (Goldman 1983, 279). *Dawanda* have replaced cult houses located in the forest as the venue in which power/knowledge is contemplated and expressed, not to affirm masculinity but to compromise it. If *ibagiya* regulated sexuality and produced bachelors in terms of a masculine ideal, *dawanda* produce men who are "fallen angels," ill and out of control. The *bisnis pati* represents unregulated sexuality in the form of prostitutes, women associated with money, consumption, and public spaces (such as markets). Located between the peripheries of the forest and the state, in spaces beyond but intruding on both the public and domestic, contemporary male sexuality is perhaps liminal.

The bachelor cult did not produce a seamless and nonproblematic Huli sexuality, in which female aquiescence to male dominance was assured and rendered "natural." The plethora of taboos surrounding coitus and its conse-quences suggest that gender was as much a domain of transgression as rule-governed behavior. Sexuality had to be managed, or illness and general decline would occur. It is likely that men were never confident in their masculinity, which was a fragile creation supported by the discourse and practice of the cult. As Glasse (n.d., 15) reports, "Huli men are fundamen-tally ambivalent and insecure in their sexual role," which the connotations of autonomy in the decoration term *yari* suggest—men can only be real men by themselves and in the absence of women. This ambivalence and insecurity have been heightened by experiences of colonialism and inde-pendence; there is no modern equivalent of *ibagiya* to construct and shore up the fragility of men's identities, their sense of being "men." As suggested above, the *dawanda* perhaps deconstructs notions of Huli sexuality as much as creating it in new forms, particularly in the context of men's dependence on the state—a dangerous, uncontrollable place, unlike the forest, where men traveled with the appropriate behavior and *gamu* to replenish and re-charge their maleness.

The Good Woman of Tari

Foucault has been criticized for neglecting the ways in which the gendered body (Seidler 1987) affects the exercise of power. This raises the issue of whether Huli "sexuality" is a male-centred discourse. Do Huli women have their own constructions of sexuality which exist separately or in opposition to male constructions? The same question has been posed of gender in Mel-anesia in general (see Strathern 1987; Ortner and Whitehead 1981).[12] While women's sexuality is created by men in myth, Huli sexuality is a gendered construct. Men and women create their own sexualities but, as a set of ideas about "relations between the body, coitus, and power/knowledge," male and female sexualities are less opposed than woven out of the same cloth. Men, including those who never attended the bachelor cult, which was voluntary, were as constrained as women by its logic. Both men and women refer to the same sorts of cosmological and mythological features of Huli society to explore and explain the connections between health, power, the periphery, beauty, and knowledge.[13] To reiterate, if it was once the bachelor cult which constructed and displayed sexuality, it is now the *dawanda* which occupies this discursive space. One difference between the two institutions is that women played little active role in the actual *ibagiya* itself, except as respondents to male beauty, whereas they can now take a more dynamic part in the process, as *pamuks* or as women who belong to women's groups

which take a public stance against men's behavior as drunks, *dawanda* participants, "tribal" fighters, and so on.

Men are the clients of *pamuks,* and women seem to accept at a personal
level *pamuks* who are relatives or coresidents of the parish. Yet at the public
level both women and men are equally condemnatory of the *pamuk* as an
amoral person, responsible for the descent of Huli society into disorder and
illness. These ideas are similar to notions of the witch, and indeed there are
similarities between the deviant figures of witch and *pamuk* which link both
to the periphery or *nambis.* The prey of the witch has changed from predominantly young children to young men, paralleling the way in which
the *pamuk* contaminates the future of Huli society by leading its young
men into temptation and illness (see Clark 1995). Women continue to be
strongly attached to a self-construction based on a regulated sexuality directed towards reproduction, which the negative portrayals of women as
witches or *pamuks* only confirm. Witches are possessed by non-Huli spirits;
pamuks are characterized as mobile "foreigners," *wali tara tangaru.*

The connection between health, morality, and sexuality seems to be as
obvious to women as to men. Just as women's sexuality had to be muted
and controlled by the discursive practices of the bachelor cult, many women
continue to subscribe to a connection between their sexuality and menstruation and reproduction. A "good" woman is one who is productive and
reproductive (menstruation gets rid of "bad" blood, making a woman attractive and her skin shiny and tight; motherhood diminishes a woman's
beauty). The Huli term *baya* exploits a link between beauty and morality;
what is beautiful is also good.[14] A girl who turns into a woman at menarche,
if she follows prescriptions on her behavior to protect the health of men,
is good and therefore beautiful. In this sense, women's beauty is similar to
but intrinsically different from that of men. The small minority of women
who dress like European women and attempt to make themselves attractive
with cosmetics are not considered to be *wali bayali,* "good" or "beautiful"
women—like drunks and *pamuk,* they are products of the *nambis.* Such
women are often considered to be deviant, and may be compared to or
designated as *pamuks.* The latter are said to be found at markets wearing
scanty clothes and makeup (Clark and Hughes 1995). Women who affect
European behavior and dress, that is, who act in a non-Huli manner, align
themselves with the periphery and deviance, the *nambis* representing in this
instance a "new" boundary of power. Huli women, in their constructions
of sexuality, often invoke Christian notions of the family and describe themselves as hard workers and providers of nurture and care to their children.
They wear sensible, unrevealing clothes with little in the way of jewelry or
decoration. Being a "mother," that is, menstruating and reproductive, still

seems to be an essential part of a Huli woman's sexual construction (reinforced by Christian beliefs), contrasting with the way in which men display their sexuality through their bodies and self-decoration.[15] Despite men's claims of their voracious capacity, many women claimed to enjoy sex, if at all, only insofar as it was directed towards conception.

If men's sexuality is bound up with appearance and power/knowledge, women's sexuality is intrinsically related to their fertility and reproductive ability. It is important to note that "blood" and "heat" continue to be central concepts around which women as sexual beings are defined, contrasting with substances such as "money," "medicine," and "beer," which define men's sexuality. This is not to deny that money is an essential aspect of *pamuk* sexuality, but the *pamuk* is more like a contemporary and autonomous man than a woman in her behavior. The bachelor cult and rituals of the ground were concerned to control or "cool" the "good" female blood of a young, unmarried woman, and to direct its fertility into the world. Women's sexuality, like men's, has an aesthetic of power and morality. Huli men and women concur that some women are too "hot," *pobo,* not in control of their will and passions; male sterility may be blamed on their semen being "cooked" through contact with *pamuks.* Money is a powerful substance which now vies with blood in constructing sexuality. Money may in some instances be comparable to "bad" blood (see Clark 1993), which makes sense of men's claims that women's blood is no longer as dangerous or lethal as it once was; it is now "cooled" by European medicine and will soon lose its power. In other words, these "modern" constructions signal a shift in power/knowledge to the *nambis,* creating a dependency on such things as money and medicine. These are some of the new icons of power, beyond the control of the majority of the Huli, even though a substance-based construction of sexuality persists. This point is supported by A. Strathern, who states that among the Melpa, "[i]ndividuality and choice are expressed not *in* bodily substances but *through* control over them" (1994, 50, his emphasis).

It seems that the state now controls a potency which was once primordially female, but it remains problematic whether women's sexuality has been as compromised by colonial and postcolonial experiences as men's. Women's sexuality, through its relations with the state since pacification, continues to transform, as beliefs about the *pamuk* and the Christian "mother" indicate, but women are perhaps less fragile than men in this transformation. Christianity has helped to secure women's sexual and self-identity in the face of change, despite a loss of power and autonomy that they have experienced as men have become less threatened by women's menstrual secretions. This takes into account women's claims that their blood, around which their sexuality is constructed, is "finished" more quickly today through an increase in the frequency of unregulated sex desired by men. Goldman (1983, 279) states that "male ideology that women have no *mana* must be set against those behavioral contexts where the ritual and chronological primacy of women is declared and deferred to." A problem for women is that this declaration and deferral appear to have attenuated in the postcolonial scene.

Conclusion

If the locus of precolonial power has been appropriated by the state, as indicated by Huli myths about gold, the *nambis,* and mining companies, and by beliefs in new forms of pollution (see Clark 1993; 1995), then the existence of a "tribe" within a state provides a new context of power/knowledge for the working out of male and female sexualities, one within which masculinities are not only ambivalent but possibly liminal, as is the case with the classic Highlands "rubbish man" who acts "like a woman" (Strathern 1981). The sense in which I use the concept of liminality owes as much to Foucault as to Turner.[16] Consider this quotation about the medieval Ship of Fools:

> It is for the other world that the madman set sail in his fools' boat; it is from the other world that he comes when he disembarks . . . [his voyage occurs] across a half-real, half-imaginary geography, the madman's *liminal* position on the horizon of medieval concern. . . . He is the passenger *par excellence.* . . . And the land he will come to is unknown—as, once he disembarks, the land from which he comes. He has his truth and his homeland only in that fruitless expanse between two countries that cannot belong to him. (Foucault, cited in Sheridan 1980, 18, Foucault's emphasis)

This quotation captures perfectly the way in which colonialism has changed the geography of experience to create not madmen—although madness was a response to pacification (see Clark 1992, 1993)—but alienated passengers on the fantastic and unfamiliar ground of the "other world," where the Huli are "prisoner[s] of the passage" to state incorporation. *Pasindia* ("passenger" in pidgin) is also a term for prostitutes and itinerant men, indicating the power of sexuality in evoking experiences of transition and marginality in time and space.

The bachelor cult and much of Huli ritual were responses to female sexuality, a power which had to be appropriated and controlled to impede its dangerous capacity to cause illness and death through pollution or sorcery. It seems that ritual, in conjunction with *ibagiya,* shored up men's ambivalence about their sexual identity in everyday interaction with women. Incorporation into the state simultaneously exposed masculine fragility and denied to men many of the bases for asserting their manhood. The irony is that the Huli developed institutions which created as well as coped with masculine ambivalence, but what was of their own making was undone by foreign institutional intrusion. Like Samson in his experience with the Philistine state, Huli men have to some extent become powerless. In the early days of colonialism many Huli men viewed the new power as a means of strengthening their masculinity. I was told that men could be even better bachelors, more beautiful and knowledgeable than before. This expectation was quickly dashed as local autonomy diminished and pragmatic adjustments had to be made to state incorporation. Huli men have, in a sense, lost their hair and today seldom make wigs. They are drawn into the amorphous zone of power outside of *anda/hama* boundaries where *pamuks,* those obscure objects of desire embodying the state, are the new Delilah.

The threat of AIDS looms over the Tari basin, and rumors spread of gangs of Engan men supposedly infected with HIV raping women in revenge (*Papua New Guinea Post-Courier,* 12 February 1993). AIDS is too novel for Huli people to have any firm or clear ideas about its nature. People certainly know of AIDS and relate it to an apocalyptic future in terms of the now familiar Huli equation of morality and health. Male sexuality was grounded in the purity of the forest, and it is suggestive that many men thought that the only way to avoid catching AIDS, which they believed could be transmitted through something as innocuous as sharing a cigarette, was to return to the forest and live in isolation from one's fellow human beings, like cassowaries. If the idiom of decoration points to its display of power/knowledge and health, to be like a cassowary is now to seek refuge from illness, a display of powerlessness. To become wild once more is no longer a viable alternative for the Huli since their encompassment within the boundaries of the state, a new "beyond" where men go to be "bad," and one whose dangerous resources, unlike the forest of old, prove resistant to Huli attempts at control and manipulation. The Huli say that Independence was "when everything turned around"; new spaces have been created through experiences of colonial time. It is because of this that Huli men cannot display themselves like cassowaries or, for that matter, like Europeans.

Huli sexuality is "transcultural," emerging out of the confrontation of notions of desire and power as an indigenous sexuality became caught up in the discourse of the West. This confrontation was experienced by the Huli through their interaction with Christian missions, labor migration, development programs, and more recently with health intervention measures designed to curtail the spread of STD and HIV/AIDS. While one can only applaud the efforts of insufficiently supplied and often poorly supported health workers, a kind of essentialism permeates government and mission attitudes to STD prevention, which equates sexuality with notions of the primitive while aligning moral "breakdown" with a loss of traditional values (in an ironic reflection of Huli notions that connect entropy and sexuality). The way in which the Papua New Guinea state attempts to regulate and control bodies, however inefficiently, has to be related to changes accompanying the transition from "tribalism" to state incorporation through a process of colonialism. The "tribal" body is thoroughly entangled with the body of the Christian citizen and, where the state is weak at its peripheries, processes of incorporation and resistance create subjects whose sexuality needs to be understood as thoroughly "modern" or even "postmodern." This understanding is both theoretically salient and practically urgent if effective intervention programs against STD and HIV/AIDS are to be implemented.

Acknowledgments

The research upon which this chapter is based was undertaken in 1993 as part of an Institute of Medical Research project aimed at improving awareness of the epidemiology and treatment of STD among the Huli. I wish to thank the IMR for its assistance with visas, accommodation, and transport, and for its general support of the project. The IMR project on STD/HIV education was initiated by Ms. Jan Dyke in 1990, who cowrote the interview forms which generated the data for this article and conducted interviews with Huli women in 1993. Ms. Dyke and Mr. David Whiting of the Tari Research Unit merit special thanks for their social and technical assistance during the survey. Sandra Pannell made many useful suggestions for improving the substance of the report, as did John Vail and Chris Ballard, and Paul Reser sacrificed many hours to print out copies of the interviews from a dsyfunctional database. I express my gratitude for all of their efforts and assistance. I also express my appreciation to the many Huli people who cooperated in the interview process, and especially to Hayaku Andiki and Rita Tukili. Any errors in the chapter are the author's and not the IMR's responsibility.

CHAPTER NINE

A Plague on the Borders: HIV, Development, and Traveling Identities in the Golden Triangle

DOUG J. PORTER

"Boundaries," the doctor continued, passing to and fro in front of the windows and pausing every now and then to gaze at the traffic on the river and to shake his head in wonderment at the industry of humankind, "exist to be transgressed, they are there to facilitate crossings, not to frustrate them."

Alex Miller, *The Ancestor Game*

Travelers' tales, media accounts, and various missions and investigations have carried alarming stories about the abduction, trafficking, and expulsion of young Burmese women involved in the commercial sex industry in Thailand. Many of these women are reported to be infected with HIV, and there have been persistent reports of their murder by Burmese authorities following their expulsion from Thailand as illegal aliens. Human rights organizations have argued that these responses indicate efforts on the part of the Burmese and Thai states to sequester "risk groups" from the broader population (Asia Watch and Women's Rights Project 1993).

At the same time, and perhaps galvanized by these reports, representatives of the international community have expressed great concern about the rapid transmission of the HIV epidemic through the border regions and into the central regions of Myanmar, China, and India. The border regions of eastern Shan State in Myanmar[1] and northwards into India have always been the focus of rivalry among Thailand, China, and India (Steinberg 1993), and these regions are now being transformed by unprecedented trade, investment, and the movement of people. The HIV pandemic is becoming concentrated in these borderlands. Just south of the Shan State border, the Thai town of Chiang Rai is dubiously distinguished as having the highest rates of HIV infection and AIDS in Thailand. The Yunnan border town of Ruili, central to the lucrative China-Myanmar border trade just across the Myanmar frontier on the old Burma Road, has the highest incidence of HIV/AIDS in China. And in Manipur, on the northern Myanmar border with India, more than half of all intravenous drug users, perhaps 3 percent of the population, are reported to be HIV positive (Porter 1995a).

Until recently, the international donor community opposed humanitarian assistance to Myanmar as part of a general, though largely unsuccessful, embargo on the State Law and Order Restoration Council (SLORC), the military government in power since 1988. This has now changed. The human rights violations, particularly as experienced by Myanmar's ethnic minorities moving across the Thai, Yunnan, and Burmese borders, and the problem of HIV/AIDS have finally prompted an international response. Supported by agencies such as the UNDP and UNICEF and various bilateral donors, HIV/AIDS and related development projects are underway or being planned by foreign, nongovernmental organizations (NGOs) in association with Myanmar and Thai counterpart organizations.

These interventions are being mounted with some trepidation. The dramatic accounts of the trafficking of women into the sex industry of Thailand and beyond to Europe, Japan, and the growth centers of Taiwan and Korea are but one aspect of the vile brew of narcotics trade, investment, and territorial contests among drug overlords, their militias, and the SLORC. This is Southeast Asia's new frontier, the new cowboy land of wheeling and dealing that has accompanied the liberalization of trade and economic policies in China and more recently Myanmar.

For more than three decades, these borderlands of the Golden Triangle have been like Kristof's frontiers (1959, 278), where sociopolitical relations are rudimentary and "marked by rebelliousness, lawlessness, and/or absence of laws," so-called "peripheral territories" central to struggles between ambitious states and ethnic minorities. The contest between the interests of the Burmese state and the people living in these border regions is historically deep. The Burmese state has been "inner oriented," primarily concerned with the occupation and containment of territory according to ethnic Burman conceptions of "national" sovereignty. Ethnic nationalities living in the borderlands have been "outer oriented," fashioned irrespective of and often in protest against the political boundaries of the nation state (Grundy-Warr 1993, 42).

The HIV pandemic has an especially problematic relation with frontiers and boundaries of all sorts. The spread of the virus is evidence of much more than the struggles to manifest and resist national sovereignty along territorial borders. The nexus of HIV transmission across this territory is a metaphor for the globalization of investment, trade, and cultural identity. Although the dominant realist tradition in studies of international relations conceives national territorial spaces as homogeneous and exclusive (George 1994; Walker 1984), what is referred to as the "new global cultural economy" must be seen as a complex, overlapping, disjunctive order, which cannot be adequately understood in terms of center-periphery, inner-outer, state-border models of the past (Agnew 1993, 256, 258; Appadurai 1990, 2). Nor is the HIV epidemic fully explained in terms of the push and pull factors of migration theory, or accounted for by reports of "trafficking in victims," where young women and men are mere dupes of an international economy of desire that impels them to cross borders on trajectories determined by "structural forces." Neither can it be expected that the dominant Western "bordering" of genders, bodies, and sexual identities necessarily has currency (Bell 1994, 40). The situation in the Golden Triangle involves many evident disjunctures of time and space, of local and global economies, cultures, and politics. The global HIV/AIDS epidemic is therefore a useful metaphor in other ways as well. As Mann, Tarantola, and Netter (1992, 14) note, the epidemic is "composed of thousands of epidemics—both separate and interdependent—occurring in communities; . . . even in a single city or population area, several different epidemics are usually underway, each with its own rate of spread, intensity, and special characteristics."

My own awareness of these disjunctures and of the inadequacy of conventional representations of change came as a result of work in the region with Burman and Shan researchers during 1993 (see Porter 1995a). This work investigated regional political and economic change, in particular in trade, transport, migration, market development, and investment, as well as the changing patterns of ownership and control which underlay the remarkable developments since 1989. It was obvious that the oppositional nature of theorizing that had long been taken for granted in regional development literature—the assembly of push-pulls, centers and peripheries, and so on—was a poor context for this evident telescoping of time and space. How to convey the inflections of teashop meetings with elders from high-country villages speaking a King James version of English taught by long-departed Baptist missionaries, struggling to be heard amidst a cacophany of Michael Jackson on Chinese boom boxes and snatches of Thai TV plying sinus and cough relief? How to match the eloquence of the young militia boy sporting the latest Adidas, a weary pair of traditional Shan pantaloons, and a Pakistani AK–47 while laughing about his "night in Bangkok" and gesturing, with a sweep of his arm, how much this "felt like Marlboro Country"? Although, as Appadurai (1990) notes, a vast array of studies have been brought to bear on the side of "homogenization," the dynamics of cultural heterogeneity, locality, and indigenization are beginning also to be explored in a sophisticated manner (Feld 1988; Hannerz 1989). Past and future, local and global, fragmentation and homogenization are not opposing arguments, but constitutive trends of the new global reality (Friedman 1990, 311). No adequately "representational" account of how local people like these apprehended the changes, the numbers and statistics accumulated by my research, could be fixed or definitely established.

My research was not specifically concerned with cultural identity nor sexual identities, but it was not possible to escape the epistemological and the political problems of "representation." In various ways, the politics of representation is my main concern here. Problems associated with the "duality of representation" (Duncan 1993, 39) pressed on this research. Irrespective of how one errs toward a representation which highlights the global continuity of local events and identities, or privileges their particularity and difference, the account is inevitably engaged in a distinct patterning, where relations between events, people, and stories are fixed, their positions are noted, and links are made between people's actions and more pervasive forces seen working through them, or behind their backs. This highlights the duality of representation, whereby the diversity and difference of local situations is "'recuperated' by appropriating it into a categorical framework that is familiar and useful" (39). These categories and frameworks of course did not emanate from the local situation, but traveled along with the researchers, together with a host of assumptions derived from locations and experiences that were radically different. Our concern was not just that our representations were likely to be invasive; that is inescapable (Gregory 1993, 277). Research such as this always implies a priori subjection, where "researchers," "truckers," "militias," and others met along the way are situated among and imbued with familiar attributes around which data are heaped to adorn the subject categories. More to the point, these situations, and indeed the research topic, are an intense "zone of contest" (Fforde and Porter 1994). The research, the first of its kind in the region, is highly germane to the interests of governmental, external, and local agencies that are instrumentally concerned to delimit, define, and stabilize the people who were "identified" and were "creators" of the events being researched.

Shortly after this research, I was invited to put aside these qualms about "representation" and become an expert adviser to the Australian government. Australia was about to resume bilateral development assistance in Myanmar by funding NGOs specifically concerned with HIV/AIDS. Although not yet persuaded of the probity of development assistance in this difficult political situation, I was intrigued to learn just what NGOs made of the confusing situation and agreed to participate in the appraisal of NGO proposals for funding.

Some proposals, all from large multinational NGOs,[2] focused directly on the border areas of eastern Shan State. All had three features in common that are characteristic of many HIV/AIDS projects (e.g., O'Shaughnessy

1994, 70): the ensemble of techniques they intended to apply; the centrality of categories of "risk groups" to the way local identities were understood; and their manifestly political character. Each proposal for funding included the same repertoire of techniques through which the "target group" was to be identified, subsequently influenced, and monitored, with KABP surveys, IEC,[3] and peer-group awareness activities used to identify gaps in people's knowledge and to transfer information, and with subsequent observation of behaviors intended to result from this transfer of knowledge. The second feature is also common in other HIV/AIDS projects. Despite widespread disaffection with the notion of "risk group categories," and the now-favored linguistic shift toward concern with "risk behaviors and situations," all proposals highlighted categories of particular groups of people, prominently the category "Commercial Sex Worker" (CSW). These euphemisms conveyed the sense that the HIV epidemic was attributable to small, physically and socially discernible epicenters which were populated by "core transmitters" that the project would "effectively and efficiently target." Wrapped around these categories was a particular understanding of how "risk groups" conduct their affairs.

All proposals carried a clear political analysis. Understandably, proponents put great distance between their efforts and the military SLORC. This "distance" was a requirement of the Australian government, but it was *de rigueur* for each agency to defend its decision to implement projects in Myanmar in the face of criticism from the democratic opposition forces and their supporting NGOs. The explicit distancing was underpinned by the liberal political outlook of the NGO community embodied in a participatory, community development discourse. This affirms the idea that the state and civil society (and the market/economy) are philosophically and structurally separate "spheres" of society. NGOs (and much recent scholarship) have defined an alternative beyond the state's reach where a "free market of groups and individuals" can participate, define their own strategies, and secure the means for attaining them (Porter 1995b). This rationale is most pronounced when NGOs work in situations like the eastern Shan State, where political alliances are volatile, where the state's reach, though powerful, is contested and institutionally weak, and correspondingly where it seems possible to assist weaker sections of society to carve out and enlarge spaces of control over their own affairs.

This rationale was further supported by the metaphors being applied to the HIV phenomena in the region. As one recent article remarked, HIV/AIDS in the Golden Triangle has become "The Plague without Borders" (Lintner 1994, 26), an aphorism which conveys the sense of an unbounded, seamless terrain in which humanitarian organizations must intervene, occupying it and bringing it to order. The categories by which vectors of risk were presented in these proposals were central in creating order. They are the "magic bullets" which can be transported from elsewhere to allow an understanding of people and places on the basis of stable, isolable, and inter-related properties, all essential for any developmental intervention, but doubly so in uncharted localities known only as turbulent. In this respect, the proposals had much in common with the practices of colonial health services and the occupation and marking of terrain that commonly occurs when the rationalities of development travel to new locales (Craig and Porter 1994; Porter, Allen, and Thompson 1991).

My contention in this chapter is that the entry of agencies concerned with the HIV pandemic marks a new phase in efforts to impose borders and boundaries on this contested region. I argue that these projects represent a new "plague of borders" through which externally derived identities and sexualities travel and add to the multiplicity of contests over terrain and identities that are already apparent. Further, I suggest that the un-selfconscious application of these rationalities can contradict the political intentions manifested in the proposals, and potentially disrupt and overpower the various ways in which local people are coping with their turbulent situation and the spectre of HIV/AIDS. The borders constituted by the sexual identities featured in these interventions and the ensemble of techniques and organizing strategies characteristic of HIV projects are discursive, but they can be no less pervasive than the borders of geography and political identity being contested by ethnic groups and regimes of official authority. Contrary to the assertions of NGOs and others who are intervening to "enable and ennoble" people facing the HIV epidemic, their work can become part of the technologies of government, whereby connections will be established between the aspirations of authorities and the activities of individuals and groups hitherto marginalized and beyond the reach of the state (Rose and Miller 1992).

I review the ways HIV has been mapped in the border region, drawing on official data from medical surveillance of the epidemic. I then summarize historical events to give some appreciation of the contemporary region. Following this, I look more closely at the vexed question of determination and agency in understanding the movement of people throughout this region. In some respects, this chapter parallels that by Lisa Law (chap. 10 in this volume). There is a well-developed critique of discourses in the literature on HIV and AIDS (e.g., O'Shaughnessy 1994, 21; de Zalduondo 1991) and there are critiques of neopopulist development in a similar vein (e.g., Mitchell 1991; Leftwich 1993). I will similarly note, for instance, how these categories of core transmitters, like CSWs, are representationally inadequate and force "reality to fit the model like the feet of the Ugly Sisters [forced] into Cinderella's glass shoe" (Reid 1993, 6–7).

That discourses distort or mislead and should be brought to account by other realities is well established. More important here is the realization that discourses are also, everywhere, performative and denote particular political investments. Language, as Fairclough (1992) points out, is the means by which unequal power relations are naturalized and "carried off" to become embedded in institutional practices (Foucault 1977). This point is well taken in debates on HIV interventions in Africa (Triechler 1992a, 1992b; Seidel 1993). To review this point and to focus discussion, I consider the ways in which subjectivities are fixed and stabilized through the various associations made between "poverty" and choice. I present alternate views on "poverty" and HIV/AIDS as a way of elaborating an alternate conception of subjectivity and identity that I believe is more consistent with the diverse ways in which local people account for their situation and actions. The view of subjectivity presented here does not overcome the politics of representation, for the positioning of subjects, objects, and ideas in relation to instrumental rationalities is a routine part of the way the world is managed. As Laclau (1990) has noted, however, the dislocation of identities that inevitably occurs through external interventions has contradictory effects. Resistance to stabilization and the bounding practices typical of HIV/AIDS interventions is likely to be intractable, but they can also be the foundation on which new identities and political competencies can be constituted. The quotation from Alex Miller's *Ancestor Game* at the beginning of this chapter reminds us that boundaries exist to be transgressed; they are there to facilitate crossings.

HIV/AIDS in Myanmar: A Grave and Alarming Situation

Assessments of HIV transmission in Myanmar are constrained by the paucity of data. Simple extrapolations across HIV sentinel survey sites can mask valuable insights (and limitations) of a still-developing sentinel system. Testing began in 1985 and identified high levels of infection among intravenous drug users (IDUs) in geographically distant locations throughout Myanmar. Health officials were clearly stunned by the speed of transmission (Porter 1995a). Myanmar statistics are not representative of the general population, but the country is now regarded as one of the three countries in the Asia-Pacific region with the most serious AIDS problem.

Without succumbing to the well-known "avidity for numbers" which marks global debate on the pandemic (Mann, Tarantola, and Netter 1992, 14–15), we can see that particular trends in the national data are noteworthy, including the widespread geography of the epidemic and the consistently high rates reported in localities close to the Thai and Yunnan borders. The first case was detected in 1988, and by mid-1991, 1,764 HIV cases were detected in 76,720 people tested from all social groups across the country. Since 1988, the proportion of people examined who tested HIV positive has consistently increased—to 2.39 percent in 1993, although these results may be misleading due to the small sample and low prevalence rates.

Among a population group regarded by health officials as "most likely to be affected" (drivers, trishawmen, traders, fishermen, prisoners, not including CSWs), 1992 testing indicated HIV infection rates of 9.1 percent in Tachilek on the Thai border and 9.4 percent in Muse to the north (Department of Health data, in Porter 1995a). Statistics indicate that nonsexual transmission has historically been the most important mode of transmission. Heroin use, introduced to Myanmar only in the early 1970s, has become increasingly prevalent. The levels of HIV infections among IDUs in Myanmar are among the highest in the world, jumping from 54.5 percent in 1989 to 74.3 percent in 1992; sentinel test results from 1993 range up to 95 percent at major cross-border trading centers, particularly in the north of Shan State. Data on women working in commercial sex are especially unreliable, but whereas HIV infection rates among IDUs are higher in the northern Shan and Kachin States and lower closer to the Thai border, the reverse tends to hold for HIV infection among women who report being involved in commercial sex. This is consistent with estimates of infection among prostitutes in northern Thailand, where the rate of HIV transmission is reported to be highest and where a substantial number of women working in brothels come from Burma, particularly Shan State.[4] Heterosexual behavior is regarded as the primary route of transmission in northern Thailand, and this is believed to be the case in Myanmar (Porter 1995a).

Contemporary Events: A Region of Transformation

The speed of HIV transmission reflected in these statistics and the prevalence reported in particular border areas of Shan State are only two aspects of the profound changes in the border region. Important factors in these changes have been, first, the so-called "transitional economy" in Myanmar; the changing political and economic relations between Myanmar, China, and Thailand; and the locally specific events attending the collapse of Burma's Communist Party in 1989.

During the 1980s Myanmar's national economic fortunes were unstable. Gross Domestic Product (GDP) swung from nearly an 8 percent increase in 1980–81 to an 11 percent decline in 1988–89, coinciding with the

SLORC's tumultuous takeover. Thereafter, almost all external aid ceased, tradable commodity prices dropped, and the external debt continued to increase.[5] Pressed for cash and legitimacy, the SLORC began to liberalize aspects of economic life (Cook and Minogue 1993) and to improve commercial and strategic relations with neighboring countries, particularly China and Thailand (Simon 1991). The rapid growth in the Thai economy during 1987 to 1990 led to Myanmar becoming a target as a source of "vital raw materials." A series of trade and taxation treaties between Thailand and China from 1986 to 1991 resulted in major infrastructure developments in eastern Shan State (Porter 1995a, 11–5, 31–5). Economic growth was equally rapid on the Chinese side, reaching 12 percent of GDP in 1992. Yunnan's provincial income increased fivefold between 1990 and 1991 (Yao Jianguo 1991; Wilson 1993), and cross-border trade increased by a phenomenal 20–25 percent each year from 1989 (Porter 1995a). China now dominates trade and economic life in Myanmar and, driven by a new era of economic reforms characterized by "sweeping pace and an unprecedented depth" (Xie 1993, 199), investment is now surging from the east of China to the traditionally isolated interior.

The effects in Shan State of economic policy and strategic interests were accelerated by domino-like events following the collapse of Burma's Communist Party early in 1989. Until its collapse, the BCP area extended down from west of Mong Ko in northeastern Shan State south to the Thai border near Tachilek—an area of around 20,000 square kilometres (Lintner 1990a; Smith 1991, 378–79). The civilian population reaped a peace dividend from the cessation of hostilities with the Burmese army, but this also had profound regional significance. The removal of BCP restrictions facilitated massive investments in roads to enable the direct movement of people and goods across the borders. At the same time, the formation of authoritatively and territorially distinct militias from remnants of the BCP was closely associated with dramatic increases in narcotics production and trafficking (USDEA 1993; Lintner 1994).[6] These events accelerated the extension of the cash economy well beyond urban settlements and increased the rural people's susceptibility to a devalued local currency and steadily increasing costs of living.

In summary, the various national economic policies, alignments among Chinese, Myanmar, and Thai traders and officials, and the physical links facilitated by the collapse of the BCP have moved the region from relative isolation to a position as one of the fastest growing border economies in Southeast Asia. Alongside major investments in infrastructure and communications has come also a dramatically fluid patterning of alignments between various political, entrepreneurial, and military authorities. Boundaries and identities of all sorts are constantly being drawn and redrawn; the maps spread over the walls of administrative and command centers throughout the region depict a mobile patchwork of lines delimiting who holds sway and under what conditions at the time.

The Victims and Victors

The drawing and redrawing of boundaries and scales of alliance, movement, and identities contrasts with what I term the "singularity" of debates about HIV interventions in this region. I will discuss this singularity in relation first to the fixation with numbers, and second to the homogenization of identity implied in aggregated statistics on categories of people. Finally, I present a more extended analysis of the way in which these identities and their presumed sexual practices are constructed at the level of causality.

Media and research attention has been preoccupied with the numbers involved in this jostling traffic of people and commodities across the national boundaries of the Golden Triangle. These discussions seem to convey the sense that settling on "a number" powerfully and confidently stabilizes the basic attribute of the HIV phenomena. Figures from the Thai side frequently refer to the 60,000 to 70,000 Burmese working illegally in Thailand, and officials, perhaps also deflecting the source of HIV away to some Other, have estimated that between 200,000 and 500,000 Burmese are illegally living in Thailand. Over two-thirds of the women arrested in brothel raids in 1992 and 1993 came from Burma. At the lower end, Thai NGOs estimate that 20,000 Burmese women are involved in Thai prostitution, and that 10,000 new recruits arrive every year—village surveys in Shan State suggest that between 5 and 20 percent of village populations are currently or recently have been working in Thailand (Asia Watch and Women's Rights Project 1993, 1, 31; cf. Porter 1995a, 68–77).

This focus tends to reaffirm the categories to which these data are presumed to apply. The focus on cross-border movement reinforces the "epicenter" view of HIV. Implied, and often explicit, is the idea that risk is derived from an external Other, the "sex industry in Thailand." Travelers and workers are "exposed to risks" and adopt behaviors based on "foreign" sexual identities and forms of conduct, which then travel back home. A direct "line" is drawn in mental maps between travel to this other world and return to the pristine world of home (cf. Buckley, chap. 11 in this volume). It is evident, however, that cross-border movement is not the most significant feature of the bustling travel. For instance, by far the most significant numbers of people travel within Shan State, not across the border. About 700,000 to 1.2 million people move each year along the stretch of road linking Lashio and Muse in the north, far outstripping the number of

Myanmar people moving to and from Thailand (Porter 1995a, 68). And the line of travel is seldom an unbroken movement from one world to another. Typically, people engage an array of occupational and social identities while traveling. Consider the case of Lawgu, an Akha traveler and one-time motorcycle transporter in his mid-30s, who recounted his previous four months' activities:

> Yeah, I've been to Thailand, about two months ago. I worked on a construction site doing painting. I've worked there before, sometimes for a couple of months, sometimes just a week. I left home (just north of Mong Phyat) just after harvest and went up to Mong Shu to work in the (gem) mines. There was too much trouble up there, so I worked in Keng Tung as a market labourer for a week or so, and then I joined trucking friends and worked as a turnboy on one of the Lines (cooperatively organized passenger transport). ("Is it always like that, moving from one place and job to another?"). No, sometimes I do, it depends on what's going on. I still spend a lot of time at home, my wife has a knitting machine and she makes clothes for a trader in Mae Sai.

The statistics on cross-border movement are also highly gendered. Young women tend to be the focus of discussion among health officials and NGOs, and most, if not all, are categorized as moving to Thailand for employment as full-time commercial sex workers. The reality of any bus, pick-up truck, or motorcycle load, however, is that men occupy most seats. And many, rather than traveling from one fixed place of employment to another, are "traders," normally "transporting" some item, documentation, or information, with the prospect of exploiting some comparative advantage in an array of enterprising activities within Myanmar's borders. San-san is a young Shan woman in her early twenties who remarked,

> Sometimes I work with my friend who has a motorcyle, we move and trade household items, like plastics, soap, batteries, things like that. Often we carry messages, mostly about what's needed in different village markets, or lists and things to a trader from another place. Sometimes I visit relatives in Chiang Mai area, but I'm really supposed to be at home most of the time.

This "livelihood travel" produces a bewildering network of relationships. San-san remarked about how "mixed up" things have become, telling how in the previous month designer jackets were being sold in Tachilek market bearing a "Made in Thailand" label. In fact, she said, these jackets had first been made in China, and because traders heard they were so much cheaper than in Thailand, they were transported to Thailand; new pockets, buttons and labels were stitched on, and they were exported to China as "superior Thai-made" designer jackets.

Travelers readily agree that "some women" engage in commercial sex work as their single occupation and that probably this "number" has increased. They also agree that CSWs, like everyone else on the road, are highly mobile.[7] The difficulty is that forms of commercial sex are far less structured than is conveyed by the singularity of the category "CSW." In Shan State as in Thailand, commercial sex is a camouflaged world of homes, hostels, parlors, trucks, clubs, bars, restaurants, "laundry services," truck stops, and hair salons. Just as the locations of employment are diverse, so too are the various mixes of identity that go to make up a survival strategy far less durable than can justifiably be homogenized in the "CSW category." Many, perhaps a majority of women engaged in commercial sex, could also be known as traders, laborers, entrepreneurs, truck attendants, or entertainers. For many women, "prostitution" is not a singular identity, but merely one of a range of economic and social identities that make up their livelihood strategies. Sexual servicing does not necessarily distinguish a "free woman" from a wife, a trader, or a market stall operator (see also Lyttleton 1994a).

> Thida Thein had worked in a small brothel in Keng Tung, one of six she knows of, for two months. With her four-year-old daughter, she had left her village, about 15 miles distant, four months earlier after her husband had gambled and lost all their savings. Her husband, she explained, was a motorcycle transporter, but had found it increasingly difficult to get work. Commercial sex work is, for her, quite lucrative because her brothel caters to traders, mostly from China and towns along the border, and sometimes Thai traders too. Thida Thein prefers Thais even though she is afraid of HIV, and is not keen on local people, not just because Thais offer more money, but also because she is scared her brothers will find out the work she has been doing. According to Thida Thein there's plenty of work with the increase in tourists and traders but, even though at 23 years old she could work for a long time yet, she expects to return to the village once her savings have improved.

A remark by Treichler seems to accord with Thida Thein's situation in that there is "no fixed correspondence among the components of sexual desire, actual practice, self-perceived identity and official definition; and it is culturally complicated as well" (1992b, 394). Although I cannot extend my analysis this far, it is also possible that the Western classifications of sexual desire, as discussed here and by Jackson (chap. 7 in this volume), which are undeniably wrapped into the category CSW, are better understood in terms of what Parker (1987, 161) calls the "fluidity of sexual desire." Unfortunately, the plurality of travels and occupational identities, and the temporal dimensions of travel between one identity and another, tend to be silenced by the preoccupation with "vectors of transmission" which singularly link "source" with "home," and with categories of sexual behavior presumed to exist in the West or in Bangkok (Manderson 1992b). The categories can become barricades erected around people, homogenizing the identities within, and reaffirming a "we/them" attitude in our understanding of the sociology of HIV.

The question of "choice" has become an unwelcome guest at HIV debates. The various layers of singularity observed above are underpinned in Clifford's critique (1992) of "the ethnographic present," where the local situation is conceived of as a timeless dimension in which tradition blends past and present together as one. In one guise, people's behavior is often seen as an instance of a preexisting custom (Pratt 1986, 139). People's choices in this view tend to be seen as deluged by external influences. HIV/AIDS is now often seen in terms of this view (Treichler 1992a, 398). In HIV project proposals, questions of "choice" evident in the plural motivations for travel by people like Lawgu and Thida Thein are glossed over by analyses which privilege a one-dimensional view of "poverty" and "structural determination." As others have noted (see, for example, Law, chap. 10 in this volume), women tend to be treated as victims who are unable to resist the predations of "globalization."

Obviously this is a contested issue to be approached cautiously; it would be senseless to ignore reports of the ruthlessly efficient trafficking in women, the complicity of some officials, and the appalling conditions of servitude (Gray n.d.; Muecke 1992; Asia Watch and Women's Rights Project 1993). In my research, on a village-by-village basis, both men and women migrants very frequently had left for the same Thai town/province, and males often went to the same employer. This might be attributable to "word of mouth," as travelers return with tales of fortune and opportunity, encouraging others to head for the same destinations. But there is also a sophisticated network of well-known local agents, either circulating within the region or available at Mae Sai/Tachilek, who are linked, in the case of women, with networks extending from Burmese and Thai officials to brothel owners who "distribute" them and, more currently, "circulate" them through a maze of commercial sex establishments, at least throughout Thailand. But one need not presume that choice is "determined" by a host of global and local structures operating against the travelers' wills. One researcher contends that "force and trickery" is a "myth" if extended beyond "only a small proportion of

CSWs [who] enter the sex industry under [these] conditions" (Guest 1994, 2). Others argue that there is slim evidence for widespread involuntary or forced prostitution in Thailand and remark on the "strong determination" women show when stepping into the profession (Sukanya Hantrakul 1983).

The causal relations drawn in HIV interventions between poverty, travel, and the adoption of new identities illustrate two other aspects of the singularity I have noted: the "economism" of explanations, and an unnecessarily constrained view of how people make travel and identity decisions. Popular accounts of travel to Thailand are consistent with research done a decade ago on the relations between rural conditions and prostitution in Thailand (e.g., Pasuk Phongpaichit 1982; Sukanya Hantrakul 1983). Project documentation is replete with assertions to the effect that poverty directly forces women into prostitution and unsafe sexual practices (cf. O'Shaughnessy 1994), and AIDS has been referred to as a "poverty virus," given its disproportionate effects on and situational correlation with the poor (Dwyer 1993; Panos 1992). In eastern Shan State, widespread food insecurity, the shortage of ways to generate cash to cover food-deficit periods, and the poor state of social services all point to the fact that poverty is a generalized condition among rural households. To this extent, "poverty" explains migration behavior. However, conceptions of poverty in HIV project documents tend to reflect an overwhelming concern with economic conditions, or what Chambers (1994) calls "income poverty." This has limited explanatory value. Income poverty does not explain the fact that spatial patterns of migration are highly differentiated. There does not appear to be a consistent relation between migration and the relative wealth of villages, or between the migration history of particular households and their socioeconomic status relative to other households in the same village (Porter 1995a, 72–76). Moreover, most travelers, and especially those who cross the Thai border, do not come from the poorest ethnic groups but from lowland villages in Shan.

Poverty and Travel

What has been termed "Jodha's paradox" (Jodha 1988) can help to illustrate the implications of the line of reasoning evident in HIV interventions. In Jodha's research in two villages in Rajasthan, India, rural poor people created their own categories and criteria for characterizing their identity and circumstances. Jodha compared data from fieldwork over twenty years and found that, although the households were almost 5 percent worse off in per capita real incomes, they were better off according to 37 of 38 of their own criteria. Consistently, when rural poor people are asked to focus on poverty and well-being, they use a wide-ranging web of criteria and relationships, and seldom accept narrow considerations based on economic wealth (cf. Max-Neef 1991; Rahmena 1992; Chambers 1994). In general, rural poor people's conceptions of "poverty" refer to judgments about their indepen- dence and options; put another way, they refer to their varying capacities to create and move toward new identities, to consider options and to create room to move.

These additional dimensions of "poverty" can be read into the wide- ranging stories that people in east Shan State told about their travel. In addition to "poverty of subsistence," due to lack of food or insufficient in- come, many young people travel to overcome "isolation" (which includes a sense of being marginal, peripheral, or feeling cut off geographically and socially), or to deal with "inferiority," a sense of confinement which can be ascribed, acquired, or due to age, gender, or status. At other times, or for other people, the decision to travel is inflected by a sense of "vulnerability" and "affection." People's desire to avoid or to serve oppressive, authoritarian local administrations, or family networks, is prominent, as may be their flight from being vulnerable to environmental degradation, or from the pre- dations of powerful or violent members of families and communities. As- pects of "humility" and identity are also referred to, including the many manifestations of respect and dignity typically denied or threatened by lack of economic or social independence. In some accounts, "anxiety" and "powerlessness" are evident as well, but often in twisted ways. People like Lawgu and Thida Thein are typically anxious about obligations to family. They travel, often apprehensively, to new identities to overcome power- lessness, knowing that they might ambiguously "win and lose" as a result.

If associations between travel and poverty are understood in these terms, then travel has both instrumental and idealizing dimensions. Travel fulfills a range of both pragmatic and imaginary desires. People's travel, in this sense, is about transgressing and creating the boundaries of material and ideational aspects of life. There is perhaps a useful crossover to consider between this expanded conception of poverty and its association with travel, and the notion of the "traveling subject" elaborated elsewhere (Craig and Porter 1994). The travel of subjects into and beyond new identities is necessary to and constitutive of their "emergence into presence" within the world (Nancy 1993). Travel is constitutive of the subject's identity in the world. This movement is intrinsically representational. Its mode of engagement depends on its representing itself variously and temporally—as trader, trucker, market worker, as young person traveling, as disco dancer—and, in the course of travel, representationally appropriating aspects of those identi- ties in more or less durable ways. With this conception of subjectivity, it is possible to appreciate some of the political effects of the singularity of HIV interventions. I will focus my remarks on the creation and stabilizing of boundaries and identities that is associated with these interventions by considering first what is regarded as being "inside" the boundaries of intervention, and then briefly noting other affairs considered to lie "outside."

The performative rationalities of HIV projects are defined in a range of ideals, goals, fields, and mechanisms included in project documents. Typically, they focus on "reducing risk behaviors" among "target groups and identified risk groups."[8] The population of beneficiaries is represented within social categories, each of which stabilizes and homogenizes specific subjects within larger groups. The project's subjects are not only socially and spatially located by the project, but are also defined in terms of certain "needs" or "lacks." Needs, following the materialist definitions of poverty and cause, tend to be economic and psychological. Projects promote income-generating activities, like handicraft groups or sewing collectives, which are designed to remove "constraints" and then stabilize populations by satisfying needs, thus removing the "compulsion" to travel. Information, Education, Communication (IEC) programs are designed to replace defective knowledge or remove other constraints by filling gaps in understanding, again bounding the subjects' ideational worlds. The project's subjects are further located in time, the duration of the intervention, and allocated particular "resources" (project inputs) to be used according to various "replicable practices" (as a result of counseling services) which further attempt to bound their travel. Projects of this sort do not assume that subjects will adopt these bounding practices (the social, spatial, and temporal identities carried by the project) on their own merits. Indeed, the singularity of these interventions is often "frustrated" in practice (Kanato and Rujkorankarn 1994, 30). Rather, successful embedding of these identities depends on "strengthening the capacity of management," which is "of paramount significance to the successful implementation of project activities." AIDS Control Teams, for instance, are instituted to focus and bring to bear the medical, administrative, and policing authorities of government and "the community." The teams are then trained in "risk group education," in "follow-up techniques," and in methods of surveillance, "baseline survey data collection and analysis," to enable monitoring and curtailment of the subjects' practices and ensure exposure of the risk groups to the project's resources, objectives, and outputs.

Well outside this focus of HIV interventions are aspects of the HIV phenomenon which can be only briefly noted here. Projects, like discourses, have an "outside" as well as an "inside"; in this respect, they specify what interventions and actions will be judged legitimate, what will be regarded as out of bounds and too political, and what will be seen as trouble-making (Barnes and Duncan 1992, 8). My research considered trucking and transport operations in Shan State, and two features which contrasted with conditions prevailing in neighboring Thailand can illustrate what lies "outside" as a consequence of the discourses of HIV interventions. One was the surprisingly long waiting time for truckers between loads, and the second was the apparently large number of overnight stopping points on the main routes (see figure 9.2).

Most truckers reported that the "down time" between loads was increasing. Sai, typical of small owner-drivers operating out of Muse, reported as follows:

> Now I handle only one or two loads each month between Muse and Mandalay. It used to be, about a year ago (1992), I had to wait for about 4 or 6 days in Mandalay, waiting for backloads. In Muse, there was plenty of loads, and we had to wait about a day only. But these days (the end of 1993), we can be waiting for four, maybe even ten days in Mandalay, and often I've got to wait ten days here for a load.

Common themes in all truckers' accounts were the rapid increase in the number of trucks competing for loads during 1992 and the monopolization of the trucking industry by a relatively few well-placed families in Yangon and Mandalay.[9] The pattern of overnight truck stops between Mandalay and Muse (figure 9.2) shows approximately twenty stops regularly used by drivers on this route. Research in Thailand points to remarkable differences (Sawaengdee and Isarapakdee 1991). Between the main centers of Bangkok and Chiang Mai, it appears that drivers make far fewer stops. The poor road conditions in Myanmar greatly increase comparable travel times and result in more overnight stops. But other political and commercial factors are also at play. Breakdowns are frequent as a result of smaller operating margins required by increased competition from large, family-owned companies, overloading is more common, and expenditure on routine maintenance has declined. Also significant are truck terminal facilities. The volume of trucks terminating in Muse exceeds capacity, in particular at Customs, as a result of the physical capacity of the facilities and the illicit, pecuniary activities of some officials who are quite aware of the pressure placed on harried drivers by their procrastination over "details." This has the effect of "bunching" the flow of trucks, necessitating many overnight stop points. Another feature of truckers' accounts of why they stop overnight at so many localities has to do with "avoidance." Until recently, conscription of vehicles (without compensation) by the military was common practice. It is reported that driver resistance (or, more likely, intervention by powerful Mandalay trucker/trading families) has reduced this practice. But unofficial taxation and interruption by officials still occur, and drivers tend to stay overnight at smaller villages dotted along the route where there are fewer officials. In these villages, some women earn income through the sale of sex, as part of a complex mix of livelihood activities which are required to service the situational, fluid nature of the trucking industry.

These accounts of the circumstances of trucking and servicing do not appear in priority listings of NGOs or official agencies within Myanmar, other than in terms of a category of "truckers" which essentializes the unstable, situational nature of this identity. HIV transmission is gendered—men are more likely than women to travel through a variety of social identities and locales. Truckers are required, by economic circumstances, to be highly mobile. They are marginal politically, and tend to operate in a twilight zone of illicit trading and connivance. Their stories of travel reveal a political economy of trucking which increasingly favors larger, well-placed operators who are directly linked to the regimes of political and economic power which provide trading licenses, access to capital, and market linkages. Ironically, here is a comparatively durable "community," largely of men, whose identity in part is predicated on distance from the range of ways—policing, customs, taxation—through which government surveillance is maintained. Perhaps because of this experience, people involved in trucking often express little inclination to cooperate with HIV interventions of the sort outlined earlier.

A Plague on Your Borders

I have remarked that eastern Shan State can be understood as a "zone of contest" (Fforde and Porter 1994) in which various kinds of political allegiances are being contested through struggles to manipulate and control people's social, spatial, and ethnic identities. The proposition here is that the categories deployed in projects which respond to the HIV epidemic are "translatable." Development agencies are keenly aware of the need to distance their responses to the HIV epidemic from the military administration of an unpopular government. But the way in which "the HIV/AIDS problem" is conceptualized is attributed to specific risk categories of people whose behavior needs to be "modified" and then monitored to ensure compliance with certain standards—and all these features are "translatable," so that they may become part of the ways local populations are administered by the government, the military, and local militias. First, they exhibit a mutuality between what is possible, agreeable, and subject to influence. Some things are "targeted" because they are regarded as legitimately "inside" the boundaries of "effective" responses to the epidemic. Typically, "target groups" are members of the population who exist on the edge of political power and whose behavior is believed to constitute a threat to the ordered and predictable administration of society according to centrally determined needs and interests. In contrast, the affairs of nontargeted social groups— for instance, those who allocate trading and trucking licences, who control customs gates and administer the flow of people and goods—are considered "outside" the arena of "responses" to HIV/AIDS and thereby effectively sealed off from inclusion as part of "the problem" of HIV. Translatability also involves fragmentation. The categorization process creates a false sense of the durability of identities as singular objects somehow separate from the social networks and relations of power and dependence which characterize social life in any locality. Fragmentation therefore increases the effect of the targeting process, wherein blame is assigned to particular categories of individuals who must "change behavior."

With translatability also comes legitimation, and this is a particularly marked aspect of what are regarded as otherwise "progressive" HIV interventions. The power of "government" of all sorts in this context is not that it blatantly reaches over the boundary between "the state" and "civil society" to impose a web of constraint on what NGOs or local people do. Indeed, the capacity to "govern at a distance" (Rose and Miller 1992) is that HIV interventions by NGOs are distinguished and "distant" from government. Simultaneously, however, the common configuration of "the problem," the encircling of people according to known, stable categories of risk groups, risk behaviors, or lacks and constraints, binds the HIV interventions to a rule of governance. A "successful project" can, by definition, be seen as one that successfully reproduces the identities constituted by the project in the local population. As Rose and Miller (1992, 184) note, "To the extent that actors have come to understand their situation according to a similar language and logic, to construe their own goals and their fate as in some way inextricable, they are assembled into mobile affiliations of governance."

Consistent with the global discourse of "democracy," most interventions are now "participatory" and go to considerable lengths to ensure that the beneficiaries participate in project implementation. This can have a doubly legitimizing effect. In effect, once identified as "CSWs" or "traders," people are encouraged to dress these categories with "local knowledge." Their participation thereby becomes part of what Latour (1987) calls the "inscription process," whereby categories of claims, identities, goals, and fates are inscribed into the local situation. To the degree that such inscription processes are participatory, they can lead people to reaffirm the categories by which they are to be known, strengthening them by participating in the refinement of the boundaries and by calibrating their expectations and behaviors to the identities defined by the project.

Conclusion: Can It Be Other Than This?

While it may be true that "for many marginalized communities with little access to government services, NGOs represent their only hope of AIDS prevention and care" (Aboagye-Kwarteng and Moodie 1995), there is also room to consider the ironic ways in which "empowerment" can, when wrapped in project rationalities, become "encirclement" and deny such hopes. As conceptual devices, "travel" and "boundaries" have been useful throughout this discussion and, by way of summary, I want now to consider how HIV interventions might pay more attention to the various ways they could avoid sealing off "lines of flight" (Deleuze and Guattari 1987) for the people they intend to work with in places like eastern Shan State.

First, it would seem necessary to review some features of current thinking about development practice, of which HIV interventions are only one part. This would require awareness of the ways in which boundaries between one set of political interests and another are not immutable. Paradoxically, the concern of donors and NGOs to be distant from the military government of Myanmar finds them neglecting the translatability of their endeavors, through various categories and procedures, in terms of the concern of this pariah state to stabilize and monitor peoples of the border regions. Assumptions which view "the state" and "civil society" as separate spheres would need review, for instance. In practice, as Schmitter (1985, 13) remarks, the state is better understood as "an amorphous complex of agencies with ill-defined boundaries performing a great variety of not very distinctive functions." In addition, following Kumar (1993, 390), it would be useful to understand the ways in which civil society is "a realm of association interpenetrated by the state."

At another level, this challenge to conventional boundaries would also cut through the "crisis of representation" remarked on earlier. From a representational point of view, the problems confronting HIV interventions may appear intractable. As recent theorizing teaches us, there is no privileged vantage point; there is no unambiguous way to unite our representations with those of others, nor are there any singular identities. If this is so, then neither is there any way of understanding and making intelligible other people's practices without in some way colonizing and invading their identities. But stabilizing is a routine part of our engagement in the world. This is the point of my remarks about "traveling subjectivity," the suggestion that the subject's mobility is something primal. If this is so, then resistance to stabilization and the bounding practices of the state and development agencies is likely to be intractable. The subject is not automatically constructed by every discourse or rationality that comes along. People readily size up the nature of interventions; they can be enthusiastic in their reception, or they can be hostile and rely at various times on what Scott (1987) has called "weapons of the weak"—foot-dragging, flight, and other forms of passive resistance.

This does not imply that HIV interventions should, for example, try to organize CSWs, pretending they represent durable identities, and merely see what happens, although in some instances and for some issues women may temporarily participate in such activities. Rather, it should be noted that the possibilities of interventions are always contradictory, that the boundaries carried by the intervention are always likely to become the sites of political antagonism (Mouffe 1993, 3). Laclau (1990, 39) notes how "every identity is dislocated insofar as it depends on an outside which both denies that identity and provides its conditions of possibility at the same time. [This] means that the effects of dislocation must be contradictory. If on the one hand they threaten identities, they are the foundation on which new identities are constituted." One lesson of discourse analysis is that institutional practices do not only operate in a "top-down" direction but are constantly challenged and recreated by people in everyday life. This has material effects on the way people deal with events like HIV/AIDS. But to realize this, in practice, requires a step beyond some of the conventional features of HIV interventions. It requires recognition that project "success" is not usefully judged in terms of the degree to which local people reproduce the categories, objectives, inputs, and information of the project, but in terms of how these are used to enable people to adopt identities and forms of conduct they define as viable ways of dealing with HIV in their survival strategies. Clearly, this kind of development practice must allow for, and foster, people's ability to cross the boundaries imposed by taken-for-granted conceptions of HIV/AIDS, motivation for travel, and notions of sexuality.

Acknowledgments

The research on which is chapter is based was done during 1991 and 1992, but principally during October through December 1993 with colleagues from the Institute of Economics in Yangon who prefer not to be acknowledged by name. The research was supported by the UNDP HIV and Development Program, New York, and the Australian National University, Canberra. The author is solely responsible for the views expressed in this chapter. The assistance of John Ballard, David Craig, Christine Tabart, and Nigel Duffy, and the counsel of the editors are gratefully acknowledged.

CHAPTER TEN

A Matter of "Choice": Discourses on Prostitution in the Philippines

LISA LAW

Introduction

This chapter examines the role of development aid in contemporary debates on prostitution and AIDS in the Philippines. More specifically, it argues that the activities and discursive practices of development-aid agencies—which include foreign donor agencies and foreign and local nongovernment organizations (NGOs) carrying out AIDS education projects—are challenging the dominant representation of prostitution in the Philippines. Historically, prostitution has been situated within the political economy of colonialism, militarism, and sex tourism (Azarcon de la Cruz 1985; Miralao, Carlos, and Santos 1990; de Leon, Contor, and Abueva 1991). In the effort to slow the spread of HIV, however, and with the influence of foreign organizations, the types of intervention programs for sex workers and the language used to describe prostitution are changing. For this reason, the terms *sex worker* and *prostitute* will be used interchangeably throughout this chapter. Although *sex worker* has a more specific meaning associated with debates on prostitution in the West (Jenness 1993), it is randomly used here to highlight these changing discursive themes.

Many writers problematize the historical construction of prostitution in academic literature and government documents, arguing that it victimizes women, denies agency, and fails to recognize the variability of experience (Lyttleton 1994a; Perkins 1991; Sullivan 1994; Truong 1990; White 1990). In contemporary debates on prostitution and AIDS, there is conflict between those who privilege the free will of women to enter prostitution (agency) versus those who privilege the more deterministic constraints (structure) that make prostitution a job opportunity for women (cf. Bell 1987). These assumptions about agency have implications for the types of programs which empower women to protect themselves from HIV. Following Bourdieu (1977), Giddens (1979, 1981), and Thrift (1983), who share a nonfunctionalist view of social action which asserts a mutual dependency of social structures and human agency, this chapter asserts that representations which privilege either aspect are problematic.

The dichotomy between victim and agent paradigms is evident in the current debates on prostitution and AIDS in the Philippines. This chapter draws from the experience of Australian and Filipino NGOs which receive foreign funding for AIDS education activities, and of the sex workers for whom programs are designed. Initially, these NGOs had made contrasting assumptions about the agency of women working in the sex industry, with Australian NGOs asserting the agency of sex workers and Filipino NGOs asserting the more structural determinants of prostitution. While this contrasts somewhat with the colonialist tendency for Western women to author themselves as agents and Third World women as victims (Spivak 1987, 1988; Mohanty 1988), the dichotomous tendency itself has been a regular feature in descriptions of Third World women.

The contrasting representations of Australian and Filipino NGOs relate to more generalized representations of prostitution in the West and in the Philippines. For example, while Western prostitutes have been represented as deviant, abnormal, or as victims of a patriarchal society (Perkins 1991), such women were viewed as "individually" pathological, and victimhood was personalized, individuated, rather than seen in structural terms. Emergent sex worker organizations also stressed the individual agency of prostitutes (cf. Nelson 1985), while resisting the legal stigma and victim language which excluded prostitution from legitimate employment, and the medical discourse which allowed HIV/AIDS to reinscribe the "pool of infection" label of earlier public health models (Jenness 1993). Most recently, prostitution has been linked to broader discussions of sexuality and sexual identity (Trumbach 1991; Weeks 1985, 1987). This perspective has influenced the AIDS education projects carried out in Australia and the Philippines.

The dominant representations of prostitution in the Philippines, however, are situated within the political economy of the country, and not necessarily within legal, public health, or sexual identity discourses. While this may ostensibly deny the agency of prostitutes, it is useful in highlighting the structural impediments to empowerment while popularizing anticolonial sentiment. These themes will be elaborated in this chapter, highlighting the difficulty of utilizing accounts which emphasize the political economy, and bringing to life the unfamiliar points of view of women in the sex industry of Cebu City. All this meshes with the local construction of prostitution by ordinary Filipinos, where the Catholic labeling of women as whores or madonnas plays an important role in defining, identifying, or being "the *other* Mary."

This chapter is organized as follows. First, I introduce the major participants and themes in the discourse on AIDS in the Philippines, situating the discourse of NGOs and highlighting their importance in shaping public perceptions of women in the sex industry. Second, to contextualize both the perceptions of NGOs and women working in Cebu City's sex industry, I provide the background to contemporary development issues in Cebu, emphasizing the popular association between tourist development and sex tourism, and the dilemmas posed by rapid capitalist expansion. Third, I recount the stories of three women in Cebu's sex industry, to reveal the tensions in their subjectivities regarding "choice." Finally, the experiences of four NGOs highlight changing discursive themes—specifically in the way the issue of "choice" is handled—and explore the links between NGO discourse and the subjectivities of bar women. This leads to discussion of strategies for rethinking sex tourism and the types of projects designed for HIV/AIDS education.

The Philippine AIDS Discourse: Major Participants and Themes

In 1984 the first Filipino national, a returning overseas contract worker, was diagnosed with AIDS. In the same year, eight prostitutes working around the American military bases at Angeles and Olongapo were diagnosed HIV positive. These and similar cases, and the subsequent designation of such people as "high risk" groups by both the media and government agencies, led to almost a decade of portraying the spread of HIV in the Philippines as a problem of foreigners. Although the new and popular Secretary of Health addresses AIDS as an issue for the general public, and the media now publishes critiques of the Church's position on condoms as well as human interest stories of people with AIDS, prostitutes remain the target of much social hostility. This was most recently evidenced in Mayor Lim's "clean-up" campaign, which saw the closure of Manila's famous sex tourism belt in Ermita and the dislocation of the women employed there (see figure 10.1).

Major participants in the Philippines AIDS discourse include the Catholic Church, the Department of Health (DOH), the World Health Organization (WHO), and various international donor agencies (especially the United States Agency for International Development, USAID, and the Australian Agency for International Development, AusAID) and their recipient NGOs. The Catholic Church and its lay groups are internationally renowned, and are involved in what can be termed "medico-moral" discourse (Seidel 1993). They seek to control sexuality generally, condemn what are termed the "three P's"—premarital sex, promiscuity, and prostitution—and as depicted in figure 10.2, inspire great debate about whether or not condoms promote promiscuity and legitimize prostitution, or control the spread of HIV. The debate between the government and the Church on AIDS has a longer history related to artificial birth control, but recent stud-

Figure 10.1. P. del Rosario Street, Ermita, Manila. The signs posted above the former entrances to bars such as the "Australian Club" highlight popular perceptions about women who work as prostitutes catering to white, Western men. From *South China Morning Post,* Hong Kong, 13 April 1994.

ies (Amante 1993; Dañguilan 1993) and the election of President Ramos, the first Protestant and pro-family planning head of state, suggest that the influence the Church once had over sexuality and contraception is decreasing.

Due to prevention, control, and surveillance functions, the WHO and DOH are involved in medical discourses of control which feature "high risk groups," "seropositives," and a homogenous group of "commercial sex workers" (CSWs). Such a rigid construction of HIV/AIDS has led to the control and harassment of prostitutes; not only must prostitutes undergo mandatory blood testing in government Social Hygiene Clinics, they are subjected to the kind of harassment evidenced in Ermita. Furthermore, despite the DOH's initiative in 1993 to eliminate mandatory testing on the grounds that it was expensive and ineffective in slowing the spread of HIV, the devolution of health services now allows this decision to be made by local governments.

Lastly, NGOs have been acknowledged as being crucial in slowing the spread of HIV (WHO 1989). In the past five years dozens of Filipino NGOs have become involved in HIV/AIDS education activities throughout the country. Some critics have gone so far as to call it AIDS "profiteering" on the part of some organizations (Remedios AIDS Foundation 1993). These NGOs, primarily community-based organizations, have reached groups otherwise neglected by government programs (the urban poor, sex workers,

Figure 10.2. The Department of Health versus the Church position on condoms. This critique of the opposing stances of the Department of Health (DOH) and the Catholic Church highlights an important debate in the Philippines. In the cartoon, Secretary of Health Flavier declares, "This is protection for the AIDS crisis," while Cardinal Sin argues, "This promotes sexual permissiveness."

gay men, men who have sex with men), and have actively participated in discussions on national policy and human rights (Litong et al. n.d.). NGOs working with sex workers in Manila, Angeles, Cebu, and Davao (see map, figure 10.3) have also been instrumental in changing the way prostitution is conceptualized within the country.

Background: Cebu City

Cebu City is the second largest city in the Philippines, with a metropolitan population of approximately one million people. Since the mid-1980s, Cebu province has registered positive growth in terms of exports, investments, and gross regional domestic product, prompting the local government to sell Cebu to local and foreign investors as the "rising economic superstar of the south" (WRCC 1992). Economic growth has not necessarily been equally distributed, however, nor has it led to the improved livelihood of the local population. As of October 1992, Cebu City had an unemployment rate of 10.28 percent, an underemployment rate of 14.62 percent, and a total of 37,857 urban poor families (WRCC 1992).

The most internationally known economic boom in Cebu, locally

Figure 10.3. Map of the Philippines.

termed "Ceboom," occurred from 1987 to the present and is clearly related to the Ramos administration's plans to make the Philippines into a Newly Industrializing Country (NIC) by the year 2000. The current Medium-Term Development Plan, which introduced this strategy as "Philippines 2000," is a plan inspired by the World Bank and International Monetary Fund that aims to further integrate the Philippines into the global capitalist economy. Cebu has become a pilot project for Philippines 2000, building on the city's long tradition as a major trading center, which began before the coming of the Spanish and experienced a resurgence in the nineteenth century (Mojares 1991), and more specifically since the mid-1980s (Clad 1988). Cebu now has a lucrative export-processing zone with forty-three firms (Ballescas 1993), and an international airport receiving direct flights from Australia, Taiwan, Hong Kong, and Japan.

Although the province does not have an official tourism master plan, foreign investment and direct international flights have helped to make Cebu a popular tourist destination for both Western and Asian tourists. According to Department of Tourism (1992) statistics, as of 1991, 314,583 tourists visited Cebu, 109,830 of whom were from foreign countries, most prominently from Japan (43,348), Taiwan (15,336), and the United States (12,015). Other Western countries (Australia, Canada, France, Germany, Italy, Switzerland, and the United Kingdom) accounted for 20,230 visitors.

Tourism as a development strategy has a long history of being tied to political agendas and economic strategies and not necessarily concerned with its socioeconomic and cultural effects (Richter 1989). Women's organizations in particular blame tourism, combined with the uneven distribution of "Ceboom" wealth, for the magnitude of the sex industry in Cebu (de la Cerna 1992; Dioneda 1993). According to statistics for 1992 from the Cebu City STD-AIDS Detection Center, 84 establishments were engaged in the sex industry; there were 12 *casas* (brothels) that voluntarily sent "clients" (sex workers) to the center, a total of 2,152 registered "clients," and 163 "free-lancers" who were examined regularly (Cebu City Health Department 1992).

Increased concern over HIV/AIDS emerged when the first case of HIV was diagnosed in Cebu in 1991. The sex industry came under close scrutiny, with many reports in local and national papers about the increasing numbers of sex workers migrating to Cebu due to the eruption of Mount Pinatubo and the closing of the American military bases at Angeles and Olongapo (*Philippine Daily Inquirer* 21 March 1992, 16 February 1992; *Sun Star Daily* 11 March 1992). Due to the concentration of HIV cases detected around these areas, these women were either presumed to be infected or seen as "luring" a foreign sex industry and therefore HIV/AIDS to Cebu. The situation worsened in 1993 when an experimental clinic for HIV and AIDS patients, treating seventeen foreign patients, "mostly Americans and Australians," was raided by the police. The mayor panicked and suggested a twenty-four-hour test center for anyone who had had contact with foreigners in the preceding weeks (*Sun Star Daily* 23 March 1993). The construction of HIV/AIDS as a problem of foreigners persists in Cebu; as one paper recently noted, "With the growing number [of HIV cases], Cebu is far from safe from AIDS, what with the place as a tourists' haven. The AIDS virus in the Philippines was first brought in from outside the country" (*Sun Star Daily* 15 February 1994).

As mentioned above, the sex industry in Cebu is composed of approximately 84 registered establishments and 12 unregistered *casas,* or a total of 96 establishments. Registered establishments can be roughly divided into seven different types: karaoke bars, bikini bars, music lounges/sing-alongs, cocktail bars, beer houses, dance halls/discos and massage parlors. More than half of Cebu's sex industry workers are employed in karaoke bars, bikini bars, and massage parlors, and these establishments are most frequently visited by tourists.

Very little has been written on the spatial aspects of prostitution. A pioneering work by Curtis and Arreola (1991) examines the typology and spatial characteristics of Mexican prostitution zones at regional and intraurban levels. Their focus is on towns along the American border, where both tourists and the local population participate in the sex industry. Their findings reveal that such zones have historically been segregated on racial, ethnic, and socioeconomic lines, and that their location within the town has been related to political, economic, and social changes in both Mexico and the United States.

Some parallels can be drawn with Cebu. Karaoke bars are confined to the growing uptown of Cebu, for example, and cater to Japanese tourists and businessmen investing in the tourism industry. Bikini bars are not confined to one area, however. Uptown bars cater primarily to white, Western men and emerged in the 1980s during Cebu's era of mail-order brides and the development of uptown Cebu. Bars downtown cater to Filipino locals and tourists, and have a long history tied to Cebu's port and its associated recreational activities (see Hilario 1932). While there is some overlap between the two areas—some foreigners frequent up-market Filipino bars and some Filipinos visit down-market foreigner bars—most Filipinos suspect uptown bars to be too expensive, and foreigners suspect Filipino bars to be too dangerous.

Three Women

The following stories collected at intervals from November 1992 to March 1994 are from three women who work, or have worked, as dancers and prostitutes in Cebu's bars catering to white, Western men. The most famous of these bars—the Brunswick, the G Bar, and the Side Bar—are Australian- and German-owned and have emerged with the development of uptown

Cebu. Dancers in these establishments dance on a stage at intervals and, while not dancing, entertain customers in exchange for "ladies drinks." "Receptionists" entertain customers and do not dance. Public sex performances like those described by Cass (1991) in the Philippines or Manderson (1992b, 1995) in Thailand do not exist, partially due to the cost of "bribes" paid to the local police. "Bar fines" are paid to take women out of the bar, mostly for one night but occasionally for days or weeks at a time. While the women who work in these establishments engage in sex for money, many perceive their employment as encompassing a variety of functions, including tour guide, interpreter, girlfriend, and prospective wife.

Virgie: *My son has made me very strong.*

Virgie is twenty-eight years old and was born and raised in rural Negros. When she completed high school, a visitor from Cagayan de Oro, Mindanao, suggested that Virgie migrate to Cagayan to seek employment. She agreed and worked in Cagayan as a domestic helper for several months, until the death of her mother caused her to return to Negros. After the funeral, her father was disappointed with Virgie's decision to continue her employment—being the oldest daughter, Virgie should, by tradition, have assumed the responsibilities of her mother—and this issue caused her to lose regular contact with the family.

In Cagayan Virgie befriended another domestic helper, and together they decided to migrate to the growing city of Cebu. After a series of low-paying jobs in restaurants, Virgie resorted to the classified advertisements in the local newspaper. One was for a waitress in a restaurant for tourists in Boracay, with a salary of 2,000 pesos (about 80 U.S. dollars) per month. She took a twenty-hour boat ride to the island, but soon after arriving learned that her salary would only be P700 per month. Virgie and her coworkers were earning small salaries for harsh labor, and sometimes vented their frustration by attending a disco after work. It was here that Virgie met the Filipino father of her son:

> But one night we decided we're going to leave this job. What I re-
> member is that we were throwing our things down from the upstairs
> and jumping down after them. We went to my friend's house and they
> call [my boyfriend] for me. He took us to his house and I lost my
> virginity. But his family is rich and I didn't feel comfortable, so we say
> we'll meet in Cebu. But I never saw him again.

Upon returning to Cebu, she was unemployed and realized she was pregnant. A former employer had opened a small restaurant, and she worked there until she was ready to deliver her son. After the birth, she was in desperate need of money and began work as a security guard. She'd been working for one day when she passed by the Brunswick and noticed the sign on the door which said "receptionists wanted." She inquired, was hired, and agreed to start immediately.

Her first night she was bought five "ladies drinks," so she earned a P30 salary and P100 in commissions on drinks that night (US$5.20). This relatively large amount of money she spent on milk and other things for her son. She met an American on her third night, they "fell in love," she stopped working, and he supported her for five months. She's unsure as to why he discontinued the relationship, but thinks it may have been sabotaged by her jealous housemate.

> Working in a bar is OK because I have self-respect. Some women are in despair thinking that no one will love them any more. They drink, take drugs, and see no problem with what they're doing because, anyway, they have no future. I'm always positive in my thinking, I'm praying and saying "help yourself." Sometimes a lot of people are helping you, and you don't know how to help yourself.

Eventually Virgie's savings ran out, and she applied to work at the G Bar, another bikini bar for foreign white men in the district around the new plaza. She was a go-go dancer there for several months and cultivated emotional/sexual relationships with two tourists, one American, and the other Australian. The American sent her money on a regular basis, and with this money she rented and furnished a house she felt was suitable for her son. The Australian, on the other hand, did not give her money until she resigned because of a hastily introduced bar policy which prohibited the use of stockings while dancing (Virgie did not shave her legs and had always worn stockings to disguise this fact). He supported her for six months. At present she has made amends with her father, moved back to the province, and is waiting for the Australian to send money for her to join him.

Filipina/Australian couples are a common phenomenon. In 1989–90 alone, 729 Filipina wives and 893 Filipina fiancées were sponsored to enter Australia (Smith and Kaminskas 1992). Mail-order brides are common (Wall 1983; Kaminskas and Smith 1990; Tapales 1990), but as in this case, Australian men also find marriage partners while traveling or working in various capacities in the Philippines. Success stories of women who married customers and are now overseas are common.

When asked if she thought women would transfer to another job if given to opportunity, Virgie said,

Why should she go back to the hard life? She's already been there, that's why she's in the bar. Why be a martyr? Working in a bar is OK if you work hard. It makes you smarter. If a woman has low education, like grade 3 or 4, then if she works in a bar she becomes smarter. She gets to meet professional men, go to expensive restaurants, more than even a teacher can. She has more chances to experience and learn. Me, I'm just like this, but I've met the owners of the big hotels here, and we've been talking. Sometimes I say to myself, if I was staying in my province, I would not meet the owner of the S. Hotel. He knows where I come from. . . . My friend, she's only grade 4, but she learned English and became more confident. She got a new hairstyle, some new clothes, and people started calling her ma'am. She dresses in white and goes to the casino. When people ask her what she's doing on the jeepney, she says she's working the night shift at Chong Hua Hospital.

Virgie maintains that life as the oldest sister in the rural Philippines is difficult and worth getting away from if you have ambition. When Virgie says she has "no choice," she relates this to lacking a college education—which is increasingly necessary even for unskilled jobs—but more so to needing money to raise her son. With neither an extended family nor an adequate welfare state, her son's future, and ultimately her own, were uncertain. She looks at her entry into the sex industry as being difficult, but as providing her with an opportunity to experience more than she would have experienced had she stayed at home. Furthermore, through her work she had the opportunity to meet men and "fall in love." Sex work in this form is seen as more than a job, and resembles what has been described by Hochschild (1983) as "selling personality" and "emotional labour."

May: *It's the bar that needs me, not me who needs the bar.*

May was born in 1959 in a poor *barangay* (suburb) of Cebu City. Because her mother left the family in the mid-1960s (she married an American serviceman who was stationed in Cebu at the time of the Vietnam War), May was raised by her father and her father's sister:

> The side of my father, that auntie I have, I really hate her because I'm not supposed to be like this now, you know, if not for her. Because when I was a kid she really treated me bad. . . . I've lived on my own since I was 13. Until now, I am 34, I am all by myself unless I have somebody like this (she motions to her sleeping boyfriend), you know, he don't have a job.

When May was thirteen years old she rebelled against her family by going to Bacolod, Negros. At this time, it was a long boat ride—more than twelve hours—to travel to this neighboring island.

> And I was very lucky that I met some guy there then. A very old guy, he got 3 kids, they're girls also. And I am the fourth one, you know? Until I was 17 I stayed with them. So when I come back here . . . when my father and my auntie saw me there in the port, they called the police and then they take me home. And I remember that they take me to the hospital . . . to see if I am still a virgin. But I'm still a virgin at that time. So when I can, I get away from them again. I went to Zamboanga. . . . I was just looking for a job there, but not this kind of job. And what I remember before, I hate 19. That's when I lose my virginity. And after that I worked because all my friends are saying "come on you know how to dance, there is a club there that just opened." I said no because . . . I never say that I am beautiful, OK? So I said "No, maybe they don't want me." They said, "No you can do it." So I said "OK, let me try." So that's where I stayed then, and that's my first job in Zamboanga.

In 1979 May returned to Cebu to find that her father had died, and she began work at the Side Bar. After one year she met a German man, went to Germany with him, and stayed there for seven years:

> Then in 1980 I went to Germany, I met this guy in the Side Bar and he wanted to take me. I said "Why not?" I went with him, and when we got there we stayed for six months together before he let me know that I wasn't allowed to stay for six months. . . . I did not find out until I asked my girlfriend about my visa. . . . And then after that I asked my boyfriend if he's going to marry me . . . and he said no he cannot yet because we are just staying together for a while, not a long time. . . . And then I said "What am I doing here? You have to let me go." And he don't want me to go home, so that's why he found me a husband. And it took about two years before we get married . . . all my paperwork is in the Philippines. . . . And then I could not get along with him . . . before our first anniversary I asked him for a divorce . . . and it takes him about three years before he decides he wants a divorce.

May returned to Cebu in 1987 and started a small food business at her house. In 1988, realizing that she could not support the lifestyle she had been accustomed to in Germany, she began work at the G Bar. Here she met an Englishman who enticed her to come to Abu Dhabi on a fiancée visa.

I went there (Abu Dhabi) in 1992. I was only there for six weeks. I did
not know that we were not compatible, because he was very nice to
me when he was here. And also, while I was here, I can get his money,
because he sent it to me. But then when I got there I don't get any. . . .
That's the problem, because if you're inside the house—and I got a
problem about that—but if he's outside talking to his friends, he get
everything, you know.

After six weeks May returned to Cebu and resumed work at the bar, and
has been working on and off since:

I'm not looking to my future. I've tried my best already before but it
didn't work. . . . As soon as possible, if I can make money without it, I
will stop. What happens tomorrow, I will take it. Some people say you
have to take this money, it's for tomorrow. No. Same with my boyfriend. You cannot keep everything. Some people ask "Why don't you
have savings, maybe you'll get sick and won't have it?" I will take it.

Few employees are allowed to work on again, off again without repercus-
sions, but May's philosophy—"it's the bar that needs me, not me who needs
the bar"—allows her great freedom. She sees the bar as convenient for her
profession, which is nothing more than paid sex. This causes some tension
among the women in the bar, and those who are striving for a "better life"
(i.e., a husband) almost resent May's outlook. As Virgie said,

Talk to May, she's been married once and then engaged. We ask her,
"May, why do you always keep coming back to this place?" Then May
says, "My first husband, we have a nice family, but I don't know. He's
so . . ." May, she's always going out bar hopping in Germany, but her
husband doesn't like. So she's not happy and came back to the Philippines. She gets engaged to an Englishman and moved to Saudi Arabia.
The same problems, and she came back. We ask her, "Why you not
ashamed May?" But she doesn't care. He didn't give her money, she's
always staying at home. Because if you're a wife its different, you're
not going out any more. But May's like a single woman. . . . We ask
her what about when you're 50, May, you can't dance any more. May
says she's already had a happy life, even if she dies tomorrow. She's not
helping herself . . . there's no future if you're always dancing.

May's entry into the sex industry is a common one. Once a woman loses
her virginity or has a child out of wedlock, she is classified as a whore.
Nonvirgins and single mothers often work in the sex industry because they
are considered "loose" and therefore unmarriageable. Although May found
two Western marriage partners in the bar, men who marry Filipinas some-

times expect them to be "not only physically beautiful and sexually exciting but also caring, compliant, submissive, and *not* 'Western' or modern"
(Manderson 1995, 309). This contradiction, and May's experiences in Germany and Abu Dhabi, taught her that life in a bar allows you more freedom
than being confined to the house as a wife is.

Edna: *My mother didn't want us to marry a Filipino who doesn't work.*

> It's hard working in a bar. It's hard to go with customers, especially if
> he's a sadist and wants to see blood first. It's hard if he's a married man.
> I hope I find a man so I can stop working. Sometimes I feel bad for 2
> or 3 days. I feel bad about my job, I'm always thinking. But every-
> where you need a college education. For me I'd like to work in a
> department store and not go out with customers, but I have only grade
> 6 [schooling]. It's a nice life working in a store. . . . It's not like America
> where it doesn't matter. My sister's a chamber maid at the Hyatt and
> she's only grade 4.

Edna's extended family can be traced to a sugarcane plantation in Negros,
but when she was four years old, her parents migrated to Cebu to seek
employment. She finished grade six education and began piecework in her
community, producing shellcraft for sale. She continued in shellcraft until
she was eighteen, when she decided to join her sisters; all three of them
were working in bars catering for American servicemen in Angeles City. As
she says, "My mother didn't want us to marry a Filipino who doesn't work."

Many studies document the history and ill effects of military bases on
women in the Philippines (Buklod 1990; Enloe 1983, 1989; Lee and WED-
PRO 1992; Miralao, Carlos, and Santos 1990; Moselina 1979; Ryan 1991;
Stoltzfus and Sturdevant 1990; Sturdevant and Stoltzfus 1992). In general,
the militarization of prostitution is seen as a complex relation of domination
involving questions of national sovereignty, racism, class inequalities, and
sexual politics. Although the American bases at Angeles and Olongapo had
their heyday during the Vietnam War, in the first quarter of 1990 there
were a total of 1,567 registered entertainment establishments in Angeles and
615 in Olongapo, with a total of approximately 55,000 "hospitality
women" in both cities (Santos 1992). The "new world order" and the expi-
ration of the US–RP Military Base Agreement spelled the end for the bases,
but the Mount Pinatubo eruption in 1991 saw the unequivocal departure
of American servicemen. This event also displaced thousands of sex workers
in both cities, many of whom came from communities such as Edna's.

Edna's two oldest sisters are in the United States, having married American servicemen they met in Angeles. Both sisters send remittances to Cebu,

although often at irregular intervals. The third oldest sister also worked in Angeles, but feels unsuccessful, as she did not find a husband. She now lives with Edna, taking care of her needs and corresponding with international pen pals in the hopes of going overseas. Edna is the youngest and, apart from the remittances from the United States, carries primary financial responsibility for the family. "I get angry sometimes, but everyone understands," she says, as her sister returns from a gambling session after losing the P25 that Edna had given her for cigarettes.

Edna was twenty-three when her two eldest sisters migrated to America, and she decided to work in a bar too. After four months a man asked if he could take her out for the night:

> My sisters had left and I had no job. So I danced for four months as a virgin. I was just strong because no one can help me. Everyone left me. . . . Then this man wants to take me out. They told me you go, it's only dinner and dancing. I didn't know at that time because I was innocent. He was a flier man in the military. He's forcing me. I'm screaming. The hotel doesn't care because he's a guest.

When Edna was twenty-four, she fell in love with an American serviceman in the bar, resigned from her job, and became pregnant. He wanted her to abort the child, but when she refused, he ended the relationship. They "weren't compatible and [were] always arguing," she remembers, and "he was butterfly, always going around with other girls in front of me." She gave birth to a daughter and stopped working for two years. When Mount Pinatubo erupted the father's financial support ended, and she returned to Cebu without an income.

> When we were there in Angeles the Base made him pay me support. But then after Mount Pinatubo nobody is there to make him pay me. . . . Now he's married to another Filipina and they're in the U.S. His mother told me that he don't have any daughter there, but he will not send money for his daughter here in Cebu.

Edna returned to Cebu because the physical destruction and sudden departure of the American servicemen decreased the demand for sex workers in the city. Liza, a friend from Cebu and Angeles, had taken a job in the G Bar and introduced Edna to the owner. She worked there for a year, but transferred to the Brunswick after having problems with the owner, who had wanted her to be a witness in a case against the disk jockey, cashier, and bartender, all presumed guilty of taking money and sleeping on the job. Edna didn't want to be involved, however, so it was easier to change bars. She's been there since: "I don't like to talk to customers. I'm ashamed even though I've been working in the bar a long time. Even [the owner] says I'm losing my salary. . . . People look down on you. That's why I just don't listen to the [gossip]. I stay in the house and work for my daughter."

Edna is one of the many women who have returned to Cebu from Angeles and are working in Cebu's bars. As Virgie once said, "People were saying that the Philippines could protect itself, but I don't think so. I was so angry at them, I remember all those people like Edna on the TV crying or throwing things because they were so angry. . . . Some people they say Mount Pinatubo went up because of all the prostitutes there. I don't think so."

Although there are no published statistics on the number of women from Cebu who migrated to Angeles, Miralao, Carlos, and Santos (1990) noted the increased number of women migrating to both Angeles and Olongapo from semiurban or urbanizing areas in the Visayas (e.g., Cebu, Negros, Leyte, Samar) during the late 1980s, suggesting that urban poverty is changing the profile of women in the sex industry (see also Sturdevant and Stoltzfus 1992, Santos 1992).

Edna's seaside community was considered part of "the province" in the 1960s and 1970s, but Cebu City's rapid growth has enveloped the area. It is a squatter community that has traditionally relied on the resources from the surrounding land and sea. The first settlers harvested *nipa* (thatch) for the construction of houses; later the community collected shells for export, but now that the shell resource is endangered from overuse and dynamite fishing, many are engaged in woodcraft. The supplies for woodcraft come from illegal logging activities, however, so the future of this activity is questionable.

The community has an extensive history of women migrating to Angeles to work. The first "bar girl" is rumored to have migrated in the late 1960s, after which time a series of personal recruitments produced a steady flow of women to both Angeles and Olongapo. As Edna's own history indicates, many families rely on remittances from daughters working elsewhere in the Philippines. The number of "Amerasian" children in her community, many with mothers that have Afro-American accents, is testimony to the liaisons established while American troops were stationed in the Philippines. Many families are now dependent on remittances from their children living in the United States, however, and although this money is primarily used to keep up with the inflationary prices of goods and services in Cebu, some families have built foundations for their houses or started small businesses.

As the stories of Virgie, May, and Edna indicate, women clearly vary in their sense of power and their capacity to change their situation. While Virgie affords herself the greatest degree of agency—she knows how to "help herself"—she also cites the effects of oppressive family responsibilities, her loss of virginity, and the limited employment opportunities for high school graduates as contributing factors to her entry into the sex industry ("I don't have enough education, I have no choice. . . . I have no family here"). May also perceives her familial background as a site of oppression, suggesting that her entry into sex work is a product of being poorly brought up by her aunt ("I'm not supposed to be like this now if not for her"), but also of her loss of virginity ("I hate 19. That's when I lose my virginity. And after that I worked"). At thirty-four years of age, her unsuccessful relations with foreign men have contributed to her perception of bar work as sex work, a convenient occupation for a good lifestyle. Lastly, Edna's family encouraged her to work in Angeles ("My mother didn't want us to marry a Filipino who doesn't work"), and her loss of virginity played no role in her entering the sex industry, although it contributed to her loss of "innocence." She continues in the sex industry despite feeling "ashamed," however, due to a lack of alternatives ("I'd like to work in a department store . . . but I have only grade 6").

The women presented here have strong overseas contacts: Virgie plans to migrate to Australia, May has lived in Germany and Saudi Arabia and has a mother in the United States, and Edna's sisters and the father of her daughter live in the United States. These women do not author themselves as part of a global sex traffic, however, largely because their work is perceived as about "love." Furthermore, they perceive their "foreign relations" in benign terms (although foreigners are often nice in the Philippines and turn nasty overseas), particularly when compared to the perceptions of outside analysts in nationalist, anticolonialist or feminist modes, as discussed below.

Representations of the Sex Industry in the Philippines

In 1985, Azarcon de la Cruz (1985, 42) suggested that widespread prostitution in the Philippines stemmed from the following causes: an export-oriented economy which strengthens the dependence on foreign investments and loans; an unjust tenancy system displacing the peasantry; uneven development in the rural and urban areas; the presence of U.S. military bases and their built-in R & R industry preventing people from developing other sources of income; foreign loans spent on tourism and infrastructure projects, resulting in devaluation and galloping inflation; a crisis in leadership maintained by militarization and a growing dissident movement, especially in the countryside; and a neocolonial and semifeudal culture and orientation that peddles women as commodities and propagates their status as inferior to men, especially to foreign men.

These elements quite precisely situated sex work within the political economy of colonialism, militarism, and sex tourism, and this perspective dominated the discourse of prostitution in the media and amongst activists and academics during the 1970s and 1980s (see Lewis 1980; Doyo 1983; Enloe 1983, 1989; Aquino Sarmiento 1988; Tapales 1988). The American military bases, the international sex traffic, and sex tourism were instrumental in highlighting these issues and in shaping the way prostitution was constructed both within the Philippines and internationally. While the American bases dominated the discourse on prostitution in the 1980s, their departure, combined with the persistent demands of the World Bank and International Monetary Fund to integrate into the global capitalist economy, changed the focus of debates to sex tourism, the traffic in women, and most recently, aesthetic issues relating to the negative image of Filipinas abroad. These four themes will be taken in turn.

First, the important debate of the 1980s, which continued until the departure of the U.S. bases in 1991, revolved around the proliferation of bars catering to American servicemen in Angeles and Olongapo. Women like Edna were seen to epitomize the country's problems as urban and rural poverty forced young women into prostitution. Because Edna was from a poor urban community, she was portrayed as being forced into prostitution to support her family, with little choice but to succumb to the whims of American men. This representation was a means to popularize the anticolonial, anti–military base sentiment that permeated the Philippine middle class (Ryan 1991), and prostitution was seen as a metaphor for the broader relations between the Philippines and the United States (Enloe 1989; Miralao, Carlos, and Santos 1990; Sturdevant and Stoltzfus 1992).

Second, many claim that sex tourism was institutionalized during the time of President Marcos when the government defined and promoted a "hospitality business" to attract foreign tourists. By 1973, women's groups in Seoul and Tokyo staged demonstrations against sex tours throughout Southeast Asia, and in 1981 Filipina women's organizations staged political protests highlighting the structural inequalities that made sex tours possible for Japanese men (Mackie 1988). Throughout the 1980s and 1990s, and as a result of the vicious circle of indebtedness to the International Monetary Fund and World Bank, sex tourism has been perceived as a product of a foreign-dominated economy that relies on tourism dollars to repay debts (Azarcon de la Cruz 1985; de Leon, Contor, and Abueva 1991). In the case of Cebu—where Virgie, May, and Edna worked for a number of years— prostitution is highlighted as a problem of government policies which attract foreigners to the city, symbolized by the construction of an international airport (de la Cerna 1992). The *Laya Feminist Quarterly* noted that "the tale of prostitution is ever present. Today, however, prostitution has been stretched to its most exploitative scale and form with government's implementation of 'tourism' and 'rest and recreation' industries. A case in point is Cebu" (Laya Women's Collective 1993, 1).

There has been much debate among NGOs and national and local government agencies on Cebu's future growth. Under "Philippines 2000," Cebu is one of the Philippines' Regional Industrial Centers, and NGOs fear that the center will be import-based, export-oriented, inspire unnecessary land conversions, and contribute little to sustainable development (Lacorte 1993; Mongaya 1993a, 1993b). Members of the Japanese development agency contracted to develop Cebu's Integrated Master Development Plan have stressed the importance of foreign direct investment and linkages with the NICs of Asia (Villamor 1993), and this, combined with new government legislation to promote foreign investment in tourism projects (*Sun Star Daily* 20 September 1993), is seen as contributing to the magnitude of the sex industry in Cebu.

Third, while sex trafficking usually implies forced sexual slavery (de Stoop 1994), in the Philippines it is facilitated by institutionalized labor migration (Fernandez 1993). As depicted in figure 10.4, poor Filipinas often grasp the double-edged sword of overseas employment, only to be maltreated or end up in prostitution. According to estimates by David (1991, 16), 347,570 women migrate to other countries annually, primarily to work as domestic helpers, nurses, and entertainers, and "every other Filipino in Japan today is a young woman, between 15 and 24 years of age, has violated the terms of her visa (either by working without permit or by overstaying), is therefore deportable, and makes a living as an entertainer." This popular representation amongst Filipino activists—the "Japayuki"—is of a poor woman who travels to work in one of the bars in Tokyo and, once she realizes her employment is nonexistent or that her visa is invalid, is coerced into prostitution (Mackie 1988; Ballescas 1992). Annual remittances from overseas contract workers are estimated at anywhere from US$800 million to $2.5 billion (David 1991, 16), and this representation is used to highlight the negative consequences of government imperatives for foreign exchange and to argue that government support for overseas workers legitimizes prostitution.

Fourth and more recently, Filipinos have also been concerned about the negative stereotypes of Filipinas abroad. Because the 1993 scandal of Filipina models and actresses engaging in high-class prostitution in Brunei—gratuitously dubbed the "Brunei Beauties" case by the local press—refuted the point that all women are economically deprived and forced into prostitution, the focus of this debate was on the negative images of Filipinas abroad

Figure 10.4. Poverty and overseas employment opportunities facilitate the rape, prostitution, and maltreatment of Filipinas.

(see figure 10.5). These stereotypes were said to encourage the mistreatment, rape, and sexual slavery of Filipinas in foreign countries; the Brunei Beauties case prompted a congressional inquiry into these issues (Jumilla 1993). While some criticized the inquiry and excessive media attention given to the case, others remarked that it had done a "service" to Filipinas, changing the stereotype to "expensive whore, sought after by royal studs" (Cacho Olivares 1993).

As the Brunei Beauty case demonstrates, the conditions under which women enter prostitution are highly variable. The dilemma is that despite constraints on alternative development, the privileging of the structural aspects of prostitution minimizes the complexity of life choices and agency available to women in the Philippines. Simplifying prostitution to an uncomplicated relation of domination casts women as victims, a portrayal which marginalizes agency and the reality of everyday life.

NGOs, HIV/AIDS and Sex Workers in the Philippines

In 1987 there were 79 recorded HIV and AIDS cases in the Philippines. The majority of these had been detected in women working as entertainers around the American military bases, and women's organizations involved in the anti-bases campaign—led by Gabriela, an umbrella feminist organiza-

Figure 10.5. The "Brunei Beauties" scandal. From *Sun-Star Daily*, Cebu City, Philippines. August 26, 1993.

tion—brought this to the attention of the national government (see Enloe 1989, 88):

> Who are the producers of AIDS in the Philippines? Why does prostitution exist and proliferate in the military bases and our tourist spots? *The danger and damage of AIDS to women and the existence of prostitution are, in fact, crimes against women.* We are the products, the commodities in the transaction. . . . Who, then, we ask, are the real criminals of AIDS and prostitution? Indict them, not us. (Enloe 1989, 88).

From the mid-1980s to the early 1990s, HIV/AIDS was easily assimilated into the discourse of American bases, overseas contract workers and sex tourism. It was perceived as another product of a foreign-controlled economy, but one with the opportunity to directly affect all Filipinos. The construction of AIDS as a problem of foreigners thus inscribed the feminist and nationalist agenda, and has persisted to do so until the early 1990s (cf. Tan et al. 1989). By 1991 there were a total of 298 HIV and AIDS cases, however, and this combined with the nomination of a new and enthusiastic Secretary of Health inspired several AIDS education projects. These were carried out primarily by health NGOs, and not feminist or nationalist organisations. With these projects came the involvement of international "experts," and challenges to the dominant discourse.

This section begins with a vignette from the Women's Education, Development, Productivity, and Research Organisation (WEDPRO), because its internal discussions highlight the changes in the prostitution discourse. WEDPRO has worked with women entertainers around the former American military bases in Angeles and Olongapo for a number of years. In 1990 it was commissioned by the Legislative-Executive Bases Council—a body constituted to address the issue of base conversion after the servicemen left—to look at alternative employment, economic livelihood, and development needs for women in the entertainment industry. The organization's views on prostitution were specified in its preliminary report (Santos in Miralao, Carlos, and Santos 1990):

> The problem of prostitution is a complex sociocultural, political and economic issue which must be addressed in the overall context of genuine social transformation that takes into account the questions of national sovereignty and democracy and women's liberation from all forms of oppression and exploitation . . . if the bases are seen by a growing number of Filipinos as an encroachment of foreign powers upon national sovereignty, the question of institutionalized bases prostitution is a question of social justice and national dignity particularly of our women, our children, and collectively our people.

Following an extensive period of research in both Angeles and Olongapo, WEDPRO submitted a "participative bases conversion" proposal to the Bases Council (Lee and WEDPRO 1992, 1), which included educational and training projects for prostitutes to ensure they would not be left out of the restructuring of the local economies. No action was taken in response to these recommendations, however.

Presently, WEDPRO continues its work in Angeles, where sex tourism has undergone a modest revival, partly due to its proximity to Manila (particularly since Ermita's bars have been closed), but also because of a lack of education and training programs for former entertainers. WEDPRO's major undertaking has been to assist the development of LAKAS, a sex worker cooperative involved in a livelihood project of food stalls. The stalls—strategically located adjacent to the bars—are seen as an opportunity for women to organize and discuss issues. Simultaneously, they are providing alternative livelihood skills for women who choose to leave the industry. Increasingly, however, WEDPRO is looking to HIV/AIDS education activities: "Donors don't want to give money for livelihood projects any more, so we're thinking about an AIDS education project" (Linda, WEDPRO representative). Linda suggested that funding priorities for HIV/AIDS marginalize the role of socioeconomic programs, which are now seen as moralistic and not helpful in preventing the spread of HIV. She recounted, as an example, a recent conference her colleague attended, at which a Western woman espoused the "prostitution as choice" perspective, claimed that these were her findings in both developed and developing countries, and argued that organizations such as WEDPRO, in proposing livelihood activities, implied that women should leave their work. This was frustrating and perplexing to the WEDPRO representative, who felt that accepting prostitution as a "choice" peripheralized important feminist and nationalist issues. This conflict thus again was between structure and agency paradigms; that is, about whether or not the entry into prostitution is a matter of free will or forced choice. Given the complexity of the issue of choice itself, the debate merely became an articulation of opposed ideologies and sterile dichotomies.

Nonetheless, a recent survey conducted by WEDPRO in the major urban centers of the Philippines incorporated these perspectives. Still grappling with the prostitution as "free choice" perspective, Linda queried: "But what do I do if the women tell me they enjoy their work?"

It is within this context that three Australian-funded organizations carrying out AIDS education activities for sex workers in the Philippines will be described: the Visayas Primary Health Care and Services in Cebu, Kabalikat in Manila, and Talikala in Davao. Under AusAID's "AIDS Initiative," these NGOs are currently "partnered" with an NGO from Australia, creating what AusAID perceives as a more democratic process of evaluation. At the same time, this relationship allows for a productive exchange of ideas and experience. While it is true that Australian organizations have much experience with "community-based" HIV/AIDS prevention programs—particularly with the sex worker and homosexual communities in Australia—they also have a culturally distinct view of commercial sex. It is this distinctly Western construction, enmeshed in Western legal and social theory, that comes into conflict with the Filipino perspective described throughout this chapter.

While the issue of "choice" in prostitution has played a role in discussions on prostitution in Australia, the dominant discourse has historically focused on prostitutes as deviant, or abnormal, or as victims of a patriarchal society (Perkins 1991). Throughout the 1980s, however, and in concert with an international movement which politically mobilized prostitutes, sex worker organizations sought to remove the "victim" label through decriminalization and law reform. While similar cases were documented in the United States (Jenness 1993) and Europe (Pheterson 1989), Australian organizations were particularly successful in working with state governments and obtaining funding for their efforts. Since 1985, for example, sex worker organizations in Australia have received government funds for AIDS education projects.

AIDS education projects for sex workers in Australia have been inspired by activities in the gay community. One model in particular—"peer education"—has been adopted by Australian sex worker organizations. Peer education is a community-based model for AIDS prevention encompassing recent advances in health intervention projects: the project must be designed, implemented, and evaluated by the "target" community, and through this participatory process, the community is empowered to safeguard its own health. The centrality of community has been documented elsewhere (see McKenzie 1991; Altman 1993) and will not be elaborated here. That community-based strategies work so well in homosexual communities is not surprising given that

> [i]n reality the lesbian and gay community has always been a network of communities, primarily split between a political community which pursues an ideal of political power and representation, and the communities of the night, which encompass the genuine diversity which political activists seek to represent (Alcorn, in Watney 1993a, 13).

In the case of gay men, the community-based peer education method worked very well, at least for the men who identified as gay and were part of an established network (magazines, newsletters, organizations) through which HIV/AIDS information could be channeled. Sex worker organizations that adopted this model emulated these networks, through organizing, producing newsletters, and advocating legislative reform.

The Australian Federation of AIDS Organisations (AFAO) has been contracted by AusAID to be "partners" with a number of Filipino NGOs working with sex workers and gay men (Altman 1991). Both Kabalikat and Talikala, for example, are partnered with AFAO and use the peer education model. The Visayas Primary Health Care and Services is partnered with the Australian People for Health, Education, and Development Abroad (APHEDA) and does not use the peer education model, for reasons described below.

Prostitution Is a Structural Problem: Visayas Primary Health Care and Services

The Visayas Primary Heath Care and Services (VPHCS) is a health-based organization, and has been involved in the formation and establishment of functional health committees in poor communities in Cebu province since its inception in 1989. An important part of its objectives is to highlight the structural problems of government which affect urban poor communities. In the case of AIDS, an integral part of its information campaign is to highlight the amount of money that the government and foreign agencies spend on AIDS, and to discover why the money does not reach the grass roots.

In 1991, the VPHCS began HIV/AIDS education activities. As well as incorporating this aspect of health into existing programs among Cebu's urban poor communities, some members also initiated seminars in Cebu's bars catering to Western men. No attempt was made to integrate with the sex worker community, nor facilitate a peer education program, primarily because the organization had other projects as its focus. The organization gave seminars in two establishments:

> Because Visayas Primary Health Care is basically a community-based program, we just chose two clubs to extend our program. But we do not wish to concentrate on them because City Health is doing that already. I think they are doing a good job because whenever I go to these clubs to conduct lectures, the girls are quite knowledgable already (Jennifer, VPHCS representative).

Educational activities in the bar included basic information on what HIV/AIDS is, its transmission and prevention, and a condom demonstration. The women were able to demonstrate that they were very familiar with HIV issues, and if they faced problems in terms of protecting their own health and minimizing risk of infection, it was for reasons that went far beyond educational information. Such seminars—primarily a one-way education campaign—gave sex workers the status of objects and not subjects of the prevention of HIV/AIDS, and as Edna commented after a seminar we attended, "AIDS is a problem in my kind of job."

The issue of choice is not explicitly addressed by the Visayas group, but prostitution is accepted as a structural problem of government, and sex tourism is accepted as a colonial legacy. The agency of sex workers is lost in ideological discussions, and the "sex worker" becomes merely a victim of structures and a vector of infection. Such a representation poses a problem to empowerment in the broad sense, where AIDS is perceived as a "problem" resulting from particular social structures instead of an issue around which sex workers can be mobilized to protect themselves from HIV. The cases of Kabalikat and Talikala, described below, reject this overly determined social context by using the agency-centered "peer education" model, yet at the same time ignore the issues highlighted by the VPHCS.

Mandatory HIV Testing and the Issue of Choice: Kabalikat

Kabalikat is a health-based organization that has been in operation since 1979 conducting community-based projects on oral rehydration, water and sanitation, family planning, and more recently HIV/AIDS. Its first HIV/AIDS education activities began in 1989 and coincided with the identification of a number of women infected with HIV working in the sex industry.

Because at that time only sex workers were being tested for HIV, it was not surprising that Kabalikat decided to focus on these women, and its target group was the women in the tourist bars of Ermita, Manila. After a period of research on this area, and particularly after the executive director visited Australia on a study tour of AIDS education projects, the organization decided to use the "peer education" model.

Kabalikat's methodology was to visit the bars and establish contact with what they described as the "sex worker community." Kabalikat's delineation of the community was what its members called the "working system," the sex industry of Ermita, which included sex workers, managers and bar owners, clients, law enforcers, and the relatives of the women. In practice, however, Kabalikat's primary focus was on sex workers, so sex workers were identified with what might not necessarily reflect their community—that is, their neighbors, family, and friends. As Edna once said, "Even your best friend in the bar you cannot trust. Maybe one night she needs the extra (money) and she takes your boyfriend and tells him you've been going around with other men. Then they're going to the hotel and forget about you. . . . Me, I just work there and come home to my house."

Kabalikat's framework, however, highlighted the current imperative of establishing "community-based" AIDS education projects. The use of the term *community* is, however, problematic, since it presumes a common (sexual) identity. While this may be the case for some men in the Philippines, it is less so for women working in the sex industry, who arguably have little common purpose and who lack an established network of organizations or newsletters. In the rhetoric of development, "community-based" frameworks are privileged, and there has been little questioning of the existence or nonexistence of a community as a base from which to work.

When the mayor of Manila closed the bars of Ermita in a rather moralistic crusade, Kabalikat discontinued its original program (see figure 10.1). It continued its commitment to sex workers, however, by representing them on the government's AIDS Council, where they discussed issues such as mandatory testing. As one Kabalikat representative said,

> [Sex workers] are usually the ones infected more often than they spread it . . . these women do not choose to be in their profession. . . . That is why we are hurrying up the resolution that makes no mandatory testing a national policy, so that all local ordinances can be revoked. . . . Even if you force them to take the test: one, you cannot forcibly bring them to the facility; two, is the facility equipped to manage all the cases it finds positive whether for STDs or HIV? It does

not put the responsibility on the person who puts [himself] or herself at risk. It puts control over them by some other group.

These comments highlight how HIV/AIDS is altering the discourse on prostitution in some sectors of the Philippines. On the one hand, sex workers "do not choose to be in their profession." This view has a long history in the country, privileging the structural issues as described above. On the other hand, however, they should be "responsible" for protecting themselves since they "put" themselves at risk, without "control over them by some other group." One statement denies, and the other enhances, the agency of sex workers. Although seemingly contradictory, this represents a shift in the way Filipinos think about prostitution, and undoubtedly has been influenced by experience with Western organizations.

The Right to Health: Talikala

> Realizing the miserable plight of hospitality women in Davao City, a Maryknoll lay missionary in 1986 took the initiative of forming a group composed of herself, a social worker, and a girl coming from the ranks of hospitality women precisely to respond to the deteriorating condition of women engaged in the flesh trade. At the very start the group was very much aware that their main task was not to tell these women to quit their jobs, for such a task would require them to assume the state's inherent obligation to provide alternative jobs. On the other hand they understood that their mission was to assist women [to] regain their self-respect and to attain the power to dictate the course of their lives and shape their own destiny. (Desquitado 1992, 126)

This statement, published in 1992, reflects the new types of programs being carried out by NGOs in the Philippines. It places the responsibility for prostitution squarely on the state, and acknowledges that asking women to leave a profession they entered for financial reasons would be counterproductive. While Talikala does not entice women out of the sex trade, it is insinuated that they should be in other jobs where they could find "self-respect" and "attain the power to dictate the course of their lives and shape their own destiny."

Since its inception, Talikala has aspired to empower women in Davao's sex trade through health issues. Its original program of information dissemination was replaced in the early 1990s, however, when a member participated in an AIDS study tour in Australia. It was at this time that the organization took on a peer education project: "They were really selling it to us, you know. . . . Anyway, we were using an exhausting systems method, it was boring. We had to do something. There were the same girls, the same costumes, the same customers. . . . Before we couldn't get the same participation and enthusiasm" (Anabelle, former Talikala representative).

Talikala's primary goal is "empowerment," and it is believed that this can be achieved by using the peer education model: "Being [peer educators], the women themselves can relate freely with one another, because they come from the same work, they have similar aspirations and dreams. There are no barriers and no fears of being stigmatized" (Arlene, Talikala representative).

Talikala began the organization with a former sex worker as one of its three staff members and has continued incorporating sex workers into the project. The peer group staff members—all former or present sex workers—have been responsible for collecting the data on the sex industry in the city (Talikala 1993). This core group has also been responsible for facilitating the formation of a self-help group, which is separate from the activities of the NGO, and headed by the former sex worker who began the NGO; that is, it is a branch of the organization strictly composed of sex workers. This group examines employment issues such as working conditions, problems with customers and owners, and so on.

The decision to adopt the peer education model and the subsequent changes in the nature of program activities are understood in the structure/agency framework. In the case of both Talikala and Kabalikat, the complexity of the dualism has been displaced by opting for an agency-centered framework. While this allows for a more participatory development project, and sex workers are becoming involved in defining prostitution as a "social problem"—both of which are progressive achievements in development projects—such an approach denies the complexity and context of prostitution, in addition to the constraints on alternative employment such as a lack of skills, the social circumstances providing the personal context to sex work, and the lack of control over sexuality generally and hence over the freedom to work or not work in the sex industry.

Conclusion

The presumed universality of the concepts of prostitution and sexuality requires interrogation if they are to be used in transcultural contexts (Caplan 1987) and particularly for HIV/AIDS intervention projects (Vance 1991; de Zalduondo 1991). Issues of translation and the differing interpretations of concepts such as peer education cannot be separated from politics, and transcultural relations such as those evidenced in development aid—where foreign and local NGOs jointly create and evaluate projects for "others"—are entangled in a global structure which is hierarchical.

Paradoxically, it is precisely this context which makes the issue of choice both enlightening and symptomatic. It is enlightening because it makes room for a more fluid world of subjectivity to be included within the analysis of prostitution and in the types of projects which help to slow the spread of HIV. At the same time, however, it is symptomatic because this world simultaneously appears to displace the "real" world of political economy. The issue is not whether prostitution is a "choice," however, but how to find a progressive politics that bridges both of these worlds.

The stories of Virgie, May, and Edna illustrate that women in the sex industry perceive a negotiated tension between their free will to enter prostitution and the more deterministic constraints that make prostitution a job opportunity for them. Organizations which neglect this complexity and privilege one aspect initiate discursive practices which deny the reality of lived experience, making empowerment difficult. The tension between paradigms becomes most pronounced in the activities of development agencies involved in HIV/AIDS education, where Filipino NGOs have historically privileged the more structural aspects of prostitution, and Australian "partner" NGOs have privileged agency. Peer education within this context is an agency-centered model deployed in a structural discourse. Perhaps it is self-help groups like Talikala that will help to understand Virgie and her own experience of sex work when she says, "I don't have enough education, I have no choice. It's easy money. I have no family here . . . " Virgie highlights complexity and context, not merely structural determinants. Simply shifting the debate from no choice to free choice—and all the Western capitalist politics and ideology that go with it—would be a step in the wrong direction.

CHAPTER ELEVEN

The Foreign Devil Returns: Packaging Sexual Practice and Risk in Contemporary Japan

SANDRA BUCKLEY

On 29 November 1993, *Asahi shimbun,* Japan's major daily newspaper, ran a story featuring the exhibition of Japan's first AIDS Memorial Message Quilt. It consisted of just twenty quilts. The patches were prepared by the friends and families of individuals who had died of AIDS, as well as persons with AIDS (PWA).[1] A second story, embedded and highlighted within the first, focused on a story of "a certain Japanese hospital," where some twenty-six patients had died of AIDS. The staff attempted to convince the bereaved families to support the production and contribution of quilts to the Memorial Message Quilt, but the next of kin were extremely reluctant to become involved. Hospital officials reported that the main concern appeared to be the public naming of the family member, and hence the risk of the family being identified as having been "exposed" to the AIDS virus.

Finally, one of the families contributed two white quilts sewn together; the upper left-hand corner of the top quilt was embroidered with the initials KW, the same corner of the bottom quilt with the initials KH. These were the initials of the names of a husband and wife. Otherwise the surfaces of the quilts were starkly empty, a marked difference from AIDS memorial quilts produced in the United States, Europe, and Australia in the same year, where each square included items of personal history, eulogies, portraits, photos, and favorite childhood toys sewn into the cloth in a collage of memory and loss. This Japanese family's reluctance to be publicly associated with AIDS was mirrored in the refusal of the hospital itself to be identified, a fear not restricted to this one medical institution. Another *Asahi shimbun* article (24 November 1993) published a few days earlier under the headline "Medical Examination of AIDS Patients Hasn't Progressed Much . . . ," included a cartoon image of a very worried doctor and nurse, beads of sweat dripping from their brows, with the caption "AIDS examination . . . " over their heads (see figure 11.1). Less than a year later another article detailed the refusal of some hospitals to be listed in government information booklets as having experience or expertise in AIDS testing or medical care. The title of this article summarized the perspective of the hospitals succinctly: "Image-down. Other Patients Won't Come" (*Asahi shimbun*, 2 August 1994).

This chapter aims to link the two AIDS memorial quilts, marked by initials only, with the comments of Japanese critics of the Tenth International Conference on AIDS and STD held in Yokohama in August 1994. A spokesperson for the Tokyo office of the HIV and Human Rights Communication Center expressed his disappointment that the conference had not attracted the broad support or participation of Japanese people who were HIV-positive or had AIDS. He noted that when one of the keynote speakers, in an emotional moment, asked that all PWAs in the audience stand, he saw almost no Japanese among those standing. He related this to the conference's failure to appeal to the interests of PWAs in the host country. A Japanese AIDS researcher from Osaka University, Professor Kurimura, expressed a similar concern that the conference had shown little understanding

Figure 11.1. AIDS examination.

for the specific conditions of the lives of PWAs in Japan, and that the decision to locate the conference in Japan had been a calculated move by the
organizers to place pressure on Japan to fund future AIDS research and
education in the region. Kurimura asserted that "[r]ather than allowing others to determine the distribution of funds, we should support international
co-operative efforts that have an understanding of the Japanese point of
view." What might be meant by "the Japanese point of view" and what is
at stake in the drawing of this boundary will be the major focus of this
chapter. Through the redeployment of specific examples of the contemporary packaging and circulation of AIDS discourses in Japan, I seek to develop the context of production for both the silence of the white space of
the two AIDS memorial quilts and the static of media coverage of criticism
of the conference.

The Story in the Statistics

The major Japanese centers for the collection, collation, and distribution of
AIDS-and HIV-related information are the semigovernmental Japan Foundation for AIDS Prevention and the Ministry of Health and Welfare Com-
mittee for AIDS Surveillance. The official statistics for confirmed cases of
AIDS/HIV and HIV seropositive individuals are given in the following
table, published in 1994:

	AIDS	HIV Seropositive
Heterosexual transmission	91	597
Homosexual transmission	88	211
Drug-related transmission	2	9
Foetal transmission	5	4
Iatrogenic transmission	418	1771
Other	96	373
Total	*700*	*2965*

Source: Japan Foundation for AIDS Prevention 1994.

Official statistics can function both to mask and foreground marked shifts
in the emergence of new patterns of transmission. By law in Japan, individuals who contract the virus from infected blood products must be listed under
a distinct category. They qualify for benefits not available to other HIV-
positive individuals, (e.g., in 1993, all hemophiliacs were declared eligible
for a monthly compensation payment of 33,000 yen regardless of serostatus.
Spouses who tested seropositive were eligible for the same benefit.) A new
compensation settlement is currently under negotiation in Tokyo on the
basis of the recent admission of responsibility from the Green Cross and key

pharmaceutical companies. The legal separation of hemophiliacs from other persons who are seropositive confirms an official narrative of passive innocence and active guilt.

The distinctive status of hemophiliacs in Japan is a direct government response to extensive and effective lobbying through powerful political constituencies and interest groups, who support the status of hemophiliacs as innocent victims of a government failure to develop and implement adequate blood-screening procedures. The effectiveness of the campaign was dramatically enhanced by emphasizing that the bulk of the infected blood supply was imported into Japan—a fact which Japanese officials used to partly deflect responsibility back onto the United States, from which over 90 percent of the contaminated blood was imported. Both the official defense against claims of negligence and the organized campaigns by hemophiliac groups have been firmly grounded in a rhetoric of unknowing innocence as against guilt and culpability. Even pediatric AIDS is not granted a similar, separate status. Up until February 1995, there had been thirteen cases of pediatric AIDS outside the hemophiliac community (*Japan Times,* 1 February 1995). While all these infants were "passively" exposed to the virus, they still appear to be categorized as "guilty" by association. Hence the concerns of members of families of Japanese PWAs that, in the present climate, the concept of PWA has been extended to a notional category of Families with AIDS—FWA (my term).

Japanese government sources and the media are quick to differentiate the context of AIDS in Japan from that of other countries, pointing out that hemophiliacs represent by far the largest group of people with HIV or living with AIDS.[2] However, the figures for infected hemophiliacs did not change over 1993 and 1994, and no new cases were reported for this period. This suggests a stabilization as a result of new and stringent procedures for screening domestic and imported blood supplies. If this stabilization is maintained, as predicted, while the rate of nonhemophiliacs testing positive continues to increase, then Japan will face a dramatic shift in the national AIDS profile over the next several years, requiring a major transformation of official policy and practice, and of public awareness and attitudes.

In some Japanese government HIV/AIDS statistics, the official figure is followed by a second figure in parenthesis, representing the number of foreigners included in that category. This separate identification of foreigners is officially explained as a reflection of the large numbers of illegal immigrant workers employed in the entertainment and sex industry in Japan. But this is more than a question of numbers. Justice Ministry statistics estimate that there are up to 300,000 illegal immigrant workers in Japan today. ("Foreigners Overstay[ing] Visas Seen Near 300,000," *Japan Times,* 30 August

1993).[3] Feminist labor activists and human rights groups claim that this figure grossly understates the number of illegal foreign workers, although current statistics are much more reliable than the estimates of the mid-1980s.

The makeup of the illegal foreign worker population has changed dramatically over the last decade. In 1986 the Immigration Bureau identified 8,000 foreign workers in Japan, two-thirds of whom were Filipinos, mostly working as prostitutes or hostesses (Yamanaka 1993, 83). While the majority of illegal female workers are still employed in the entertainment and sex industry, women now constitute only 36 percent of the illegal workers in Japan. Thai women constitute the largest national grouping (*Japan Times*, 30 August 1993) and Filipinos the second largest group, but that is changing relative to arrivals from Korea, Taiwan, and China. Thai officials estimated that approximately 70,000 Thais were working in prostitution in Japan in 1993 ("Arrests Crack Alleged Sex Syndicate," *Japan Times*, 13 August 1993). An additional 90,000 legal immigrant workers are employed in the entertainment and sex industry, the majority again Thai (Yamanaka 1993, 77), contradicting the widespread impression in much popular and academic writing outside Japan through the 1990s that this population is predominantly Filipino.

By mid-1993 the Japanese media had begun reporting that relative to foreigners, Japanese were being infected in greater numbers than before. Some articles overtly stated that foreigners were "to blame." The increase in Japanese infections as a proportion of total new cases relates to an overall decrease of 26 percent in confirmed HIV infection, a major shift from annual increases of more than 50 percent in 1990–91 (from 97 to 238) and 1991–92 (from 238 to 493) ("Eizu hokoku sakunen 364 nin" ["364 AIDS cases last year"], *Asahi shimbun*, 28 January 1994). This decrease has to be interpreted against a correspondingly large reduction in the number of foreigners in the figures—a fall from 332 in 1992 to 181 in 1993—despite the continuation of a pattern of annual increase in foreigners working in the sex industry, where most of the infected foreigners are employed. The media were quick to sensationalize this documented shift as a sign that AIDS was no longer a foreign disease and was "penetrating" the Japanese population. While HIV infection has increased among Japanese, the decline in reported cases among foreigners is most likely the result of a decrease in testing of foreign males and females in the sex industry. Improved understanding of safe sex methods by sex workers might also explain the decrease.

However, there is a far more likely explanation, as blood testing has become a mechanism for extending the policing of illegal immigrant labor. This policing is intended to "protect" Japanese male clients against "exposure" to HIV-positive sex workers. Sex workers commonly report that blood tests are far more actively encouraged, some indeed would say enforced, among foreign sex workers than among Japanese nationals in the same industry. Testing functions more as an aggressive process of screening than as a cooperative process of education, prevention, and treatment, resulting in workers' fears of job loss and deportation, fueled by media reports of nationwide raids, with up to three thousand being deported at a time. ("Thousands Deported in Recent Clampdown," *Japan Times,* 4 October 1993; "July Raids Send 2,700 Illegals Home," *Japan Times,* 9 October 1994). Such extensive publicity might represent an official attempt to reassure the public that the government is acting to "protect" against any further incursion by the "foreign disease." This seemingly concerted campaign has led both illegal immigrant workers and their employers to adopt a less cooperative stance towards voluntary testing and reporting.

The Japanese figures for confirmed cases of HIV for January and February 1994 continue the pattern of 1993–94, with the highest total number of new cases occurring among "heterosexuals" (30, including 11 foreigners) (Japan Foundation for AIDS Prevention 1994). However, the rate of increase among "homosexuals" is far greater as a percentage of the total male homosexual population (16, including 1 foreigner). No new cases were confirmed among intravenous drug users, hemophiliacs, or children. However, a further category of "Other/Uncertain" lists 20 new cases (including 16 foreigners) for which there is either no information or no single condition/practice identifiable as the site of exposure. This insistence on identification of originary sites or contexts of exposure is linked to conventions used by WHO/GPA (Global Programme on AIDS, World Health Organization) in the collation and dissemination of AIDS data and the formation of international AIDS policy (see below).

Not only is the rate of newly confirmed cases higher as a percentage of the total population of homosexual men than is the case for the heterosexual community, but the overall rate of increase is also higher. An increase of 26 from 1993 (571) to 1994 (597) in the category of heterosexual transmissions and 12 from 1993 (199) to 1994 (211) in the category of homosexual transmissions translates into a 1994 increase over 1993 of 4.5 percent in heterosexual and 16.5 percent in homosexual transmissions (Japan Foundation for AIDS Prevention 1994). While the figures for heterosexual cases appear to have been distorted since 1993 due to the downturn in testing and reporting among illegal immigrant sex workers, still the rate of increase in homosexual transmissions is high, and this must have serious implications for the national AIDS profile. Since the decline in testing among illegal immigrants is also assumed to extend to foreign male sex workers, homosexual and bisexual, this would in turn lead to underreporting and a downward distortion of figures for the categories of homosexual transmission and "Others/Uncertain." Even at present levels of reporting, the representation of foreigners in this category is high–79 percent of confirmed cases in 1994 (Japan Foundation for AIDS Prevention 1994).

Another listing offered in the annual figures for Japan is for newly confirmed cases and accumulative totals per annum. This is a statistical breakdown into three site-of-transmission categories—domestic, foreign, and uncertain—for the accumulative totals according to gender and age groupings. This data is potentially unreliable, since it assumes that HIV-positive individuals are able to accurately identify the specific situation in which they contracted the virus. If, for example—as is common in Japan—an individual tests positive and has had unprotected sexual intercourse in both foreign and domestic contexts (heterosexual and/or homosexual), it could prove extremely difficult to ascertain the carrier. At present there is a breakdown of those who contracted HIV outside Japan and of those who contracted it domestically, but it is not recorded whether domestic transmissions were traced to foreigners or Japanese nationals. The absence of these distinct categories for cases of transmission within Japan implies that domestic exposure to AIDS is assumed to be linked almost exclusively to foreign sex workers. This in turn assumes that the high percentage of foreigners represented in both the homosexual and heterosexual transmission categories reflects the reality and not a failure of the system to identify accurately the levels of transmission among Japanese nationals. Some Japanese feminists have insisted that the present focus on AIDS education for high school and tertiary-age students and the screening of foreign sex workers effectively bypass adult heterosexuals and homosexuals who are not sex workers and may be at risk of infection through unprotected sex with spouses and lovers involved in unprotected, high-risk activities. AIDS-related educational and medical materials consistently list three main conditions of "high risk": unprotected sex with a person whose sexual history is unknown or who has multiple sexual partners, shared use of hypodermic needles, and vertical transmission (mother/child) (Legal Foundation for AIDS Prevention 1994, 5).

High levels of corruption in the Japanese medical profession are suspected to contribute to the underreporting of seropositive Japanese nationals, creating a further distortion in the official statistics.[4] In addition to unnecessary surgical procedures and overprescription of drugs, the practice of disguising or not reporting certain medical conditions (e.g., STDs) and procedures (e.g., abortion and gender screening of pregnancies) has long been subject to media scrutiny in Japan. There is considerable potential for doctors, patients, and families to conceal serostatus and disguise AIDS-related deaths, purportedly to protect the reputation of the family from any association with "risky" sexual practice—heterosexual or homosexual—or to avoid the family's categorization within an emerging unofficial identity of Families with Aids. In addition, many doctors do not inform patients of their serostatus. Nondisclosure of terminal illness to a patient, and sometimes the patient's family, is common in Japan,[5] and has gained considerable attention in relation to cancer in medical journals, publications of patients' rights groups, and the media. Doctors argue that nondisclosure is in the best interests of the patient, who is more likely to respond to treatment if unaware of the terminal nature of the condition. Critics argue, however, that nondisclosure is an example of the tremendous discretionary power of Japanese doctors, and the practice is often linked also to issues of unnecessary procedures and overbilling. In a Ministry of Health and Welfare survey of medical institutions dealing with AIDS patients, only 43 percent stated that they always informed patients of their serostatus ("Jissai wa hokoku no 8.7 bai: Eizu uirusu no kansenshasu" ["Real statistics as much as 8.7 times higher than reported: The rate of AIDS infection"], *Asahi shimbun*, 28 July 1993); 28 percent responded that they sometimes did so ("AIDS Spread Outlined in Poll," *Japan Times*, 10 November 1994). Institutions that admitted to not informing offered two dominant explanations: the patient was a minor and the parents chose for the information to be withheld, or the patient him/herself did not want to know. No information is offered as to how this latter preference was established, or if it was simply assumed by the physician/institution. It is estimated that among people who have been infected by spouses who are HIV positive and hemophiliac, in 39 percent of cases the spouses had not been informed that they themselves were infected, and the virus was transmitted unknowingly ("Spouses Were Not Told About HIV," *Japan Times*, 17 July 1993).

Whether because of corrupt disguise of serostatus or nondisclosure by doctors, there is good reason to consider official AIDS statistics for Japanese nationals to be unreliable. The government continues to focus on identifying potential carriers, and within official statistics that category is always marked implicitly as "foreign," whether the site of transmission is assumed to be domestic or overseas. In December 1994, a government-funded educational publication entitled rather inappropriately *Laughing AIDS* (*AIDS wa warau*) described Thailand as the "major AIDS power in the world."[6] This was withdrawn from circulation after extensive campaigning by gay activists. There appears to have been little change in the official framing of AIDS since the 1992 controversy over a Japan Foundation for AIDS Prevention poster that showed a Japanese with a passport shielding his face, with the caption "Have a nice trip, but be careful of AIDS." Once the source of "contagion" is marked as non-Japanese (whether internal or external), then the goal is to protect innocent Japanese by identifying and expelling "carri-ers." The "othering" of contagion, represented by this deeply entrenched stereotyping of the carrier as foreign, inhibits the accurate profiling of new transmission trends among both foreigners and Japanese across the range of current official categories of classification. These very categories mask intensely differentiated community and individual experiences of living with AIDS and therefore warrant extensive interrogation (see Clatts and Mutchler 1989; Watney 1989b; Patton 1990; Farmer 1992). I return to this issue later.

The Ministry of Health and Welfare predicts that the number of seroposi-tive Japanese will reach twenty-seven thousand by the end of 1997 (*Asahi shimbun,* 28 July 1993), although official figures for 1993 and 1994 are not consistent with this level of increase. The Ministry itself has suggested that the discrepancy may reflect a fall in official reporting and self-identification of symptomatic individuals as well as shortcomings in the screening and educational processes across the full range of potential "risk groups." In July 1993, the Ministry stated publicly its concern that actual levels of infection in Japan could be 8.7 times higher than reporting suggests (*Asahi shimbun,* 28 July 1993). The implications of such high levels of underreporting are obviously significant for the development and implementation of successful policies and programs for the prevention and treatment of AIDS. I now turn to two official attempts to educate Japanese children and adults about HIV/AIDS.

The Story in Education

In 1993 the Japan Education Foundation produced a video in their Home Room Series entitled *AIDS: What Is Really So Frightening?* (Japan Education Center and TAO Communications, Tokyo 1993) for classroom use in high schools. The project focused on AIDS awareness activities at the Interna-tional Christian University High School, and most of the footage is of a classroom workshop, structured around brief information sessions presented by teachers and AIDS researchers, followed by open question periods. As the video voice-over states, this school was selected because of its reputation for an internationally diverse student body, and both the high proportion of female to male students and their racial and ethnic backgrounds combine to make this a quite atypical classroom environment in the Japanese context. While generational difference may account for some of the marked contrast in attitudes towards AIDS expressed in broader public surveys and in the views held by these students, the internationally mixed environment among students and faculty at ICU and its affiliate high school may also explain the more open climate of nondiscrimination. None of the students considered any need to adjust daily interaction and practices should a fellow student be diagnosed as HIV-positive, and exposure to blood in case of an accident was the only contact issue discussed as a potential area for modification of behavior. These responses contrast with those of an *Asahi shimbun* survey (21 October 1993) which indicated that 70 percent of respondents would not change their daily interactions, 20 percent would modify their interactions, and 10 percent would cease all contact with a fellow worker who was seropositive. A broader Ministry of Health and Welfare survey of public opinion, also conducted in 1993, suggests that the level of behavioral modification may be even higher, given the lack of basic AIDS-related knowledge demonstrated by respondents. The brochure indicated that 41 percent believed that entering the same bath or using the same toilet could lead to infection; 45 percent identified drinking from the same cup as a risk behavior; 62 percent believed that they could contract AIDS from a mosquito bite (*What Is AIDS? Correct Knowledge and Practice Will Protect You*, Ministry of Health and Welfare and Japan Foundation for AIDS Prevention 1993a, 1). The Ministry survey underlined the need for enhanced public education programs, and in the same year the government allocated a total of 10.3 billion yen to AIDS education, surveillance, and treatment (*Far Eastern Economic Review*, 7 January 1993). The Japanese Education Foundation video and classroom teaching kits for high school use are consistent with the designation of high school students as a key target group of AIDS education resources.

The video *AIDS: What Is Really So Frightening?* is thirty minutes long. In that time the Japanese word *homo* (male homosexual) is heard only once when a student is asked what he would feel personally if he was diagnosed as HIV-positive: "There wouldn't be much I could do about it if I'd ended up becoming a homosexual." The implication is that, in the mind of this young student, AIDS is a homosexual disease, and that one "becomes" a homosexual. The only other reference to homosexuality is a brief view of the traditional term *dooseiai* ("same sex love") written on a blackboard, but the camera focuses on the word just as the characters are being erased.[7] This video is almost exclusively about heterosexually transmitted AIDS in Japan. The fact that the student comment was left in the video raises concern that its inclusion might be intended to reinforce a notion that AIDS among gay men is unpreventable ("there wouldn't be much I could do about it"), while heterosexual AIDS is avoidable. Antihomosexual content in official AIDS publications is not without precedent. The controversial brochure *Laughing AIDS* outraged Japanese gays with its statement that Japanese should avoid traveling to Germany because it has been infested with homosexuals since ancient times (*Far Eastern Economic Review,* 7 January 1993). The fact that *dooseiai* was clearly a topic of discussion within the workshop but was edited out of the materials for school distribution raises the worrying issues of censorship and the misrepresentation of the changing national AIDS profile. The target audience of the video is not the atypical ICU classroom but students across rural and urban Japan where the understanding and willingness to discuss homosexuality and AIDS are likely to be lower and the levels of ignorance or prejudice higher.

In an early scene in the video, a teacher asks if it is possible to contract AIDS from a single act of unprotected sexual intercourse. The students respond correctly that it is not 100 percent certain. The teacher agrees but then turns to one of the foreign students and asks her to recount a story she had heard of a young foreigner who contracted AIDS this way. Both Hong Kong and the United States are mentioned in the scenario that follows. The students are also asked if they have ever seen a condom. The teacher does not demonstrate condom fitting, but goes on to assert that a condom should be worn "from the very beginning." She stated that she had been taught how to get condoms and even fit them, but no one had taught her how to ask a man to wear one or get him to agree. This is an important distinction, an issue not addressed in the video. In the absence of any discussion of sexual practices (homosexual or heterosexual) that might not focus on vaginal penetration alone ("from the very beginning"—penetration—to the end—ejaculation) there is little scope to expand notions of safe sex beyond condom use. It is interesting to observe that the teacher's nonverbal gestures and eye contact direct these remarks on condom use to female rather than male students in the classroom. The weight of responsibility falls on women to protect themselves.[8]

The final segment of the video records a meeting at a neighborhood youth information center between young teenage students and Hirata Yutaka. In October 1992, Hirata became the first Japanese to publicly identify as having been infected through sexual transmission rather than contaminated blood. As late as mid-1993 he was one of only three nonhemophiliacs in Japan to speak openly in public forums about their personal experience of AIDS. In his on-video exchange with the students, Hirata emphasized the importance of reducing ignorance and fear. He asked a student what she would do if her lover was diagnosed with AIDS. "If we were really in love and still wanted to have sex?," she asks. "Yes, and that person you love is diagnosed as HIV seropositive . . . what would you do?" She couldn't respond. Hirata stepped into the silence his question had created and explained that it was ignorance and uncertainty that led to fear, and fear left many PWAs battling their illness alone.

But the video does not include details of safe sex methods or alternative sexual practices to intercourse. In his exchanges with the students, Hirata also avoids gendering the words *lover* and *person* through gender-specific pronouns or inflections. His tactic is intentionally to keep open the possibility of both homosexual and heterosexual love and sexual relations in his discussions with the students. There is tension between Hirata's deliberate ambiguity and the dominant strategy in the video to place such ambiguity within a normative heterosexual model. Although the video attempts to present a realistic picture by recognizing that an increasing number of young Japanese engage in heterosexual relations prior to marriage, it neither addresses the issue of unprotected sex (either marital or extramarital) after marriage, nor the possibility that some students who might watch this video may be gay or may engage in both homosexual and heterosexual activities.

One student makes a comment in the classroom that performs a smooth appropriation of the empowering strategy of the identity politics of PWAs. The student, speaking as a non-PWA, comments that the real issue is not how "we" live with AIDS (*tomo ni ikite iku*) but how we give life (*ikite ageru*) to PWAs for the remainder of the time *they* have to live. In this transition from the history of PWA as a designation for those who have AIDS to this use of the term to describe those who live with people who have AIDS, *AIDS: What Is Really So Frightening?* begins to answer its own question. The video goes to great lengths to silence or erase any evidence of sexual identity or practice that falls outside very limited parameters of "appropriate" heterosexual behavior for young Japanese.

Laughing AIDS?

The Japan Foundation for AIDS Prevention and the Ministry of Health and Welfare prepare a range of adult educational materials for wide public distribution. The brochures are mailed out in response to phone or mail requests for information and are distributed through clinics, hospitals, and counseling services offering AIDS-related services. The very name "Japan Foundation for AIDS Prevention" resonates with the emphasis of the home room video. Protection and prevention are used synonymously in these materials. The question "What is really so frightening?" begs the question "Who is frightened of what?" and in turn, "What or who specifically is protected through the strategies of prevention?" The adult education materials leave no doubt that at the heart of the matter is the healthy heterosexual family.

Three of the more widely distributed brochures for adult AIDS education are *What You Need to Know about AIDS: Basic Knowledge for Protection and Co-*

Existence (Legal Foundation for AIDS Prevention 1994), *What Is AIDS? Correct Knowledge and Practice Will Protect You* (Ministry of Health and Welfare and the Japan Foundation for AIDS Prevention 1993a) and *The AIDS Reader* (Ministry of Health and Welfare and Japan Foundation for AIDS Prevention 1993b). The front covers of the first and the last of these carry an image of a happy and loving heterosexual couple holding hands. *What Is AIDS?* features a more science-oriented cover with a "through the microscope view"—rendering visible the invisible. All three cover images show the design influence of the extremely popular graphic style of the comic books (*manga*). The style of presentation aims to capture as wide a readership as possible by utilizing the familiar design and graphics of the most widely read printed medium of popular culture, the *manga* (Buckley 1996). The only non-*manga* images in the brochures are occasional maps of the global distribution of AIDS, photographs of healthy and unhealthy cells, statistical graphs, and lists of AIDS information contact numbers.

It is worthwhile to look more closely at the images that illustrate every page of these brochures. The choice of the *manga* style is easily open to misunderstanding outside Japan. In a country where the most popular biweekly and monthly *manga* sell two to three million copies per edition, and where leading *manga* artists have the status of media stars, the decision to use the graphic style of the comic books in AIDS-related materials is not at all unlike the logic behind U.S. and European AIDS awareness and education campaigns that employ high-profile figures from the worlds of entertainment and sport as spokespeople.[9] In Japan, the prevailing reluctance to be publicly associated with AIDS has reduced the viability of this as a serious option. The use of one of the most popular forms of contemporary consumer culture as a medium for communicating AIDS-related information amounts to the same basic strategy. Although today the *manga* are at the center of an ongoing public debate over censorship and pornography laws, since the mid-1960s, *manga* have been the key cultural site for testing and stretching strong taboos and legal restrictions that have limited the open discussion or imaging of sexual practices. The body, sexuality, and desire are not easily spoken into public discourses in Japan. The cultural territory of the *manga* offers a rare space for the uncomplicated and unapologetic presentation of images and content that may be "masked" or diffused by more familiar forms of official communication.

To anyone unfamiliar with the *manga* market, the graphics may seem an inappropriate form for AIDS information, but this is far from true. Calls for the withdrawal of the controversial *manga*-style *Laughing AIDS* brochure were not based on any objection to the format, but on its offensive title and antigay and racist content. Gay men, lesbians, feminists, A-bomb survivors, environmentalists, conservative politicians, right-wing promilitarist groups, the Ministry of Education, and new religious sects have all used *manga* as a medium to communicate their messages to the public in a popular and accessible format. The *manga* are often far too serious in content to fit the implications of humor implied by the English translation of "comic book." While there are many *manga* on the market that are extremely humorous, it would be incorrect to think that the use of *manga* graphics implies a lack of seriousness or undermines the legitimacy of the information conveyed. In the context of AIDS publications, the *manga* style is a strategic choice of a familiar, accessible, and nonalienating form.

Another potential misunderstanding relates to the highly stylized, apparently Western appearance of many *manga* characters. Since the first boom in teenage *manga* in the 1960s, the imaging of characters, male and female, has involved a complex and highly inflected movement across a range of physical and racial characteristics or markings that have emerged into a virtual repertoire of identity codings. Readers of the *manga* are extremely fluent in interpreting these codes as an extra level of textual depth. Shape of eyes, skin tone, hairstyle, type of shoes, fit and style of clothes, shape of hands, type of moustache, length of eye lashes, and shape of smile combine, as in a police identikit, to disclose character and personality as the reader's eye scans the narrative off the visual mix of text, image, and white space on the page.[10] The presence of a large number of advertisements for plastic surgery, slimming techniques, body building, and so on in many of the adult genres of *manga* for men and women suggests that the notion of beauty and the role of racial and other differentiating characteristics in the construction of identity in the *manga* warrant closer attention (Buckley 1991). However, it is important to emphasize that the interpretation of this representational practice as a substitution of Western figures for Japanese is too simple and misreads the multiple layers of interpretation and displacement through which a Japanese reader articulates an identification with these images as Self and not Other.

A typical example of the potential for misinterpretation occurs in one critic's description of the content of a Japanese AIDS education poster: "The dress and coiffure are clearly Western, reinforced by the coffee bar and french bread" (Hill 1994, 16; see figure 11.2). But the designation of french bread and coffee as Western, reinforcing the foreign influences associated with AIDS, makes little sense. Notions of ownership or origin of the objects of everyday life cannot be applied so unproblematically in the global cultural economy in which Japan is a high-end user and producer. What could be more "Japanese" than smart, stylish dress and modern, sophisticated consumer habits? The real issue is the appropriateness of the image for its target audience.

It is crucial to intepret Japanese AIDS education materials in the context of their production and circulation, not to read these images through the lens of a lingering Othering of Japanese identity. The style of dress in the poster is consistent with specific fashion codes popular in the romantic and "soft porn" genres of *manga* for older teenage girls and young married women. This particular graphic style and the grammatical inflection of the caption identifies the primary target group for this poster as female and heterosexual, somewhere between senior high school and early motherhood. The style of the popular genre of *Reedeezu Komikku* (Ladies Comics) has been selected specifically for its nonalienating ability to trigger identification.

Figure 11.2. Japanese AIDS education poster, 1990.

Certain patterns are repeated across the *manga*-based AIDS education publications mentioned above. For instance, the person represented as worried about possible symptoms, anxious after unprotected sex, undergoing a blood test, or receiving medical treatment is always a male heterosexual (see figure 11.3). The notable exception is the image of a pregnant woman. Two of the brochures include such an image, together with some description of the risks of vertical transmission. One of the images leaves no doubt as to the general attitude toward vertical transmission. An HIV-positive infant points accusingly at the mother, and the bubble-caption over the infant's head reads simply "You" (figure 11.4). Sweat forms into exclamation marks over the mother's head. This uncomplicated attribution of responsibility and guilt to the mother is consistent with the tone of recent media coverage relating to "AIDS babies" in the United States.

None of the brochures include an image of a man who could be identified as gay within the standardized codings of *manga* reading. The heterogeneously heterosexual context of the imaging and packaging of this AIDS information is so complete that it would be essential to offer some mark of difference if any of the male figures were intended to be identified as gay. Visual codification of gay identity in the *manga* style is well established and easily recognized. The visual coding of the sexual identity of the male characters that inhabit the pages of these brochures is unambiguously heterosex-

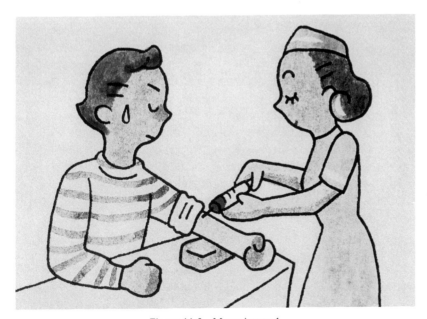

Figure 11.3. *Manga* image 1.

Figure 11.4. *Manga* image 2.

ual. While there is discussion and imaging of the various activities that are described as constituting a "high risk" of transmission, such as unprotected (heterosexual) sex with someone whose sexual history is not known, needle sharing, pregnancy when HIV-positive, and direct contact with blood of an infected individual, any reference to homosexual practices is avoided. The brochures mention body fluids as a potential source of contamination, and the *What Is AIDS?* (Ministry of Health and Welfare and the Japan Foundation for AIDS Prevention 1993a) brochure includes anal sex together with intercourse without a condom and shared use of sex aids (vibrators, etc.) as "high-risk" activities. However, only one of the brochures uses the word *homosexual*. It occurs in the context of a brief response to the question "Isn't AIDS a homosexual disease?": "Of course this is wrong. Anyone can contract AIDS. Because it was initially limited to male homosexuals, a misconception spread across the world that this was a disease that only certain people can contract" (*What You Need to Know about AIDS: Basic Knowledge for Protection and Co-Existence,* Legal Foundation for AIDS Prevention 1994, 12).

The question and answer reinforce the fact that in this brochure AIDS is treated as a heterosexual issue. In clarifying that AIDS is not a homosexual disease, the statement also appears to reinforce a negative and deviant marking of male gay identity by uncritically linking discrimination toward PWAs with gay identity. It criticizes the negative marking of AIDS while apparently accepting and participating in the negative marking of gay men. Although other focused materials are prepared and circulated within gay communities, largely by AIDs action groups, it remains disturbing that gay men who have AIDS or are seropositive are omitted from key educational materials prepared by the two major AIDS education and prevention organizations in Japan. This is particularly significant, given that increased HIV infection and AIDS in the gay community were already evident in 1993 and 1994 when these brochures were in production. Even if the brochures were designed specifically for a heterosexual audience, the absence of any reference to AIDS in the context of male homosexuality suggests that the boundaries between homosexual and heterosexual identities are clearly drawn and not crossed. This would imply, for example, that there is no sexual contact between female heterosexuals and men who may or may not self-identify as gay and have sex with other men, an assumption that is not supported even by official statistics. I return to this point towards the end of the chapter.

In addition, the brochures lack any reference to hemophiliacs or the transmission of AIDS through infected blood products. This is consistent with the Japanese government's agreement with lobby groups representing infected hemophiliacs that they be treated separately from other PWAs in Japan (see above). In the context of educational materials, the risk is that in recognizing the specificity of the history of transmission in the hemophiliac community and protecting the rights of HIV-positive hemophiliacs, there is a restriction placed on the open flow of information to the general public about what was, until recently, the largest group of HIV-positive individuals in Japan. An implicit message in this absence of references to hemophiliacs in general AIDS-prevention educational materials goes beyond the separate legal status of these individuals: the "risk of contagion" is identified as located elsewhere, without. When the brochures attempt to identify high-risk sites of transmission, these usually fall into one of two clear categories: (1) exposure of Japanese to non-Japanese "carriers," and (2) transmission through objects and practices of everyday life (e.g., sharing towels, toothbrushes, razor blades, needles and syringes, and having unprotected intercourse). The images in the brochures position these two categories as primary and secondary sites of exposure. Within this framework the point of "origin" of AIDS—what is represented as the primary level of exposure that must be protected against—is always located "outside" or on/in bodies that cross from "outside" to "inside" Japan. Hemophiliacs can be located within this construction of a narrative of Japanese AIDS on the basis that the contaminated blood supply was predominantly imported. However, activists within this community have resisted this framing of their history to avoid any disclaimer of responsibility by the Japanese government.

Japanese represented in the educational materials as having been "infected" are most frequently shown as having participated in "high-risk" activities with a non–Japanese "carrier." Those people are in turn represented as potential sites of secondary infection for other Japanese with whom they come into contact in daily life and share the use of everyday objects. In one illustration a Japanese man and woman sit under a palm tree on an island surrounded by the mounting statistics for confirmed cases of HIV seropositivity in Japan (see figure 11.5). The image can be interpreted as showing either island-Japan at risk, or the risks of venturing abroad to tropical paradises only to bring AIDS back to Japan. Either way the message of "inside" and "outside" is explicit. In the brochure *The AIDS Reader* (Ministry of Health and Welfare and the Japan Foundation for AIDS Prevention 1993b), the first page is a full-page *manga* image of a medical laboratory with a man looking into a microscope and taking notes. The reader turns to the next double-page to find a second full-page image of an airport scene with four young Japanese, two men and two women, sitting on their suitcases (marked with United States tourist stickers), reading a guidebook for Hawaii while they wait for their flight. The caption reads "Recently AIDS has been spreading in Asia" (figure 11.6). The image appears on the left-hand page; on the right are two graphs based on WHO statistics: the rate of increase of HIV infection and AIDS in Japan from 1989–1992, with a prefectural breakdown of the distribution of HIV and, below these figures, a map of the world showing selected regional statistics. The lower image/graph shows a statistic of 1,500 confirmed AIDS cases on the Chinese mainland and 25 on the Korean peninsula, but there is no indication of which regions these two figures represent in total or whether Japan is included at all. In combination, the map of global AIDS statistics and the cartoon image of Japanese tourists visually reinforce the message that the "problem" lies elsewhere. The statistics represent the arrival of something foreign that is carried in from the outside.

The Frontier of AIDS in Asia

Articles that appeared in the *Asahi shimbun* in July and early August 1994, prior to the International Conference on AIDS, reinforce this notion of AIDS arriving in an innocent or passive Japan that exists outside a newly emerging Asian AIDS epidemic. This particular Japanese conceptualization of AIDS replicates WHO/GPA models for the patterning of the AIDS epidemic.[11] The earlier WHO model was based on a geographic clustering of

Figure 11.5. Islands of risk.

countries into six administrative regions: Pan-America, Europe and the United Kingdom, the Western Pacific, Southeast Asia, Sub-Saharan Africa, and the Eastern Mediterranean. In response to widespread criticism of this model, WHO/GPA developed a different clustering based on the notion of the temporal "emergence" of densities of AIDS of differing "origins," defined not only by geographic space but also by specific forms of transmission and a notion of an epidemiological time line. This model has met with extensive criticism, but it continues to have a significant impact on the conceptualization of AIDS in much public discourse, both official and popular. It is this model which offers a legitimation of the dominant narrativization of AIDS in Japan. The WHO/GPA model describes three "patterns." Pattern One is called simply AIDS, and describes the transmission category of male homosexual intercourse, most closely associated with North America. Pattern Two is African AIDS and describes heterosexual transmission. Pattern Three describes Asia, "where AIDS arrived late." The criterion in the case of Asia is not a dominant transmission pattern but a temporal categorization grounded in an initial state of absence. As the predictions for the rate of increase of HIV seropositivity across Asia continue to rise, the significance of the historically late "arrival" of AIDS is rapidly being displaced by the magnitude of the problem facing the governments of Asia.

Critics of the WHO/GPA patterns argue that the notion of the "lateness" of the Asian AIDS "pattern" conveniently fed into both international and

Figure 11.6. Recently AIDS has been spreading in Asia.

local strategies of inaction. Instead of being treated as a major opportunity for the development of preventive preemptive strategies, official inaction effectively promoted the conditions for the rapid spread of infection through specific communities, in particular intravenous drug users, prostitutes, and gay men. Japan's own self-representation in relation to regional and international discourses of "Asian AIDS" has remained firmly grounded in the same assumptions of epidemiological progression made in the WHO/ GPA model—even as the enormity of the AIDS epidemic in Asia has rendered that model historically redundant. Japan continues to insist on framing itself out of the picture, a last frontier on the margin of Asia.

An *Asahi shimbun* article (7 August 1994), "How AIDS Is Transmitted," shows a map tracking the global transmission of AIDS. It depicts three distinctive strains of the AIDS virus "arriving" in Japan—two from Thailand

and one from North America and Australia. In this map AIDS is always represented as moving unilaterally. Multilateral movements of bodies (Japanese and non-Japanese) along complex and extensive networks of power and influence are reduced to simple unilateral black lines, with an arrow at the end of each to mark a progression into Japan from an external point of origin. Similarly, in an article entitled, "AIDS Threatens Asia," the subtitle, "Country-by-Country Fact Report," leads the reader to a series of minifeatures on Thailand, the Phillippines, Singapore, India, and Korea (*Asahi shimbun*, 15 July 1994). In an almost full-page feature article, the only mention of Japan is in relation to policies for the global containment of AIDS. Japan is offered as an example of a developed nation that must help those countries where the "battle" against AIDS is still to be won. Those countries are generalized as representative of Asia, and are grouped into a larger category of countries where the fight has not yet been won. Japan however is located among the ranks of the developed nations, where things are described as "under control."

In North America, the epidemiological lines of Japan's "defense" converge with the boundaries drawn by the language and practice of protectionist economic infrastructure on that other popular "front" of the so-called United States—Japan Trade War. The attack-defense rhetoric of both economic and epidemiological discourses is consistent. However, a very different and intensely contradictory picture emerges in the case of Japan's positioning of itself in relation to Asia. Within that framework, popular if controversial categories of economic development based on chronologically sequential progress—underdeveloped or late-developing Third World nations versus developed First World nations—become the basis for a conflation of patterns of epidemic transmission and economic status. Again the military metaphor predominates. Most significantly, Japan is marked as not Asian, in favor of a closer affiliation—political, economic, and cultural—with Europe and North America. The familiar historical description of the Japanese as "the whites of Asia" is rooted in this desire for a politico-cultural (and even racial) distancing from a geographically defined identity.

Resort to military metaphors when describing the human experience of disease and epidemic has already been widely and effectively critiqued by others (see Sontag, Watney), but there are some distinctive details in Japan. The Japanese "Battle Against AIDS" identifies the "enemy" or source of threat not just as the virus itself, but as specific strains of the virus that are linked to designated originary geographic spaces, North America and Asia in particular. The underlying principle is not dissimilar to that of the original WHO regional groupings, but the implications are played out with profoundly different consequences. AIDS has certainly been deeply implicated in the racist politics of Othering elsewhere, as in the treatment of Haitian and Dominican blacks in the United States, misleading depictions of black Americans as the channel of epidemiological contagion between Africa and the United States, and so on (Clatts and Mutchler 1989; Watney 1989b; Patton 1990; Farmer 1992).

What is striking in Japanese discourses on AIDS is the contradiction between the metaphor of regional and international epidemiological warfare and the contemporary policies of Japanese politico-economic integration with Asia. Both in the media and official rhetoric, the "Asianization" of Japan has gained tremendous currency in the 1990s. The concept is underpinned by the same assumption that Japan is not Asian, and therefore needs to be "Asianized" to take its place at the center of what is popularly predicted to be the coming Asian millennium. At the heart of this model is a rhetoric of open borders and free flows of trade and capital. In stark contrast, in the epidemiological battle against AIDS, a prosperous Japan is located on the outside looking in at the uncontrolled spread of the epidemic in the developing countries of Asia. The lines of inside and outside are clearly drawn to be maintained. Race and HIV-positivity (non-Japanese "carrier" and Japanese "victim") are easily conflated within this framework. The focus becomes one of prevention and protection against a "spread" of contagion into Japan, and the isolation and expulsion of contagious non-Japanese bodies found within.[12] The tension between the isolationist discourse of AIDS and that of the Asianization of Japanese economies is played out around the increasingly controversial and contested body of the illegal, female, immigrant sex worker and the fear generated by the perceived threat of her presence "inside" Japan—fluid movement, border crossings, lines broken, illicit flows.[13]

Not the Official Story

It is the Japanese male who is identified in the educational materials as anxious and worried; it is he who may have contracted AIDS and be putting his Japanese female partner at risk. Women are also handed a considerable burden of responsibility to protect themselves against potential "secondary infection." As early as 1990–91, AIDS-prevention posters for community distribution focused on the heterosexual couple and the need for men to avoid "secondary infection" of Japanese women. One poster showed an image of the lower torso of a man and a woman inverted in a position reminiscent of the water ballet movements of the female synchronized swimmers so popular in Japanese sport at that time. The caption read simply "Are you emotionally prepared? Take responsibility together." The language is clearly marked as female speech, and specifically it suggests the tone a young woman might use when speaking to a male rather than a female friend. The message to Japanese men is twofold: be prepared to enter into committed long-term relationships (emotional preparedness), and wear condoms (shared responsibility).

In Japan condoms have been widely used throughout the postwar period, and are frequently described as the most common form of contraceptive (Atoh 1989; cf. Valdiserri et al. 1989; see figure 11.7). While it has been argued that this is one of the reasons why HIV infection rates remained so low for so long in Japan, despite the size of the domestic sex industry and the popularity of overseas sex tourism, this is only part of the picture. Japanese feminists have frequently pointed out that the use of condoms among young, unmarried couples is widely accepted, but that contraception and protection from STDs remain significant problems for women in two other contexts: marriage and the sex industry. While official surveys may indicate that condoms are the main form of contraception in Japan, feminists, on the basis of community research, find a quite different picture, and abstinence and abortion appear to be major reasons for Japan's continuing low birthrates (Valdiserri et al. 1989; Oaks 1994). Until the contraceptive pill is fully legalized, Japanese women must depend on the cooperation of their partners if condoms are to be used, and this is far more difficult after marriage than before. Absolute conjugal rights of the husband still blur the legal viability of the concept of marital rape, and various court cases have verified judicial support for a husband's right to "enforce" conjugal access.[14] Too often Japanese women describe their sexual relations with their husbands as being only occasional, frequently taking place under circumstances beyond their control. It is not uncommon for a husband to come home drunk from after-work hours with colleagues in the bars and clubs. The combination of drunkenness and a lack of private spaces, separated from children or the ears of neighbors, leads many wives to take the path of least resistance. The feasibility of insisting on condom use in the context of marital sex is simply dismissed by many Japanese married women. Even though they know that their husbands may have unprotected sex with sex workers, they do not feel that they have the power or even the opportunity to insist that their husbands use condoms maritally or extramaritally.

In the AIDS education brochures described above, the "originary" source of domestic sexual transmission among Japanese men is explicitly identified as female foreign sex workers. One typical *manga* illustration of "high-risk" activities depicts a man surrounded by three separate images—a hypodermic needle; a woman with dark skin, foregrounding her non-Japanese identity, and wearing stiletto shoes (the standard marker of a bar hostess in the

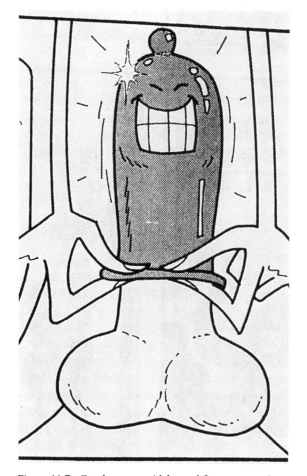

Figure 11.7. Condoms are widely used for contraception.

manga); and two drops of blood (figure 11.8). The woman's physical pose and the two heart shapes that decorate the image reinforce the codification of a "sexy" body. Thai and Filipino women constitute the two largest groups of illegal immigrant workers in the Japanese sex industry. In the popular media they are often collapsed into a single category characterized/ caricatured by darker skin. In the imagistic codification of the *manga*, foreign sex workers are designated by identifying markers of occupation and race. In another illustration in the same brochure (*What You Need to Know about AIDS*, Legal Foundation for AIDS Prevention 1994), a female is shown singing—an activity that links her to the performative space of the bar world. She winks as she asks "Me?" The image appears with a text explaining that even though one may not show symptoms of AIDS and is therefore unaware of having contracted it, there is still a high risk of infecting others. The language is constructed so as to make it clear that the target reader is not a bar worker but her potential male client. Another image of a double bed and a quilt marked with a pattern of multiple hearts links AIDS risk to the sex industry yet again.

In the genre of Ladies Comics, double beds and hearts are popular motifs of the love hotels where unmarried young couples, sex workers and their clients, and illicit lovers can all retreat for privacy. The couple sitting up in the double bed point accusing fingers at each other (see figure 11.9). The brochures unambiguously link unsafe or "high-risk" sexual practices with the bar world and sex industry while setting in place the contrast of safe "low-risk" sex within a monogamous, long-term relationship. The motif of the heart symbol appears in a very different context in *What Is AIDS?* (Min-

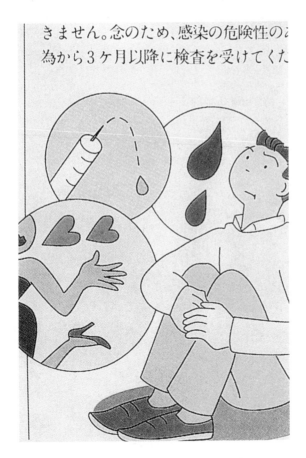

Figure 11.8. The female foreign sex worker.

istry of Health and Welfare and the Japan Foundation for AIDS Prevention 1993a), where a large single heart adorns the double *futon* of a happy couple (figure 11.10). The text on the page features a list of "safe" activities, and the caption under this particular image reads "Sex with a long-term partner who has tested negative." Paired with the traditional *futon* in this context, the monogamous single heart acts to reinforce the contrast between home and the hotel bed.

The fallacy of the monogamous single heart on the matrimonial quilt is exposed in the following anecdote. A Japanese friend recently described with some pride how she had handed her husband a box of condoms and requested that he wear one when having intercourse with any prostitute or bar hostess.[15] She described how difficult it had been for her to raise the issue, and was relieved when he responded good humoredly that she did not have to worry about him wearing a condom because he and his colleagues from work were also worried about AIDS, and had stopped patronizing bars that employed foreign hostesses. A number of assumptions underpin both the request and the response, other than the obvious one that the husband is engaged in extramarital sex: that he is likely to be involved in extramarital sex with sex industry workers; that only foreign sex workers might be infected; and that he need only wear a condom when having sex with a foreign sex worker.[16] These assumptions fit very neatly within the

Figure 11.9. Risks of multiple partnerships.

Figure 11.10. Monogamy.

framing of AIDS promoted in official documentation and popular media in Japan. My friend perceives that she carries a responsibility to seek to protect herself; her husband accepts that his extramarital sexual activity can place his wife at risk; he acknowledges a responsibility to protect her against that risk; and the source of the risk is identified as the sex industry—more specifically foreign women sex workers. Unfortunately the picture is not so straightforward or so neatly contained within a simple, single narrative.

The most widely used Japanese word for wife is *okusan. San* is an honorific suffix attached to names, ranks, and functions to designate respect on the part of the speaker. *Oku* is translated in the *Kenkyusha New Japanese English Dictionary* as "the innermost recess," "the heart." The primary motivation of the range of cultural materials considered here has been the protection of this "person at the heart." The healthy body that is represented as vulnerable to "attack" is arguably nothing less than the body politic of Japan. The most vulnerable organ of that "body" is the family; and at the heart of that organ is the mother body (figure 11.11). The strategies of prevention and protection of Japanese AIDS policy and educational materials are aimed at isolating the mother and her body, gatekeeper of the heart/hearth of the Japanese family, from any threat of contagion. Within the rhetoric of homogeneous, pure Japanese identity, the "antibody" is never imagined as an internal site of immunity but always an external force of invasion. In figure 11.4 when the HIV-positive child stares accusingly at the mother, the child addresses her not in Japanese but in English: "You." The single English word designates more than just an attribution of blame. An infected and infecting mother body is denied the mother tongue. She is now addressed in the popular language of trade of the foreign sex worker. The seropositive Japanese mother body is a foreign body.[17]

The lines of defense are drawn around the potential or actual mother body of the heterosexual female. The black lines of contagion on a map trace the movement of "carriers" across the border of "inside" and "outside." The simplicity of this narrative of invasion masks the fluidity of the identities that may be performed by a single body across a multitude of spatiotemporal migrations. Yet a Thai woman working as a hostess in Tokyo

Figure 11.11. Hearth and home.

is also a mother of five in Bangkok. A Japanese man dancing in a tight embrace with a male transvestite in a Singapore bar is husband and father back home. The Japanese hostess pouring another whiskey for her lunch-time client has to hurry or she won't have time to pick up her husband's business suit from the dry cleaners and still get home before the children arrive from school. A Japanese school teacher embraces his male Filipino lover before they each catch the last train home to their wives. The perva-siveness of images of happy, risk-free, heterosexual, domestic scenes in AIDS educational materials ignores the reality of the constant movement of bodies across boundaries (home/sex industry, heterosexual/homosexual, wife/sex worker) and works to create a mythology of highly differentiated unsafe and safe territories.

The everyday stories of sexual identity and practice are written in the cracks of the statistics and categories of the official story. Boundaries are always porous and permeable; fluid identity oozing through the cracks. Identity is often multiple but seldom predictable, a statistician's nightmare. The official categories cannot keep the bodies in their "proper" places. Per-haps the only credible category is "Other/Uncertain." As we begin to ex-plore the cracks and tell these "other" stories, we paint over the official stories, the stories of the Othering, and the simple black lines of maps and statistical tables begin to fade to a palimpsest.[18]

⟢ NOTES ⟣

Preface

1. The meeting at the ANU was convened by Margaret Jolly and Kalpana Ram, and coincided with a series of other meetings and seminars held in 1993 on sexualities and cultures, including a series of conferences organized by the Humanities Research Centre, ANU. The meeting at UCLA was convened by Lenore Manderson, Helen Hardacre, and Francesca Bray.

Introduction

1. Connell (1987, 68–70) has a parallel reflection on debates about sex and gender. Biological essentialism is not confined to the vulgar sociobological dictates of Lionel Tiger or Desmond Morris, or Goldberg's hormonal evidence for the inevitability of patriarchy. It is also present in those softer forms of psychology devoted to the study of sex roles and sex differences. As Connell notes, this adds a dramaturgical metaphor to a biological substrate of difference. Biological theories are dedicated to finding differences where similarities are more usual and to sliding from average differences between overlapping continua to bounded categorical differences (7–73). His goal is not to deny how the body is implicated in gender relations, but to suggest that the body is involved in every kind of social practice, and that this does not render any social practices natural or inevitable. Feminist theorists have of course wrestled long and hard with the body, and many espouse the centrality of sexual difference and the corporeal embodiment of being a woman. Certain radical feminists have vaunted an essentialism which merely inverts the patriarchal values—men are perforce aggressive rapists and warmongers, women innately nurturing and maternal. But others such as Gatens (1983) and Grosz (1994) perceive their stress on difference and embodiment as consonant with a view of the body as historically and culturally constructed.

2. Some essays which follow in this volume attempt this more than others; see especially those of Clark and Jackson.

3. To quote her at greater length, "Across a range of otherwise incompatible theories, sexuality and gender have been viewed as in some sense superstructural. Whether they referred to roles, scripts, ideologies, or representations, they implicitly referred back to some physical, biological, bodily base, known in both cases as "sex" (Pringle 1992, 88).

4. A comparison might be made with Rubin's sex/gender system (1975).

5. Vance and Snitow (1984) were writing at a particularly bitter moment in the sex debates in the United States, when the factions were blithely labeled "pro-sex" and "anti-sex." As they argue, the debate was less about promotion or repression of sexual expression than about "deeply different views about women's sexual agency, the theory

of social construction, the connections between sex and gender, and the nature of representation" (127). They criticize how the antipornography movement conflated violent pornography with pornography, pornography with sex, and sex with violence. If misogyny was everywhere, they ask, why focus on the most sexually violent portrayals of women? Sex is perceived wrongly as the root cause of gender oppression.

6. The significance of the layering in Freud's theory is much debated, including whether his concepts of sexual urge and instinct relegate them to the natural. A "hydraulic" theory of desire (Vicinus 1982) can be detected not just in Euro-American notions of sexuality, especially of male sexuality as a natural urge, but also in popular reworkings of psychoanalytic theories of sexuality as central to the construction of self. In some reworkings, the metaphor of levels from the unconscious to the conscious, from id to the superego, a metaphor of depth and surfaces, relies on the idea of a fluid in a deep reservoir, which perforce, if repressed and not released through heterosexual intercourse, then gushes and spills through irregular courses—the perverse fistulae of homosexuality, of fetishism, and hysteria.

7. Gay machismo and lesbian chic challenged such caricatures by inversion, but whether they thereby erased or underlined heterosexist caricatures was hotly debated. Gay men and lesbians were often lumped uncomfortably together in political alliances and academic theorizing—a discomfort which often turned on the differences between abandonment and restraint or amoral versus moral approaches to pleasure (Rubin 1992 [1984]).

8. Herdt's work, together with the historical works of Weeks (1985, 1987) and Halperin (1990), was central in challenging Eurocentric models of the relationships among biological sex, gender, and sexual orientation. Herdt's ethnography of the Sambia, and of male homoeroticism in the context of male initiatory cults there and elsewhere in Melanesia (Herdt 1981, 1984, 1987), posed some very graphic and basic questions. First, it was apparent that such ritual acts in which younger men fellated older men, and older men penetrated younger, neither constituted men with a certain identity as "homosexuals" nor in any way compromised their status as men. The debate about the Sambia was not just about the nature of sexual orientation or sexual object choice, but also about the implications of homoerotic behavior for gender identity. Herdt argues that for the Sambia, sexuality between men does not perforce make them less than "men," and indeed, may be seen rather as constitutive of their masculinity. Weeks (1985, 1987) argued similarly for the recent English past, and Halperin (1990) for the ancient Greek past that same-sex practices did not establish a set identity as a homosexual, nor were such practices seen as devalued acts or a perversion to be cured. Like Foucault, Weeks finds the origin of such identity constructs in the medicalization of perverse pleasure in the nineteenth century. The negativities of Krafft-Ebing's categories of "perversions" have been reversed by late-twentieth-century identity politics, as homosexual men and lesbian women have positively affirmed their identities, "come out," and celebrated being "gay" in contexts ranging from AIDS campaigns to the Mardi Gras—celebrated in Sydney and claimed to be the largest gay festival in the world.

9. Connell and Dowsett (1992, 50) coin the term *nativist,* a term which, though it has much in common with *essentialist,* in their view rather stresses the notion of origins in a presocial state. They detect nativist presumptions in many rival theories of sex, as laid down by God as lust or sin, as achieved by evolution, or as settled by the hormones. One could also apply this term to narratives about origins of sexual exploitation or oppression, or to psychoanalytic accounts about the origins of the law of the father.

10. Rubin in her paper "Thinking Sex" (1992 [1984]) plots a sexual hierarchy in terms of which certain acts and partners are privileged and others punished. Heterosexual, conjugal, and procreative sex are rewarded and others less so. However, within the feminist movement there has been sometimes an inversion of such values whereby lesbianism is not only the privileged practice, but in the view of some, feminism and heterosexuality are incompatible. Segal's *Straight Sex* (1994) is both a polemical defence of her right to be heterosexual and feminist, and an argument that seeking pleasure with men does not necessarily empower men at women's expense.

11. Most obviously and most crudely perhaps in Hyam (1990). He maintains that the distance between home and colonial posting, and the freedom from social, moral, and familial restrictions, gave soldiers, traders, and administrators considerable freedom for sexual experiment (see Stoler in this volume for a critique). Canonically these were sexual relations between European men and local women, relations which included coercive rape, prostitution, concubinage, and long-standing domestic relations and marriages. Relations with local women were, however, often controversial and contested, and sexual commerce particularly so (Hyam 1990; Warren 1993).

12. McClintock's recent book (1995) also challenges such simple stories. She critiques a view of phallic penetration of passive spaces, suggesting that this was often accompanied by terror of an unknown, female interior.

13. He also notes how missionaries and colonial officials differed in their allocation of blame—the former more than the latter castigated fallen white men.

14. Rushton and Bogaert's contentious paper (1989) on race and HIV risk is a contemporary controversial example. In it, they draw on diverse and noncomparable studies to argue that size of internal sexual organs can be correlated with differences in libidinal levels, twinning rates, and vulnerability to and incidence of sexually transmitted diseases. See Leslie (1990) for criticisms of their use of material and their sociobiological argument.

15. Of course postcards were but a small part of erotic imagery which circulated from the colonies. Victorians assiduously collected Oriental erotica—India prints of *kama sutra* couples, for instance, and Japanese erotic woodcuts—alongside other exotic curiosities. Erotic and exotic images and artifacts of the Orient and the Pacific were thus appropriated and domesticated back home: wallpaper showing the varieties of the Pacific islands, willow-patterned china, Persian and Chinese carpets, camphor boxes, screens, and fans. The visual and performing arts such as opera similarly appropriated the imagery and imputed sensuality and sexuality of Asia and the Pacific (see Manderson in this volume; Broinowski 1992). Thus the erotics of the exotic were imagined in the metropolis of Empire.

16. Very often, notions of allure and desire were as much about fecundity as they were about sexuality. In many societies in both Asia and the Pacific, parenthood was (and is) an essential component of securing adult status and often of securing status as a dead ancestor to be revered and celebrated. Thus the aesthetics of generational fecundity was as crucial as the sexual beauty of a particular body, male or female. Even when heterosexual conjugality was construed as dangerous, debilitating, or polluting, and indigenous ideas emphasized corporeal states or sexual substances, this rarely predicated a notion of a sexed subject with an urge (see Clark in this volume).

17. This may seem preposterous, yet the positioning of women as objects rather than subjects of desire has been replicated even in local film industry (e.g., in Thai film; see Hamilton 1992). Images of the exotic Orient are also incorporated into indigenous texts, including those fed back to both Western consumers and locals (Hamilton 1992).

18. This is the caption provided by the filmmaker, Dennis O'Rourke, to accompany a still of the central character Aoi (see chapter 5, figure 5.3). Manderson and other authors query this simple interpretation, as discussed within the chapter.

19. See among others Pasuk Phongpaichit (1982); Gronewold (1985); Lai Ah Eng (1986); Rule (1987); Hesselink (1987); Warren (1993); and Garon (1993).

20. Here we do not wish to pursue the difficulty of applying Freudian theories to ethnographic materials (but see Coward 1983; Malinowski 1922, 1929; Spiro 1977; Herdt 1981 and papers in Herdt 1984).

Chapter One

1. Judith Butler puts Foucault's position this way: "The law that we expect to repress some set of desires which could be said to exist prior to law succeeds rather in naming, delimiting, and thereby giving social meaning and possibility to precisely those desires it intended to eradicate" (1987, 218). Other attempts to define what is distinctive about Foucault's notion of desire offer only a sparse roadmap to it; see for example Lash (1984).

2. For Foucault, "instinct" emerged as a medical object in the 1840s (1978, 221).

3. In the introduction to *The Use of Pleasure* (1985), volume 2 of *The History of Sexuality,* Foucault explains the shift in his analytic trajectory and why he will "recenter [his] entire study on the genealogy of the desiring man." While this recentering on "the hermeneutics of the self" and a "general history of the 'techniques of the self'" is described as a new venture, one could argue that there is already strong evidence of this concern in volume 1. There the *dispositif* of sexuality forms the basis on which the cultivation of the [bourgeois] self is predicated, evinced in a bourgeois concern for governing and conveying how to live. A focus on "the cultivation of the self" is already there: the shift is in the larger frame in which Foucault historicizes that phenomenon. In volume 1, Foucault identified "the cultivation of [the bourgeois] body" as crucial to the bourgeoisie's dominance (1978, 125). In volume 2, the nineteenth-century management of "how to live," described in the last of his 1976 Collège de France lectures, provides the analytic focus for a broader inquiry, not confined to nineteenth-century bourgeois culture. It is reformulated as the key to a deeper historical genealogy and another agenda. What is *not* set out in volume 1 is a "history of desiring man" (Foucault 1985, 6).

4. Foucault's notion of power shared with, and was clearly influenced by, Deleuze and Guattari's understanding of desire (1987) as embodying productive and generative properties (as opposed to Freud and Lacan's psychoanalytic emphasis on "lack"), and it was Foucault who wrote the laudatory preface to *Anti-Oedipus.* But Deleuze and Guattari's approach influenced Foucault's conception of power rather than his treatment of desire. For *La volonté du savoir* is *not* about what desire produces but what produces desire, that is those regulatory discourses of sexuality that have made us believe that true knowledge of ourselves is accessible if we know our "inner sexual drives." Despite this debt, there were differences. According to Butler (1990a, 215, 219), Deleuze and Guattari, unlike Foucault, retained a "precultural notion of 'true desire,'" thereby undermining their historical sense of it. Eribon too (1994, 249, 257), who otherwise describes Lacan and Foucault's pre–1976 relationship as one of "affinity" more than influence, holds that Foucault's formulation of the repressive hypothesis "targeted" *Anti-Oedipus,* Lacanian psychoanalysis, and represented a clear break with Lacan.

5. Others have also noted the lack of an analysis of desire in volume 1. Baudrillard

(1977, 17–18), for very different reasons, has argued that "in Foucault power takes the place of desire. It is there in . . . a network, rhizome, a contiguity diffracted ad infinitum. That is why there is no desire in Foucault: its place is already taken."

6. This is not to suggest that the notion of "sexual instinct" first appeared with Freud. On the contrary, representations of African sexuality at least from the 1500s attributed primal lust, licentious instincts, unbridled sexual appetite, and a propensity for "venery" to the racialized Other long before Freud theorized the place of the libido in the workings of the human unconscious (e.g., Newman 1987). Gilman (1993) argues that what Freud did was to treat those sexual and mental pathologies, long associated with the Jew and the black, not as racial attributes but as consequences of civilization itself. It would be interesting to explore further how these earlier discourses on racialized lust were, *malgré* Freud, recuperated in a nineteenth-century racial discourse that drew on Freud to lend added credence to arguments that the racialized Other was driven by sexual instincts that required a civilizing imperial mission to control and contain.

7. Clearly not all students of colonialism (myself included) who have attended to European colonials' anxieties in the face of their illegitimate rule have read or intended to draw on Freud's arguments. My point is to acknowledge how much a Freudian and more general, psychologically oriented vocabulary have underwritten what are ostensibly very different sorts of economic, political, and sociological analyses.

8. Among the best of the numerous recent reengagements with Freud via Fanon, see Diana Fuss's critique (1994) of Fanon's treatment of interracial rape, femininity, and homosexuality.

9. As they explain, "Life overseas, away from family and friends, may have presented more opportunities or pressures to be promiscuous, officials had great power over the people they ruled, and black flesh may have seemed attractive merely because it was forbidden or was thought to be more "natural" (Gann and Duignan 1978, 240).

10. Fanon's scathing assault in *Black Skin, White Masks* (1967, 83–108) on Mannoni's misguided analysis of the "so-called dependency complex of colonized people" coupled with Mannoni's gross generalizations about the roots of Malagasy national character both conspired to relegate him to the uncited and unworthy of critical review. Nevertheless, it is Mannoni who worked closely with Lacan, whose revisions of Freud have in turn figured so prominently in some postcolonial theory. Turkel (1992, 259) notes that Octavio and Mannoni were considered among "the great barons," the "old guard of the Lacanian clinical tradition," and among "Lacan's loyal followers since the schism of 1953."

11. Although published in 1980, most of Drinnon's study was written in the mid-1970s just before *The History of Sexuality* appeared. Drinnon acknowledges his debt to Foucault's notion of a "carceral" society, but remains firmly fixed in Freud's repressive hypothesis (Drinnon 1980, xv–xvi).

12. Roediger (1991, 101) writes, "Some concept of projection is necessary to understand the growth of a sense of whiteness among antebellum workers, who profited from racism in part because it enabled them to displace anxieties within the white population onto Blacks. But the process of projection was not abstract. It took place largely within the context of working class formation and addressed the specific anxieties of those caught up in that process."

13. Tiffany and Adams (1985) discuss fully these discourses on eroticized native women. Malleret (1934) offers a wonderful analysis of the erotics of the exotic and a comprehensive bibliography. For a recent take on the representation of the sexualized,

passive Asian female "in the patriarchal Western psyche" and the long genealogy of it, see Kang (1993).

14. In Gay's (1993) Freudian analysis, racism and manliness provide the "alibis" for bourgeois aggression; deeply dependent on the notion of projection, he pointedly omits any reference to Foucault.

15. In a more recent postcolonial critique of late colonial discourse, Behdad similarly notes that "the negative vision of the Oriental is important to the colonizer's identity because it provides him [sic] with an 'imaginary' Other onto whom his anxieties and fears are projected" (1994, 79).

16. These images of an unrestricted libido let loose on colonial and postcolonial terrain remain tenacious leitmotifs in contemporary analyses of homoeroticism. See Silverman's analysis of T. E. Lawrence's homoerotic voyages (1989) and Green's exploration (1992) of the sensual delights and opportunities for pleasure in postwar Tangiers for Paul Bowles and his compatriots.

17. For a very different use of this notion of the "revenge of the repressed," see Alloula's *Colonial Harem,* where he analyzes, and to some extent reproduces, the pornographic pleasures and power infused in erotic postcards of Algerian women as "illustrated forms of colonialist discourse" (1986, 120).

18. For a sharp assault on Hyam's attention to genitalia not gender, and to great white men not the racial politics of sexuality, see White (1992). On Hyam's euphemisms for sexual exploitation, see Berger (1988).

19. For a review of a recently published set of books that work off this repressive model, see Robbins (1992, 212–13) where he similarly asks, "[I]s the Empire to be conceived, as a number of the authors in these volumes seem to conceive it, as the 'unconscious' of nineteenth-century culture, a repressed but definitive truth that is always already obliged to return? Or does an allegorical Freudianism of this sort soften the hard fact that the Empire *could* be successfully ignored, even by what has been judged highest in nineteenth-century culture? . . . Or to take another example of displaced Freudianism, is everything said by the colonizer about the colonized to be understood as a projection of the colonizer's anxieties? If imperialism required not just a rationale (the inferiority of the natives), but working knowledge of a certain objectivity that would aid in conquering and ruling, then projection probably is not the whole story."

20. Bhabha (1994) credits Fanon with having identified these colonial dislocations, but I think Bhabha himself does it with much more subtlety and care. It is also, of course, Bhabha who exemplifies a welding of Foucauldian and Freudian analyses, via Lacan. Also see Rogin's fine analysis (1994) of how blackface musicals drew on racial images to secure and resolve a nostalgic narrative of national identity.

21. Thus, in *The Hidden Force,* by Louis Couperus, sexual craving and passion activated by the Indies causes the demise of the main character and representative figure of colonial paternalism, Resident Van Oudjick, because "he is susceptible to it." See Beekman's superb analysis of this work (1984) and Buruma's review of the English edition, *Revenge in the Indies* (1994).

22. See also *Verbaal* 29 December 1903, no. 47, Minister of Colonies, quoted in Ming (1983).

23. Ingelson (1986) notes that interracial sexual relations were more than a problem among low-level civil servants and the military rank and file. He also notes that in Surabaya in the 1860s there were brothels "owned by Europeans, employing European women, and catering for European men" (1986, 126).

24. See especially de Braconnier (1913), who provides a summary history of the sexual arrangements of European soldiers since the seventeenth century.

25. Those who supported concubinage argued that lifting the prohibition on marriage would increase military expenses by three to five times what they were under the concubinary system (see Weijl and Boogaardt 1917b, 11). In 1913, it was estimated that out of thirty-four thousand European and native soldiers, 40 percent of those classified as European had contracted some form of venereal disease, as opposed to only 10 percent of the soldiers classified as native.

26. While the dangers of "unnatural desires" between men were more often assumed than discussed, this was not always the case. In a debate over the merits of retaining barrack concubinage, one military official in 1893 noted that in the absence of women at the Gombong military compound, "far more than half of the young men quartered there were guilty of practicing unnatural vices [with other men]" (postscript to report dated 1893, in Verbaal 21–1–1903, quoted in Ming 1983, 69). Twenty years later the abolition of concubinage was again debated, and the Archbishop of Batavia held that "unnatural desires" could be "strictly controlled" but "not rooted out" (81). For a comparable discussion for British Malaya, see Manderson 1996.

27. Algemeen Rijksarchief, Report on officers and civil servants living with a concubine from the Government-Secretary to the Governor-General of the Netherlands Indies, 8 March 1904. Also see Kern 1905.

28. Again, see Couperus's *The Hidden Force,* where sexual passion circulates in a creole, Eurasian, Javanese world of illicit liaisons around the transgressions of Leonie, the creole wife of a colonial resident, not Eva, the woman who is educated, cultured and truly European.

29. Re-presentations of that mode have appeared in the form of postcolonial critique for some time, and some might argue that there is no longer reason to give space to such degradations here. The University of Minnesota Press's high-gloss, coffee-table format for Alloula's *Colonial Harem*—which literally takes the viewer through the progressive baring of Algerian women's bodies—is a case in point of this "double-exposure." Gilman's study of the iconography of prostitutes and Hottentot women (1986) might be cited on similar grounds. While my analysis of the "scientific" study below omits both the photos accompanying that piece and its most explicit descriptive obscenities, I do not hold that such pornographic texts should be buried or effaced from view. At issue is how we use them and write against their prurient grain.

30. Given that all of Stratz's models are nude, the reader would have little reason to doubt his claims, but it is a strange observation for anyone familiar with urban and rural women's dress in Java since the *setagen;* a long "abdominal sash" wound snugly several times around the body from the pelvis to up above the waist, is a crucial part of their toilet.

31. On contagion as a dominant metaphor in Victorian culture, see Vrettos, 1995.

32. Also see Hunter's analysis of "personality as a vocation" in the making of liberal education (1993).

33. Levitas (1990) draws on E. P. Thompson's use of this term to describe nineteenth-century utopian projects. I use the "education of desire," rather, as a way of understanding why parental, and specifically maternal, affection was so central to the racial and nationalist visions of the Dutch colonial state.

34. In chapter 3 of *Race and the Education of Desire* (Stoler 1995), I illustrate how Foucault described that discourse of race in the seventeenth century as one which bifur-

cated society into an "upper" and a "lower" race, with the latter representing the "reappearances of its own past" (Foucault 1990, 54), reminding us of Rawick's notion that Englishmen in the seventeenth century saw West Africans as a "pornography of their former life." But Rawick's account, I suggest, is indebted to Freud's notion of repression, not to Foucault.

35. Gilman's recent work (1993) on Freud and race, where he argues that Freud's theories of sexual instinct were *responsive* to a common and earlier racial discourse that pathologized the sexual instincts of Jews, could add further credence to my claim. Gilman (90–91) holds that Freud generalized a sexual pathology that had been discursively construed as a predisposition of Jews and made it into one of civilization, allowing Freud to reformulate "the illness attributed to the Jew's body [as] the disease of all human beings."

Chapter Two

1. Reverend Field was on the *Lord of the Isles,* the ship carrying the first Methodist missionaries to the area in 1891 (Colwell, 1914, 548).

2. The Massim region spread across most of three administrative districts: the Eastern Division, the South-Eastern Division, and the North-Eastern Division. In the first there were 163 Europeans, in the second 97,, and in the last 8 (Papua Annual Reports 1911, 49).

3. In the same year the Methodists claimed to have 24,582 church attendants; an incredible figure considering the Massim population was estimated at 60,000 (Colwell, 1914, 554).

4. Kwato island was situated between the Papuan mainland and Samarai. The station was administered as an industrial mission by Reverend Abel until his death in 1930. By then it was run independently as the "New Guinea Evangelisation Society." In 1933 it controlled twenty-seven out-stations in the surrounding district (Abel 1934, 251).

5. The model Anglican station was however at Boianai, where the indigenous community attended church services every night, ran their own council, and had access to confession for three hours each day (Gill n.d., 6).

6. I use the generic term *European* when I feel that missionaries, settlers, administrators, and ethnographers conjoin in constructing a sexual image.

7. In 1914 there were 67 mandated children in Papua: 15 in the care of Methodists, 25 with the Roman Catholic missions, 12 with the Anglicans, and another 15 placed with colonial officials (Papua 1914, 29).

8. Most villages in the Massim had a school, under the charge of a native pastor, which taught basic reading, writing, and arithmetic (Burton 1949, 103–5). Brighter students would go on to the station school and be instructed by a European missionary. A small proportion of these would then proceed to the parish or central training institution at the head station. In 1924 there were over six thousand pupils at Methodist schools and another fifteen hundred in Anglican schools (Burton 1926, 91).

9. Fellows Papers, date of entry 16 July 1893. Fellows arrived at Kiriwina in the Trobriands in 1891 and stayed until 1901.

10. The quotation is from correspondence sent by the missionary Rich to the London Missionary Society headquarters. The letter is dated 7 August 1905.

11. Sister Minnie Billing was in charge of the girl's school at the Methodist head station on Dobu (Australasian Wesleyan Methodist Church 1895, 5, 2).

12. Salamo was constructed by the Methodists in 1921 as a technical school and training center for native teachers and their wives (Burton 1926, 82).

13. This quote is by a Miss M. Hodge and appears in Fellows' papers as a cut-out from page 12 of *The Missionary Review*, 5 July 1941 (Fellows n.d.).

14. In 1924 venereal diseases were no longer the primary concern of medical officers. Those traveling officers who administered medical care across rural Papua reported the application of 22,996 hookworm treatments, 2,233 yaws treatments, and only 90 venereal treatments (Papua 1925, 49).

Chapter Three

1. Martha Kaplan (1995) has written a detailed ethnographic history of Navosavakadua, the Tuka, and the aftermath of British punishment for these putative "dangerous and disaffected natives" and their descendants to the present. She is also preparing a paper about A. B. Joske's self-transformation from foreign-named outsider to gentleman of empire via his published writings (published under the name A. B. Brewster (see Brewster 1922, 1937), which combine memoir, ethnography, and evocations of ancient Rome and Kipling's India (Kaplan n.d.).

2. The Supreme Court tried all charges of violent crime; the charges laid by the various Magistrate's Courts now reside in the National Archives of Fiji.

3. In colonial Fiji the term used for whites was *European,* regardless of whether the person had ever set foot there, and European was generally regarded—and still is, there—as the name of a "race" in a world in which race discourse was fundamental to social relations.

4. When Gill was appointed overseer, or *randi-wallah,* to the women's gang on Vitongo plantation, he was required to live several miles away from the lines, apparently at the insistence of the senior cane inspector's wife (Gill 1970, 33). Later, after he was assaulted by Moti, an indentured man to whom he had assigned additional work, Gill had difficulty convincing the investigating constables that it was one of the less frequent cases in which the root of the violence was related to work and not sex: "The first questions from His Khaki and Silver Gorgeousness were: did Moti have a wife or daughters? If either or both, when had I last 'taken them the cane?' He made it sound like a dissolute game of 'Who's in who?' Unfortunately for his hopes, Moti vehemently denied possessing either. He said he had tried to kill me because the senior overseer kicked him. 'One sahib or another, it was all the same to him.'" (Gill 1970, 43). Gill provides far more detail about sexual relations on the plantations than any other "European" writer, writing half a century after his years as an overseer there. But if he loves (and is selling) salacious stories, his stories are more likely to be embellished than simply invented, and contrast in style, not substance, with both Indian accounts (see especially Sanadhya 1991 and Ali 1979) and Christian accounts (see especially Burton 1910; for a bibliography, see Kelly 1991b). The most common motif of the Indian accounts is the narrative of a virtuous woman struggling against the evil pressures of the system; the signal tropes of the Christian accounts are assertions of "the low character of these women" (Bavin 1914, 182) and the indescribability of their lives: "[L]ife in the lines is unspeakably corrupt. . . . The degradation of such a life may be better imagined than described" (Garnham 1918, 14–15).

5. Gill saw animalistic motives, not only but especially in the Indians: "Unfortunately, the system and the conditions bred men to administer them. That I was one worried me

not at all. The pattern had been set and for all I knew would persist after me. Unfortunately, it also changed a section of the importees, those who had been the dregs of their homeland when they left [not true, JK], into something in the ape class, and in the end it succeeded in reaching out to drag us all into a jungle of its own contriving" (Gill 1970, 38–39). Especially when in this Laborite register, Gill foregrounds the economic order as the prime villain, but leaves no doubt that the Indians, in his vision, both started lower and descended lower down the chain of animal classes in this particular jungle.

6. Mitchell (1988) discusses "enframing" in particular from pp. 176–79. To be clear here about Mitchell's own representation of the agency of the colonized, his argument is not that the colonized are always entirely transformed. Instead, "there always remained regions of resistance and voices of rejection" (171). In Mitchell's vision this mere resistance is destined only to slow a process that he does not, exactly, call modernization: "Colonial or modern politics will seek to create for this subject a continuous theatre of certainty, unknown to pre-colonial politics. . . . The reorganization of towns and the laying out of new colonial quarters, every regulation of economic or social practice. . . . Such projects were undertaken as an enframing, and hence had the effect of re-presenting a realm of the conceptual, conjuring up for the first time the prior abstractions of progress, reason, law, discipline, history, colonial authority, and order" (178–9). The difference between older modernization theories and Mitchell's vision is that modernity is here no longer the telos; instead, the telos is the newer consciousness capable of seeing that this "enframing" is a trick—and also capable of imagining a world in which no one before European colonization really had planned cities or irrigation systems, law, order, discipline, or history.

7. The 1909 report also contained the only dramatic exception I have seen to the silence of the annual reports about European and sardar involvement in this violence. The governor, on the advice of the chief justice, commuted the death penalty of a convicted murderer to penal servitude for life: "the Chief Justice commented strongly on the conduct of a plantation sardar who had taken or enticed away the woman from her man, as pointing to the necessity for steps being taken to prevent such cases of scandalous oppression."

8. As Stoler (1989, 1991) in particular has argued, white women frequently got the blame across the European empires for the very change in colonial practice that led to their presence, an increasing insistence on separated European social and moral spaces, an insistence that here, in late indenture Fiji, Gill could still semiopenly resist.

9. How many scholars of India, for example, seek the effects of Macaulay's effort to become India's Roman-style law-giver, compared to those who trace the effects of census and statistics in the objectification of caste? How many scholars studying conflicts over the founding of New Zealand fully understand the significance of the explicitly Austinian positivist determination of New Zealand's Supreme Court, in 1877, that the original Treaty of Waitangi between the Maori and the British crown was "a simple nullity," because no sovereign actually ruled in New Zealand before British arrival? What Macaulay, with his famous minute on education and his law code for India, and Chief Justice Prendergast, with his clean sweep in New Zealand, had in common was a commitment to the replacement of unsatisfactory public order founded on efforts to respect some kind of existing social order among the colonized, a commitment to a new will to order.

10. A principal way in which Vedic-orthodox Indian philosophical systems distinguish themselves from each other is according to what *pramana,* "means of knowing,"

they will accept; *pramana* itself is a tactile metaphor, "measure," from the verb complex *pra* + *ma,* "to measure, to form, to arrange." *Grahana* means both "seizing" or "grasping," and "conceiving or understanding." *Satyagraha,* the Sanskrit name Gandhi promoted for his political style of direct, symbolic, confrontational action, was frequently translated into English by Gandhi himself as "insistence on the truth." It can also be translated differently, with more literal fidelity to its Sanskrit verb root, as "seizing hold of the truth." In English also, grasping can readily be used as a metaphor for knowing, but I know of no one in the history of Western discourse who has elevated mastery of the metaphor of the grasp into a knowledge power capable, say, of colonizing Egypt. Although some important Western philosophers, notably Derrida, make much of hearing as a knowing power, more generally, Westerners think they know it when they see it.

11. "There was no crime in the Colony to speak of until the Indian coolies made their appearance. Although on the whole they were a useful and estimable body, there was a considerable sprinkling of criminals among them, and seldom a quarterly sessions passed without the infliction of the capital punishment. The intercourse of Fijian and Hindu prisoners in the various jails must in time inevitably lead to the contamination of the former, and call for sterner discipline than that of the old native system" (Brewster 1922, 139–40).

12. Details of this case can be found in Colonial Secretary's Office minute paper 692/11, in the Fiji National Archives.

Chapter Four

1. This is also discussed by Lutz and Collins in *Reading National Geographic* (1993, 134–144). They compare representations of Micronesia in 1967 and 1986 and suggest the consistency of the trope of sensual women and of men as skilful navigators (between the islands and between tradition and modernity).

2. In part my comment here challenges the simple dichotomy between license and repression which Foucault and other theorists have rightly criticized (see Introduction). Sexuality was core to ancestral Polynesian cosmologies and cosmogonies, in the explication of the creation of the world from a primordial act of sexual intercourse or from the separation of merged conjugal bodies. (See Oliver 1974, Valeri 1985, Linnekin 1990, and Ralston 1988, 1990, Sahlins 1995).

3. See Jolly (1996), which focuses on the Cook voyages and in particular the way in which Islander-European sexual relations were pervaded by concerns about venereal disease.

4. Cook was not the first European navigator to "discover" Tahiti, but was preceded by Wallis in 1767 and Bougainville in 1768. Says Porter "Tahiti possessed a ravishing beauty which disarmed its first discoverers" (1990, 123)—connecting as usual the beauty of landscape and women's bodies. But the "discoverers" were only metaphorically disarmed for, when Wallis arrived, there was violent confrontation at first, which left several local men dead. The offering of the sexual services of women ensued soon after, perhaps in peace-making as much as hospitality. George Robertson, master of the *Dolphin,* reported that elderly men encouraged women to have sex with the sailors in return for presents of iron, especially nails (a trade which generated much sexual innuendo then and since, see Porter 1990, 124–5). Thus when Bougainville and later Cook arrived in Tahiti there was already an expectation of a beautiful landscape, beautiful women and sexual license.

5. In Jolly (1993a) I consider in far greater depth the agency of Pacific women in these early texts from the Cook voyages. There is, I argue, a tendency to vaunt the eagerness and the lascivious license of women in the eastern islands, which though it might be true in part, also elides aspects of force and strenuous persuasion in sexual exchanges. Simultaneously, representations of sexual sequestration of women in the western islands (now Vanuatu and New Caledonia) and sexual exchanges in New Zealand deny women agency and depict them as "beasts of burden" and "pawns" of their male kin. I am not denying that differences existed between the situation of women in various places nor in how Pacific women related to foreigners at "first contact," but these differences were amplified to create a dichotomy which contrasts the "lascivious ladies" of the east with the "beasts of burden" of the west.

6. There was much public interest in and contemporary debate about the Pacific voyages in Europe, and also much subversive satire. Smith documents this beautifully in both of his major books (1985 [1960], 1992).

7. At this point I should acknowledge how my title and this question echoes that of Porter (1990). Although there is considerable overlap between the texts that we use, and Porter also suggests that the formulation of Polynesian eroticism reinforced "phallic imperialism," his argument is rather different to my own. Ulitmately he argues the opposite thesis, that "more typical among English travellers was not the exoticization of Tahitian sexuality but its normalization" (1990, 138). He considers both the earlier voyages of Wallis and Bougainville as well as Cook, and is at pains to stress the differences among observers, and between them and the savants in Europe.

8. Smith depicts the exotic as a "fringe dweller among the aesthetic categories" in eighteenth century European thought. By this he means that the exotic was differentiated both from the beautiful and the ugly. The exotic was "what the European was not and thus helped Europe define itself" (Smith 1992, 10). He stresses that it reduces the real diversities of others into a convenient polarity with Europe. I should stress that my use of exoticism is very different to the concept of "primitivism" as discussed by Torgovnick (1991) which relies more on a strategy whereby the strange or foreign is identified with earlier *or* more "savage" elements within the European self.

9. The Orientalist and classical aspects of these images have again been explored by Smith (1985 [1960], 41–3, 1992, 173–5) who also notes the overlap between the two— the drapery evoking both middle Eastern robes and turbans and Roman or Grecian togas. The portrait of Omai by Reynolds is probably the best example.

10. The picture I allude to here is *The Landing at Erromanga, One of the New Hebrides,* by William Hodges. The oil painting is, like much of Hodges' work in the National Maritime Museum in London, and is more widely known through the published engraving by Sherwin after Hodges (see reproductions at plates 181–2, in Smith 1992, 200–201, and my discussion of both versions in Jolly 1992).

11. Webber does not even include, in the official record, an image of Cook's death at Kealakekaua Bay, although he did do an engraving after images by Barlozzi and Byrne. The event has been visualized innumerable times since (Smith 1992, 232–240).

12. This was a Summer School on Colonialism and Postcoloniality in February 1993 organized by Nicholas Thomas and Dipesh Chakrabarty and co-sponsored by the Humanities Research Centre, The Australian National University and the University of Melbourne.

13. Grimshaw had very different views of Polynesian and Melanesian women which reflect her overall aestheticization of the former and bestialization of the latter. The

journey through the Pacific is broken at precisely this point—*In the Strange South Seas* deals with the Polynesian islands and *From Fiji to the Cannibal Islands* with Melanesia. Evans notes how in the novels, Melanesia was constructed by Grimshaw as the site of blackness, evil and the unknown. See Branigan (1993) also on Grimshaw's travel writing.

14. This fearful fantasy is often evoked in her novels, but is hardly unique for the period. In Papua in 1926 The White Women's Protection Ordinance was issued. As Amirah Inglis (1974) demonstrates, this was passed despite the fact that sexual advances by Papuan men towards white women had been few.

15. Evans' subtle thesis (1993) looks at the complexities of Grimshaw's position in straddling the tensions between being British and Irish, and being British and Australian, as well as being a white woman in a colonial context. She perceives antitheses between Britain and Australia but then combines these as the sites of "civilization" versus the South Seas. Within the latter, Polynesia and Melanesia are divided into good and bad sites.

16. She was engaged to William Little, a pioneer prospector and later a tax collector in Papua. He died in 1920 before they could be married (see Jolly 1993b, 122–3).

17. In a paper which appeared as this was going to press, O'Dwyer has considered both Michener's text and film as colonial discourses inscribing an "American identity across the Pacific" (1995, 123). She argues that in both the sexualization of race and gender perpetuates the power of the United States, in moments of imperial expansion and neo-colonial exploitation. Michener won the Pulitzer Prize for his *Tales,* which O'Dwyer suggests like his later *Hawaii,* combines "colonial-settler mythology, sexual fantasy and frontier-hero narrative" (1995, 123), if in a more nervous liminal space. This anxiety is, she suggests, not just due to the war setting but to doubts and fears about American superiority. O'Dwyer focuses only on the Cabel-Liat romance (and ignores the Forbush-de Becque romance), but is concerned as I am with the difference between indigenous and migrant, Pacific Islander and Tonkinese. Bloody Mary she reads as the repulsive aspect of the 'other' woman, displaying a disconcerting almost masculine authority.

18. I am alluding both to documentary and fictional genres, Flaherty's *Moana* (1927), *White Shadows of the South Seas* (1928), and *Tabu* (1931), the latter two from which he dissociated himself from. They were completed subsequently by Van Dyke and Murnau respectively (Bergan 1982, 45–6, 96, 149). Note also King Vidor's *Bird of Paradise* (1932), the lurid plot of which casts Dolores del Rio as a South Sea women, doomed to be sacrificed by her kin in a volcano to rescue her lover, an American sailor. Shohat and Stam (1994, 142) have noted how yet again the woman comes to embody the island and nature, both in its paradisical and threatening aspects.

19. These are, of course, the words of the song "I'm in Love with a Wonderful Guy," which is a celebration of convention as much as heterosexual romance.

20. Burgin (1994) has depicted *South Pacific* as not just heterosexual but heterosexist, focusing as it does on "family romance," by which he means not just monogamous reproductive marriages but nationalist imaginings. I find his artistic reinscriptions intriguing, especially in how he situates the film in the context of racial politics in the United States. Little Rock is not just Nellie Forbush's home town but also the place where just before the film's release a black teenager, Elizabeth Eckford, had been denied entry to a white high school by the National Guard and a mob of whites. Burgin also detects "overtones" in the film, "with all these sailors living together on this island" (Bhabha and Burgin 1994, 458) and implies a connection between fears of the differences of race

and sexual orientation; in conversation with Bhabha about the "between" and the "third space," he talks of transforming the images of *South Pacific* on his computer screen, re-coupling and reconjugating characters. In their talk about the "latent content" of the film, they deploy psychoanalytic theories to suggest that though superficially it seems to be "dealing" with race, the film rather works through elisions and denials (see my discussion of this). Their conversation drifts through a number of other sites, until they return to the imaged horizon in *South Pacific,* and the uncertainty of whether the sun is rising or setting, evoking perhaps the end of the American frontier "the anxiety of having reached the limit of that quest" (1994, 463).

21. Large numbers of "Tonkinese" (Vietnamese) were brought by the French from Indochina to work their Pacific plantations in both New Caledonia and Vanuatu (then the New Hebrides/Nouvelles Hebrides), and thus this has some historical veracity (see Henningham 1995).

22. Despite the war setting, there is little military action in the film. This pervasive aestheticization of violence is both indulged and internally acknowledged in the film. At one point, Nellie observes clouds on the horizon, and Emile retorts, "Those lovely little white clouds could be gunfire."

23. In one of their duets they croon, "Born on opposite sides of the sea, we are as different as people can be."

24. After announcing to Emile that she can't marry him, Nellie admits that the problem is his previous Polynesian wife, saying, "I can't help it—there is no reason. This is something that's born in me, I can't help it." After her tearful departure, Emile asks Joseph, "What makes her talk like that? Why do you have this feeling you and she?" Joseph's song announces "It's not born in you. You have to be carefully taught to hate and fear. . . . to hate all the people your relatives hate." After Cabel dies and she is praying that Emile comes back alive, Nellie concludes, "the woman you had before . . . her color . . . what piffle!"

25. He also does Nellie's laundry for her and is extremely fussy about her ironing.

26. Sandra Buckley has commented on the homosexual suggestions about Billis, and his recuperation by gay men in North America, where *South Pacific* has a new cult status.

27. Her romance with Emile can also be read in terms of the military alliance—of Americans joining the war and the liberation of France through the allied war effort.

28. As for example the wonderful art work by Jim Vivieare, incorporating a cheap reproduction of Gauguin and a colonial postcard with the caption *6 Tahitians, 2 in Leningrad, 4 in Papeete* (see Thomas 1995a, 206–7; 1995b).

29. This is of course a rhetorical question. Other forms of relation are possible and necessary, in the broader cultural politics of the Pacific. Nor am I completely damning the tourist industry in this, although transcending colonialist spectatorship here is much harder, despite the best efforts of indigenizing the industry and culturally sensitizing the tourists (see Jolly 1995). Clearly the important dynamic is Islanders actively asserting their subject positions as much as Euro-Americans relinquishing theirs. But the assertion of agency is not always an act of resistance.

Chapter Five

1. This is true for other generic Asian stories, such as "action films" relating to the Vietnam war, in which context Vietnamese are "(un)represented as invisible Orientals" (Tasker 1993, 100–103).

2. This is a continuing tradition, sometimes satirical, as in the funny and fantastic Scene 5, Act 1 in the opera *The Ghosts of Versailles* (Coriglian and Hoffman, 1991). It is important to note, however, that European composers have always been extremely catholic in their choice of theatrical setting; hence while there are plenty of examples of Orientalism, there are parallel traditions of the use of the ancient world, and other times both past and fantastic: for example, *Dido and Aeneas* (Purcell 1689), *Nabucco* (Verdi 1836), *Les Troyens* (Berlioz 1863), *Troilus and Cressida* (Walton 1954), *Tristan und Isolde* (Wagner 1865), numerous versions of the myth of Orpheus and Eurydice, and so on.

3. *The Romance of the Harem* was first published in 1873 by James R. Osgood and Co., Boston. The title was changed when it was published in London; see Morgan 1991, xxi–xxiv.

4. Andrew Lloyd Webber's *Cats* includes an embedded "Thai" dramatization ("Growl Tiger") that is reminiscent in its staging of "Small House of Uncle Thomas" in *The King and I*; the songs in *Cats*, like those in *Joseph and His Amazing Technicolour Dreamcoat*, parody a variety of musical genre and presentational styles.

5. I am presuming the version described in this chapter *is* a theater version; it is definitely the version screened in Australia in cinemas in the 1970s. Frances Bonner (1994, personal communication) tells me that there are at least four versions of this film. In one other version, trailers of which precede the video versions of the two later films of the trilogy, the focus is on Marie-Ange's seduction by Emmanuelle and Jean together.

6. In the 1960s and 1970s in Australia at least, perhaps thousands of high school students enacted this musical; I was one of the wives of Mongkut in a high school production of the musical in 1966 and one of the "three little maids" in *The Mikado* a few years earlier.

7. Morgan (1991, xx) describes Anna as "a Victorian woman in her early thirties" at the time of her arrival at Court. However, if Morgan is correct (xiv) and Anna's maternal grandmother was herself Indian, then her own account (e.g., in *The Romance of the Harem*, 1873a) takes on rather different nuances.

8. See also Enloe (1989) and Sturdevant and Stoltzfus (1993) on prostitution and the military in the Philippines, Korea, and Japan.

9. Reynolds (1994, 76) expresses some surprise at the absence, to date, of attention to issues of sex and gender in Thai historiography, even at the most obvious level of the roles of the elite women of the court.

10. Played to the full in the film version of *The King and I* by Yul Brynner and Deborah Kerr, with the aid of close camera work: the advantages of the cinematic medium are obvious in such candid and sympathetic moments. It is worth noting too that she is consistently summoned to see the King at night, when she is either asleep or preparing for bed.

11. As noted above, there has been little attention to issues of gender in the historiography of Thailand (Reynolds 1994). This would seem to hold true not only with respect to social and political history, but also with respect to the history of ideas. The contrast is Java, for which there has been considerable research exploring the development of Kartini's feminism in light of her links with Dutch feminists; see, for example, Geertz 1964; Zainu'ddin 1980.

12. See Stoler (1995), on notions of the unenculturated sexuality of the child.

13. This is the world of Flaubert, among others (see also Marcus 1992). There are certain differences in this genre of film, as well as in other accounts, of Orientalist fantasies set in the "Middle East" compared with those of the "Far East," for example, but

these are exotic details only, like the choice between camels and elephants as the beasts of porterage. The precise location is of little greater account.

14. This was, according to Berry (1994, 24–25), fortunately tempered in its execution or editing; it was originally to have included the filmmaker putting on a condom, and inserting his penis. In the end, O'Rourke maintains his physical presence and his voice in rather muted forms only.

15. This includes *Half Life: A Parable for the Nuclear Age* (1986) and *Cannibal Tours* (1987). In both films O'Rourke is a continuing presence as participant as well as film-maker. Camera shots, conversations between the filmmaker and subjects, conversations alluding to the production of the film (its profits as well as its processes, as in *The Good Woman*) all establish the subject's complicity, rather than their accidental inclusion in the film (see Lutkehaus 1989; MacCannell 1994).

16. See, for example, Kerr (1992). The reviews of the film leave much to be desired. Kerr begins with an apparently negative review of the film, which he describes as "voy-euristic, contrived and subjective," leaps to supposition (e.g., Aoi is "obviously spaced out from drugs or sheer exhaustion of both" and "virtually all the interviewees . . . appear to be under the influence of alcohol or a narcotic"), collapses with a plea for greater explicitness in the name of "honesty" ("for all the project's candid honesty, it does not actually show Aoi, its centre-piece, working" [!]), and then valorizes the lead ("she remains poised and stoic throughout"). See also Adams (1992).

17. Among criticial audiences, voyeurism has two slants: one which emphasizes the personal dimensions and propriety of O'Rourke's and Aoi's relationship (hence also speculation about O'Rourke's personal integrity), and another which emphasizes O'Rourke's integrity as filmmaker, provoked by the invasiveness of the camera and his presumed professional "insensitivity."

18. This is not new in O'Rourke films: compare with *Cannibal Tours* (1987), which mixes Mozart, an Iatmul flute, and short-wave radio messages as the soundtrack.

19. Cf. MacDougall (1994, 34, 36, n.10), who draws attention to the "variously di-rected discourses" of ethnographic film, its subjects speaking, *inter alia,* with the anthro-pologist working with the filmmakers, with each other, and through film, with aborigi-nal and nonaboriginal audiences (in the case of *Familiar Places*).

20. This contrasts with Australian women's responses, which, like the critical re-sponses summarized by Berry (1994, 24–32), divide between positive response (the film is seen to document and expose sex tourism) and negative response (O'Rourke is voy-euristic and the film another example of male gaze/female object; (Berger 1972, 47; Mulvey 1989, 23). Thai responses have also varied. Typically arguments have been made against the film because it is not "really right for people to see such things" (either because of its explicitly sexual material or because of its portrayal of prostitution and other commercial sex work in Thailand), and Thai audiences have complained that the film did not make clear (1) that not all Thai women are like Aoi, and (2) that the government is taking action to reduce sex work and to rehabilitate prostitutes. Thai students of Annette Hamilton (1995, pers. comm.) felt that the film had been scripted and that Aoi was not talking with the "natural speech of a prostitute from the north-east." In addition, they could see no reason to make a film about a Thai prostitute, and were upset that Australians (or others) who viewed the film would now have a false impression of Thailand. Against this, a number of my own Thai female students found *The Good Woman of Bangkok* profoundly distressing, not because it lied, but because it spoke the (partial) truth.

21. However, I do not wish to make too much of this apparent national difference. In *Foreign Bodies,* it is an American bar owner in Pattaya, Tim Dragoo, who claims that "old and ugly and unloved" American men discover in Thailand "a nice stable relationship and . . . the woman feels very grateful that he's helping her family—getting tractors, drinking water, mosquito nettings, etc.—everyone has a good time here."

Chapter Six

1. This paper is not intended to perpetuate the stereotype of evil Western males dominating helpless girls sold into sex slavery by impoverished parents. The economic factors behind the sex trade cannot be discounted, and the mode of its recruitment and organization may be ruthlessly exploitive and often violent. Nevertheless the interpersonal relationships between Thai girl and *farang,* whether short-or long-term, are complex and cannot be reduced to some simplistic dominance-submission equation. This paper should be read as a companionpiece to Hamilton (in press).

2. A classic example is found in *Siamese-English Conversation Self-Taught* by K. K. (n.d.). This is one of many cheaply produced Thai conversation books aimed at the foreigner wishing to obtain a smattering of Thai. Many of these language manuals are constantly reprinted. This would seem to be one: the section entitled "At the Beer-Hall" would today probably be more appropriately called "At the Bar," but the contents are just as useful. The following conversation items are suggested *inter alia* on p. 150:

7. You are very pretty.
8. Come and sit here.
9. What is your name?
10. How old are you?
16. Do you love me?
17. Yes, I love you very much.
18. Will you go to enjoy yourself with me?
19. Yes, but we must go after 12 o'clock.
21. Can you be my wife?
22. I want a woman.
23. Yes, I shall find one for you.
24. Do you like this one?
25. Yes, I like her very much.
26. Call me a tricycle.

3. The term *Western* is of course a misnomer here. The Thai sex trade has been just as appealing to Japanese men on organized sex tours, while ethnic Chinese from Malaysia provide the major clientele for the brothels, bars, and hotels of the southern Thai border regions. While a variety of cultural differences among clients are recognized by women in the sex trade, the particular cluster of behaviors apparent among *farang* indicate a common source, presumably in the Judaeo-Christian heritage. I will use the term *Western* here while recognizing that in the contemporary global flows of desire, the term is limited, being both too general (obscuring differences among "Western" groups) and too specific (failing to identify changes in attitudes among "non-Western" groups).

4. The term *farang* refers to white-skinned Westerners, and Thais maintain it is a translation of the word *français* (French). It is not dissimilar from the Persian and Urdu terms *ferangi* and *feringhee,* however (and the English *foreign*), and so could alternatively have a Sanskrit derivation.

5. There has been increasing public attention within Thailand in the context of HIV/ AIDS. Some women's groups in Thailand are working actively with prostitutes on health and anti-AIDS campaigns: recently efforts to stamp out the trade in underage (below sixteen) girls have been highly publicized and appear to be effective, at least officially. The public face of prostitution has been subject to more rigorous scrutiny by police, social-workers, and academics. "Brothels" became at least temporarily less visible, but this only intensifed the importance of coffee-shops, bars, nightclubs, and barber-rooms. Supposedly the more lurid of the live sex shows were to be closed down, although at the end of 1994 touts were still pressing illustrated brochures on passing tourists near Patpong (see Manderson 1992b, 1995). The deep problems involved in controlling or limiting the sex trade include above all the role of the police force, many members of which make substantial sums in exchange for protecting these establishments.

6. Many Thai, both men and women, say they are mystified by what they know of *farang* desire for love relationships with sex workers. "When man go to Patpong, he will see beautiful girl. But beautiful girl in American eyes. But not beautiful in Thai eyes. Maybe dark skin, but he love very dark skin. . . . when Thais think of love in Patpong, they think it's very stupid. But I think they can't understand about farang's [*sic*] life, because in America they don't care where you come from. But in Thailand, when I get married, I have to look back his family and education and everything. In Thai society, we care so much about background" (from "Epilogue," by Mrs. Pisamai Tantrakul, in Walker and Ehrlich 1992).

7. *Sex worker* or *service worker* are inadequate terms, although *prostitute* is equally inappropriate. The term *prostitute* in English carries a distinct set of associations, including the notion of an impersonal and purely commoditized sexual transaction. As will become clear here, this usually does not occur in the bar trade relationships between *farang* male and Thai girl. A girl in the bar scene is not obliged to have sex with her customers, at least not with all of them. This voluntarism may be overstated, of course, but it provides an important source for whatever self-esteem the bar girl may muster in her everyday life. The other component of this is her ability to send substantial sums of money back to her family, often funded by one or more *farang* "boyfriends" remitting money from overseas, the amounts being far in excess of anything a girl could earn in the normal Thai sex trade or in any other occupation.

8. Many expatriates working in the Middle East also take their holidays in Thailand, swelling the number of "Middle-Eastern" visitors who turn up in the tourist statistics. Mining companies in remote Australia are also reported to provide leave in Bangkok for their workers, as are Malaysian companies engaged in logging in Papua-New Guinea (Andrew Lattas, personal communication).

9. *Tuk-tuk* is Thai for a small, three-wheeled, motorized vehicle.

10. During 1994 a lively correspondence concerning the appropriateness of the Trink Page in the age of AIDS took place in the Bangkok Post. There is no sign to date however that Trink's contributions will be terminated.

11. Use of the term *Thai girl* (or *Thai woman*) is common in these discourses. For most Thais, the equation of Patpong bar girl with Thai womanhood is incomprehensible and insulting; impoverished rural people are not taken as representative of "Thai-ness" except insofar as they conform to rural stereotypes of the cheerful farmer. I use the term here because it is used in the literature, while being aware of the problems inherent in it.

12. None of these, to my knowledge, have been translated into Thai, again indicating

the extent to which educated Thai people have been "screened" from the proliferation and consequences of the sex trade in their country.

13. The idea of the "Old Hand"—the Westerner who lives his life out in the East—has a long history in novels and stories. Of course many Westerners lived in Thailand for years: for example the famous Jim Thompson, who pioneered silk-weaving in Bangkok and whose house is currently a major tourist attraction for foreign visitors. However, men such as Thompson do not conform to the current version of the Old Hand; it goes without saying that today's Old Hands are not going to be remembered by the tourist industry of the future. It seems clear from most of these stories that an extraordinary foreshortening occurs when the whole country is viewed through the bottom of a beer glass in a Bangkok bar. Many men are indeed taken "up-country" by their girlfriends, sometimes for geniunely sociable reasons but usually with the intention of illustrating graphically the suffering at home which the *farang* may care to relieve by his generous contributions. This creates a double image, an oscillation between impoverished village and Bangkok demimonde, as if nothing else exists or matters. The entire society, its religious forms and activities, political struggles, media and popular culture, natural features, provincial town life, literary and poetic expressions, formal occasions, festivals, and national events seem simply not to exist for the bar habitué. The *farang* may be dragged unwillingly into "superstitious" activities, such as making offerings at a shrine, to keep his girlfriend happy, but nothing else seems to "touch" him. Perhaps this is central to the constitution of primal pleasure; a world within, and beyond, the "real" world.

14. As I noted in "Mistaken Identities" (Hamilton, in press) the issue of speech and speaking is central to the construction of the relationship between Dennis and Aoi in *The Good Woman of Bangkok*. The filming of her speaking the "truth" of her suffering provides the most discomforting (if perhaps the most poignant) aspect of the film to many viewers. But as I have argued, this is in fact not "her" speech at all, but the conventional tropes and accents of the "suffering woman" of Thai popular film and television melodramas. The woman will not "reveal" the inner self which the Western concept of personhood demands; she avoids, displaces, and finally seems to accede to male demands (here, Dennis O'Rourke), but only by using "another" speech. This issue has been commented on by Thai viewers, many of whom believe the entire film was scripted and that Aoi was indeed "acting."

15. The implication of this ending is that the American is devoting himself to another kind of "rescue"—this time the salvation of lepers; but Vilai is only there with him because she'll be able to skim the profits, bankrupt his project, and move on to her next victim.

16. Where women marry foreigners and go to live with them outside Thailand, they are generally fluent in the husband's language, and a closer accommodation between them is much more likely. It seems to go without saying that it is up to the woman to transform herself. Where couples remain in Thailand, however, there is much less need or possibility for the woman to change herself to suit her husband's requirements, and the likelihood that the man will learn to speak and understand Thai is very slight.

17. Elsewhere I suggest (Hamilton, in press; see also Berry 1994) that a masochistic position is adopted by the Western male, through a process of identification with the woman whom he wishes to rescue. The "subordinate" woman, on the other hand, engages in a "masquerade," through which she disguises herself before the man who seeks her, while identifying him with abundance and power, which she seeks to obtain

through sexual and social transactions with him. The theoretical issues underlying these relations require further consideration.

Chapter Seven

1. I use a modified version of the Thai Royal Institute (Ratchabanditthayasathan) system of transcribing Thai (e.g., *j* instead of *c*, and *or* instead of *o'*.) The Royal Institute system does not mark tones or vowel length.

2. The approximate pronunciation of *kathoey* is "gatuhy."

3. The term *kathoey* appears to have no Thai cognate. It may be derived from a pre-Angkorian Khmer intransitive verb variously represented in inscriptions as *dai* or *doej* (*dai* or *toej* in modern Khmer), which meant "to be other/different" (Jenner 1981, 152). The modern Khmer term for the transgender category is *katoey*, with an unaspirated second consonant. *Kathoey* is now the dominant term for the male transgender category in Thailand's other language regions because of the growing use of Central Thai as the national language. While it is possible that *kathoey* originally had the sense of "a person whose gender is different [from that of other males]," the notions of "having a mixed gender" (e.g., Northern Thai *pu-mia*) or "a male who acts like a woman" (e.g., Southern Thai *tham mia*) have long been the only meanings attached to the term by Central Thai speakers. In other words, if *kathoey* did displace a preexisting Central Thai term, it nevertheless assumed the cross-gender meanings that attached to that now lost term and are retained in indigenous terms in other Thai dialects. The term *kathoey* thus appears to have perpetuated Thai cultural notions and attitudes that no doubt predated its borrowing from Khmer. (Thanks to Tony Diller for assisting with the comparative linguistic information in this note).

4. For example, *len phu'an* ("to play with friends") and *ti ching* ("to clash cymbals") denote lesbian sex between gender-normative females.

5. The expression "woman" in inverted commas here denotes the Thai sex/gender category *phu-ying*, while the expression "man" denotes the sex/gender category *phu-chai*.

6. The Royal Institute Thai language dictionary (Ratchabanditthayasathan 1982, 72) defines a *kathoey* as "A person who has both male and female genitals; a person whose mind [i.e., psychology] and behavior are the opposite of their sex/gender (*phet*)." In his *Photjananukrom Thai* (Thai dictionary), Manit Manitcharoen (1983, 70) defines *kathoey* as denoting either a man or a woman, and he attempts to correct popular Thai misconceptions that homosexuals and *kathoeys* are the same with his definition: "Homosexuals or the sexually perverted (*wiparit thang phet*) are not *kathoeys*. The characteristic of a *kathoey* is someone who cross-dresses (*lakka-phet*), a male who likes to act and dress like a woman and has a mind like a woman, or a female who likes to act and dress like a man and who has a mind like a man."

7. A Buddhist monk, while renouncing sexuality, is a type of Thai "man," and his asexual status does not associate him with the stigmatized, demasculinized position of the *kathoey*. The clear ritual distinction between monks and *kathoeys* is shown by the fact that *kathoeys* are ritually barred from ordination (see Jackson 1993).

8. In this chapter I refer only to the sexuality of lay people in Thailand. All forms of sexuality, including heterosexual, homosexual, and autosexual, are prohibited for Buddhist monks. I have analyzed Thai Buddhist attitudes to homosexuality elsewhere (Jackson 1993).

9. Williams (1990, 130) observes, "Though it is widely acknowledged [in Thailand] that General Prem [Tinsulanonda] has relationships with his handsome young military aides, he never felt the need to marry a woman or to deny that he is homosexual . . . his particular sexual behaviour is just accepted without comment."

10. Attempts to "out" Thai public figures are almost always criticized as "cowardly," or as demonstrating the scurrilous and disreputable character of the accuser, and such attempts tend to generate sympathy for the accused and contempt for the accuser. The *Bangkok Post Weekly Review* (10 June 1994, 5, "Politician slams attack on unwed ministers") recently reported that an anonymous attempt to "out" six ministers in the cabinet of former Prime Chuan Leekpai was severely criticized.

11. Confusion about the meaning of recently borrowed or newly coined terms is common among less educated Thais. Thousands of new terms have been added to the Thai language in this century to describe new technologies or represent ideas borrowed from Western discourses, and even many educated Thais have trouble keeping up with many of the neologisms. Current confusion about the meaning of "gay" parallels earlier uncertainty in the general Thai populace about the meaning of terms for such novel concepts as "(parliamentary) constitution" (*ratthathammanun*), "democracy" (*prachathipatai*) and "(socioeconomic) development" (*kan-phatthana*).

12. Unlike personal classified advertisements in most Western gay magazines, which maintain the anonymity of the advertiser, Thai gay classifieds can include the name and address and often also a photograph of the advertiser. This suggests the weaker character of sanctions against male homosexuality in Thailand compared to Western societies, where the consequences of exposure can be severe.

13. Thai lacks terms for the English notions of "sexual identity" and "gay identity." However, the expressions *pen gay* ("to be gay" or "being gay") and *khwam pen gay* ("gayness") are often used to refer to what English authors call "gay identity."

14. Contemporary Thai gay parlance draws many terms from English, but often applies particularly Thai nuances. "Man" (Thai: *maen*) denotes a masculine-identified male homosexual who would usually be expected to be the inserter in anal sex. Among Thai gay men the indigenous term for "man/male" (*phu-chai*) is most commonly used to refer to male biological sex and to heterosexual men. Thus in Thai the sentence, "He is a man (*phu-chai*)," may mean either "He is male" or "He is a (masculine) heterosexual man." In contrast, the sentence, "He is a man (*maen*)," means that "He is a (masculine) homosexual man." *King* denotes a preference for insertive anal sex, while *queen* denotes a preference for receptive anal sex, but unlike English, the Thai term *queen* carries no necessary connotation of effeminacy, and *king* does not necessarily imply strongly expressed masculinity. The distinctively Thai but English-derived compound terms *man-queen* and *man-king* emphasise the masculine appearance and demeanor of homosexual men who prefer receptive and insertive anal sex, respectively. To denote effeminacy, Thai relies on terms from its own vocabulary, not English, with the noun *kathoey* and the verbal adjectives *kratung-krating* and *tung-ting* ("to be ostentatiously effeminate") being common derogatory terms for effeminate male homosexuals. That Thai has indigenous terms for effeminate but not for masculine male homosexuality follows from the fact that the traditional cultural stereotype of exclusive male homosexuality has been that of a feminized man. The English-derived term *bai* ("bi-") and the Thai-English compound *seua-bai* ("bi-tiger") denote a bisexual man, the latter term describing strongly expressed performative masculinity.

15. In Thai Buddhism sex/gender identity is believed to vary through different

rebirths, with a person variously being born as a man, women, or *kathoey* in different incarnations, depending on his or her *karma*.

16. Note, however, that the Thai gay man's openness about his homosexuality does have a historical precedent in the visible sexuality of the *kathoey*. That is, Thai culture is not without precedents for the public visibility of exclusive male homosexuality.

Chapter Eight

1. The ideas which encouraged the cult's reception remain vital, however and continue to influence Huli history; see Clark (1995).

2. All foreign terms both in Huli language and *tok pisin* (Melanesian pidgin) are italicized.

3. These problems are connected by some Huli to the granting of independence to Papua New Guinea before Highlanders were prepared, especially in contrast to coastal peoples who had longer experiences of colonialism.

4. The inclusion of coitus in this definition may appear to support Heider's connection of sexuality with "penile penetration," yet coitus is not what defines sexuality. Rather it is a forum in which the aesthetics of desire is negotiated.

5. *Ibagiya* would have operated, in terms of its structure, location, and disocurse, in a similar way to the panopticon described by Foucault (1979), which "ideally" produced subjectivity through the control of discourse and nondiscursive space. But I would lay more stress on agency in the production of discourse.

6. Many useful references to sexuality are, however, found throughout Goldman's monographs on the Huli (1983, 1988, 1995).

7. It is only in this amorphous sense that the *nambis* can be partially equated with the state, which in its Western definition is too concrete and overdetermined a concept to capture the nuances and ambiguities of the Huli notion of *nambis*.

8. At least institutionally, although the cult still seems to play an important, albeit reduced, ideological role.

9. From women's perspectives, men "contained" things, principally through their actions in building fences and ditches (Chris Ballard, personal communication, 1994).

10. Telefol people near the Ok Tedi mine make a similar connection between Europeans and a trickster figure (Dan Jorgensen, personal communication, 1993).

11. Ordinarily sensible men, when drunk, are said to be controlled by beer, totally without willpower as if possessed, and will do things they normally would not do, such as having sex with *pamuks* or with menstruating women. Succumbing to temptation, drunk or sober, is described as *damene minaya*, "caught by *dama*/Satan," so that a lack of willpower—a male characterization of women—can be rationalized as not being totally a man's fault.

12. For a discussion of the distinctions between the concepts of sexuality and gender, see Pringle (1992) and the introduction to this volume.

13. See Clark (1993), where I report a myth dealing with these connections at the Mt. Kare goldfields that was first related to me by a woman.

14. This has to be related to men's preferences for extramarital sex with young, attractive and "clean" women (sometimes referred to as "holy"). Many men said that if the woman was good looking, then they wouldn't use a condom, which can be related to the Huli equation of beauty, morality, and health. Men's beliefs that young, attrac-

tive women should also be "clean" can be related to their claims about women keeping things hidden from men. A hidden or covert quality is an attribute associated with women, particularly in relation to illicit sex. I was often told by men that women kept the "true" talk about sex "hidden" from us, and that they conspired to mislead us in response to our questions. Interestingly, I was informed by men that if we wanted to hear "true" talk, then we should seek out and interview *pamuk* women, who had no grounds to lie to us. If a man had sex with a young, "clean" woman and afterwards developed symptoms of STD, he invariably suggested that the woman had kept her illness (or the fact that she had had sex with other men) hidden from him. This relates to men's claims that they cannot "see" STD on a woman, and that she cannot be relied upon to tell the truth of her condition (this applies to *pamuks* as well as to young, local women). Woman are again blamed for male illness.

15. It has been suggested that there was no monolithic form of "traditional" Huli sexuality, and of course this also applies to "modern" forms which exist along a continuum now influenced by the *dawanda,* not *ibagiya.* In light of this, the term *sexuality* invariably refers to "sexualities."

16. Liminality in Victor Turner's (1967) usage implies not only being between structures but also a transition towards another state, and it may be that Huli men, to adapt a phrase used by Howlett (1973) about the "terminal development" of a Highlands peasantry, are stuck in an "infinite pause" of masculine liminality. Descriptions of men as ill-featured, unkempt, with short and dusty hair, capture some of the bizarre features which Turner attributes to monsters which appear in liminal stages of ritual. What has not been considered in this article is the way in which prostitutes may be liminal women, whose role is similar to that of gender-liminal men in parts of Polynesia, who satisfy men's sexual desires outside of "normal" heterosexual channels (Besnier 1994).

Chapter Nine

1. The State Law and Order Restoration Council (SLORC) changed the name of the state from Burma to Myanmar in 1989. Opposition groups have not accepted this change. Myanmar is used here without political implications for the state under the present leadership. Burmese is used as an adjective and Burman to indicate the ethnic majority.

2. For reasons of confidentiality, these cannot be identified, nor can details be quoted from these proposals.

3. Knowledge, Attitude, Beliefs, Practices; and Information, Education, Communication. See O'Shaughnessy (1994) for a review of these techniques in HIV/AIDS projects.

4. In 1988 there were only 186 known cases nationally; by the end of 1990, there were 27,030. Late in 1993, the number was estimated at 600,000 with up to 1,200 cases expected daily. Data from Chiang Rai province indicated that none in the commercial sex industry were infected with HIV in August 1986; a year later, it had risen to 1 percent; by June 1990, 54 percent (data reported in Porter 1995a, 5–8).

5. Aid levels through the 1980s fluctuated between US$129 milllion to US$402 million each year. By 1989 this plummeted to US$17 million. Debt rose from US$1.6 million in 1980 to US$5.3 million in 1989 (cf. Steinberg 1990, 591).

6. Opium poppy production, for instance, is reported to have increased from 600 tonnes in 1987 to 2,575 tonnes in 1993 (data sourced in Porter 1995a).

7. CSW mobility was earlier revealed in studies by health workers in Myanmar, Myo Thet Htoon et al. (n.d.), and Khin Win Thin et al. (n.d.).

8. These quotations come from NGO project proposals, but for reasons of confidentiality cannot be sourced.

9. Other factors exacerbate this trend, including the downturn, late in 1993, in cross-border trade, restrictions on imports and exports of some commodities, and so on.

Chapter Eleven

1. Japanese usually differentiate between people infected with HIV, using the untranslated English acronym, and people with AIDS, transliterated into Japanese and pronounced "EIZU." The term *seropositive* is widely used in explanations of HIV infection. In 1993 and 1994, PWA, but not PLWA (persons living with AIDS), was in common use.

2. Japan is not the only country to argue its uniqueness in relation to the AIDS epidemic; however, the predominance of hemophiliac infections in the early stages of the documentation of AIDS cases in Japan became an important factor in masking the potential for other groups in the population to be exposed also to the virus in other contexts.

3. For an excellent historical overview, see Yamanaka (1993). See also Spencer (1992) and Morita and Saskia (1994).

4. See Buckley (1994), where I discuss levels of overprescription and unnecessary surgery among Japanese women, and see Lock (1993) for discussion of questionable practices within the medical profession in relation to the diagnosis and treatment of menopause in Japan.

5. For an overview of various aspects of Japanese doctor/patient relationships, see Lock (1980) and Norbeck and Lock (1987).

6. I have been unable to locate a copy of the brochure. Information is anecdotal and drawn from the article "Fatal Error" (*Far Eastern Economic Review*, 1993).

7. For a detailed discussion of traditional constructions of male homosexual relations, see the introduction to Sharlow's translation of Saikaku's *The Great Mirror of Male Love* (1990).

8. That is, women must persuade men to wear them.

9. The 1994 Stop AIDS campaign did use individual media personalities in both television and poster advertising for AIDS prevention.

10. For a more detailed analysis of the *manga*, see Buckley (1992).

11. This discussion of WHO/GPA models is strongly indebted to the work of Cindy Patton in her various works in preparation on AIDS and the politics of WHO/GPA policy and practice.

12. For an early and still influential discussion on the positioning of Inside/Outside and Victim/Carrier, see Treichler (1988). See Lingis (1994) for an interesting extension of Foucault's concepts of power, sexuality, and discipline, an extension which functions as a useful theoretical framework for the discussion of the location of the body of the female immigrant sex worker in contemporary Japan.

13. Watney (1993a, b) discusses the mobilization of the category of homosexual in the policing of home and family in contemporary Britain. This offers an interesting point of contrast to Japan, where similar dynamics can be observed in relation to the female immigrant sex worker.

14. I thank Cathy Burns for drawing my attention to the excellent analysis of judicial rulings on questions of the sexual freedom of prostitutes and married women in Japan, in the work of Yunomae Tomoko (1989).

15. My friend agreed to the publication of this anecdote, but wishes to remain anonymous.

16. Many non-Japanese readers may find the assumptions worrying and be surprised by the open attitude towards the sex industry and its pervasiveness. For an overview in English, see Allison (1994).

17. My thanks to Kaye Broadbent for pointing out the use of English rather than Japanese in this caption.

18. My research assistants Minako Sakai, Keiko Mukai, Kaye Broadbent, and Cathy Burns provided me with essential support at different stages over the three years of research for this project.

BIBLIOGRAPHY

Abel, C. W. 1902. *Savage Life in New Guinea: The Papuan in Many Moods*. London: London Missionary Society Press.

Abel, R. W. 1934. *Charles W. Abel of Kwato: Forty Years in Dark Papua*. New York: Fleming H. Revell.

Aboagye-Kwarteng, T., and R. Moodie. 1995. *Community Action on HIV: A Resource Manual of HIV Prevention and Care*. Melbourne: Macfarlane Burnet Centre for Medical Research, International Health Unit.

Abu-Lughod, L. 1990. The romance of resistance: Tracing transformations of power through Bedouin women. *American Ethnologist* 17, 41–55.

Adams, P. 1992. Prostitution, pretence and pious prattle. *The Weekend Review*, 31 October–1 November, 12.

Agnew, J. 1993. Representing space: Space, scale and culture in social science. In *Place/Culture/Representation*, edited by J. Duncan and D. Ley, 251–271. London and New York: Routledge.

Ali, A., ed. 1979. *Girmit: The Indenture Experience in Fiji*. Suva: Fiji Museum.

———. 1980. *Plantation to Politics: Studies on Fiji Indians*. Suva: University of the South Pacific and Fiji Times and Herald.

Allen, J. 1992. Frameworks and questions in Australian sexuality research. In *Rethinking Sex: Social Theory and Sexuality Research*, edited by R. Connell and G. Dowsett, 5–31. Melbourne: Melbourne University Press.

Allison, A. 1994. Nightwork: Sexuality, pleasure and corporate masculinity in a Tokyo hostess club. *The Journal of Asian Studies* 54, no. 1: 213.

Alloula, M. 1986. *The Colonial Harem*. Minneapolis: University of Minnesota Press.

Allyn, E. 1991. *Trees in the Same Forest: the Men of Thailand Revisited. Thailand's Culture and Gay Subculture*. Bangkok: Bua Luang Publishing.

———, ed. 1992. *The Dove Coos (Nok Kao Kan): Gay Experiences by the Men of Thailand*. Translated by Nukul Benchamat and Somboon Inpradith. Bangkok: Bua Luang Publishing.

———, ed. 1994. *The Dove Coos II: Gay Experiences by the Men of Thailand*. Translated by David Jonathon. Bangkok: Floating Lotus Books.

Altman, D. 1982. *The Homosexualization of America, the Americanization of the Homosexual*. New York: St Martin's Press.

———. 1991. The primacy of politics: Organising around AIDS. *AIDS* 5, suppl. 2, 231–238.

———. 1992. AIDS and the discourses of sexuality. In *Rethinking Sex: Social Theory and Sexuality Research*, edited by R. Connell and G. Dowsett, 32–48. Melbourne: Melbourne University Press.

————. 1993. Expertise, legitimacy and the centrality of community. In *AIDS: Facing the Second Decade,* edited by P. Aggleton, P. Davies, and G. Hart, 1–12. London: The Falmer Press.

————. 1995. The new world of gay Asia. In *Meridian: Asian and Pacific Inscriptions,* edited by Surendrini Perera, 121–138. Melbourne: Meridian Press.

Amante, I. D. 1993. Fear of side effects, not religion, prompts women to pick natural method. *Sun Star Daily* 4 August, 1, 18.

Appadurai, A. 1990. Disjuncture and difference in the global economy. *Public Culture* 2, no. 2: 1–24.

Aquino Sarmiento, M. 1988. Love for sale (like cigarettes). *Sunday Inquirer Magazine* 3, no. 3: 12–13.

Arnold, D. 1993. Sexually transmitted diseases in nineteenth-and twentieth-century India. *Genitourinary Medicine* 69: 3–8.

Asia Watch and Women's Rights Project. 1993. *A Modern Form of Slavery: Trafficking of Burmese Women and Girls into Brothels in Thailand.* New York: Human Rights Watch.

Atoh, M. 1989. Changes in fertility and fertility control behavior in Japan. In *Basic Readings of Population and Family Planning in Japan,* edited by M. Minoru and K. Tameyoshi, 40–60. Tokyo: Institute of Population Problems.

Austen, L. 1934–35. Procreation among the Trobriand Islanders. *Oceania* 5: 102–113.

Australasian Wesleyan Methodist Church. 1892a. *Australasian Methodist Missionary Review* 1, no. 11: 3.

————. 1892b. *Australasian Methodist Missionary Review* 1, no. 12: 6.

————. 1895. *Australasian Methodist Missionary Review* 4, no. 11: 3.

————. 1902. *Australasian Methodist Missionary Review* 11, no. 9: 11.

————. 1911. *Australasian Methodist Missionary Review* 20, no. 10: 17.

Australia. 1904. *British New Guinea Annual Report for 1902–03, presented to Parliament of the Commonwealth of Australia.* Melbourne: R. Brain, Government Printer.

Azarcon de la Cruz, P. 1985. *Filipinas for Sale: An Alternative Philippine Report on Women and Tourism.* Manila: Aklat Filipino.

Baldwin, B. n. d. Papuan notes and Trobriand Island linguistic material. MS. 1031, Pacific Manuscripts Bureau. Research School of Pacific and Asian Studies, Australian National University, Canberra.

Ballard, C. 1994. The death of a great land. Ph.D. dissertation, Department of Prehistory, the Australian National University, Canberra.

Ballescas, R. P. 1992. *Filipino Entertainers in Japan: An Introduction.* Quezon City: The Foundation for Nationalist Studies.

————. 1993. Reconciling growth and development: The labour situation in Cebu. *Data Links* 2, no. 2: 1–8.

Ballhatchet, K. 1980. *Race, Sex and Class under the Raj.* New York: St. Martin's Press.

Bamber, S. D., Hewison, K. J., and Underwood, P. J. 1993. A history of sexually transmitted diseases in Thailand: Policy and politics. *Genitourinary Medicine* 69: 148–157.

Barnes, B. 1993. Emotional hell of predators who fall for their exotic prey. *The Australian,* 14 May, 11.

Barnes, J., and Duncan, J., eds. 1992. *Writing Worlds: Discourse, Text and Metaphor in the Representation of Landscape.* London: Routledge.

Baudrillard, J. 1977. *Forget Foucault.* New York: Semiotext.

Bavin, C. 1914. The Indian Fiji. In *A Century in the Pacific,* edited by J. Colwell, 175–197. Sydney: William H. Beale, Methodist Book Room.

Beall, J. 1990. Women under indenture in colonial Natal, 1860–1911. In *South Asians Overseas: Migration and Ethnicity,* edited by C. Clarke, C. Peach, and S. Vertovec, 57–74. Cambridge: Cambridge University Press.

Beekman, E. M. 1984. The Passatist: Louis Couperus' interpretation of Dutch colonialism. *Indonesia* 37: 59–76.

Behdad, A. 1994. *Belated Travelers: Orientalism in the Age of Colonial Dissolution.* Durham: Duke University Press.

Bell, L. 1987. *Good Girls/Bad Girls: Sex Trade Workers and Feminists Face to Face.* Toronto: The Women's Press.

Bell, S. 1994. *Rereading, Writing and Rewriting the Prostitute Body.* Bloomington: Indiana University Press.

Bergan, R. 1982. *An A–Z of Movie Directors.* Melbourne and Auckland: Oxford University Press.

Berger, J. 1972. *Ways of Seeing.* Harmondsworth: Penguin.

Berger, M. J. 1988. Review of Hyam, "Empire and Sexual Opportunity." *The Journal of Imperial and Commonwealth History* 17, no. 2: 83–89.

Berry, C. 1994. *A Bit on the Side: East-West Topographies of Desire.* Rose Bay: Empress Publishing.

Berry, C., Hamilton, A., and Jayamanne, L., eds. In press. *The Good Woman of Bangkok: The Debate.* Sydney: The Power Institute.

Besnier, N. 1994. Polynesian gender liminality through time and space. In *Third Sex, Third Gender: Beyond Sexual Dimorphism in Culture and History,* edited by G. Herdt, 285–328. New York: Zone Books.

Bhabha, H. 1994. Remembering Fanon: Self, psyche and the colonial condition. In *Colonial Discourse and Post-Colonial Theory,* edited by Patrick Williams and Laura Chrisman, 112–123. New York: Columbia University Press. First published 1986, in *Black Skin, White Masks,* by F. Fanon. Foreword to reprint.

Bhabha, H., and Burgin, V. 1994. Family romance. In *Visualizing Theory. Selected Essays from V.A.R., 1990–1994,* edited by L. Taylor, 453–462. New York and London: Routledge.

Black, R. H. 1957. Dr. Bellamy of Papua. *The Medical Journal of Australia* 2: 189–197, 232–238, 279–284.

Bourdieu, P. 1977. *Outline of a Theory of Practice.* Cambridge: Cambridge University Press.

Branigan, E. 1993. Heavenly Bodies and Hideous Hags: Representations of Polynesian and Melanesian Women in Beatrice Grimshaw's 1907 Pacific Travelogues. Ph.D. dissertation, Department of Anthropology and Sociology, La Trobe University, Melbourne.

Brecht, B. 1970. *Parables for the Theatre: The Good Woman of Setzuan, The Caucasian Chalk Circle.* Harmondsworth: Penguin.

Brewster, A. B. 1922. *The Hill Tribes of Fiji.* Philadelphia: J. B. Lippincott.

———. 1937. *King of the Cannibal Isles.* London: Robert Hale and Company.

Broinowski, A. 1992. *The Yellow Lady: Australian Impressions of Asia.* Melbourne: Oxford University Press.

Bromilow, W. E. 1909. Some manners and customs of the Dobuans of south east Papua. *Australasian Association for the Advancement of Science* 12: 470–485.

———. 1929. *Twenty Years among Primitive Papuans.* London: Epworth Press.

Brown, G. 1904. *A Brief Account of Methodist Missions in Australasia, Polynesia and Melanesia, their Past History, Present Conditions, and Possibilities.* Sydney: Methodist Missionary Society of Australasia Press.

Buchbinder, D. 1993. Straight acting: Masculinity, subjectivity and (same-sex) desire. Paper presented at *Forces of Desire Conference*, August, Humanities Research Centre, Australian National University, Canberra.

Buckley, S. 1991. Effacing the feminine. In *Bodies and Boundaries East and West*, edited by S. Buckley and B. Massumi. *Social Discourse* 3: 3–4.

———. 1992. "Penguin in bondage": A graphic tale of Japanese comic books. In *Technoculture*, edited by A. Ross and C. Penley, 163–195. Minneapolis: University of Minnesota Press.

———. 1994. A short history of the feminist movement in Japan. In *Women of Japan and Korea: Continuity and Change*, edited by J. Gelb and M. L. Palley, 150–186. Philadelphia: Temple University Press.

———. 1996. *Broken Silence: Voices of Japanese Feminism*. Berkeley: University of California Press.

Buklod Centre. 1990. *Hospitality: What Price? The U.S. Navy at Subic Bay*. Olongapo: Buklod Centre.

Burgin, V. 1994. Paranoic space. In *Visualizing Theory. Selected Essays from V.A.R., 1990–1994*, edited by L. Taylor, 230–238. New York and London: Routledge.

Burton, J. W. 1910. *The Fiji of To-Day*. London: Charles H. Kelly.

———. 1912. *The Call of the Pacific*. London: Charles. H. Kelly.

———. 1926. *Papua for Christ*. London: The Epworth Press.

———. 1949. *Modern Missions in the South Pacific*. London: London Missionary Society Press.

———. 1955. *The First Century of Missionary Adventure 1855–1955*. Sydney: Methodist Overseas Missions Press.

Buruma, I. 1994. Revenge in the Indies: Review of *The Hidden Force*, by Louis Couperus. *New York Review of Books* 41, no. 14: 30–32.

Bushell, K. 1936. *Papuan Epic*. London: Seely, Service, and Co.

Butler, J. 1987. *Subjects of Desire: Hegelian Reflections in Twentieth-Century France*. New York: Columbia University Press.

———. 1990a. Gender trouble. In *Feminism/Postmodernism*, edited by L. J. Nicholson, 324–340. New York: Routledge.

———. 1990b. *Gender Trouble: Feminism and the Subversion of Identity*. New York: Routledge.

Byam, W., and Archibald, R. 1921. *The Practice of Medicine in the Tropics*. London: Henry Frowde, and Hodder and Stoughton.

Cacho Olivares, N. 1993. Maceda, Coseteng did a "service" to Filipinas. *Philippine Daily Inquirer*, 28 August.

Cadet, J. 1981. *Occidental Adam, Oriental Eve*. Chiang Mai: Charles Browne Publications.

———. 1987. *Venusberg Revisited*. Chiang Mai: Charles Browne Publications.

Callaway, H. 1987. *Gender, Culture and Empire: European Women in Colonial Nigeria*. London and Oxford: Macmillan and St. Anthony's College.

Caplan, P., ed. 1987. *The Cultural Construction of Sexuality*. London: Routledge and Tavistock Publications.

Cass, A. M. 1991. Sex and the Military: Gender and Violence in the Philippines. Ph.D. dissertation. Department of Anthropology and Sociology, University of Queensland, Brisbane.

Cebu City Health Department. 1992. *Present Situation*. Cebu: AIDS Prevention and Control Program, STD-AIDS Detection Centre.

Chambers, R. 1994. Poverty and livelihoods: Whose reality counts? Paper presented at

Stockholm Roundtable on *Change: Social Conflict or Harmony?* Mimeograph. New York: United Nations Development Program, Overview Paper 2.

Chignell, A. K. 1911. *An Outpost in Papua.* London: John Murray.

Clad, J. 1988. Cebu sets the pace: Island province leads Philippine economic recovery. *Far Eastern Economic Review,* 10 November: 82–4.

Clark, J. 1992. Madness and colonization: The embodiment of power in Pangia. *Oceania* 63: 15–26.

———. 1993. Gold, sex and pollution: Male illness and myth at Mt. Kare, Papua New Guinea. *American Ethnologist* 20, no. 4: 742–757.

———. 1995. Highlands of history: Images of deviance and desire. In *Papuan Borderlands: Huli, Duna, and Ipili Perspectives on the Papua New Guinea Highlands,* edited by A. Biersack, 379–400. Ann Arbor: University of Michigan Press.

Clark, J., and Hughes, J. 1995. A history of sexuality and gender in Tari. In *Papuan Borderlands: Huli, Duna, and Ipili Perspectives on the Papua New Guinea Highlands,* edited by A. Biersack, 315–340. Ann Arbor: University of Michigan Press.

Clatts, M. C., and Mutchler, K. M. 1989. AIDS and the dangerous other: Metaphors of sex and deviance in the representation of disease. *Medical Anthropology* 10: 105–114.

Clifford, J. 1992. Travelling cultures. In *Cultural Studies,* edited by L. Grossberg, C. Nelson, and P. Treichler, 96–116. London: Routledge.

Cohen, E. 1982. Thai girls and *farang* men: The edge of ambiguity. *Annals of Tourism Research* 9, no. 3: 403–428.

———. 1986. Lovelorn *farangs:* The correspondence between foreign men and Thai girls. *Anthropological Quarterly* 59, no. 3: 115–127.

———. 1988. Tourism and AIDS in Thailand. *Annals of Tourism Research* 15, no. 6: 467–486.

Coleman, E., Colgan, P., and Gooren, L. 1992. Male cross-gender behavior in Myanmar (Burma): A description of the Acault. *Archives of Sexual Behavior* 21, no. 3: 313–321.

Colwell, J. 1914. *A Century in the Pacific.* London: Charles H. Kelly.

Comaroff, J., and Comaroff, J. 1991. *Of Revelation and Revolution: Christianity, Colonialism and Consciousness in South Africa.* Chicago: University of Chicago Press.

Comte, A. 1830–42. *The Essential Comte: Selected from Cours de Philosophie Positive.* London: Croom Helm.

Connell, R. W. 1987. *Gender and Power.* Cambridge and Oxford: Polity Press and Basil Blackwell.

Connell, R. W., and Dowsett, G. 1992. "The unclean motion of the generative parts": Frameworks in western thought on sexuality. In *Rethinking Sex: Social Theory and Sexuality Research,* edited by R. Connell and G. Dowsett, 49–75. Melbourne: Melbourne University Press.

Cook, J. 1967. *The Journal of Captain James Cook on his Voyages of Discovery. The Voyage of the Resolution and Discovery, 1776–1780.* Vol. 3, Part 1. Edited by J. C. Beaglehole. London: The Hakluyt Society.

Cook, M. 1993. Cry freedom. *Good Weekend,* 27 November, 12–16, 18, 20.

Cook, P., and Minogue, M. 1993. Economic reform and political change in Myanmar (Burma). *World Development* 21, no. 7: 1151–1161.

Couperus, L. 1924. *The Hidden Force: A Story of Modern Java.* New York: Dodd Mead and Company.

Coward, R. 1983. *Patriarchal Precedents: Sexuality and Social Relations.* London: Routledge and Kegan Paul.

Craig, D., and Porter, D. 1994. The phoenix of the subject in development. Paper presented at symposium, *Why Psychology for Developing Worlds?* 29th annual conference of the Australian Psychology Society, 29 September, Wollongong.

Curtis, J. R., and Arreola, D. D. 1991. Zonas de tolerancia on the northern Mexican border. *The Geographical Review* 81, no. 3: 333–346.

Dañguilan, M. J. 1993. *Making Choices in Good Faith: A Challenge to the Catholic Church's Teachings on Sexuality and Contraception.* Quezon City: Woman Health.

Daniel, H., and Parker, R. 1993. *Sexuality, Politics and AIDS in Brazil.* London: The Falmer Press.

Dauncey, H. M. 1913. *Papuan Pictures.* London: London Missionary Society Press.

David, R. D. 1991. Filipino workers in Japan: Vulnerability and survival. *Kasarinlan* 6, no. 3: 9–23.

Dawson, A. 1988. *Patpong: Bangkok's Big Little Street.* Bangkok: Thai Watana Panich Press.

de Braconnier, A. 1913. Het Kazerne-Concubinaat in Ned-Indie. *Vragen van den Dag* 28, 974–995.

de Certeau, M. 1984. *The Practice of Everyday Life,* translated by S. Rendall. Berkeley: University of California Press.

de la Cerna, M. L. 1992. Women empowering women: The Cebu experience. *Review of Women's Studies* 3, no. 1: 51–73.

de Lauretis, T. 1984. *Alice Doesn't: Feminism, Semiotics, Cinema.* London: Macmillan Press.

———. 1986. *Feminist Studies/Critical Studies.* Bloomington: Indiana University Press.

———. 1987. *Technologies of Gender: Essays on Theory, Film, and Fiction.* Basingstoke: Macmillan Press.

———. 1994. *The Practice of Love: Lesbian Sexuality and Perverse Desire.* Bloomington: Indiana University Press.

de Leon, A., Contor, E., and Abueva, A. 1991. Tourism and Child Prostitution in the Philippines. *Caught in Modern Slavery: Tourism and Child Prostitution in Asia.* Bangkok: The Ecumenical Coalition on Third World Tourism.

Deleuze, G., and Guattari, F. 1987. *A Thousand Plateaus: Capitalism and Schizophrenia.* Minneapolis: University of Minnesota Press.

Department of Tourism. 1992. *Tourist Traffic to Cebu.* Unpublished Department of Tourism Statistics. Cebu: Cebu City Regional Office.

Desquitado, M. 1992. *Behind the Shadows: Toward a Better Understanding of Prostituted Women.* Davao: Talikala.

de Stoop, C. 1994. *They Are So Sweet, Sir: The Cruel World of Traffickers in Filipinas and Other Women.* Manila: Limitless Asia.

de Zalduondo, B. O. 1991. Prostitution viewed cross-culturally: Toward recontextualising sex work in AIDS intervention research. *Journal of Sex Research* 28, no. 2: 223–248.

Dioneda, L. C. 1993. Women in the flesh industry. *Bakud* 3, no. 2: 6–7.

Donaldson, L. 1992. *Decolonizing Feminisms: Race, Gender and Empire-Building.* Chapel Hill and London: The University of North Carolina Press.

Dowsett, G. W. 1990. Reaching men who have sex with men in Australia. An overview of AIDS education: Community intervention and community attachment strategies. *Australian Journal of Social Issues* 25, no. 3: 186–198.

Doyo, C. P. 1983. The prostitution problem must be viewed from a national, even global, perspective. *Philippine Panorama* 12: 36–40.

Drinnon, R. 1980. *Facing West: The Metaphysics of Indian-Hating and Empire-Building.* Minneapolis: University of Minnesota Press.

Duncan, J. 1993. Sites of representation: Place, time and the discourse of the other. In *Place/Culture/Representation*, edited by J. Duncan and D. Ley, 39–56. London: Routledge.

Durkheim, E. 1915. *The Elementary Forms of the Religious Life*. New York: The Free Press.

Dwyer, J. 1993. Foreword. In *Economic Implications of AIDS in Asia*, edited by D. Bloom and J. Lyons, v–vi. New Delhi: United Nations Development Program.

Eckhardt, J. 1991. *Waylaid by the Bimbos and Other Catastrophes in Thailand*. Bangkok: Post Publishing.

Eddy, P., and Walden, S. 1993. Terror in the land of smiles. *The Australian Magazine*, 19–20 September, 10–14, 16, 18.

Ellis, H. 1923 [1897]. *Studies in the Psychology of Sex*. Vol. 2. *Sexual Inversion*. Philadelphia: Davis.

Embree, J. F. 1950. Thailand: A loosely structured society. *American Anthropologist* 52: 181–193.

Enloe, C. 1983. *Does Khaki Become You? The Militarisation of Women's Lives*. London: Pluto Press.

———. 1989. *Bananas, Beaches and Bases: Making Feminist Sense of International Politics*. London: Pandora.

Epstein, J., and Straub, K. 1991. *Body Guards: The Cultural Politics of Gender Ambiguity*. New York: Routledge.

Eribon, D. 1994. *Michel Foucault et ses Contemporains*. Paris: Gallimard.

Evans, J. 1993. Feminism, postcolonialism and Beatrice Grimshaw. M. A. thesis, Women's Studies, La Trobe University, Melbourne.

Fairclough, N. 1992. *Discourse and Social Change*. Cambridge: Polity.

Fanon, F. 1967. *Black Skin, White Masks*. New York: Grove Press.

Farmer, P. 1992. *AIDS and Accusation: Haiti and the Geography of Blame*. Berkeley: University of California Press.

Fauconnier, H. 1931. *Soul of Malaya*. Harmondsworth: Penguin.

Feld, S. 1988. Notes on World Beat. *Public Culture* 1, no. 1: 31–37.

Fellows, S. B. n.d. Papers, 1883–1900. MS. 601, Pacific Manuscript Bureau. Research School of Pacific and Asian Studies, Australian National University, Canberra.

Fernandez, L. 1993. Slaves. *Philippines Free Press,* 28 August, 12, 49, 55, 78.

Fforde, A., and Porter, D. 1994. Public goods, the state, civil society and development assistance in Vietnam: Opportunities and prospects. Paper presented at *Vietnam Update Conference*, 11 November, Australian National University, Canberra.

Fiji. 1896. *Report of a Commission Appointed to Enquire into the Decrease of the Native Population, Colony of Fiji*. Suva: E. J. March, Government Printer.

Fildes, V., Marks, L., and Marland, H., eds. 1992. *Women and Children First: International Maternal and Infant Welfare 1870–1950*, 154–177. London: Routledge.

Firth, S. 1987. *Nuclear Playground*. Honolulu: University of Hawaii Press.

Fordham, G. 1993a. The social and cultural context of the AIDS epidemic in Thailand. Paper presented at *Fifth International Conference on Thai Studies*, July, School of Oriental and African Studies, London.

———. 1993b. Northern Thai male culture and the assessment of HIV risk. Paper presented at *AIDS Impact and Prevention in the Developing World: The Contribution of Demography to Social Science*, December, Annecy, France.

Forster, G. 1968 [1777]. *George Forster's Werke—Band 1 [A Voyage Round the World in his Britannic Majesty's Sloop, Resolution]*. Edited by Robert L. Kahn. Basel. Originally published London: B. White. Berlin: Academie Verlag.

Forster, J. R. 1778. *Observations Made During a Voyage Round the World on Physical Geography, Natural History and Ethic Philosophy.* London: G. Robinson.

———. 1982. *The Resolution Journal of Johann Reinhold Forster.* Edited by Michael E. Hoare. 4 volumes. London: The Hakluyt Society.

Foucault, M. 1973a. *The Order of Things.* New York: Vintage Books.

———. 1973b. *Madness and Civilization: A History of Insanity in the Age of Reason.* New York: Vintage Books.

———. 1977. *Discipline and Punish: The Birth of the Prison.* London: Penguin.

———. 1978. *The History of Sexuality—An Introduction.* Vol. 1. London: Penguin Books.

———. 1980. *The History of Sexuality—An Introduction.* Vol. 1. Translated by Robert Hurley. New York: Vintage Books.

———. 1981. *The History of Sexuality—An Introduction.* Vol. 1. Harmondsworth: Pelican Books.

———. 1985. *The History of Sexuality.* Vol. 2. *The Use of Pleasure.* New York: Pantheon.

———. 1990. *Difendere la societa.* Florence: Ponte alle Grazie.

France, P. 1969. *The Charter of the Land.* Melbourne: Oxford University Press.

Frankel, S. 1986. *The Huli Response to Illness.* Cambridge: Cambridge University Press.

Frayser, S. G. 1985. *Varieties of Sexual Experience: An Anthropological Perspective of Human Sexuality.* New Haven: Human Relations Area Files Press.

Fredrickson, G. 1981. *White Supremacy: A Comparative Study in American and South African History.* Oxford: Oxford University Press.

Freud, S. 1953 [1905]. Three essays on the theory of sexuality. In *Complete Psychological Works.* Standard Edition. Vol. 7. London: Hogarth Press.

———. 1961. *Civilization and Its Discontents.* New York: Norton.

———. 1963 [1930]. *Civilization and Its Discontents.* Translated by J. Rivière, revised by J. Strachey. London: Hogarth Press.

Freyre, G. 1946. *The Masters and the Slaves.* New York: Knopf.

Friedan, B. 1965. *The Feminine Mystique.* Harmondsworth: Penguin.

Friedman, J. 1990. Being in the world: Globalization and localization. *Theory, Culture and Society* 7: 311–328.

Fuss, D. 1994. Interior colonies: Frantz Fanon and the politics of identification. *Diacritics* 24, nos. 2–3 (special issue): 20–42.

Gallop, J. 1988. *Thinking Through the Body.* New York: Colombia University Press.

Gann, L. H., and Duignan, P. 1978. *The Rulers of British Africa, 1870–1914.* Stanford: Stanford University Press.

Garber, M. 1992. The occidental tourist: *M. Butterfly* and the scandal of transvestism. In *Nationalisms and Sexualities,* edited by A. Parker, M. Russo, D. Sommer, and P. Yaeger, 121–146. New York and London: Routledge.

Gardner, S. 1977. For love and money: Early writings of Beatrice Grimshaw, Colonial Papua's woman of letters. *New Literature Review* 1: 10–36.

———. 1987–88. A "'vert to Australianism": Beatrice Grimshaw and the Bicentenary. *Hecate* 13, no. 2: 31–68.

Garnham, F. 1918. *A Report on the Social and Moral Condition of Indians in Fiji.* Sydney: Kingston Press.

Garon, S. 1993. The world's oldest debate? Prostitution and the state in Imperial Japan, 1900–1945. *American Historical Review* 98, 3, 710–732.

Gatens, M. 1983. A critique of the sex/gender distinction. In *Beyond Marxism? Interventions after Marx,* edited by J. A. Allen and P. Patton, 143–160. Sydney: Intervention Publications.

————. 1991. *Feminism and Philosophy*. Bloomington: Indiana University Press.

Gay, P. 1993. *The Cultivation of Hatred: The Bourgeois Experience, Victoria to Freud*. New York: Norton.

Geertz, H. 1964. Kartini: An introduction. In *Letters of a Javanese Princess*, edited by R. A. Kartini, and translated by A. L. Symmers, 7–26. New York: W. W. Norton.

Genovese, E. 1974. *Roll Jordan Roll*. New York: Pantheon.

George, J. 1994. *Disourses of Global Politics: A Critical (Re)introduction to International Relations*. Boulder: Lynne Rienner.

Giddens, A. 1979. *Central Problems in Social Theory: Action, Structure and Contradiction in Social Analysis*. London: Macmillan.

————. 1981. *A Contemporary Critique of Historical Materialism*. London: Macmillan.

Gill, W. 1970. *Turn North-East at the Tombstone*. Adelaide: Rigby.

Gill, R. n. d. Letters 1897–1928. MS. 40, Pacific Manuscripts Bureau. Research School of Pacific and Asian Studies, Australian National University, Canberra.

Gilman, S. L. 1985. *Difference and Pathology: Stereotypes of Sexuality, Race and Madness*. Ithaca: Cornell University Press.

————. 1986. Black bodies, white bodies: Toward an iconography of female sexuality in late-nineteenth-century art, medicine and literature. In *"Race," Writing and Difference*, edited by H. L. Gates, 223–261. Chicago and London: University of Chicago Press.

————. 1988. *Disease and Representation: Images of Illness from Madness to AIDS*. Ithaca and London: Cornell University Press.

————. 1993. *Freud, Race, and Gender*. Princeton: Princeton University Press.

Glasse, R. 1992. Encounters with the Huli: Fieldwork at Tari in the 1950s. In *Ethnographic Presents: Pioneering Anthropologists in the Papua New Guinea Highlands*, edited by T. Hays, 232–248. Berkeley: University of California Press.

————. n.d. *Report on the Huli*. Manuscript.

Goldman, L. 1983. *Talk Never Dies: The Language of Huli Disputes*. London: Tavistock Publications.

————. 1988. *Premarital Sex Cases among the Huli: A Comparison between Tradition and Village Court Styles*. Oceania Monograph, no. 34. Sydney: University of Sydney.

————. 1995. The depths of deception: Cultural schemas of illusion in Huli. In *Papuan Borderlands: Huli, Duna, and Ipili Perspectives on the Papua New Guinea Highlands*, edited by A. Biersack, 111–138. Ann Arbor: University of Michigan Press.

Gray, J. 1990. The road to the city: Young women and transition in Northern Thailand. Ph.D. dissertation, Anthropology, Macquarie University, Sydney.

————. 1993. HIV/AIDS in the hills: A crisis just waiting to happen. Paper presented at the *Fifth International Conference on Thai Studies*, July, School of Oriental and African Studies, London.

————. n.d. "We never thought it would turn out like this": HIV/AIDS, prostitution and sex tourism in Thailand. Mimeograph. Sydney: National Centre for HIV Social Research, AIDS Research Unit, Macquarie University.

Great Britain. 1891. *British New Guinea No. 6. Annual Report for 1889–90, presented to Houses of Parliament*. London: Eyre and Spottiswoode, Her Majesty's Stationary Office.

————. 1892. *British New Guinea No. 37. Annual Report for 1890–91, presented to Houses of Parliament*. London: Eyre and Spottiswoode, Her Majesty's Stationary Office.

————. 1893. *British New Guinea No. 68. Annual Report for 1891–92, presented to Houses of Parliament*. London: Eyre and Spottiswoode, Her Majesty's Stationary Office.

————. 1904. *British New Guinea Annual Report for 1902–03, presented to Parliament of Commonwealth Australia*. Melbourne: R. Brain, Government Printer.

Green, M. 1992. *The Dream at the End of the World: Paul Bowles and the Literary Renegades in Tangiers*. New York: Harper.

Gregory, D. 1993. Interventions in the historical geography of modernity: Social theory, spatiality and the politics of representation. In *Place/Culture/Representation*, edited by J. Duncan and D. Ley, 272–313. London: Routledge.

Grimshaw, B. 1907a. *In the Strange South Seas*. London: Hutchinson and Company.

————. 1907b. *From Fiji to the Cannibal Islands*. London: Hutchinson and Company.

————. 1921. *My South Sea Sweetheart*. London: Hurst and Blackett.

————. 1922. *Conn of the Coral Seas*. London: Hurst and Blackett.

Gronewold, S. 1985. *Beautiful Merchandise: Prostitution in China, 1860–1936*. New York: Harington Park Press.

Grosz, E. A. 1989. *Sexual Subversions: Three French Feminists*. Sydney: Allen and Unwin.

————. 1994. *Volatile Bodies: Towards a Corporeal Feminism*. Sydney: Allen and Unwin.

Grundy-Warr, C. 1993. Coexistent borderlands and intra-state conflicts in mainland southeast Asia. *Singapore Journal of Tropical Geography* 14, no. 1: 42–57.

Guha, R. 1989. Dominance without hegemony and its historiography. In *Subaltern Studies VI*, edited by R. Guha, 210–309. Delhi: Oxford University Press.

Guillon, E. 1991. The ultimate origin of the world, or the Mula Mula, and other Mon beliefs. *Journal of the Siam Society* 79, no. 1: 22–30.

Hackshaw, F. 1989. Nineteenth-century notions of Aboriginal title and their influence on the interpretation of the treaty of Waitangi. In *Waitangi: Maori and Pakeha Perspectives on the Treaty of Waitangi*, edited by I. H. Kawharu, 92–120. Auckland: Oxford University Press.

Halperin, D. 1990. *One Hundred Years of Homosexuality and Other Essays on Greek Love*. New York: Routledge.

Hamilton, A. 1991. Rumours, foul calumnies and the safety of the state: Mass media and national identity in Thailand. In *National Identity and Its Defenders: Thailand, 1939–1989*, edited by C. J. Reynolds, 341–375. Monash Papers on Southeast Asia, no. 25. Clayton, Victoria: Centre of Southeast Asian Studies, Monash University.

————. 1992. Family dramas: Film and modernity in Thailand. *Screen* 33, no. 3: 259–273.

————. in press. Mistaken identities: Art, truth and dare in "The Good Woman of Bangkok." In *The Good Woman of Bangkok: The Debate*, edited by l. C. Berry, A. Hamilton and L. Jayamanne. Sydney University: Power Institute.

Hannerz, U. 1989. Notes on the global ecumene. *Public Culture*. 1, no. 2: 66–75.

Haraway, D. J. 1991. Situated knowledge: The science question in feminism and the privilege of partial perspective. In *Simians, Cyborgs, and Woman: The Reinvention of Nature*, by D. J. Haraway, 183–201. New York: Routledge.

Havanon, N., Bennett, A., and Knodel, J. 1993. Sexual networking in provincial Thailand. *Studies in Family Planning* 24, no. 1: 1–17.

Hawkes, S. J., and Hart, G. J. 1993. Travel, migration and HIV. *AIDS Care* 5, no. 2: 207–214.

Haylock, J. 1990. *A Touch of the Orient*. Chiang Mai: Silkworm Books.

Heider, K. 1976. Dani sexuality: A low energy system. *Man* 11, no. 2: 188–201.

Henningham, S. 1995. Labour resistance and a challenged colonial order: The Asian workforce in New Caledonia and the New Hebrides at the time of the Second World War. Special Issue on Labour in the Pacific edited by D. Munroe. *Journal of Pacific Studies*, 18: 151–183.

Herdt, G. 1981. *Guardians of the Flutes: Idioms of Masculinity.* New York: McGraw-Hill.

———, ed. 1984. *Ritualized Homosexuality in Melanesia.* Berkeley: University of California Press.

———. 1987. *The Sambia: Ritual and Gender in New Guinea.* New York: Holt, Rinehart and Winston.

———. 1992. Semen depletion and the sense of maleness. In *Oceanic Homosexualities,* edited by S. O. Murray, 33–68. New York: Garland Publishing.

Herdt, G., and Lindenbaum, S., eds. 1992. *The Time of AIDS. Social Analysis, Theory and Method.* Newbury Park: Sage.

Herdt, G., and Stoller, R. 1990. *Intimate Communications: Erotics and the Study of Culture.* New York: Columbia University Press.

Hesselink, L. 1987. Prostitution: A necessary evil, particularly in the colonies. Views on prostitution in the Netherlands Indies. In *Indonesian Women in Focus: Past and Present Notions,* edited by E. Locher-Scholten and A. Niehof, 205–224. Dordrecht-Holland: Foris Publications.

Hilario, C. 1932. Night life in Cebu. *Progress,* 1 May, 4–5, 22.

Hill, P. 1994. Safe sex and synchronised swimming: Cultural constructions of AIDS. *Venereology,* 7, no. 1: 12–19, 10.

Hinds. J. 1989. *Faces of the Night.* Bangkok: Editions Duang Kamol.

Hirschfeld, M. 1935. *Women East and West.* London: William Heinemann.

Hochschild, A. R. 1983. *The Managed Heart: Commercialisation of Human Feeling.* Berkeley: University of California Press.

Hollington, S. 1993. Destination sex. *Cosmopolitan,* November, 92–96.

Hoorn, J. 1993. Hostage taking in the Pacific: The case of Poedua. Paper presented at David Nichol Smith Seminar IX, Voyages and Beaches, Discovery and the Pacific, 1700–1840, 24–28 August, University of Auckland.

Howlett, D. 1973. Terminal development: From tribalism to peasantry. In *The Pacific in Transition,* edited by H. Brookfield, 249–273. London: St.Martin's Press.

Hunter, I. 1993. Personality as a vocation: The political rationality of the humanities. In *Foucault's New Domains,* edited by M. Gane and T. Johnson, 153–192. London: Routledge.

Hurst, H. L. 1938. *Papuan Journey.* London: Angus and Robertson.

Hyam, R. 1990. *Empire and Sexuality: The British Experience.* Manchester: Manchester University Press.

Ingelson, J. 1986. Prostitution in colonial Java. In *Nineteenth-and Twentieth-Century Indonesia: Essays in Honour of Professor J. D. Legge.* Clayton, Victoria: Monash University Press.

Inglis, A. 1974. *Not a White Woman Safe: Sexual Anxiety and Politics in Port Moresby, 1929–1934.* Canberra: Australian National University Press.

Irigaray, L. 1985. *This Sex Which Is Not One.* Ithaca: Cornell University Press.

Jackson, M. 1989. *Paths Toward a Clearing: Radical Empiricism and Ethnographic Inquiry.* Bloomington: Indiana University Press.

Jackson, P. 1989. *Male Homosexuality in Thailand: An Interpretation of Contemporary Thai Sources.* New York: Global Academic Publishers.

————. 1993. From kamma to unnatural vice: Thai Buddhhist accounts of homosexuality and AIDS. Paper presented at Fifth International Conference on Thai Studies, July, School of Oriental and African Studies, London.

————. 1995. *Dear Uncle Go: Male Homosexuality in Thailand*. Bangkok: Bua Luang Books.

Japan Foundation for AIDS Prevention. 1994. *Statistics*. Tokyo: Ministry of Welfare.

Jenner, P. N. 1981. *A Chrestomathy of Pre-Angkorian Khmer II, Lexicon of the Dated Inscriptions*. Southeast Asia Paper, no. 20, Part 2, Southeast Asian Studies. Honolulu: Centre for Asian and Pacific Studies, University of Hawaii.

Jenness, V. 1993. *Making It Work: The Prostitutes' Rights Movement in Perspective*. New York: Walter de Gruyter.

Jiwani, Y. 1992. The exotic, the erotic and the dangerous: South Asian women in popular film. *Canadian Woman Studies/Cahiers de la femme* 13, no. 1: 43–46.

Jodha, N. 1988. Poverty debate in India: A minority view. *Economic and Political Weekly*, November 24, 21–28.

Jolly, M. 1992. "Illnatured-Comparisons"? Racism and relativism in European representations of ni-Vanuatu from Cook's second voyage. *History and Anthropology* 5, no. 3: 331–364.

————. 1993a. Lascivious ladies, beasts of burden and voyaging voyeurs: Representations of women from Cook's voyages in the Pacific. Paper presented at David Nichol Smith Seminar IX, Voyages and Beaches, Discovery and the Pacific, 1700–1840, 24–28 August, University of Auckland.

————. 1993b. Colonizing women: The maternal body and empire. In *Feminism and the Politics of Difference*, edited by S. Gunew and A. Yeatman, 103–127. Sydney: Allen and Unwin.

————. 1994. Introduction. In *Women's Difference: Sexuality and Maternity in Colonial and Postcolonial Discourses*, edited by Margaret Jolly. *The Australian Journal of Anthropology* 5, nos. 1 and 2: 1–10.

————. 1995. "Kastom" as commodity: The land dive and tourism in Vanuatu. In *Culture-Kastom-Tradition: Developing Cultural Policy in Melanesia*, edited by G. White and M. Lindstrom, 131–144. Suva: Institute of Pacific Studies, University of South Pacific.

————. 1996. Desire, difference and disease: Sexual and venereal exchanges on Cook's voyages in the Pacific. In *Exchanges*, edited by R. Gibson, 187–217. Sydney: Museum of Sydney.

————. n.d. Metropolitan liaisons. In *Engendering Colonialism: European Visions of Women in Vanuatu, 1606–1920*. Manuscript.

Jordan, W. 1968. *White Over Black*. New York: Norton.

Jumilla, L. T. 1993. Brunei beauties probed. *Philippine Daily Inquirer*, 5 August, 1, 10.

Kabbani, R. 1986. *Europe's Myths of the Orient*. Bloomington: Indiana University Press.

Kaminskas, G., and Smith, A. 1990. Brides or women? Female Filipino migration to Australia. Paper presented at the Second National Conference of the Australian Women's Studies Association, Melbourne.

Kammerer, C. A., and Symonds, P. V. 1992. Hill tribes endangered at Thailand's periphery. *Cultural Survival Quarterly* Fall: 23–25.

Kanato, M., and Rujkorankarn, D. 1994. Cultural factors in sexual behaviour, sexuality and sociocultural contexts in the spread of HIV in the Northeast Thailand. Paper presented at Workshop, Cultural Dimensions of AIDS Control and Care in Thailand, Chiangmai.

Kang, L. Hyun-Yi. 1993. The desiring of Asian female bodies: Interracial romance and cinematic subjection. *Visual Anthropology Review* 9, no. 1: 5–21.

Kaplan, M. 1989. *Luve ni wai* as the British saw it: Constructions of custom and disorder in colonial Fiji. *Ethnohistory* 36: 349–71.

———. 1995. *Neither Cargo Nor Cult: Ritual Politics and the Colonial Imagination in Fiji.* Durham, NC: Duke University Press.

———. n.d. From Jew to Roman: Imaging self and other in colonial Fiji. Manuscript.

Kaplan, M., and Kelly, J. D. 1994. Rethinking resistance: Dialogics of disaffection in colonial Fiji. *American Ethnologist* 21, no. 1: 123–151.

Kelly, J. D. 1989. Fear of culture: British regulation of Indian marriage in post-indenture Fiji. *Ethnohistory* 36: 372–391.

———. 1990. Discourse about sexuality and the end of indenture in Fiji: The making of counter-hegemonic discourse. *History and Anthropology* 5: 19–61.

———. 1991a. Appendix: Fiji Indians and the law, 1912. In *My Twenty-One Years in the Fiji Islands,* edited by T. Sanadhya, 154–210. Suva: Fiji Museum.

———. 1991b. *A Politics of Virtue: Hinduism, Sexuality and Countercolonial Discourse in Fiji.* Chicago: University of Chicago Press.

———. 1992. "Coolie" as a labour commodity: Race, sex, and European dignity in colonial Fiji. *Journal of Peasant Studies* 19: 246–267.

Kempton, M. 1992. A new colonialism. *New York Review of Books,* November 19, 39.

Kern, R. A. 1905. De kontroleurs en 't concubinaat. *Tijdschrift voor het Binnenlandsch Bestuur* 28: 1–6, 250–252.

Kerr, G. 1992. Review of "The Good Woman of Bangkok." *Cinema Papers* 86: 52–53.

Khin Thitsa. 1980. *Providence and Prostitution: Image and Reality for Women in Buddhist Thailand.* London: Change International Reports.

Khin Win Thin, Yu Yu Lwin, Naing Naing Myint, May Khin Soe. n.d. *A Study on Knowledge, Attitude, Practice and Behaviour (KAPB) of Commercial Sex Workers: Implications for HIV/AIDS.* Mimeograph. Yangon: Department of Health.

Kinsey, A. C., Pomeroy, W. B., and Martin, C. E. 1948. *Sexual Behavior in the Human Male.* Philadelphia: Saunders.

Kinsey, A. C., Pomeroy, W. B., Martin, C. E., and Gebhard, P. H. 1953. *Sexual Behavior in the Human Female.* Philadelphia: Saunders.

K. K. [pseud.] n.d. *Siamese-English Conversation Self-Taught.* Bangkok: n.p.

Kleiber, D. 1991. AIDS und (sex-)tourismus. In *AIDS und Tourismus,* edited by Niedersachsisches Sozialministerium, 1–28. Hanover: Edition AIDS 11.

Knapman, C. 1986. *White Women in Fiji, 1835–1930: The Ruin of Empire?* Sydney: Allen and Unwin.

Kohlbrugge, J. F. H. 1901. Prostitutie in Nederlandsch-Indie. *Indisch Genootschap,* Algemene vergadering van 19 Februari, 2–36.

Kondo, D. 1990. "M. Butterfly": Orientalism, gender and a critique of essentialist identity. *Cultural Critique* 16: 5–29.

Krich, J. 1989. Here come the brides: The blossoming business of imported love. In *Men's Lives,* edited by M. S. Kimmel and M. A. Messner, 382–392. New York: Macmillan.

Kristeva, J. 1991. *Strangers to Ourselves.* New York: Columbia University Press.

Kristof, L. 1959. The nature of frontiers and boundaries. *Annals, Association of American Geographers* 49: 269–82.

Kuaytaek, R. 1993. *Dogmouth Blues, Soulmates and Holistic Practices.* Bangkok: Toad Press.

Kulick, D., and Willson, M., eds. 1995. *Taboo: Sex, Identity and Erotic Subjectivity in Anthropological Fieldwork.* London and New York: Routledge.

Kumar, K. 1993. Civil society: An inquiry into the usefulness of an historical term. *British Journal of Sociology* 44, no. 3: 375–395.

LaCapra, D. 1989. History and psychoanalysis. In *Soundings in Critical Theory,* edited by D. LaCapra, 30–66. Ithaca: Cornell University Press.

Laclau, E. 1990. *New Reflections on the Revolution of our Time.* London: Verso.

Lacorte, G. A. 1993. Coalition of NGOs to oppose import-dependent export sector. *Sun Star Daily* 4 October, 218–232.

Lai Ah Eng. 1986. Peasants, proletarians and prostitutes: A preliminary investigation into the work of Chinese women in Colonial Malaya. Manuscript.

Lal, B. 1985a. Kunti's cry: Indentured women on Fiji plantations. *Indian Economic and Social History Review* 22: 55–71.

———. 1985b. Veil of dishonour: Sexual jealousy and suicide on Fiji plantations. *Journal of Pacific History* 20: 135–55.

Lambert, S. M. 1941. *A Doctor in Paradise.* London: J. M. Dent and Sons.

Landon, M. 1944. *Anna and the King of Siam.* New York: John Day and Co.

Laracy, E., and Laracy, H. 1977. Beatrice Grimshaw: Pride and prejudice in Papua. *Journal of Pacific History* 12, no. 3: 154–175.

Lash, S. 1984. Genealogy and the body: Foucault/Deleuze/Nietzsche. *Theory, Culture, Society* 2, no. 2: 1–17.

Latour, B. 1987. The powers of association. In *Power, Action and Belief: A New Sociology of Knowledge?* edited by J. Law, 264–280. Sociological Review Monograph, no. 32. London: Routledge.

———. 1992. *The Pasteurization of France.* Cambridge, MA: Harvard University Press.

Laya Women's Collective. 1993. Special issue. Prostitution: Old tale, new face. *Laya Feminist Quarterly* 2, no. 3: 56.

Leavitt, S. 1991. Sexual ideology and experience in a Papua New Guinea society. *Social Science and Medicine* 33, no. 8: 97–907.

Lee, L., and WEDPRO. 1992. *From Carriers to Communities: Alternative Employment, Economic Livelihood and Human Resource Development for Women in the Entertainment Industry.* Manila: Women's Education, Development, Productivity and Research Organisation (WEDPRO).

Leftwich, A. 1993. Governance, democracy and development in the Third World. *Third World Quarterly* 14, no. 3: 605–624.

Legal Foundation for AIDS Prevention. 1994. *What You Need to Know about AIDS: Basic Knowledge for Protection and Co-Existence.* Brochure. Tokyo: Japan Stop AIDS Fund.

Le Guin, U. 1992. *Dancing at the Edge of the World: Thoughts on Words, Women, Place.* London: Paladin.

Leonowens, A. 1870. *The English Governess at the Siamese Court: Being Recollections of Six Years in the Royal Palace at Bangkok.* London and Cambridge, MA: Trubner and Co.

———. 1873a. *The Romance of the Harem.* Boston: James R. Osgood and Co.

———. 1873b. *Siamese Harem Life.* London and Cambridge, MA: Trubner and Co.

Leslie, C. 1990. Scientific racism: Reflections in peer review, science and ideology. *Social Science and Medicine* 31, no. 8: 891–905.

Lett, L. 1945. *The Papuan Achievement*. Melbourne: Melbourne University Press.

Levitas, R. 1990. *The Concept of Utopia*. New York: Philip Allan.

Lewis, J. 1980. A boom Japan does not want. *Diliman Review* 28: 44–5.

Lindstrom, L., and White, G. M. 1990. *Island Encounters: Black and White Memories of the Pacific War*. Washington and London: Smithsonian Institution Press.

Lingis, A. 1994. *Foreign Bodies*. New York: Routledge.

Linnekin, J. 1990. *Sacred Queens and Women of Consequence: Rank, Gender and Colonialism in the Hawaiian Islands*. Ann Arbor: University of Michigan Press.

Lintner, B. 1990a. *The Rise and Fall of the Communist Party of Burma*. Ithaca: Cornell University Southeast Asia Programme.

———. 1990b. A fatal overdose: Civilians butchered in fighting between drug gangs. *Far Eastern Economic Review*, 3 June 1990: 26–7.

———. 1994. Plague without borders. *Far Eastern Economic Review* 157: 29, 26.

Litong, G. T., Espartero, J., Pinchay, N., Goyena, M., Ursua, E. and Reyes, S. n. d. Philippine laws and jurisprudence relevant to the AIDS/HIV problem. Manila.

Lock, M. 1980. *East Asian Medicine in Urban Japan: Varieties of Medical Experience*. Berkeley: University of California Press.

———. 1993. *Encounters with Aging: Mythologies of Menopause in Japan and North America*. Berkeley: University of California Press.

London Missionary Society. n.d. Reel 101. Archives, London Missionary Society.

Lutkehaus, N. C. 1989. "Excuse me, everything is not alright": On ethnography, film, and representation. An interview with filmmaker Dennis O'Rourke. *Cultural Anthropology* 4: 422–437.

Lutz, C. A., and Collins, J. L. 1993. *Reading National Geographic*. Chicago: University of Chicago Press.

Lyttleton, C. 1994a. Knowledge and meaning: The AIDS education campaign in rural northeast Thailand. *Social Science and Medicine* 38, no. 1: 135–146.

———. 1994b. The "Love Your Wife" disease: HIV/AIDS education and the construction of meaning in northeast Thailand. Ph.D. dissertation, Department of Anthropology, University of Sydney, Sydney.

MacCannell, D. 1994. Cannibal tours. In *Visualizing Theory: Selected Essays from V.A.R., 1990–1994*, edited by L. Taylor, 99–114. New York and London: Routledge.

McClintock, A. 1995. *Imperial Leather: Race, Gender and Sexuality in the Colonial Context*. New York and London: Routledge.

MacCormack, C., and Strathern, M. 1980. *Nature, Culture and Gender*. Cambridge: Cambridge University Press.

MacDougall, D. 1994. Whose story is it? In *Visualizing Theory: Selected Essays from V.A.R., 1990–1994*, edited by L. Taylor, 27–36. New York and London: Routledge.

McKenzie, N. F. 1991. *The Aids Reader: Social, Political and Ethical Issues*. New York: Penguin Group.

Mackie, V. 1988. "Division of labour: Multinational sex in Asia." In *The Japanese Trajectory: Modernisation and Beyond*, edited by G. McCormack and Y. Sugimoto. Cambridge: Cambridge University Press.

MacKinnon, C. A. 1987. *Feminism Unmodified: Discourses on Life and Law*. Cambridge, MA: Harvard University Press.

McMorran, N. V. 1984. Northern Thai ancestral cults: Authority and aggression. *Mankind* 14, no. 1: 308–314.

Malinowski, B. K. [1922] 1961. *Argonauts of the Western Pacific*. New York: E. P. Dutton.

————. 1927. *Sex and Repression in Savage Society*. London: Routledge and Kegan Paul.

————. 1929. *The Sexual Life of Savages in North Western Melanesia*. London: Routledge and Kegan Paul.

————. 1967. *A Diary in the Strict Sense of the Term*. New York: Harcourt, Brace and World.

Malleret, L. 1934. *L'Exotisme Indochinois et la Littérature Française*. Paris: Larose.

Manderson, L. 1992a. Maternal and child health in colonial Malaya. In *Women and Children First: International Maternal and Infant Welfare, 1870–1950*, edited by V. Fildes, L. Marks, and H. Marland, 154–177. London: Routledge.

————. 1992b. Public sex performance in Patpong and explorations of the edges of imagination. *Journal of Sex Research* 29, no. 4: 451–475.

————. 1994. Drugs, sex and social science: Social science research and health policy in Australia. *Social Science and Medicine* 39, no. 9: 1275–1286.

————. 1995. The pursuit of pleasure and the sale of sex. In *Sexual Nature/Sexual Culture: Theorizing Sexuality from the Perspective of Pleasure*, edited by P. R. Abramson and S. D. Pinkerton, 305–329. Chicago: University of Chicago Press.

————. 1996. *Sickness and the State: Health and Illness in Colonial Malaya, 1870–1940*. Cambridge and Melbourne: Cambridge University Press.

Manit Manitcharoen. 1983 (2526) *Photjananukrom Thai* [Thai dictionary]. Bangkok: Ruam-san.

Mann, J., Tarantola, D., and Netter, T., eds. 1992. *AIDS in the World*. Cambridge, MA: Harvard University Press.

Mannoni, O. 1950. *Prospero et Caliban: Psychologie de la Colonisation*. Paris: Seuil.

Marcus, G. E. 1994. The modernist sensibility in recent ethnographic writing and the cinematic metaphor of montage. In *Visualizing Theory: Selected Essays from V.A.R., 1990–1994*, edited by L. Taylor, 37–53. New York and London: Routledge.

Marcus, J. 1992. *A World of Difference: Islam and Gender Hierarchy in Turkey*. Women in Asia Publications Series. Sydney: Allen and Unwin.

Marcuse, H. 1955. *Eros and Civilization*. Boston: Beacon Press.

Mason, P. 1958. *Birth of a Dilemma: The Conquest and Settlement of Rhodesia*. London: Oxford University Press.

Masters, W. H., and Johnson, V. E. 1966. *Human Sexual Response*. Boston: Little, Brown.

Matthews, J. 1992. The "present" moment in sexual politics. In *Rethinking Sex: Social Theory and Sexuality Research*, edited by R. Connell and G. Dowsett, 117–130. Melbourne: Melbourne University Press.

Max-Neef, M., with Elizade, A., and Hopenhayn, M. 1991. *Human Scale Development: Conception, Application and Further Reflections*. New York: The Apex Press.

Mayuree, R. 1990. When children are sold as sex slaves. *Bangkok Post*. 27 December.

Mead, M. 1923. *Coming of Age in Samoa*. New York: Morrow.

Meggitt, M. 1964. Male-female relationships in the highlands of Australian New Guinea. *American Anthropologist* 66, no. 4: 204–224.

Melanesian Mission. 1904. *Handbook of the Melanesian Mission*. Auckland: Phoenix Press.

Mellman, B. 1992. *Women's Orients: English Women and the Middle East, 1718–1918: Sexuality, Religion and Work*. Ann Arbor: University of Michigan Press.

Michener, J. 1947. *Tales of the South Pacific*. New York: Macmillan.

Mill, S. 1991. *Discourses of Difference: An Analysis of Women's Travel Writing and Colonialism*. London: Routledge.

Miller, A. 1992. *The Ancestor Game*. Melbourne: Penguin.

Millett, K. 1972. *Sexual Politics*. London: Abacus.

Ming, H. 1983. Barracks-concubinage in the Indies, 1887–1920. *Indonesia* 35: 65–93.

Ministry for Welfare and the Japan Foundation for AIDS Prevention. 1993a. *What Is AIDS? Correct Knowledge and Practice Will Protect You*. Brochure. Tokyo: Ministry for Welfare and the Japan Foundation for AIDS Prevention.

————. 1993b. *The AIDS Reader*. Brochure. Tokyo: Ministry of Welfare and the Japan Foundation for AIDS Prevention.

Mintz, S. 1985. *Sweetness and Power*. New York: Viking.

Miralao, V. A., Carlos, C. O., and Santos, A. F. 1990. *Women Entertainers in Angeles and Olongapo: A Survey Report*. Manila: Women's Education, Development, Productivity and Research Organisation (WEDPRO) and Katipunan ng Kababaihan Para Sa Kalayaan (KALAYAAN).

Mitchell, T. 1988. *Colonising Egypt*. Berkeley: University of California Press.

————. 1991. The limits of the state: Beyond statist approaches and their critics. *American Political Science Review* 85, no. 1: 77–96.

Mohanty, C. 1988. Under western eyes: Feminist scholarship and colonial discourses. *Feminist review* 30: 61–88.

Mojares, R. B. 1991. The formation of a city: Trade and politics in nineteenth-century Cebu. *Philippine Quarterly of Culture and Society* 19: 288–95.

Monckton, C. A. W. 1921. *Some Experiences of a New Guinea Resident Magistrate, First Series*. London: John Lane, The Bodley Head.

Mongaya, E. N. 1993a. NGOs coalition sees massive land conversions with setting up of RIC. *Sun Star Daily*, 5 October.

————. 1993b. NGO sector divided on response to RICs, Philippines 2000. *Sun Star Daily*, 4 October.

Moore, C. 1993. *Asia Hand*. Bangkok: White Lotus.

Morgan, S. L. 1991. Introduction. In *The Romance of the Harem*, edited by S. Morgan. Charlottesville and London: University Press of Virginia.

Morita, K., and Saskia, S. 1994. The new illegal immigrants in Japan, 1980–1992. *International Migration Review* 28, no. 1: 153–163.

Morris, R. C. 1994. Three sexes and four sexualities: Redressing the discourses on gender and sexuality in contemporary Thailand. *Positions* 2, no. 1: 15–43.

Moselina, L. M. 1979. Olongapo's rest and recreation industry: A sociological analysis of institutionalised prostitution with implications for a grassroots-oriented sociology. *Philippine Sociological Review* 27: 176–188.

Mosse, G. L. 1985. *Nationalism and Sexuality: Middle-Class Morality and Sexual Norms in Modern Europe*. Madison: University of Wisconsin Press.

Mouffe, C. 1993. *The Return of the Political*. London: Verso.

Muecke, M. A. 1992. Mother sold food, daughter sells her body: The cultural continuity of prostitution. *Social Science and Medicine* 35, no. 7: 891–901.

Mulvey, L. 1989. *Visual and Other Pleasures*. Basingstoke: Macmillan.

Murray, H. J. 1912. *Papua or British New Guinea*. London: T. Fisher Unwin.

————. 1925. *Papua of Today, or an Australian Colony in the Making*. London: P. S. King and Son.

Murray, S. O., ed. 1992. *Oceanic Homosexualities*. New York: Garland Publishing.

Murray, A., and Robinson, T. 1996. Minding your peers and queers: Female sex workers in the AIDS discourse in Australia and South-east Asia. *Gender, Place and Culture*, 3, no. 1: 43–59.

Myo Thet Htoon, Myat Thu, Thein Myint, Min Thwe and Saw Edward Zan. n.d. *A Study on the Social and Behavioural Pattern of Commercial Sex Workers Returning from Thailand*. Mimeograph. Yangon: Department of Health.

Nagata, J. 1984. *The Reflowering of Islam: Modern Religious Radicals and Their Roots*. Berkeley and Vancouver: University of California Press.

Nancy, J-L. 1993. *The Birth to Presence*. Translated by B. Holmes. Stanford: Stanford University Press.

Nandy, Ashis. 1983. *The Intimate Enemy: Loss and Recovery of Self under Colonialism*. New York: Oxford University Press.

Nelson, R. 1985. Strategies for change, from the Australian Prostitutes Collective. In *Being a Prostitute*, edited by R. Perkins and G. Bennett, 279–287. Sydney: George Allen and Unwin.

Neumann, A. L. 1979. "Hospitality girls" in the Philippines, *Southeast Asia Chronicle-Pacific Research* 66/7, no. 5: 18–23.

Newman, K. 1987. "And wash the Ethiop white": Feminist and the monstrous Othello. In *Shakespeare Reproduced: The Text in History and Ideology*, edited by J. E. Howard and M. F. O'Connor, 143–162. New York and London: Methuen.

Nichols, B. 1994. The ethnographer's tale. In *Visualizing Theory: Selected Essays from V.A.R., 1990–1994*, edited by L. Taylor, 60–83. New York and London: Routledge.

Norbeck, E., and Lock, M. 1987. *Health, Illness and Medical Care in Japan: Cultural and Social Dimensions*. Honolulu: University of Hawaii Press.

Noyes, J. K. 1992. *Colonial Space: Spatiality in the Discourse of German South West Africa, 1884–1915*. Chur, Switzerland: Harwood Academic Press.

Oakley, A. 1972. *Sex, Gender and Society*. London: Maurice Temple Smith.

Oaks, L. 1994. Fetal spirithood and fetal personhood: The cultural construction of abortion in Japan. *Women's Studies International Forum* 17, no. 5: 511–523.

Obeyesekere, G. 1992. *The Apotheosis of Captain Cook*. Princeton: Princeton University Press.

O'Dwyer, C. 1995. American identity across the Pacific: Culture, race and sexuality in *South Pacific* and tales from the South. *Antithesis, A Postgraduate Journal of Interdisciplinary Studies* 7, no. 2: 123–137.

Odzer, C. 1994. *Patpong Sisters*. New York: Blue Moon Books/Arcade Publishing.

Oliver, D. 1974. *Ancient Tahitian Society*. 3 volumes. Canberra and Honolulu: Australian National University/University of Hawaii Press.

O'Merry, R. 1990. *My Wife in Bangkok*. Berkeley: Asia Press.

O'Neill, E. 1989. (Re)presentations of eros: Exploring female sexual agency. In *Gender/Body/Knowledge: Feminist Reconstructions of Being and Knowing*, edited by A. M. Jaggar and S. R. Bordo, 68–91. New Brunswick: Rutgers University Press.

Ong, A. 1990. State versus Islam: Malay families, women's bodies, and the body politic in Malaysia. *American Ethnologist* 17, no. 8: 258–276.

O'Rourke, D. (Writer and Director). 1991. *The Good Woman of Bangkok* (See Filmography).

Ortner, S. B. 1974. Is female to male as nature is to culture? In *Woman, Culture and Society*, edited by M. Z. Rosaldo and L. Lamphere, 67–88. Stanford: Stanford University Press.

Ortner, S. B., and Whitehead, H. 1981. *Sexual Meanings: The Cultural Construction of Gender and Sexuality*. Cambridge: Cambridge University Press.

Orwell, G. 1950. *Shooting an Elephant and Other Essays*. London: Secker and Warburg.

O'Shaughnessy, T. 1994. Beyond the Fragments: HIV/AIDS and Poverty. *Issues in Global Development*, 1 November. Melbourne: World Vision Australia.

Panos, 1992. *The Hidden Cost of AIDS: The Challenge of HIV to Development*. London: The Panos Institute.

Papua. 1908a. *The Parliament of the Commonwealth of Australia, Territory of Papua Annual Report for the Year 1906–7*. Melbourne: A. J. Kemp, Government Printer.

———. 1908b. *The Parliament of the Commonwealth of Australia, Territory of Papua Annual Report for the Year 1907–8*. Melbourne: A. J. Kemp, Government Printer.

———. 1909. *The Parliament of the Commonwealth of Australia, Territory of Papua Annual Report for the Year 1908–9*. Melbourne: A. J. Kemp, Government Printer.

———. 1911. *The Parliament of the Commonwealth of Australia, Territory of Papua Annual Report for the Year 1910–11*. Melbourne: A. J. Kemp, Government Printer.

———. 1912. *The Parliament of the Commonwealth of Australia, Territory of Papua Annual Report for the Year 1911–12*. Melbourne: A. J. Mullet, Government Printer.

———. 1914. *The Parliament of the Commonwealth of Australia, Territory of Papua Annual Report for the Year 1913–14*. Melbourne: A. J. Mullet, Government Printer.

———. 1920. *The Parliament of the Commonwealth of Australia, Territory of Papua Annual Report for the Year 1918–19*. Melbourne: A. J. Mullet, Government Printer.

———. 1921. *The Parliament of the Commonwealth of Australia, Territory of Papua Annual Report for the Year 1919–20*. Melbourne: A. J. Mullet, Government Printer.

———. 1922. *The Parliament of the Commonwealth of Australia, Territory of Papua Annual Report for the Year 1920–21*. Melbourne: A. J. Mullet, Government Printer.

———. 1923. *The Parliament of the Commonwealth of Australia, Territory of Papua Annual Report for the Year 1921–22*. Melbourne: A. J. Mullet, Government Printer.

———. 1924. *The Parliament of the Commonwealth of Australia, Territory of Papua Annual Report for the Year 1922–23*. Melbourne: H. J. Green, Government Printer.

———. 1925. *The Parliament of the Commonwealth of Australia, Territory of Papua Annual Report for the Year 1923–24*. Melbourne: H. J. Green, Government Printer.

———. 1926. *The Parliament of the Commonwealth of Australia, Territory of Papua Annual Report for the Year 1924–25*. Melbourne: H. J. Green, Government Printer.

———. 1927. *The Parliament of the Commonwealth of Australia, Territory of Papua Annual Report for the year 1925–26*. Melbourne: H. J. Green, Government Printer.

———. 1928. *The Parliament of the Commonwealth of Australia, Territory of Papua Annual Report for the year 1926–27*. Canberra: H. J. Green, Government Printer.

———. 1934–35. *The Parliament of the Commonwealth of Australia, Territory of Papua Annual Report for the Year 1934–35*. Canberra: L. F. Johnston, Government Printer.

———. 1936–37. *The Parliament of the Commonwealth of Australia, Territory of Papua Annual Report for the Year 1935–6*. Canberra: L. F. Johnston, Government Printer.

Parker, R. 1987. Acquired Immunodeficiency Syndrome in Brazil. *Medical Anthropology Quarterly* 1, no. 2: 155–75.

Pasuk Phongpaichit. 1982. *From Peasant Girls to Bangkok Masseuses. Women, Work and Development*, no. 2. Geneva: International Labour Office.

Patton, C. 1990. *Inventing AIDS*. London: Routledge.

Peltier, A. 1991. *Pathamamulamuli: The Origin of the World in the Lan Na Tradition*. Chiang Mai: Suriwong Book Centre.

Perkins, R. 1991. *Working Girls: Prostitutes, Their Life and Social Control*. Canberra: Australian Institute of Criminology.

Pheterson, G., ed. 1989. *A Vindication of the Rights of Whores*. Seattle: Seal.

Piprell, C. 1989. *Bangkok Knights.* Bangkok: Editions Duang Kamol.

———. 1991. *Kicking Dogs.* Bangkok: Editions Duang Kamol.

———. 1993. *Bangkok Old Hand.* Bangkok: Post Books.

Porter, D. 1995a. *Wheeling and Dealing: HIV/AIDS and Development in Eastern Shan State Myanmar.* UNDP HIV and Development Issues Papers. New York: United Nations Development Program.

———. 1995b. Scenes from childhood: The homesickness of development discourses. In *The Power of Development,* edited by J. Crush, 63–86. London: Routledge.

Porter, D., Allen, B., and Thompson, G. 1991. *Development in Practice: Paved with Good Intentions.* London: Routledge.

Porter, R. 1990. The exotic as erotic: Captain Cook at Tahiti. In *Exoticism in the Enlightenment,* edited by G. S. Rousseau and R. Porter, 117–144. Manchester and New York: Manchester University Press.

Powdermaker, H. 1933. *Life in Lesu: The study of a Melanesian Society in New Ireland.* London: Williams and Norgate.

Pratt, M. 1986. Scratches on the face of the country or, what Mr. Barrow saw in the land of the Bushmen. In *Race, Writing and Difference,* edited by W. Sachs, 138–62. Chicago: Chicago University Press.

———. 1992. *Imperial Eyes: Travel Writings and Transculturation.* London and New York: Routledge.

Price, G. 1939. *White Settlers in the Tropics.* New York: American Geographical Society.

Pringle, R. 1992. Absolute sex? Unpacking the sexuality/gender relationship. In *Rethinking Sex: Social Theory and Sexuality Research,* edited by R. Connell and G. Dowsett, 76–101. Melbourne: Melbourne University Press.

Rahmena, M. 1992. Poverty. In *The Development Dictionary: A Guide to Knowledge as Power,* edited by W. Sachs, 158–176. London: Zed Books.

Rajchman, J. 1985. *Michel Foucault: The Freedom of Philosophy.* New York: Columbia.

Ralston, C. 1988. "Polyandry," "pollution," "prostitution": The problems of Eurocentrism and androcentrism in Polynesian studies. In *Crossing Boundaries, Feminism and the Critique of Knowledges,* edited by B. E. Caine, E. A. Grosz, and M. de Lepervanche, 71–81. Sydney: Allen and Unwin.

———. 1990. Deceptive dichotomies, private/public and nature/culture: gender relations in Tonga in the early contact period. *Australian Feminist Studies* 12 (Summer): 65–82.

Ram, K. 1993. The female body of puberty: Tamil linguistic and ritual perspectives on theories of "sexuality." Paper presented at conference, Human Research Centre, Australian National University.

Ram, K., and Jolly, M., eds. In press. *Maternities and Modernities: Colonial and Post-Colonial Experiences in Asia and the Pacific.* Cambridge: Cambridge University Press.

Ratchabanditthayasathan (Royal Institute). 1982 (2525). *Photjananukrom Chabap Ratchabanditthayasathan* [Royal Institute Edition Dictionary]. Bangkok: Royal Institute.

Rawick, G. 1972. *The American Slave: A Composite Autobiography.* Westport, CT.: Greenwood Publishing.

Reid, E. 1993. *Approaching the HIV Epidemic.* Mimeograph. New York: United Nations Development Programme.

Remedios AIDS Foundation 1993. AIDS Profiteering. *Remedios Newsletter* 1, no. 3: 2.

Rentoul, A. 1931. Physiological paternity and the Trobrianders. *Man* 31: 152–154.

Reyes, L. I. 1995. *Made in Paradise: Hollywood's Films of Hawaii and the South Seas.* Honolulu: Mutual Publishing.

Reynolds, C. J. 1994. Predicaments of modern Thai history. *South East Asia Research* 2, no. 1: 64–90.

Reynolds, J. 1992 [1956]. *A Woman of Bangkok.* Bangkok: Editions Duang Kamol.

Richter, L. K. 1989. *The Politics of Tourism in Asia.* Honolulu: University of Hawaii Press.

Robbins, B. 1992. Colonial discourse: A paradigm and its discontents. *Victorian Studies* 35, no. 2 (Winter): 209–214.

Roberts, S. H. 1927. *Population Problems of the Pacific.* London: George Routledge and Sons.

Roediger, D. 1991. *Wages of Whiteness.* London: Verso.

Rogin, M. 1971. Liberal society and the Indian question. *Politics and Society* 1, no. 3 (May): 269–312.

———. 1994. "Democracy and burnt cork": The end of blackface and the beginning of civil rights. *Representations* 46 (Spring): 1–34.

Rosca, N. 1995. Participant observer. Review of C. Odzer, "Patpong Sisters." *The Women's Review of Books* 12, no. 6: 17.

Rose, N., and Miller, P. 1992. Political power beyond the state: Problematics of government. *British Journal of Sociology* 43, no. 2: 173–205.

Rubin, G. 1975. The traffic of women: Notes on the political economy of sex. In *Toward an Anthropology of Women,* edited by R. Reiter, 157–210. New York: Monthly Review Press.

———. 1992 [1984]. Thinking sex: Notes for a radical theory of the politics of sexuality. In *Pleasure and Danger: Exploring Female Sexuality,* edited by C. S. Vance, 267–283. London: Pandora Press.

Rule, P. 1987. Prostitution in Calcutta, 1860–1940: The pattern of recruitment. In *Class, Ideology and Women in Asian Societies,* edited by L. Manderson and G. Pearson, 65–80. Hong Kong: Asian Research Service.

Rushton, J. P., and Bogaert, A. F. 1989. Population differences in susceptibility to AIDS: An evolutionary analysis. *Social Science and Medicine* 28, no. 12: 1211–1200.

Ryan, K. 1991. Sex, sin and work: Changing perspectives on women, development and prostitution with a focus on Filipinas. M. A. thesis, Flinders University, Adelaide.

Sahlins, M. 1988. Cosmologies of capitalism: The trans-Pacific sector of "The World System." *Proceedings of the British Academy* 74: 1–51.

———. 1995. *How "Natives" Think: About Captain Cook, For Example.* Chicago: University of Chicago Press.

Said, E. W. 1978. *Orientalism.* London: Penguin.

Saikaku, I. 1990. *The Great Mirror of Male Love.* Translated by P. G. Sharlow. Stanford: Stanford University Press.

Sanadhya, T. 1991. *My Twenty-One Years in the Fiji Islands.* Suva: Fiji Museum.

Santos, A. F. 1992. Gathering the dust: The bases issue in the Philippines. In *Let the Good Times Roll,* edited by S. Sturdevant and B. Stoltzfus, 32–44. New York: The New Press.

Savage, A. 1996. "Vectors" and "protectors": Women and HIV/AIDS in the Lao People's Democratic Republic. In *Maternity and Reproductive Health in Asian Societies,* edited by P. L. Rice and L. Manderson. Chur, Switzerland: Harwood Academic Press.

Sawaengdee, Y., and Isarapakdee, P. 1991. *Ethnographic Study on Long-Haul Truck Drivers for Risk of HIV Infection.* Mimeograph. Bangkok: Institute for Population and Social Research, Mahidol University.

Schmitter, P. 1985. Neo-corporatism and the state. In *The Political Economy of Corporatism,* edited by W. Grant, 1–31. Cambridge: Cambridge University Press.

Schneider, B. 1992. Popular theatre in northern Thailand. In *A Northern Miscellany,* edited by Geoffrey Walton, 187–202. Chiang Mai: Silkworm Books.

Scott, J. 1987. *Weapons of the Weak: Everday Forms of Peasant Resistance.* New Haven: Yale University Press.

Segal, L. 1994. *Straight Sex: The Politics of Pleasure.* London: Virago.

Seidel, G. 1993. The competing discourses of HIV/AIDS in Sub-Saharan Africa: Discourses of rights and empowerment vs. discourses of control and exclusion. *Social Science and Medicine* 36, no. 3: 175–194.

Seidler, V. 1987. Reason, desire and male sexuality. In *The Cultural Construction of Sexuality,* edited by P. Caplan, 82–112. London: Routledge.

Shapin, S. 1994. *A Social History of Truth.* Chicago: University of Chicago Press.

Sheridan, A. 1980. *Michel Foucault: The Will to Truth.* Routledge: London and New York.

Shohat, E., and Stam, R. 1994. *Unthinking Eurocentrism, Multiculturalism and the Media.* London: Routledge.

Shore, B. 1981. Sexuality and gender in Samoa: Conceptions and missed conceptions. In *Sexual Meanings: The Cultural Construction of Gender and Sexuality,* edited by S. B. Ortner and H. Whitehead, 192–215. Cambridge and New York: Cambridge University Press.

Shrage, L. 1992. Is sexual desire raced?: The social meaning of interracial prostitution. *Journal of Social Philosophy* 23, no. 1: 42–45.

Silverman, K. 1989. White skin, brown masks: The double mimesis, or With Lawrence in Arabia. *Differences* 1, no. 3: 3–54.

Simon, S. 1991. China and Southeast Asia: Suspicion and hope. *Journal of East Asian Affairs* 5, no. 1: 195.

Singh, B. 1984. *My Father's Land: Fiji.* New Delhi: Tamavua Enterprises.

Smith, A., and Kaminskas, G. 1992. Female Filipino migration to Australia: An overview. Paper presented at the Fourth International Philippine Studies Conference, 1–3 July, Canberra.

Smith, B. 1985 [1960]. *European Vision and the South Pacific.* 2d ed. Sydney: Harper and Row.

———. 1992. *Imagining the Pacific: In the Wake of the Cook Voyages.* Carlton: Melbourne University Press at the Miegunyah Press.

Smith, H. E. 1971. Thai-American intermarriage in Thailand. *International Journal of Sociology of the Family* 1: 127–136.

Smith, M. 1991. *Burma: Insurgency and the Politics of Ethnicity.* London: Zed Books.

Smithies, M. 1993. *Bight of Bangkok.* Singapore: Heinemann Asia.

Sone, S. 1992. The Karayuki-san of Asia, 1868–1938: The role of prostitutes overseas in Japanese economic and social development. *Review of Indonesian and Malayan Affairs* 26, no. 2: 44–62.

Sontag, S. 1989. *AIDS and Its Metaphors.* New York: Farrar, Straus & Giroux.

Spencer, S. 1992. Illegal migrant workers in Japan. *International Migration Review* 26, nos. 3–4: 754–805.

Spencer, M. 1964. *Doctor's Wife in Papua.* London: Robert Hale.

Spiro, M. 1977. *Kinship and Marriage in Burma.* Berkeley: University of California Press.

Spivak, G. C. 1987. *In Other Worlds: Essays in Cultural Politics.* New York: Methuen.

———. 1988. Can the subaltern speak?. In *Marxism and the Interpretation of Culture,* edited by G. Nelson and L. Grossberg, 271–313. Urbana: University of Illinois Press.

Stacey, J. 1994. *Star Gazing: Hollywood Cinema and Female Spectatorship.* London and New York: Routledge.

Stamford, J., ed. 1977. *Spartacus 1977 International Gay Guide.* 7th ed. Amsterdam: Spartacus.

Steinberg, D. 1990. International rivalries in Burma: The rise of economic competition. *Asian Survey* 30 (June): 587–601.

———. 1993. Myanmar as nexus: Sino-Indian rivalries on the frontier. *Terrorism* 16: 1–8.

Stimpson, C. R., and Person, E. S., eds. 1980. *Women: Sex and Sexuality.* Chicago: University of Chicago Press.

Stoler, A. 1989. Rethinking colonial categories: European communities and the boundaries of rule. *Comparative Studies of Society and History* 31, no. 1: 134–61.

———. 1991. Carnal knowledge and imperial power: Matrimony, race, and morality in colonial Asia. In *Gender at the Crossroads: Feminist Anthropology in the Postmodern Era,* edited by M. de Leonardo, 51–101. Berkeley: University of California Press.

———. 1992. Sexual Affronts and Racial Frontiers. *Comparative Studies in Society and History* 34, no. 2: 514–51.

———. 1995. *Race and the Education of Desire: Foucault's History of Sexuality and the Colonial Order of Things.* Durham: Duke University Press.

Stoller, R. 1968. *Sex and Gender.* London: Hogarth Press.

Stoltzfus, B., and Sturdevant, S. 1990. From Samar to the Seventh Fleet: Women's experiences of sexual labour in Olongapo. In *Critical Decade: Prospects for Democracy in the Philippines in the 1990s,* edited by D. Flamiano and D. Goertzen, 137–142. Berkeley: Philippine Resource Centre, Center for Southeast Asian Studies, University of California.

Strathern, A. 1994. Keeping the body in mind. *Social Anthropology* 2, no. 1: 43–53.

Strathern, M. 1981. Self-interest and the social good: Some implications of Hagen gender imagery. In *Sexual Meanings: The Cultural Construction of Gender and Sexuality,* edited by S. B. Ortner and H. Whitehead, 166–191. Cambridge: Cambridge University Press.

———, ed. 1987. *Dealing with Inequality: Analysing Gender Relationships in Melanesia and Beyond.* Cambridge: Cambridge University Press.

———. 1988. *The Gender of the Gift: Problems with Women and Problems with Society in Melanesia.* Berkeley: University of California Press.

———. In press. The mediation of emotions. In *Conflict and Control in the New Guinea Highlands,* edited by W. Wormsley.

Stratz, C. H. 1897. *De Vrouwen op Java: Eene Gynaecologische Studie.* Amsterdam: Scheltema and Holkemas; Samarang: G. C. T. van Dorp.

Sturdevant, S. P., and Stoltzfus, B. 1992. *Let the Good Times Roll: Prostitution and the U.S. Military in Asia.* New York: The New Press.

Sukanya Hantrakul. 1983. Prostitution in Thailand. In *Women, Aid and Development,* edited by L. Melville, 61–63. Proceedings of a Workshop Co-sponsored by Women and Development Network of Australia, Australian Council for Overseas Aid, and Development Studies Centre of the Australian National University. Canberra: Women and Development Network of Australia.

————. 1984. Dutiful daughters on society's lower rungs. *Far Eastern Economic Review,* 5 (January): 39–40.

————. 1988. Prostitution in Thailand. In *Development and Displacement: Women in Southeast Asia,* edited by G. Chandler, N. Sullivan, and J. Branson, 115–136. Monash Papers on Southeast Asia, no. 18. Clayton, Victoria: Centre of Southeast Asian Studies, Monash University.

Suleri, S. 1992. *The Rhetoric of English India.* Chicago: University of Chicago Press.

Sullivan, B. 1994. Rethinking prostitution. Paper presented at the Women's Studies Seminar, 20 May, Australian National University, Canberra.

Talikala. 1993. *A Comprehensive Survey on Davao City's Entertainment Industry and the Hospitality Women.* Davao: Talikala .

Tan, M., de Leon, A., Stoltzfus, B., and O'Donnell, C. 1989. AIDS as a political issue: Working with the sexually prostituted in the Philippines. *Community Development Journal* 24, no. 3: 186–193.

Tapales, P. D. 1988. The commercial chain of prostitution. *Philippine Currents* 3: 9–11.

————. 1990. Women, migration, and the mail-order bride phenomenon: Focus on Australia. *Philippine Journal of Public Administration* 34, no. 4: 311–312.

Tasker, Y. 1993. *Spectacular Bodies: Gender, Genre and the Action Cinema.* London and New York: Routledge.

Taussig, M. 1987. *Shamanism, Colonialism, and the Wild Man.* Chicago: University of Chicago Press.

————. 1992. *The Nervous System.* London: Routledge.

Teaiwa, T. K. 1994. Bikinis and other s/pacific n/oceans. *The Contemporary Pacific* 6, no. 1: 87–109.

Thanprasertsuk, S.,, and Sirprapasiri, T. 1991. Probability of HIV acquisition from HIV-exposed sex service prostitutes, Chiang Mai, June—August 1989. *Thai AIDS Journal* 3, no. 2: 45–53.

Thomas, N. 1994a. *Colonialism's Culture: Anthropology, Travel and Government.* Oxford: Polity Press.

————. 1994b. Licensed curiosity: Cook's Pacific voyages. In *The Cultures of Collecting,* edited by J. Elsner and R. Cardinal, 116–136, 281–282. London: Reaktion Books.

————. 1995a. *Oceanic Art.* London: Thames and Hudson.

————. 1995b. *From Exhibit to Exhibitionism.* Paper presented at conference, Representing the Other, 2–6 May, Neiderswald, Germany.

Thrift, N.J. 1983. On the determination of social action in space and time. *Environment and Planning. D. Society and Space* 1, no. 1: 23–57.

Tiffany, S., and Adams, K. 1985. *The Myth of the Wild Woman.* Cambridge: Schenkman.

Tinney, J. n. d. Diary of Miss J. Tinney of the Methodist mission, British New Guinea, 1892–1902. MS. 633, Pacific Manuscript Bureau. Research School of Pacific Studies, Australian National University, Canberra.

Todorov, T. 1984. *The Conquest of America.* New York: Harper and Row.

Torgovnick, M. 1991. *Gone Primitive: Savage Intellects, Modern Lives.* Chicago: University of Chicago Press.

Treichler, P. A. 1988. AIDS, homophobia, and biomedical discourse: An epidemic of signification. In *AIDS: Cultural Analysis/Cultural Activism,* edited by D. Crimp, 31–70. Cambridge, MA, and London: MIT Press and October Magazine.

————. 1992a. AIDS, HIV and the cultural construction of reality. In *The Time of AIDS:*

Social Analysis, Theory and Method, edited by G. Herdt and S. Lindenbaum, 65–100. London: Methuen.

————. 1992b. AIDS and HIV infection in the Third World: A First World chronicle. In *AIDS: The Making of a Chronic Disease,* edited by E. Fee and D. Fox, 377–412. Berkeley: University of California Press.

Trumbach, R. 1991. Sex, gender, and sexual identity in modern culture: Male sodomy and female prostitution in enlightenment London. *Journal of the History of Sexuality* 2, no. 2: 186–203.

Truong, V. 1990. *Sex, Money and Morality: Prostitution and Tourism in Southeast Asia.* London: Zed Books.

Turkel, S. 1992. *Psychoanalytic Politics: Jacques Lacan and Freud's French Revolution.* New York: Guilford Press.

Turner, S., and Factor, R. 1994. *Max Weber: The Lawyer as Social Thinker.* New York: Routledge.

Turner, V. 1967. *The Forest of Symbols: Aspects of Ndembu Ritual.* Ithaca and London: Cornell University Press.

USDEA (United States Drug Eradication Agency) 1993. *Results of Early 1993 Opium Yield Survey and Poppy Cultivation Estimates,* 7 September. Mimeograph. Washington DC.: USDEA.

Valdiserri, R. O., Arene, V. C., Proctor, D., and Bonati, F. A. 1989. The relationship between women's attitudes about condoms and their use: Implications for condom promotion programs. *American Journal of Public Health* 79: 499–500.

Valeri, V. 1985. *Kingship and Sacrifice, Ritual and Society in Ancient Hawaii.* Chicago: University of Chicago Press.

Vance, C. S., ed. 1984. *Pleasure and Danger: Exploring Female Sexuality.* New York: Routledge and Kegan Paul.

————. 1989. Social construction theory: Problems in the history of sexuality. In *Homosexuality, Which Homosexuality,* edited by A. van Kooten Niekerk and T. van der Meer, 13–34. Amsterdam: An Dekker/Schorer.

————. 1991. Anthropology rediscovers sexuality: A theoretical comment. *Social Science and Medicine* 33, no. 8: 875–884.

Vance, C. S., and Snitow, A. B. 1984. Towards a conversation about sex in feminism: A modest proposal. *Signs* 10, no. 11: 126–135.

Vicinus, M. 1982. Sexuality and power: A review of current work in the history of sexuality. *Feminist Studies* 8, no. 1: 136.

Villamor, M. S. 1993. Jica urges Cebu to link up with Asian tigers for FDIs. *Sun Star Daily,* 10 November, D1, D3.

Viswanathan, G. 1990. *Masks of Conquest: Literary Study and British Rule in India.* London: Faber and Faber.

Vrettos, A. 1995. *Somatic Fictions: Imagining Illness in Victorian Culture.* Stanford: Stanford University Press.

Wahnschafft, R. 1982. Formal and informal tourism sectors: A case study in Pattaya, Thailand. *Annals of Tourism Research* 9: 429–451.

Walker, D., and Ehrlich R. S., eds. 1992. *"Hello My Big Big Honey!" Love Letters to Bangkok Bar Girls and Their Revealing Interviews.* Bangkok: Dragon Dance Publications.

Walker, R. 1984. The territorial state and the theme of Gulliver. *International Journal* 39: 529–52.

Walkowitz, J. 1980. *Prostitution and Victorian Society: Women, Class and the State*. Cambridge: Cambridge University Press.

Wall, D. R. 1983. Filipino brides: Slaves or marriage partners?—A further comment. *Australian Journal of Social Issues* 18, no. 1: 217–220.

Wallace, L. 1993. Too darned hot: Sexual contact in the Sandwich Islands. Paper presented to David Nichol Smith Seminar IX, Voyages and Beaches, Discovery and the Pacific, 1700–1840, 24–28 August, University of Auckland.

Warren, J. F. 1993. *Ah-Ku and Karayuki-san: Prostitution in Singapore, 1870–1940*. New York: Oxford University Press.

Watney, S. 1989a. Missionary positions. *Critical Quarterly* 30: 1.

———. 1989b. AIDS, language and the Third World. In *Taking Liberties: AIDS and Cultural Politics*, edited by E. Carter and S. Watney, 183–192. London: Serpent's Tale, in association with ICA.

———. 1993a. Emergent sexual identities and HIV/AIDS. In *AIDS: Facing the Second Decade*, edited by P. Aggleton, P. Davies, and G. Hart, 13–27. London: The Falmer Press.

———. 1993b. The spectacle of AIDS. In *The Lesbian and Gay Studies Reader*, edited by H. Abelove, M. A. Barale, and D. M. Halperin, 202–211. New York: Routledge.

Weber, M. 1948. *From Max Weber: Essays in Sociology*. Edited by H. H. Gerth and C. Wright Mills. London: Routledge.

Weeks, J. 1985. *Sexuality and Its Discontents: Meanings, Myths and Modern Sexualities*. London: Routledge and Kegan Paul.

———. 1987. Questions of identity. In *The Cultural Construction of Sexuality*, edited by P. Caplan, 31–51. London: Tavistock.

Weijl, S., and Boogaardt, W. 1917a. *Het Concubinaat in de Indische Kazernes*. Baarn: Hollandia.

———. 1917b. *Pro en Contra: Het Concubinaat in de Indische Kazernes*. Baarn: Hollandia.

Weinberger, E. 1994. The camera people. In *Visualizing Theory: Selected Essays from V.A.R., 1990–1994*, edited by L. Taylor, 3–26. New York and London: Routledge.

West, F. 1970. *Selected Letters of Hubert Murray*. Melbourne: Oxford University Press.

Wetherell, D. 1977. *Reluctant Mission: The Anglican Church in Papua New Guinea, 1891–1942*. Brisbane: University of Queensland Press.

White, G. 1929. *A Pioneer of Papua—Being the Life of the Reverend Copland King*. London: Society for Promoting Christian Knowledge.

White G. M., and Lindstrom, L., eds. 1989. *Pacific Theatre, Island Representations of World War II*. Pacific Islands Monograph Series, no. 8. Honolulu: University of Hawaii Press.

White, H. 1972. The forms of wildness: Archaeology of an idea. In *The Wild Man Within*, edited by E. Dudley and M. E. Novak, 3–38. Pittsburgh: University of Pittsburgh Press.

White, L. 1990. *The Comforts of Home: Prostitution in Colonial Nairobi*. Chicago: University of Chicago Press.

———. 1992. Review of "Empire and sexuality: The British experience." *The International Journal of African Historical Studies* 25, no. 3: 664–65.

Whittaker, A. 1994. Isaan women: Ethnicity, gender and health in Northeast Thailand. Ph.D. dissertation, Tropical Health Program, The University of Queensland, Brisbane.

WHO. 1989. *Collaboration with Nongovernmental Organisations: The Development of Effective*

Cooperation at National, Regional, and International Levels. Geneva: WHO, Global Programme on AIDS.

Williams, F. E. 1932–3. Depopulation and administration. *Oceania* 3: 219–226.

Williams, W. L. 1990. Review of "Male Homosexuality in Thailand—An Interpretation of Contemporary Thai Sources," by P. A. Jackson. *Journal of Homosexuality* 19, no. 4: 126–138.

Wilson, K. 1993. Yunnan wants its share of economic boom, *AP-Reuters,* 1 July.

Wiss, R. 1994. Lipreading: The story of Saartjie Baartman. In *Women's Difference: Sexuality and Maternity in Colonial and Postcolonial Discourses,* edited by M. Jolly, *The Australian Journal of Anthropology* 5, nos. 1 and 2: 11–40.

WRCC (Women's Resource Centre of Cebu). 1992. The women of Cebu: Braving the odds. *Bakud* 2, no. 3: 5–11.

Xie, Y. 1993. Retrospective of China's urbanization and regional development in the era of economic reforms. *Geojournal* 29, no. 2: 199–206.

Yamanaka, K. 1993. New immigration policy and unskilled foreign workers in Japan. *Pacific Affairs* 66, no. 1: 72–90.

Yao Jianguo. 1991. Yunnan: The gateway of southwest China. *Beijing Review,* 9–15 September: 15–21.

Young, M. 1989. Wesleyans in the D'Entrecasteaux. In *Family and Gender in the Pacific: Domestic Contradictions and the Colonial Impact,* edited by M. Jolly and M. Macintyre, 108–134. Cambridge: Cambridge University Press.

Yunomae Tomoko. 1989. *Ikebukuro Baishun Dansei Shibo Jiken kara Miete Kita Mono,* 45–53. Tokyo: Nihon Fujin Mondai Konwakai Kaihor, no. 48.

Zainu'ddin, A. T. 1980. Kartini—Her life, work and influence. In *Kartini Centenary: Indonesian Women Then and Now,* edited by A. T. Zainu'ddin, 1–29. Melbourne: Centre for Southeast Asian Studies, Monash University.

⊰ FILMOGRAPHY ⊱

The AIDS Domino. 1992. Produced by M. O'Donnell, February 17, 42 min. Series: Four Corners. Sydney: ABC (Australian Broadcasting Corporation)

AIDS: What Is Really So Frightening? 1993. Produced by Japan Education Foundation. Video: Home Room Series, 30 minutes. Tokyo: Japan Education Centre and TAO Communications.

Bird of Paradise. 1932. Produced by David O. Selznick, directed by King Vidor, 80 minutes. New York: RKO Radio Pictures.

Cannibal Tours. 1987. Produced, directed, and photographed by Dennis O'Rourke, 70 minutes. Film. Los Angeles: Distributed by Direct Cinema.

Emmanuelle. 1974. Directed by J. Jaeckin, produced by Yves Rousset-Rouard, with Sylvie Kristel, Marika Green, Alain Cuny, and Daniel Starky, 86 minutes. Film. France: Trinacra Films.

Emmanuelle L'Antiverge. 1975. Produced by Yves Rousset-Rouard, directed by Francois LeTerrier, 95 minutes. Film. France: Trinacra/ParaFrance Films.

Emmanuelle in Soho. 1981. Directed by David Hughes, 65 minutes, UK.

Foreign Bodies. 1988. Produced by A. Porteus and T. Cooper, reported by Tim Cooper, 38 minutes and 30 sec. London: Clarke Productions for Channel 4 (21 December 1987).

Goodbye, Emmanuelle. 1975. Directed by Francis Giacobetti. Film.

The Good Woman of Bangkok. 1991. Directed and written by D. O'Rourke, 82 mins. Film. Canberra: Film Australia (O'Rourke and Associates Filmakers in association with the Australian Film Commission and Channel 4).

Half Life: A Parable for the Nuclear Age. 1985. Dennis O'Rourke. Sydney: O'Rourke and Associated Filmmakers. Video recording, 86 min.

Lady Boys. 1992. Produced and directed by Jeremy Marre. London: Harcourt Films Production in Association with TVF and Channel 4.

The King and I. 1956. Directed by W. Lang, produced by Charles Brackett, music by Richard Rodgers, 133 mins. Film. Book and lyrics by Oscar Hammerstein II. Beverley Hills: Twentieth Century Fox.

Moana: A Romance of the Golden Age. 1924. Produced by R. J. Flaherty and F. H. Flaherty, directed by R. J. Flaherty, 64 minutes. Film. New York: Paramount Pictures.

The Piano. 1993. Directed by Jane Campion, produced by Jan Chapman, Alain Depardieu, and Mark Turnbull, 121 minutes. Australia, New Zealand: Ciby 2000.

Pacific Paradise. 1987. Directed by Oliver Howes, 29 minutes. Lindfield, NSW: Film Australia Video.

Rambo III. 1988. Directed by Peter MacDonald, 101 minutes. USA: Roadshow.

South Pacific. 1958. Produced by Buddy Adler, directed by Joshua Logan, 170 minutes. Film. United States: Magna/S.P. Enterprises.

Slaves of Progress. 1984. BBC (British Broadcasting Corporation). Series: World in Action. Screened in Sydney: Channel 9, 15 April 1984, 12 mins. London: Granada.

Tabu: A Story of the South Seas. 1931. Written and directed by F. W. Murnau and R. J. Flaherty, 80 minutes. United States: Colorhart Synchrotone.

The Thai Sex Industry. 1993. Produced by Giselle Portenier, directed by Susan O'Leary. Series: Foreign Correspondent, July 3, 19 mins. Sydney: ABC (Australian Broadcasting Corporation).

Trobriand Cricket: An Indigenous Response to Colonialism. 1975. Directed by J. W. Leach and G. Kildea. Papua New Guinea: Office of Information.

White Shadows of the South Seas. 1928. Directed by R. J. Flaherty and W. S. Van Dyke, 88 minutes. Los Angeles: Metro-Goldwyn-Meyer.

You Can't Buy a Wife, Can You? 1993. Written and directed by H. Lehtimaki, screened in Sydney, SBS Television, 20 May, 51 minutes. Finland: Forsti-Filmi Production.

⊸ CONTRIBUTORS ⊸

Sandra Buckley is Professor of Japanese Studies, Division of International and Asian Studies, at Griffith University. Her research areas include contemporary Japanese popular culture, contemporary cultural studies, Japanese feminism, and modern Japanese literature. These diverse interests are linked by a theoretical focus on gender, sexuality, and representation. Her publications include *Broken Silence: Voices of Japanese Feminism* (1995), a special issue of the *U.S.-Japan Women's Journal* on women and modern Japanese literature, and *Raiding Japanese Popular Culture* (forthcoming).

Jeffrey Clark was formerly Senior Lecturer, Department of Anthropology, at James Cook University of North Queensland and an Australian Research Council Fellow visiting the Department of Anthropology and Archaelogy, the Faculties, at the Australian National University, when this chapter was written. He wrote many papers on the Huli and Pangia of the New Guinea Highlands, focusing on questions of Christian conversion and the impact of capitalist economy and state incorporation on gender and sexual relations. He died in June 1995.

Annette Hamilton is Professor of Anthropology at Macquarie University, Sydney, Australia. Since 1986 she has been researching aspects of media and culture in Thailand. This led to an interest in the representations of Thailand in the tourist industry, and to a focus on the national imaginaries involved in the relations between "the West" and Thailand. She has also published on the Thai film industry, and is currently working on a study of the relations between media and culture in the southern Thai border zones.

Peter A. Jackson is Research Fellow in Thai History at the Australian National University, where he is researching the history of Thailand's sexual subcultures. He was previously Executive Officer of the National Thai Studies Centre at ANU. His book, *Male Homosexuality in Thailand* (1989, reprinted in 1995 under the title *Dear Uncle Go*), was the first major study of male homoeroticism in Thailand. His novel *The Intrinsic Quality of Skin* (1994) also deals with homosexuality in modern Thailand, and he is a member of the editorial board of the new Australian journal, *Critical InQueeries*.

Margaret Jolly is Convenor of the Gender Relations Project and Senior Fellow, Research School of Pacific and Asian Studies, at the Australian National University. Her research and publications are focused on feminist anthropology, colonial history, and the politics of tradition in the Pacific. Her major works include *Family and Gender in the Pacific* (ed., 1989), *Women of the Place* (ed., 1994), and *Women's Difference: Sexuality and Maternity in Colonial and Postcolonial Discourses* (1994).

John D. Kelly is Associate Professor of Anthropology at the University of Chicago. His recent publications include *A Politics of Virtue: Hinduism, Sexuality, and Countercolonial Discourse in Fiji* (1991) and, with Martha Kaplan, "Rethinking resistance: Dialogics of disaffection in colonial Fiji (*American Ethnologist* 1994). He is currently working on a new book, *Discourse, Knowledge, and Culture: Grammatical Philosophy in Ancient India, and Questions for an Anthropology of Knowledge*, and also plans a second volume on Fiji: *A Politics of Value.*

Lisa Law recently completed her Ph.D. in Human Geography, Research School of Pacific and Asian Studies, at the Australian National University. Her doctoral dissertation examines the globalizing discourses which currently construct the prostitute body in the Philippines and the limitations of this approach in empowering women to protect themselves from HIV/ AIDS.

Lenore Manderson is an anthropologist and social historian, and is Professor of Tropical Health in the Australian Centre for International & Tropical Health & Nutrition, at the University of Queensland. Her books include *Women, Politics, and Change* (1980), *Australian Ways* (ed., 1985), *Shared Wealth and Symbol* (ed., 1986), *New Motherhood* (with Mira Crouch, 1993), and *Sickness and the State: Health and Illness in Colonial Malaya, 1870–1940* (1996). Her primary research and publications relate to infectious disease in poor resource communities, and to gender, sexuality, and women's health.

Doug Porter researches and teaches in Development in Administration, NCDS Research School of Pacific and Asian Studies, at the Australian National University. He is coauthor of *Development in Practice: Paved with Good Intentions* (1991) and *Vietnam's Rural Transformation* (1995). His current research and development interests focus on Vietnam and the Myanmar side of the Golden Triangle. He maintains close advisory and consultant responsibilities with Australian nongovernment organizations, the United Nations Development Programme, and the World Bank.

Adam Reed has a master's degree from the University of Otago, New Zealand. His thesis dealt with colonial sexuality in the Massim, Papua New

Guinea. He is now a graduate scholar in the Department of Anthropology, Cambridge University, Cambridge, U.K., and is conducting research on prisons in Papua New Guinea.

Ann Stoler is Professor of Anthropology, History, and Women's Studies at the University of Michigan, and codirector of the Joint Ph.D. Program in History and Anthropology. Her books include: *Capitalism and Confrontation in Sumatra's Plantation Belt, 1870–1979* (1985), for which she was awarded the 1992 Harry Benda Prize in Southeast Asian Studies, *Race and the Education of Desire: Foucault's History of Sexuality and the Colonial Order of Things* (1995), and *Tensions of Empire: Colonial Cultures in a Bourgeois World*, coedited with Frederick Cooper (1996).

INDEX